THE BANK MERGER WAVE

The Economic Causes and
Social Consequences of
Financial Consolidation

Gary A. Dymski

*M.*E. Sharpe
Armonk, New York
London, England

2\00

#39756669

Library of Congress Cataloging-in-Publication Data

Dymski, Gary.
The bank merger wave : the economic causes and social consequences of financial
consolidation / Gary A. Dymski.
p. cm. — (Issues in money, banking, and finance)
Includes bibliographical references and index.
ISBN 0–7656–0382–9 (hardcover : alk.paper). — ISBN 0–7656–0383–7 (pbk : alk. paper)
1. Bank mergers. 2. Consolidation and merger of corporations.
I. Title. II. Series.
HG1722.D96   1999
332.1′6—dc21   98–37065
CIP

Printed in the United States of America

The paper used in this publication meets the minimum requirements of
American National Standard for Information Sciences—
Permanence of Paper for Printed Library Materials,
ANSI Z 39.48-1984.

BM (c)   10   9   8   7   6   5   4   3   2   1
BM (p)   10   9   8   7   6   5   4   3   2   1

Table of Contents

List of Figures and Tables

Figures

Tables

Foreword

Bank megamergers, each bigger than the last, have dominated business news for the last two years. These megamergers are simply the culmination of a merger wave that has been reshaping U.S. banking for nearly two decades: From 1981 to the present, an average of 1.7 banks have disappeared by merger each business day. Between 1981 and the end of 1997, there were 7,402 bank mergers, totaling $1.8 trillion in assets. Since the mid-1990s, bank mergers have been eliminating 5 percent or more of all U.S. banks each year. Despite U.S. antitrust laws, federal banking regulators have largely accommodated this wave. For example, in the ten years from 1982 to 1992, they approved 205 of the 211 bank merger applications that had the effect of increasing banking market concentration.

Banking analysts, economists, and the business press usually characterize the bank merger wave as inevitable, triggered by large banks' need to gain economies of scale in their banking operations, and they frequently observe that it will eliminate excess capacity without hurting banking consumers. The high rate of regulatory approvals supports this view, but this book disputes it. A careful review of the causes of bank consolidation finds that the merger wave is not being driven by economy-of-scale considerations in banking activities as such. Far more important is a shift in strategy by large banks that has made them hungry to provide new services for more upscale depositors and branches. This shift has been facilitated by regulators' sympathetic stance and by Wall Street's embrace of the equities of large banks seeking to get still bigger.

This study finds that the primary beneficiaries of bank mergers are bank executives and the suspendered shock troops of Wall Street, not consumers and small businesses along Main Street. Evidence reviewed here suggests that large banks and banks headquartered out of state charge higher fees and pay less interest on bank accounts, and large banks often make fewer loans to small business than the small banks they are replacing. Further, while megamergers are increasing bank profits, they are having little effect on bank efficiency; and while they may expand financial options for some households and businesses, for others the scope of available financial services may deteriorate. Under at least some measures, concentration levels have been trending upward in banking markets and may rise rapidly when markets digest the current round of megamergers. Also evidence presented here suggests that mortgage approval rates are systematically lower in more concentrated banking markets.

This study emphasizes the social efficiency consequences of the bank merger movement—that is, its effect on lower-income and minority households and communities that have historically encountered barriers in seeking access to credit and capital. An extended evaluation of recent home-purchase lending data finds that banking markets across the United States remain deeply affected by racial and income inequality. With some regional variation, minority applicants face higher denial rates than white applicants even after accounting for neighborhood characteristics and for the applicant's income and loan-to-income ratio. Other studies have reached this conclusion. What is distinctive about this analysis is, first of all, its scope: It uses more than 4.5 million loan applications in eighteen states and 140 metropolitan areas to establish that race and income barriers remain high in credit markets across the country. These barriers can be traced to three factors: structural inequality among applicants and between areas within cities, personal discrimination and bias on the part of lenders, and lender market power. This finding suggests that banking markets are economically inefficient in that some creditworthy borrowers apparently are not approved due to lender bias. Further, the banking system is not socially efficient in that banking outcomes do not reduce inequality of opportunity.

The model of the probability of loan approval used here differs from prior studies in several ways. First, it examines the barriers faced by *four separate categories of minority applicant*—Native American, Asian-American, African-American, and Hispanic. Second, it applies a uniform model to *markets across the United States*. We find that in virtually every market, African-American applicants are at a large, statistically significant disadvantage in applying for home-purchase loans, and Native American applicants are at a large, statistically significant disadvantage in many of these markets. Hispanic applicants usually have a large statistical disadvantage relative to other applicants, but a statistical advantage in a small number of cases. Asian-Americans are sometimes at a statistical advantage, sometimes at a statistical disadvantage.

This study is also unique in that it generates results for different types of lender separately, as a way of evaluating the likely effects of mergers on access to credit for underserved customers and areas. Comparing all large merging banks with small in-state banks, savings and loans, and mortgage companies, we find that mortgage companies perform better than the other lender groups with respect to minority and low-income. Large merging banks and small in-state banks perform very similarly, on average, vis-à-vis minority and lower-income applicants and areas. When large merging banks with and without in-state branches are evaluated separately, however, merging banks *with* in-state branches perform almost as well as mortgage companies, on average, while merging banks *without* in-state branches perform relatively poorly.

We also find that different types of lender treat similar applicant groups very differently within the same market. And in most of the markets studied, at least one category of lender served minority (or lower-income) applicants better than other lender types in that same market. These results suggest that different lenders may be evaluating creditworthiness very differently in local markets and that credit-scoring systems are not a panacea that will eliminate race and redlining effects in credit markets. A sub-study of ten California cities then finds that access to credit—the probability of loan approval—is systematically lower in more concentrated banking markets served by fewer banks.

This book recommends that regulators and the Congress reconsider the arguments for bank mergers by considering more closely, and more explicitly, their effects on economic and social efficiency. Acquiring banks should be obliged to show that they will take concrete steps to offset the higher depository costs and decreased access to credit that many affected consumers and communities will face postmerger. Fast-track approval of mergers should not be permitted; the slower review process that has been in place until now permits time for community-based groups to negotiate commitments to underserved banking and credit-market needs. To ensure a level playing field, however, nonbank financial firms that provide financial services traditionally encompassed under the umbrella of commercial banking should, like banks, be held accountable under the Community Reinvestment Act.

While large banks may be shifting away from broad-based transaction accounts and broad-based credit instruments, these remain the bedrock social functions of the banking system, and the basis of banks' special status under U.S. law. There is no reason to expect the small-niche banks now emerging to serve smaller-balance households and small businesses—that is, those left behind by large merging banks—can both be competitively viable and provide these broad-based banking services at competitive prices. If large banks are uninterested in serving broad-based customer markets with instruments that increase access to credit and low-cost transaction accounts, then the special protections these banks now receive should be withdrawn and restricted to those banks that do provide core banking services that are both economically and socially efficient. The defining protections provided to banks, of course, are deposit insurance and lender-of-last-resort protection. If a withdrawal of these public protections from large merging banks is not advisable, then banking regulators and Congress should just say no to large bank mergers until the banking system makes the same commitment to expanding social efficiency and equal opportunity as it has to increasing its owners' financial gains and expanding its managers' market reach and power.

Preface and Acknowledgments

This book began life as a short literature review in spring 1996. With the U.S. economic landscape awash in bank takeovers, it seemed an apt time to examine what economists had written on the causes and consequences of bank mergers. The "causes of" investigation would require interpreting industry studies of banking. I had already studied this voluminous literature in my dissertation work at the University of Massachusetts and in subsequent research for a 1993 book on banking and monetary policy (Dymski, Epstein, and Pollin 1993), so it was a matter of bringing my reading up-to-date.

I wasn't familiar with any "consequences of mergers" material, but imagined it would be easily found. I had done research for several years on racial discrimination in credit markets, and on bank "redlining" of inner cities. A democratic assemblage of people, ranging from street-level activists to academics, have analyzed redlining and discrimination in credit markets. This diverse set of authors reflect the great public interest in and continuing controversy over the economic and social consequences of banking and credit-market processes. I guessed that many people must have investigated the social consequences of bank mergers. To my surprise, this wasn't at all the case. Other than a Notre Dame dissertation on bank mergers and community reinvestment by Reynolds Nesiba (1995), I found no other traces of a literature on this topic. Undoubtedly I have missed studies on this topic, especially those written by activist researchers and community-based groups in U.S. cities; I apologize in advance to these authors for the overly academic character of my literature search.

So my short literature review became a substantial research project, as I began considering how to analyze the consequences of changing bank structures with available resources. The Federal Reserve surveys of bank costs and data on financial office locations were obvious sources of information; so were Home Mortgage Disclosure Act (HMDA) data, whose comprehensive geographic and lender coverage is ideal for studying complex and extensive credit-market phenomena. Initially I conducted a study of how different types of lender behave in a small set of credit markets. I chose several Western cities and tested different lender groups' sensitivity to "at risk" borrower classes—minority applicants, lower-income applicants, minority neighborhoods, and lower-income neighborhoods. While I found clear and convincing evidence of disadvantage, the patterns were complex. To interpret the multidimensional disadvantage of "at risk" classes in different markets, I created the disadvantage index proposed in chapter 9. But while this disadvantage index allowed me to compare statistical outcomes systematically, it did not yield cut-and-dried answers about different lender groups' relative performance. The lack of clear answers was due in part to regional differences in financial structures and credit-market outcomes. I therefore deepened my efforts and undertook a broad-ranging investigation of financial infrastructures and credit flows in Midwestern, Northeastern, and Southeastern banking markets. I also investigated patterns for three years' worth of HMDA data, 1992, 1995, and 1996. This volume summarizes the results of this analytical and empirical effort, which is more a work in progress than a finished effort. Hopefully others will extend and refine the work presented here.

I am solely responsible for any errors of fact or interpretation herein. Further, several debts are acknowledged with gratitude. The probit model used here is adapted from one John Veitch and I developed originally for our studies of the Los Angeles residential credit market. I am indebted to John Veitch and James Ssemekula for help in learning to program in SAS. I am ever indebted to Professor Jim Kindahl of the University of Massachusetts for helping me gain some insight into statistical and empirical analysis. Finally, the ideas about social efficiency and market processes that appear here have been developed over the past several years in joint work with Dorene Isenberg of Drew University.

My colleagues Steven Helfand, Bob Pollin, and Keith Griffin at the University of California, Riverside, and Patrick L. Mason of the University of Notre Dame helped me shape this project over the course of many conversations. I have also gained a great deal from conversations about banking and economic theory with U.C. Riverside graduate students, among whom Barbara Wiens-Tuers, Paul Woodburne, Mark Brenner, and Lisa Mohanty deserve special mention. Anne Shlay, Greg Squires, Jim Campen, and John Lind provided detailed comments on a preliminary version of the manuscript. Fernando Cardim de Carvalho, Rogerio Studart, Luiz Fernando Rodrigues de Paula, and their colleagues at the Instituto de Economia provided a kind audience and insightful comments in the first presentation of these ideas at the Federal University of Rio de Janeiro in June 1997; so did the members of the Keynesian Society at Waseda University in April 1998, and Ilene Grabel and other participants in a session at the 1998 conference of the Association for Institutionalist Thought in Denver. Eileen Appelbaum of the Economic Policy Institute has been a steadfast and wise adviser; and I have drawn continued inspiration from the example of Hyman Minsky and from Donald Harris's advice to "keep my eye on the target." My deepest professional debt is to my thesis adviser and friend, Jim Crotty of the University of Massachusets.

I appreciate the support of Jane D'Arista, who urged me to publish this study in the M.E. Sharpe series "Issues in Money, Banking, and Finance." Throughout the writing and editing process, I have benefited from the encouragement of Stephen Dalphin, Esther Clark, and especially Peter Coveney at M.E. Sharpe. Peter deserves special thanks for helping me sculpt a final manuscript from a rather ungainly preliminary draft.

I especially want to acknowledge the support of my family and loved ones during this endeavor. My children, Jamaal and Naima, have shown remarkable patience through their father's endless SAS runs. Joan Tenma has stood by me and assisted me in countless ways during this project. Finally, I dedicate this volume to my parents, Don and Therese. They have probably wondered when I would get around to writing that first book. Well, here it is. I have tried to make it a book written by the kind of economist they hoped I might become.

THE BANK
MERGER WAVE

1
Introduction

Why This Study?

This volume investigates some of the social and economic implications of the evolution of banking and financial structures, with special attention to the banking merger wave in the United States. Banks—that is, institutions that issue deposits that can be used as money, and that make loans by creating credit—are being transformed at a breakneck pace. They may not do what they once did, or they may do it differently; they have been buying one another up as if the millennium were at hand—which, indeed, it is; and they are shouldering their way into an expanding list of new businesses.[1] This investigation constitutes more a progress report than a definitive treatment. Banking and financial structures are evolving at breakneck speed; tomorrow's newspaper may undo today's assessment of the emerging financial architecture.

So if you cannot hit a moving target with a moving weapon, why write this book? Why not wait until the target has slowed down, and more definite weapons are at hand? The answer is very simple. The ongoing transformation of financial relations generally, and of banking institutions and practices specifically, is fundamentally important for the future of economic inequality and the scope of economic opportunity in the United States. The transformation of U.S. banking is being accompanied by—and in turn inducing—changes in who has access to credit, for what purpose, and on what terms; and it is redefining which financial institutions are available for local use in different sorts of communities. These shifts are not simply reactions to given inequalities of wealth and power; they also affect the evolution of these dual inequalities over time. The question of who can save and who cannot is determined not only by personal predisposition, and not just by patterns of job-holding, but also by who has access to savings vehicles.

Several reasons for the lack of attention to these implications of the transformation of U.S. finance come to mind. First, they are difficult to measure. Detailed data on the operations of the banking system is scarce enough, but data on less wealthy households and smaller businesses is scarcer still. Second, the prevailing approach to banking and financial issues among economists discourages

3

analysis of the sort conducted here. Contemporary economic theory largely abstracts from institutional structure, and assumes that markets function perfectly unless otherwise specified. Economists have accepted this norm for a variety of reasons. The mathematical techniques that have been used to advance pure economic theory give the most profound and far-reaching results when markets are assumed to work well—when supply equals demand in every market, when agents know what they want and can buy as much as they want and can afford, and so on. The idea that some creditworthy agents will be left out of the market makes many economists uncomfortable. They would rather assume that market outcomes must be efficient, since otherwise "$500 bills would be lying untaken on the street"; indeed, because one *does not* observe $500 bills, or even quarters, anywhere in the neighborhood, then what exists, is efficient. Of course, the idea that people fully exploit the economic prospects they have available—including scooping up spare change in their driveways—by no means implies that the economic prospects available to them are socially optimal.

Many economists with expertise in banking and finance hold the view that this transformation can only increase every agent's welfare. The market works best when freedom of choice is least constrained; the bank merger and consolidation movement is increasing freedom of market choice because it is introducing potent new players into existing markets. Therefore, the merger and consolidation trends are pro-market—and where is the problem? This line of argument is apparently so obvious as to require no supporting evidence.

The present study does not grant the premise that financial markets work very efficiently. This makes things rather messy; many results are obtained, but few neat conclusions. Indeed, this lack of neat conclusion suggests a final reason for the public's relative indifference to the banking consolidation wave. We find that small in-state banks' performance in serving lower-income and minority communities is worse, on average, than that of large merging banks with in-state branches (though better than large merging banks without in-state branches). Yet minorities and lower-income people are the constituencies that have fueled the waves of protest against bank and corporate disinvestment, primarily in larger cities. In effect, our results suggest that community protests against large local banks *have* had a measurable effect; indeed, large banks' efforts to merge will provide new leverage for community-based groups' ongoing negotiations with these banks over the scope and size of reinvestment efforts. In smaller cities, where small banks' role may be more unique, grassroots movements on behalf of small banks are less likely to be organized and sustained, and thus to succeed.

Plan of the Book and Methodology

This inquiry centers on two questions. First, why has the merger wave occurred? Second, what are the consequences of bank mergers and consolidation generally in banking markets? It will be useful to summarize the core methods and data used to answer these questions in this study.

Answering the first question is the task of chapters 3 to 5. These chapters primarily describe historical developments, synthesize other authors' studies, and interpret evolving policy decisions. Chapter 3 first provides some historical background on the banking industry and bank regulation. Chapter 4 then launches into a detailed investigation of the possible causes of bank mergers: the widespread distress of many banks in the 1980s, operational factors such as banks' costs and risks, equity-market forces, and banks' evolving profit-making strategies. Since U.S. banking regulators must approve or deny all proposed mergers, chapter 6 explores the evolving stance of bank regulators in this merger wave.

The second question, the consequences of banking consolidation, is addressed in chapters 6 to 10. Chapter 6 first reviews evidence published in other studies, which has focused on the relationship between banking consolidation and bank costs, and between consolidation and small-business lending. To ascertain the effect of bank size and out-of-state banks on checking account fees, we analyze data on banking fees collected by the Federal Reserve Board in surveys spanning the period 1989–1996. Trends in these data on fees are contrasted for in-state and out-of-state banks, and for large and small banks.

Chapters 7 to 10 then develop evidence unique to this study. Chapter 7 contrasts the ideas of economic and social efficiency in banking, and explores the links between local markets and financial structures. This chapter then explores economic and social-efficiency aspects of banking markets in sixteen selected Western and Eastern cities. Social efficiency in banking markets is explored first with the "fair-share" measure used in sociological studies. However, fair-share measures alone prove inadequate because of regional differences and because this study explores the social efficiency of banking as a multidimensional phenomenon encompassing four categories of minority applicant, as well as area effects. To permit a richer analysis of these various factors, a probit model of the probability of home-purchase loan approval for these sixteen cities is developed in chapter 8. This probit model permits us to identify some structural differences in how different lenders—including acquiring banks, large out-of-state banks, and small in-state banks—react to income and race differentials (among both individual applicants and geographic areas) in the residential credit market.

Chapters 7 and 8 establish that regional variations are important in banking structures, but the simple East/West contrast therein is too broad. The last portion of chapter 8 presents evidence on financial infrastructure in a nationwide selection of thirty-five cities. A statistical test on these data then shows that regional differences explain more of the variance in financial infrastructure than does city size or city minority population.

Given this result, that regional patterns are important in U.S. banking structures, the sixteen-city East/West model of chapters 7 and 8 is extended to the nation as a whole on a region-by-region basis. Chapter 9 explores financial structures and credit-market outcomes in five distinct national regions—Southwestern, Mountain/Great Plains, Midwestern, Northeastern, and Southeastern. Probit analysis is used to evaluate patterns in approximately 4.7 million home-purchase loan applications in 140 metropolitan areas in eighteen states. These probits evaluate whether a set of independent variables, including economic factors such as applicant income and loan-to-income ratio, and social factors such as applicant race, systematically affect the probability of loan approval.

Probit analyses of home-mortgage data are nothing new; the first such analyses were done two decades ago. What is innovative about the analysis conducted here is the use of probit equations to compare the performance of different types of lender in extensive market areas typically encompassing more than one metropolitan area. The types of lenders analyzed are: (1) small in-state banks; (2) all large merging banks; (3) large merging banks with branches in-state; (4) large merging banks without in-state branches; (5) savings and loan associations and mutual savings banks; and (6) mortgage companies. Running distinct equations for different lender groups allows us to conduct "horse races" evaluating which types of lenders do better or worse in terms of racial and income difference.

Interpreting and comparing results in this broader investigation constitutes two challenges: the multi-dimensional character of minority and lower-income disadvantage; and the fact that the relative number of minorities and lower-income applicants varies among regions and states. To handle these problems of comparison, a "disadvantage index" is developed. Chapter 9 uses this disadvantage index to compare and contrast the relative performance of different kinds of lender in the five regions (and eighteen states) encompassed in this study.

Chapter 10 then explores a different influence on credit-market outcomes— whether market concentration affects the probability of loan approval. In the view of many analysts, the importance of local market structures is dwarfed by the emergence of integrated centralized markets to which many people have access. So does local market structure still matter? Data on banking market structure in ten California cities in 1982 and 1992 are combined with 289,000 home-purchase loan applications reported under the Home Mortgage Discolsure Act (HMDA) in 1995 and 1996. The probit method is then used to analyze the effects of banking market structure, including the degree of market concentration, on loan approval—in an equation that takes account of variables commonly included in redlining and discrimination studies of the home-loan market. The banking market structure variables tested for each California city are: concentration as measured by the Herfindahl–Hirschman Index (HHI)—a standard measure of concentration—in 1982; the change in the HHI from 1982 to 1992; the change in the number of banks from 1982 to 1992; and the volume of 1992 deposits. Chapter 11 then recapitulates some of the key results of this study; and chapter 12 sets out some policy implications.

Some important aspects of the transformation of banking are not treated here. The possibility that cash may be supplanted by cash cards is not discussed, and the implications of computer-based banking are discussed only summarily. Neither the activities of overseas banks in the United States nor the overseas activities of U.S. banks are analyzed.

This study is innovative in several ways. First, its treatment of economic literature is somewhat unique. Typically, studies of bank consolidation and bank efficiency rely exclusively on industrial-organization literature. However, this study integrates the industrial-organization approach with insights rooted in the empirical literatures on bank discrimination and bank redlining in urban credit markets. The sociological and economic approaches to whether banks treat different areas and borrowers differently are reviewed briefly and compared in these pages. In a sense, this book's challenge is to integrate industrial-organization studies of banking, which ignore questions about differential access to capital, with studies of unequal access to capital, which ignore the industrial and organizational aspects of banking.

Also new with this study are the "horse-race" probit approach developed here; the probit model incorporating market-concentration and race and lower-income effects on the probability of loan approval; and the nationwide regional approach taken in this probit analysis.

Another innovative idea here is the notion of the "social efficiency" of the banking system. This idea results from an adaptation of the familiar concept of economic efficiency, which measures the ability of an economic organization to generate outputs or revenues for a given volume of inputs or costs. The "social efficiency" of the banking system, by extension, measures the extent to which a given organization or set of organizations facilitates the access to capital of borrower groups that have faced historical barriers limiting this access. The historical barriers emphasized here are those faced by minority applicants, by applicants with lower incomes (among those applying for loans), and by applicants seeking home loans in either minority or lower-income neighborhoods.

Also new here is the disadvantage index proposed in chapter 9. This index is designed to facilitate comparisons of different lenders' performance in different market areas despite two vexing problems. One is that barriers to credit-market access are multi-dimensional—that is, barriers may be faced both by individuals and by areas, and may pertain both to race and to income status. A second element making comparisons difficult is that the proportion of minority and lower-income applicants and residents typically varies from one market area to another. Some means of normalizing these differences is required before comparing barriers in one market with barriers in others.

Economic Theories of Banking and Financial Markets

An economy's financial structure is defined here as consisting of two elements: the local financial infrastructures that meet the demand of households and businesses for credit and for the means of making monetary transactions; and the pattern of credit flows, that is, the level of capital and credit demanded and obtained by different segments of the household and business sectors. The two elements obviously fit together: It is primarily the local financial infrastructure that creates and channels patterns of credit flows. How important is financial structure in economic outcomes? Why does it matter what the financial structure is, or how it might be changing?

Economists have argued over these questions for centuries. Two broad lines of debate have formed. Terminology introduced in the early-nineteenth century debate over the powers of the Bank of England still serves today: On one side are the proponents of the "Currency School," for whom money is primarily a medium of exchange, the volume of which is controlled by either the Crown or the cost of mining gold; on the other are the proponents of the "Banking School," who view money as consisting largely of credit, the volume of which varies with the demands of commerce and the capacity of the banking system. While the differences between these approaches are frequently subtle, all monetary economists eventually find themselves on one side of this line or the other.[2]

In the Currency School view, credit is a passive and residual category in economic dynamics; by extension, so too are the institutions that specialize in the creation of credit. The volume of money is exogenous and fixed; businesses and households will adjust price levels to accommodate whatever volume is in circulation. In the modern era, the Currency School view is reflected in monetarist economics and in Walrasian general equilibrium, wherein the economy's financial aspects are purely secondary. In the Banking School view, credit is an active force in economic dynamics, the volume of which (and by extension that of money) is endogenous. The volumes of credit and money can be "wrong," in the aggregate or for individual units, given the level of income and of prices. In this event, individual agents may have to make do with less credit than they deserve (or conversely, may be empowered to spend more money than is prudent), and the economy as a whole may suffer a turndown.

The Currency and Banking Schools take opposite sides in the continuing debate over whether financial markets should be viewed as largely efficient or inefficient. In the Currency School view, financial markets are characteristically efficient—agents exploit all available information in deciding whether to buy or sell financial assets. Since financial assets are emitted to provide credit or capital for firms, this in turn means that the price of credit or capital for all firms is efficiently priced by the market. The market always works, and financial-asset prices reflect the fundamentals of the firms that emit them—that is, they faithfully capture these firms' ability to generate risk-adjusted earnings over time. The efficient-market view ascribes so much efficiency to the markets that banks have only a minor role in credit allocation. Indeed, in Fama's definitive 1980 article on banking in efficient markets, banks have no effect on the allocation of credit; banks' very existence is due solely to the economies of scale they enjoy in providing liquidity on demand. In this view, if commercial banks did not exist but financial markets were efficient, every one of the efficient loans that banks would have made would be made anyway by a nonbank entity.

In the Banking School view, financial-market outcomes are less than perfect because the environment in which credit and capital-market instruments are exchanged is itself flawed. These flaws typically begin with damaged information: Information may be asymmetrically distributed between borrowers and lenders; information about future outcomes may be unavailable or unreliable. Further, transactions in credit markets may be costly. These deviations from idealized conditions of economic exchange generate outcomes that deviate from those observed in efficient-markets models. All agents may not have the same opportunity to make financial contracts—indeed, some agents may be shut out of financial contracts altogether; and some agents may have to pay substantially higher rates than others in the contracts they do make. When information is costly, unevenly distributed, and/or unreliable, it is readily apparent that financial structures matter independently in economic outcomes.

Many Keynesian and institutionalist economists and other social analysts have explored the character of financial-market outcomes and dynamics when information is incomplete or unreliable and when market participation is partial or endogenous. The critics of financial-market efficiency are many and diverse. At one extreme are New Keynesian economists like Joseph Stiglitz of Stanford University, who develop sophisticated formal behavioral models assuming that all agents are fully rational. At the other extreme are sociologists such as Anne Shlay, who build non-behavioral models of implicitly inefficient credit markets. In the middle are Post Keynesian economists like Paul Davidson of the University of Tennessee, who use the analytical tools of economics but who insist that full rationality—and hence intricate formalization—is impossible because agents must operate under fundamental uncertainty.[3] For the analysis conducted here, the differences among these critics of financial-market efficiency are relatively unimportant. It is sufficient to recognize that economic exchanges, including credit-market transactions, are not precoordinated through time and space by a dispassionate and perfectly functioning, price-driven market allocation process; that the outcomes observed in any locale reflect the coevolution of financial-market structures and market and social environments over time, and that these outcomes are not preordained but reflect evolving historical opportunities.

In the Banking School perspective adopted in this book, commercial banks are not disembodied institutions that select ready, willing, and able borrowers from among applicants with readily ascertained creditworthiness; instead, commercial banks are institutions engaged in co-evolution with market areas and market participants they may or may not service. We assume that market environments are shaped by bank decisions just as bank decisions are conditioned on signals emitted by market environments.[4]

Banking, Credit Markets, and Community Development

So, contrary to the passive, efficient-markets view of financial structure, financial structures are understood here as active contributors to the formation of market choices and the market allocation of resources. Figure 1.1 demonstrates this contrast. The two-headed lines indicate mutual determination, and the one-way arrows determination. In the "passive" or "reactive" view of bank behavior, the bank lender floats above a geographic community, assessing the prospects of prospective borrowers located in this community, and the prospects of prospective borrowers who wish to locate in this community. The creditworthiness of loan applicants within the community depends to some extent on the community's own economic and possibly social characteristics. The evolution of the bank lender depends on trends and changes among all bank lenders. The bank's loan decisions affect borrowers, and indirectly the community in which these borrowers are located (or seek to locate), but the community in turn has no effect on the bank. The bank's market area is what it is, and the bank simply reacts to it in ways conditioned primarily on the evolution of the banking industry as a whole.

In the "coevolutionary" view of bank behavior, by contrast, the bank lender is viewed as embedded in the community itself. Its own decisions affect the economic outcomes of the households and businesses in its market area, and these outcomes in turn affect the bank's viability. The bank's evolution is determined in part by the trajectory of the banking industry as a whole, but also by that of the community environment it services and derives profits from.

The bank/community relationship involves dense co-respective interactions of two distinct types. First, the existence of a community means that the characteristics of some clusters of potential borrowers are tied together by their place-specific assets, whose value at any point in time reflects both these economic units' individual income flows and wealth levels, and conditions in the community. In the absence of any community effects, banks could only evaluate each borrower in isolation, since any one borrower's creditworthiness would be independent of any other borrower's. Knowledge derived from the evaluation of any one loan applicant would be of no use in determining the viability of the next. But the community environment ties together borrowers into co-related groups whose characteristics are mutually dependent, not independent. In effect, the geographic fixity of a portion of most loan applicants' assets makes the communities in which these applicants are located into spillover factories. Spillovers are replete here, at any point in time and across time.[5]

This view of urban communities as laden with market spillovers is not controversial. Neither is it controversial to note that the outcomes of borrowers' loans affect the bank's profit levels and, ultimately, operating health. A second form of bank/community interaction is not commonly acknowledged, however: the effects of bank decisions on the economic characteristics of the communities they

Figure 1.1 **Two Views of the Bank/Community Relationship**

1: The passive bank confronting a pre-given community environment

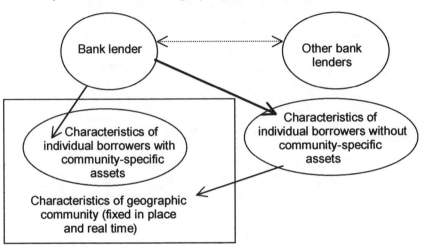

2: The bank as one component in an evolving community environment

service. The volume and terms of the loans any bank makes, the density of its branch network, the cost of its transaction services all have spillover effects for locally based economic units, borrowers and nonborrowers alike. For couldn't the cost of a business's financial transactions depend, in part, on the number and geographic proximity of banks operating in its market area? Couldn't the credit-worthiness of the loans in a given community by a given lender depend, in part, on the number and terms of loans made by that community's other lenders?

Most other analyses of banking mergers answer these questions in the negative, because they are informed by a "passive bank," Currency School view; they do not question that consumer and community opportunity sets evolve independently of banks' structural changes. This analysis, by contrast, investigates whether these questions have an affirmative answer, and hence allows the possibility that bank-ing mergers are transforming both banks and affected communities' futures si-multaneously. Determining just what these effects are, and how important they are, will require far more than this one study. Numerous studies using diverse methods of inquiry and data sets will be needed. This study contributes only some of the first pages of what promises to be an extended debate about what banking is, how banking is done, and the impact of banking practices in an increasingly diverse and complex U.S. economy.

2
Overview

Introduction: A Capsule Summary of the Issues

The laws of the United States have been hostile to market monopoly since the passage of the Sherman and Clayton Antitrust Acts in 1890 and 1914, respectively. This hostility has arisen because monopoly firms can often restrict volume and set exploitative prices that their hapless customers must pay. Given this legacy, the last fifteen years have seen a remarkable turn of events in the U.S. banking industry. For the last fifteen years, this industry has experienced an unrelenting merger wave and an unprecedented increase in concentration. This study reviews the economic evidence explaining why bank mergers are happening in such great numbers, and explores the effect of increased bank concentration and out-of-state ownership on banks' customers.

Banks have disappeared by merger at the rate of 1.7 per business day between 1981 and the present. Some 6,374 bank mergers occurred between 1980 and 1994, representing $1.2 trillion in banking assets (Rhoades 1996). According to data collected by the FDIC, another 1,748 mergers occurred between 1995 and 1997, bringing another $611 billion into new ownership. Figure 2.1 illustrates available evidence on this merger wave. The volume of assets acquired shows a steady upward trend in the 1990s. This figure also sets out two available and inconsistent sets of numbers on the volume of mergers since 1980, one published by the FDIC and one by the Federal Reserve. Both data series have two peaks, one in the late 1980s and a second in the mid-to-late 1990s.

Mergers have brought consolidation with a vengeance. All told, about half of all banks in operation at the end of the 1970s have disappeared. According to *American Banker,* the share of commercial-banking assets controlled by the twenty-five largest banks in early 1997 has grown by more than 1 percent annually from 1985 to 1995, and by over 2 percent in 1996. The twenty-five largest banks control 70 percent of all assets, and are expected to control 85 percent of bank assets in another decade—mostly via mergers.[1] Mergers have also changed the shape of the largest U.S. banking firms. Only sixteen of the top twenty-five banks as of January 1, 1992, remained in the top twenty-five on December 31,

Figure 2.1 **U.S. Commercial Bank Mergers and Assets Acquired, 1980–1997**

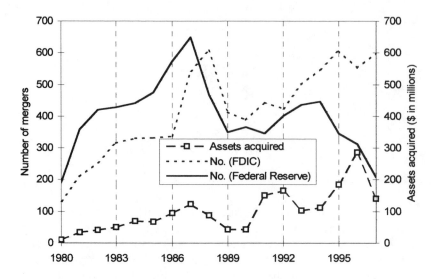

1996; and four banks in the top ten—NationsBank, PNC, Fleet, and CoreStates—five years ago were not in the top ten. These newcomers to the top ten got there by mergers, but their competitors also made ready use of the merger weapon. By December 31, 1997, Fleet and PNC had been pushed out of the top ten by other banks' mergers, notably that of First Chicago and NBD; and CoreStates was in the process of being taken over by First Union. As of mid-1998, six of the top ten end-of-1997 banks had pending megamergers with one another—BankAmerica had a merger pending with NationsBank, First Chicago NBD with Banc One, and Norwest with Wells Fargo.

This merger wave has drawn remarkably little public outcry, perhaps because the business press, bank regulators, and prominent bankers generally agree that the United States economy is "overbanked." The argument goes that market forces are bringing enhanced financial mobility, creating the need for consolidation; and without consolidation, the U.S. banking industry will be unable to compete with its nonbank and overseas competitors. Further, the bank merger movement in the United States is just one part of a global pattern of mergers and acquisitions in financial services; so megabanks' megamergers seem the more inevitable because they represent one aspect of financial globalization.[2]

Whatever the gains in "competitiveness," the legacy of U.S. antitrust law suggests that industrial concentration works against consumers' interests. Two core questions should be raised before replacing the dispersed U.S. banking system with a Canadian-style system featuring six nationwide banks: Is consolidation good for consumers, and will it enhance efficiency in banking?

The business press, bankers, and most regulators take it as settled that the answers are, respectively, yes and yes. But there may be other answers to this question from other perspectives. Indeed, advocates of the interests of consumers, small businesses, farmers, and communities have formulated more skeptical views of whether larger banks' activities enhance access to capital and leave markets better off. The reason is that bank mergers are trigger events for such evaluations. Under the Community Reinvestment Act (CRA) of 1977, consumer and community groups can challenge banks' mergers and/or their branch expansion plans if these institutions' reinvestment performance is unsatisfactory. No one standard of what constitutes satisfactory reinvestment performance has emerged in practice; but certainly satisfactory performance must include making credit as accessible to qualified minority applicants as to white applicants, to those in minority neighborhoods as well as in white neighborhoods, and to those in lower-income areas as well as in wealthy areas.

The rapid pace of merger activity has provided community advocates with numerous opportunities to put banks' CRA records under the microscope; and many independent studies of banks' reinvestment performance and of discrimination in credit markets have been done. The results of these informal and formal studies give one pause, for these studies have frequently found evidence that lenders' performance may discriminate against minority and lower-income applicants and areas. Indeed, because of precisely these less-than-stellar reinvestment results, merging banks have sometimes made substantial commitments to reinvest in lower-income neighborhoods. This does not ensure that the movement bringing about consolidation in the U.S. banking industry will simultaneously bring about a more consumer-friendly industry with better reinvestment performance. The small number of banks that engage frequently in such mergers, such as NationsBank, have shown signs of compassion fatigue vis-à-vis reinvestment promises.[3] Banking industry representatives have begun to argue that challenges to bank mergers are short-sighted because they lead to commitments that block efficiency gains; and many view activity aimed at reinvestment as socially costly because it leads to deviations from efficient market outcomes.

Is there anything to this view? Is consolidation driven by banks' race to attain operating efficiencies? Are the credit markets in which banks operate generating efficient outcomes? Will fewer but bigger banks mean improved banking services? This study answers these questions using both evidence generated by other analysts and new information compiled especially for this study. The rest of this chapter summarizes this book's findings and recommendations.

The Logic of the Bank Merger Wave

While bank mergers may have salutary effects on consumers' access to credit and on banking costs—two points we examine below—these effects do not explain why banks have been merging at so ferocious a pace. Banks' search for efficiency is not the answer. The economic literature shows that megabanks do not have greater operating efficiency than middle-sized banks. According to most studies, advantages due to size—economies of scale—disappear once a bank reaches about $250 million in assets. A few studies show small efficiencies in bank sizes of up to $3 billion in assets, and one has claimed small efficiencies of under 5 percent when banks have up to $50 billion in assets. But the ten largest U.S. banks each have assets in excess of $50 billion. Thus these megabanks are unlikely to achieve further economies of scale in banking operations by becoming even larger.

If operating efficiencies are not spurring mergers, what is fueling the bank merger wave? This book suggests three interlocking causes. The first is the rise of new banking strategies. This study suggests that U.S. banks have been forced by evolving macroeconomic and competitive circumstances to abandon their former strategies and instead adopt new ones. Some large banks are pursuing a strategy that might be termed upscale retail banking, which leads to an interest in acquiring new deposit bases. Upscale retail banking involves identifying a preferred "upscale" customer base, and then delivering to this base both traditional banking services—short-term consumer loans, long-term mortgages, depository services—and nontraditional services such as mutual funds, insurance, and investment advice. Initially, these banks can increase revenues by serving more of the financial needs of their core customers; but once they have saturated their existing customer base, they must seek out new ones. Smaller banks that have survived by serving market niches left underserved by other players may also engage in mergers; but these mergers typically are defensive.

So it is large banking firms pursuing upscale-retail strategies whose urge to merge provides the impetus for this merger wave. Where do merging banks find the means for expansion? As the literature on banking economies of scale points out, the sheer size of these megabanks leaves them with little possibility of growing more efficient by growing larger. So they are not financing mergers with retained earnings. This leads to the second piece of the interlocking merger puzzle: In its long boom period, Wall Street has been willing to augment acquiring banks' retained earnings by supporting bank stock buybacks and stock swaps. This view is confirmed in a *Wall Street Journal* article on April 14, 1998, in which reporter Steven Lipin observes, "Any investment banker worth his pinstripes and suspenders keeps a list of bank-takeover prospects on his desk, including the ages of chief executives. After all, some believe chief executives simply like dealmaking and getting big at the end of their careers." The BankAmerica/NationsBank and Banc One/First Chicago mergers, totaling $90 billion in equity, had driven Wall Street into a white-hot frenzy. Lipin observed, "One banker says the merger mania will be stoked by the latest pair of megadeals. 'Given the momentum, it's irrelevant whether it's right or wrong.'"

The slowdown of the bank merger trend after Wall Street stock prices stumbled after July 1998, especially bank stock prices, only strengthens this argument.

The provision of Wall Street capital has usually been preceded by a discussion of the inefficiency and excess capacity of the U.S. banking sector. Mergers have then been accompanied by banks' promises to cut costs dramatically by consolidating operations and laying off staff. A downward trend in bank employment has emerged in many states, especially California and New York, which can be traced in part to mergers; however, in most mergers, the cost economies and layoffs actually attained disappoint equity-market expectations. This recurring disappointment with cost-cutting has not removed the bullets from equity-market guns. For one thing, the equity market as a whole has surged through the 1990s, carrying banks along; for another, merging banks promise not just to cut costs but to create synergetic combinations of financial products sure to multiply revenues and earnings. While waiting for definitive proof of such synergies, Wall Street has supported bank expansion strategies and driven bank mergers forward. Thus far, the megabanks' check remains in the mail.[4] Indeed, the losses suffered by BankAmerica and Citigroup, among others, due to these institutions' involvement in overseas financial-market meltdowns in the 1998 global financial crisis only illustrates the two-faced nature of the new opportunities that financial consolidation creates.

The third and final impetus for the bank merger wave has been regulatory permissiveness. This study documents the clash among regulators about which criteria should govern their assessment of bank performance: old-fashioned "structure–conduct–performance" studies, or newer studies that rely on equity-market evidence about bank efficiency and effectiveness. Bank regulators appear to be operating under two maintained hypotheses: First, the industry is over-banked; second, financial innovations have made access to capital so universal for every class of economic agent as to remove it from the plate of regulatory concerns. Given these assumptions, regulators' own inaction combined with acquiring banks' market expansion strategies has fueled a merger wave that regulators and the press can attribute to "market forces."

So behind the invisible hand of the bank ownership market can be detected these three factors—regulatory acquiescence, acquiring banks' strategy, and Wall Street's underwriting. These forces have combined to create a great merger wave whose effects are simultaneously pervasive and complex. Banking firms are not necessarily less socially efficient because of the merger wave. As community activists across the country can verify, many banks have resisted any interest in social capital and community prosperity for decades. The small banks that are disappearing are not necessarily angels of social responsibility and reinvestment; the large banks taking them over are not necessarily exploitative monopolies that discriminate against minorities and serve only the rich. The pattern changes from one region to another, as the analysis in this book demonstrates. Banking performance in social-efficiency terms was not rosy before the merger wave started, and neither will the merger wave make it rosy in these terms. The merger wave has emerged for reasons only tangentially unrelated to the interests of minority and lower-income communities; and those communities will have to advocate for their interests after this wave has broken, just as they had to do before this wave first swelled.

Bank Mergers and Consolidation: Effects on Consumers and Small Business

Increased Bank Concentration Reduces Access to Home Mortgage Credit

This study finds that cities with increased banking-market concentration had lower-than-average approval rates for home loans. Conversely, home loan approval rates were above average in markets that experienced reduced concentration. Banking market structure in ten California cities is examined over a ten-year interval, and related to subsequent loan approval rates in 1995 and 1996 using probit analysis. Concentration rose in six of the cities examined, and fell in four others. Cities with higher concentration levels had consistently lower mortgage-approval rates, all else equal, than the groupwide average for comparable applicants in the same year. This was true regardless of applicant race or ethnicity.

Concentration levels changed dramatically in the ten markets during the study period. The Stockton market became significantly less concentrated, while concentration nearly doubled in Santa Barbara. Conventional home-loan applicants in Stockton, which became less concentrated, had a 5.8 percent higher-than-average likelihood of having their loan applications approved in 1996. Home-loan applicants in Santa Barbara, which became more concentrated, had a 12.6 percent lower chance of approval than similar applicants elsewhere in 1996. The range of the effect of market-structure change on home-loan approval rates for 1995 and 1996 probits, from +14 percent to −34 percent, suggests that banking market structure is a significant determinant of approval for home loans.

Large Banks and Thrifts Charge More than Small Ones for Deposit Accounts

Large banks are leading the trend toward higher bank fees. This study found that larger banks and thrifts charge higher fees than small banks and thrifts for some types of accounts and service fees. Another recent study by U.S. Public Interest Research Groups (PIRG) also found that large banks charge more than small ones. Price data reported by the Federal Reserve Board for 1995 and 1996 showed that large bank and thrift fees were higher than smaller institutions' fees on single-balance and fee-checking accounts and for NOW accounts,[5] as well as for service fees. The data show:

- Large banks and thrifts charged 46 percent more for single-balance and fee-checking accounts than did small banks and thrifts in 1995 ($8.97 vs. $6.16), and 24 percent more in 1996 ($7.59 vs. $6.13).
- NOW accounts cost consumers 31 percent more at large financial institutions than at small ones in 1995 ($10.81 vs. $8.25), and 34 percent more in 1996 ($10.12 vs. $7.56).
- Large banks and thrifts charged consumers $5.47 more per bounced check than did small ones in 1995, a 38 percent higher price, and $5.24 more in 1996, a 35 percent higher price.
- Large banks and thrifts charged their own customers 99 cents more for each money order than small banks and thrifts in 1995, a 54 percent higher price. Noncustomers seeking money orders face an even larger price differential: In 1995 they paid $1.61 more at a large bank or thrift for each money order, a 74 percent higher price.
- Out-of-state banks charged 18 percent higher monthly fees for checking accounts in 1995 than did in-state banks. Out-of-state banks also required higher minimum balances to avoid fees.
- Some checking account fees varied widely by region. The average cost to consumers for fee-only checking accounts was $2.74 among Northeastern U.S. financial institutions in 1995, but $4.88 in the South—a full 78 percent higher.

Other evidence also suggests that consumers are paid lower rates of interest in more concentrated banking markets; and that while bank mergers may generate higher profits, they do not lead to greater operational efficiency.

Bank Concentration and Small Businesses

The impact of bank mergers on smaller nonfinancial business enterprises should be a central focus of a book like this, but nothing like the home-mortgage data collected under the Home Mortgage Disclosure Act (HMDA) is available for small business loans. Instead, this study takes the much less satisfactory step of summarizing available studies on this topic.

Several studies suggest reasons to worry that increasing bank concentration will adversely affect small business. Adverse effects of three types have been developed: first, that large merging banks lend substantially less to small businesses than the smaller banks they displace; second, that small businesses will suffer because most of their financial business is conducted with locally owned financial intermediaries; and third, that small businesses will suffer because of the closure of nearby bank branches. These studies characterize the link between small businesses and banks as a relationship nurtured by proximity, with ongoing exchanges of qualitative as well as quantitative information.

These points have been disputed. Some have observed that large banks devote smaller proportions of their loan portfolios to small business, but nonetheless are able to replace smaller banks' small-business loans because of their large size; that large businesses use credit-scoring methods to make small-business loans more efficiently than small banks; that new niche banks will enter to fill in any holes in the credit market; and so on. Officials of the Federal Reserve are convinced by these latter points; but at the very least, some skepticism, and more comprehensive and extensive evidence, is wanted.

Bank Branch Location and Consolidation

Bank mergers are often accompanied by promises of branch closures and staffing layoffs. Studies have shown that bank branch closures in the wake of mergers occur at the same rate in lower-income and upper-income areas. However, since lower-income areas have smaller numbers of bank branches in the first place, their loss is greater. Further, other studies show that banks tend to open new branches in close proximity to other banks' branches; that is, bank branches cluster in some locations while avoiding others, including lower-income and minority areas. This finding sheds doubt on the notion that new banks will emerge in areas abandoned by large merging banks. The informal financial offices that replace formal banking institutions are not perfect substitutes. They provide only a partial set of banking services, and those they provide often cost more than when conducted at commercial banks.

A Nationwide Evaluation of Home Mortgage Outcomes by Race, Income, and Neighborhood

This study analyzes HMDA data from over 4.7 million loan applications in metropolitan portions of eighteen states throughout the continental United States. Having information about a very large number of loan applicants allows a comparison of how minority applicants and white applicants with similar incomes and loan-to-income ratios have actually been treated. The analysis also accounts for several neighborhood characteristics. This large sample of HMDA data was used to build a model testing whether racial or ethnic status and several other variables had an effect on loan approval independent of economic characteristics such as income and loan-to-income ratio. This method allows evaluation of the effect on race and ethnicity after controlling for key economic factors that might be expected to influence any applicant's chance of loan approval.

The study results show lending patterns by lender type for several different groups of cities. First, seven cities west of the Mississippi River are compared with eight cities east of the Mississippi River. Then, lending patterns in five regional groups of cities are compared using probit analysis: Southwestern states, including the City of Los Angeles, three other clusters of California cities, and clusters of five Texas cities and three New Mexico cities; Great Plains/Mountain states, including all the metropolitan areas in Idaho, Montana, North Dakota, South Dakota, and Wyoming; Midwestern states, including the metropolitan areas within Minnesota, Indiana, and Iowa; Northeastern states, including metropolitan areas within Pennsylvania, New York, Massachusetts, and New Jersey; and Southeastern states, including the metropolitan areas within Georgia, North Carolina, and Mississippi. The purpose of analyzing clusters of cities in each state or region is to get a large enough sample of loans to draw statistically reliable results by lender type within each regional cluster.

The study reports results for six lender groups, plus combined results for all lenders who report HMDA data. The types of lenders analyzed are: (1) small in-state banks; (2) all large merging banks; (3) large merging banks with in-state branches; (4) large merging banks without in-state branches; (5) savings and loan associations and mutual savings banks; and (6) mortgage companies. The focal point of this study is the lending records of large merging banks, defined here as the twenty-five largest bank holding companies at the end of 1997 plus four other institutions. The core result is that large merging banks do not perform consistently better than other lenders in extending home mortgages to underserved consumers and communities.

Running probit equations for each of seventeen different state and regional metropolitan clusters, for five lender types plus all lenders, generates 101 coefficients for each minority applicant category; it also generates 101 coefficients for lower-income loan applicants, and another 101 coefficients for minority areas and lower-income areas within the cities included here.[6] These coefficients all indicate how any one of these variables of interest—say, African-American applicants—is being treated in a specific regional cluster by a specific type of lender. That is, one can estimate whether applicants in a particular category are advantaged or disadvantaged relative to other applicants in applying for home-purchase loans, holding constant income, loan-income ratio, and the various other factors built into the probit model used here. A negative coefficient, such as –24 percent for a particular applicant group, means that those in this group, on average, have a 24 percent lower probability of loan approval compared with otherwise identical applicants who are not members of this group. A positive coefficient means that a particular applicant group is more likely to be approved than applicants not in this particular group.

Results for Minority and Lower-Income Applicants and Areas

The probit analysis conducted here for state and regional markets finds, for 1996 data:

- In every market tested, minority applicants are denied home mortgage credit at higher rates than white applicants with the same income and debt-to-income ratios. Except in seven cases, *every* lender type has at least one statistically significant negative coefficient for minority applicants *in every single market area* examined—that is, in 95 of 101 instances. For all lenders and lender types considered together, the four categories of minority applicant are at a statistically significant disadvantage relative to nonminority applicants in 46 percent of all instances, and at a statistical advantage in 8 percent of these instances. For 1995 data, these figures are 42 percent and 8 percent, respectively.[7] Removing Asian-Americans from these all-lender results, minority applicants are at a statistically significant disadvantage 59 percent of the time, and at a statistical advantage just 4 percent of the time.
- Taking into account all markets and all lender types, African-American applicants are disadvantaged in loan approval in 82 of 101 instances (81 percent), with coefficients as large as –95.6 percent relative to economically similar non-African-American applicants; they are never at a statistical advantage in probits for 1996 data. Across all 101 instances, African-American applicants average a loan-approval disadvantage of –36.3 percent.
- For all markets and all lender combinations, Hispanic applicants are at a disadvantage in loan approval rates in 50 of 101 lending probits (50 percent) relative to non-Hispanic applicants, and at an advantage in 10 instances (10 percent). This disadvantage is estimated as large as –59.5 percent. Across all valid instances, Hispanic applicants average a loan-approval disadvantage of –18.0 percent.
- For all markets and all lender types, Asian-American applicants are at a statistically significant disadvantage in 6 of 101 instances (6 percent), and at an advantage in 21 instances (21 percent). The estimated disadvantage in loan approval ranged as high as –28.8 percent. Across all valid instances, Asian-American applicants average a loan-approval advantage of 5.8 percent.
- For all markets and all lender combinations, Native American applicaots are at a disadvantage relative to non–Native American applicants in 47 of 101 instances (47 percent), and at an advantage in 2 instances (2 percent). The estimated disadvantage in loan approval ranged as high as –71.5 percent. Across all 89 valid instances, Native American applicants have an average loan-approval disadvantage of –36.3 percent.
- Among households that completed applications for home-purchase loans, applicants with lower incomes are at a disadvantage in getting a home loan relative to applicants with higher incomes, even after taking into account every applicant's income and loan-to-income ratio. A

lower-income disadvantage is estimated to be statistically significant in 41 of 101 cases (41 percent); and in 5 cases (5 percent), those in the lower-income portion of the applicant pool are at a statistical advantage. This lower-income effect is generally small; taking all markets and all lender types into account, it averaged −1.2 percent, independent of the applicant's ethnicity.

- Applicants who seek to finance homes in lower-income neighborhoods sometimes face more difficulty in getting a home loan. In 37 of 101 cases (37 percent), applicants from lower-income neighborhoods are at a statistically significant disadvantage relative to those applying for home loans elsewhere. In just one case are such applicants at an advantage. On average, taking all markets and all lender combinations into account, applications from lower-income neighborhoods are at a −3.8 percent disadvantage in loan approval, independent of borrower ethnicity and independent of several neighborhood features (including density and proportion of home owners).

- Applicants who seek to finance homes in neighborhoods with relatively high proportions of minority residents are at a statistically significant disadvantage in many of the markets examined here; for all lenders and all city clusters, a disadvantage is 30 of 101 times (30 percent), and an advantage 13 times (13 percent). Over all lender types and market clusters, applicants seeking homes in neighborhoods with relatively high proportions of minority residents are at an average disadvantage of −2.6 percent in loan approval, again independent of applicants' ethnicity.

In sum, our statistical investigation of regional city clusters finds a wide range of significant coefficients for minority applicants in loan approval rates, primarily negative coefficients, for all categories of lenders. Smaller but often significant levels of disadvantage and advantage in loan approval are present for lower-income applicants and neighborhoods, and for minority neighborhoods.

Results by Lender Type

Running an identical probit model of loan-approval probability for different lender types sets up a "horse race" concerning the social indicators of primary interest here—the treatment of race and lower-income in loan approval. This "horse race" reaches the following conclusions:

- When averages for all city clusters are computed using 1995 home-purchase loans, mortgage companies perform best in their sensitivity to race and lower-income variables; small in-state banks and savings and loans perform worst; and the two large merging bank categories place in the middle.

- When averages for all city clusters are computed using 1996 home-purchase loans, mortgage companies perform best in race/lower-income sensitivity, followed distantly by large merging banks with in-state branches; and large merging banks without in-state branches and savings and loans perform worst.

Table 2.1 sets out these averages for the four types of minority and lower-income variable for 1995 and 1996, thus summarizing the outcome of these "horse races." Mortgage companies attach a very low level of net disadvantage to area and applicant race, compared to the other lender types, but their income-based disadvantage is relatively large. When all large merging banks are considered together with 1996 data, their net disadvantage performance, on average, is slightly worse than that of small in-state banks in the same year.

In 1995, the two subcategories of large merging banks perform very similarly; but in 1996, large merging banks *with* in-state branches perform relatively well, whereas those without in-state branches perform poorly. Indeed, the worst net performance in the two years is by large merging banks without in-state branches, with a disadvantage sum of −27.1 percent. This −27.1 percent figure can be understood as follows. Suppose a minority applicant seeks a home-purchase loan in a minority and lower-income neighborhood—that is, whose proportion of minority residents falls into the highest 25 percent of all local census tracts, and whose residents' median income falls among the lowest 33 percent of all local census tracts. Suppose this applicant has an income that is among the lowest third of all home-purchase loan applicants for that city. If this applicant is otherwise average, she will have a 27 percent lower chance of receiving a loan after controlling for this applicant's income, loan-to-income ratio, and several other applicant and neighborhood characteristics. The −27 percent is troubling, but it differs very little from the other probabilities recorded in Table 2.1.

The reader is cautioned that no one type of lender performs uniformly well in terms of sensitivity to minority and lower-income status. Indeed, huge variations in race/lower-income sensitivity exist for any given lender type from one region to another, and also within regional markets. This leads to several additional summary points:

- No type of lender is consistently serving all minority consumers and neighborhoods better than other lender types.
- There is great variation in the treatment of minority loan applicants by different types of lenders in the same metropolitan area.
- There is wide variation in the treatment of minority loan applicants by the same type of lenders in different metropolitan areas.
- Lender groups that confer little or no disadvantage to one minority group frequently have a much poorer record in serving other minority groups in the same market.

Consider the seventeen city-cluster probit equations run here, counting each minority applicant category separately. In probits using 1996 HMDA data, small banks have positive applicant-race coefficients indicating loan-approval advantage in 2 out of 68 instances (2.9 percent), and negative coefficients (indicating disadvantage) 27 times (40 percent). Large merging banks with in-state branches have positive coefficients in 4 instances out of 60 (6 percent), and negative coefficients in 25 trials (39 percent). Large merging banks without branches have positive coefficients 3 times (4 percent) and negative coefficients 27 times (40 percent). Savings and loans record positive coefficients 2 times and negative coefficients 36 times (53 percent). Mortgage companies record positive coefficients 10 times (15 percent) and negative coefficients 30 times (44 percent).

The estimated coefficients for minority neighborhoods are also extremely variable. All categories of lender except merging banks with in-state branches record a positive coefficient at least once for minority neighborhoods among the 17 equations run. All categories also have two or more negative coefficients among the 17 equations; merging banks without branches in-state have negative coefficients 10 times. Less variability is found in lenders' response to lower-income applicants and areas—lower-income applicants have positive coefficients only four times among the 85 equations for lender subgroups, and lower-income areas only once. The lower-income variables otherwise are either statistically insignificant or negative for every lender type.

Conclusions and Recommendations

Table 2.2 summarizes the evidence presented in this study about the relative performance of different types of lenders in meeting the needs of consumers and small businesses, and especially those of minority and lower-income borrowers and areas. This table shows that in serving minority and lower-income applicants and areas, mortgage companies perform better than banks in residential credit markets; that overall, large merging banks perform about the same vis-à-vis minority and lower-income applicants and areas as do small in-state banks. Large banks may also perform less well in meeting small business credit and banking needs than do small banks. Large banks charge higher fees than do smaller ones; and banks owned out-of-state charge higher fees than banks owned in-state. Bank branch location patterns tend to disadvantage lower-income and minority areas.

Recommendations Concerning Mergers and Bank
Concentration

This study finds that mergers may have a large impact on consumers and communities. Insofar as mergers increase banking market concentration, they may hurt consumers and communities by increasing the chance of denial for loan applicants. The pricing data evaluated in this study suggests that the spread of larger

Table 2.1 **Effect of Race and Lower-Income Status on Loan Approval, Averages by Lender Type, Home-Purchase Loans, 1995 and 1996.**

	Minority applicant	Minority area	Lower-income applicant	Lower-income area	Cumulative race, lower-income impact
1995 Home-purchase loans					
All lenders	-13.2	-1.2	-6.8	-3.9	-25.1
Small in-state banks	-14.4	-2.2	0.9	-4.9	-20.6
Large banks with in-state branches	-13.7	-2.1	-0.4	-2.8	-19.0
Large banks without in-state branches	-12.4	-4.8	0.5	-2.0	-18.7
Savings and loans	-12.1	-1.9	-4.1	-1.6	-19.8
Mortgage companies	-8.0	0.1	-5.4	-3.3	-16.6
1996 Home-purchase loans					
All lenders	-12.1	-1.9	-2.0	-4.3	-20.3
Small in-state banks	-18.9	-1.8	-0.2	-3.9	-24.8
Large banks with in-state branches	-9.8	-4.0	-1.3	-1.9	-17.0
Large banks without in-state branches	-14.0	-8.6	-1.2	-3.3	-27.1
Savings and loans	-17.6	-0.7	-1.3	-6.7	-26.3
Mortgage companies	-7.5	1.5	-1.7	-2.6	-10.2
All large banks	-12.6	-5.8	-1.8	-5.4	-25.6

Note: The cumulative impact column on the right sums the figures in the other columns, which are derived from probit equations for the probability of loan approval, using 1995 and 1996 home-purchase loans reported under HMDA. Figures are averages using only statistically significant coefficients, with insignificant coefficients set to zero. The minority applicant figures are averages for four minority categories. The probit model and data used to generate these coefficients are discussed in chapters 8 and 9.

banks will lead to higher consumer prices for checking account services. It also indicates that replacing banks headquartered in-state with out-of-state banks raises banking prices. Mergers may especially reduce access to home-mortgage credit for minority borrowers and for lower-income borrowers: By changing the mix of lenders offering home-mortgage credit in different markets, merger activity alters the probability that applicants will be disadvantaged based on individual or neighborhood ethnicity or lower-income status.

Regulators must evaluate more carefully the impacts of proposed mergers on consumers and on underserved communities. Regulators should deny approval to large-bank mergers unless the banks prove that they will help and not hurt consumers. Regulators should take the following actions:

- Reject proposed bank mergers unless the acquiring bank commits to, or can prove the existence of, tangible benefits to consumers who are likely to be harmed by the merger. This study shows that there is real harm to consumers from larger and more concentrated markets in two important areas: fees and home-mortgage credit. Regulators should require banks that want to merge to prove that the merged bank will provide real benefits to affected consumers that more than offset these demonstrated harms. Regulators should evaluate the effect of every proposed merger on consumers and on underserved communities, and should approve more large bank mergers only if real benefits for consumers are proven.
- Abandon streamlined approval of bank mergers. The new federal Regulation Y puts some bank mergers on a fast track to approval, if several conditions are met. Those conditions are that the increase in concentration is below a certain threshold amount; most of the banks owned by the merging bank holding company had satisfactory CRA ratings; there are no substantial community comments filed; and the transaction is up to $7.5 billion in size. However, streamlined merger approval should be abandoned, because U.S. banking markets for consumers remain local markets in ways documented in this study. Bank fees vary among U.S. regions, and lender performance for minority and low-income applicants varies widely among regions. Lender types who have good records in one part of the United States perform poorly in other regions. So the "one-size-fits-all" approach permitted under Regulation Y should be rejected in favor of a careful examination of the probable effects of proposed mergers on consumers in each affected market. Further, disallowing fast-track approval permits community-based groups to develop pertinent comments more effectively; these, in turn, are more likely to lead to meaningful preapproval commitments by lenders.
- Require merging banks to propose definite plans and timetables to eliminate racial loan approval gaps. Every lender, whether or not it is merging, should have and implement a plan to lend to qualified minority and low-income applicants at levels comparable to white applicants.
- To ensure a level playing field, nonbank financial firms that provide financial services traditionally encompassed under the umbrella of commercial banking should, like banks, be held accountable under the Community Reinvestment Act.

Recommendations Concerning Access to Credit and Racial and Income Inequality

Our extensive analysis of available data and of the determinants of the probability of home-purchase loan approval suggests there is room for significant im-

Table 2.2 **Overall Assessment of Relative Performance by Banking Sector**

	Banks vs. non-banks	*Large merging banks*	*Small in-state banks*
Residential lending market			
Denial rates	Thrifts have lower rates than banks, mortgage companies higher rates	Merging banks without in-state branches have higher denial rates on average. Large	Small in-state banks have very low denial rates.
Minority-area fair share for loans made	Mortgage companies outperform banks.	banks headquartered in-state do best, large banks headquartered out-of-state worst.	Medium-level performance.
Lower-income area fair share for loans made	Mortgage companies outperform banks.	Large banks hdqtred in-state do best; large banks hdqtred out-of-state do worst.	Medium-level performance.
Loan approval race and lower-income effects	Mortgage companies do better than banks, thrifts worse.	Large banks in-state do relatively well, large banks out-of-state relatively poorly.	Small in-state banks perform the same as all merging banks.
Total race/income disadvantage	Mortgage companies do better than banks, thrifts worse.	Large banks in-state do relatively well, large banks out-of-state relatively poorly.	Small in-state banks perform the same as all merging banks.
Other evidence: banking fees, small-business effects, and branch locations			
Banking costs and fees	Most commercial bank fees are higher than those charged by savings associations.	Large banks charge more for fees and accounts than other banks; banks owned out-of-state charge more for fees and deposits.	Small banks charge less for accounts and have lower fees than large and medium banks.
Small business and bank credit	The informal loan market has unfavorable terms for those outside the formal market.	Large banks make a large volume of loans to small business, but these are less important than for smaller banks.	Small business loans are very important for small banks, on a relational basis.
Bank branch locations	Informal financial offices have replaced bank branches in lower-income areas.	Large banks often close branches when merging, especially in overlapping markets. They locate new branches close to other banks' branches, leaving geographic gaps.	

provement in lenders' treatment of loan applications from minority and lower-income applicants and areas—that is, for more socially efficient credit-market outcomes. It also shows that significant differences arise between different types of lender in the same market, and between similar lenders in different markets. Both lenders and regulators need to do more to improve access to home mortgage credit for minority applicants. Lenders should work hard to improve, and regulators should push every lender to bring its record of lending to minority applicants at least up to the standard set by the lender in its market with the best record. This leads to several conclusions:

- Lenders should seek to improve in every market. In the home-purchase loan analysis conducted here, no one lender group treats applicants from every major minority group the same as white applicants in any of the seventeen markets analyzed. The possibility of improvement is readily seen: In each of the seventeen city clusters, at least one type of lender approved Hispanic, Asian-American, or Native American applicants at the same rate as white applicants. In twelve of the seventeen city clusters, at least one type of lender also showed no disadvantage for African-American applicants relative to white applicants with similar economic characteristics.

   The existence of at least one lender group loaning to minority consumers without a higher probability of denial suggests room for improvement in the treatment of minority applicants in *every* market. Lenders should alter their practices to bring their own records up to the standards of others in their own markets that already have had success in making socially efficient as well as economically efficient loans.

   Lenders commonly respond to poor or mediocre HMDA records by asserting that racial and ethnic disparities in denial rates are an industry-wide problem. This excuse should be soundly rejected. The broad variation in performance by different lender types in the same market shows that most lenders can do a far better job of serving minority applicants. Lenders should look at the statistics for their own cities. They should determine which type of lender is best serving each minority population in their own area. Each lender should evaluate how its own underwriting and application-processing practices differ from those of lender types with better records in its market.

   The treatment of Asian-American applicants in Texas in 1995 offers an example of the room for improvement in lenders' performance within a market. In Texas, one lender category approved Asian-American applicants at the same rate as non–Asian-American applicants; four lender types at a higher rate; and one lender type at a lower rate. The effect from an Asian-American applicant in Texas ranged from a reduced probability of approval of 45.2 percent to an increased probability of approval of 15.2 percent (–15.2 percent to +45.2 percent). This range shows that there is room for very significant improvement by those lenders in the groups scoring negatively.

The treatment of Hispanic applicants in California in 1996 offers an example of the possibility of improvement across markets. Hispanic applicants were treated very differently in the four city clusters evaluated in California. In every city cluster, Hispanic applicants had at least one instance of statistically significant advantage vis-à-vis other applicants with at least one lender group, and at least one instance of disadvantage with at least one other lender group. Overall, however, Hispanic coefficients for most lender groups in the northern and southern California cities were negative and significant; Hispanic coefficients for most lender groups in inland California cities were statistically insignificant; and Hispanic coefficients for most lender groups in Los Angeles County were positive and significant. California lenders outside of Los Angeles may have something to learn from at least some lenders in Los Angeles.

- Regulators should hold lenders to the highest standard that the best lenders in their own market and their peers in other U.S. markets are achieving vis-à-vis racial and lower-income disadvantage. There is a continuing need for regulatory attention to fair-lending issues. This attention should be given in fair-lending reviews, as part of Community Reinvestment Act examinations, and in the convenience and needs test in reviews of merger applications. In each of these reviews, regulators should heighten their fair-lending scrutiny in market areas in which some types of lenders have much higher minority and lower-income disadvantage levels than do other types of lenders in the same market.

Regulators should demand that lenders raise their level of performance in serving minority and lower-income borrowers at least to that of their competitors in the same market. In addition, regulators should demand that lenders find ways to match the successes achieved by their counterparts in other parts of the United States.

- Regulators should separately review the sensitivity of any lender to race and lower-income disadvantage in every market that the lender serves, especially when considering merger or branching applications.

Our analysis of HMDA data finds that banking market outcomes are local. That a lender has a good record in one state does not guarantee its good performance in any market it may want to enter. This is particularly true if the demographics of the new market differ widely from the demographics of the existing market. For example, large merging banks with in-state branches showed no statistically significant disadvantage for African-American applicants in New Mexico and Indiana, but had significant levels of disadvantage for African-American applicants in 1996 in nearby Texas and Minnesota (–41.3 percent and –53.1 percent, respectively). This implies that a large bank with a good record in serving minority applicants in one market will not necessarily provide good service to minority applicants in another market without studying and adjusting to that new market.

- Special steps should be taken to address African-Americans' systematic disadvantage in obtaining home loans, and to understand the extent of Native Americans' disadvantage.

This analysis of data on over 4.5 million loan applications came to one conclusion common to many other studies of HMDA—African-American home loan applicants still face the largest disadvantage in having their loan applications approved, compared with white applicants of similar income and similar loan-to-value ratios, seeking homes in similar neighborhoods. These results cry out for scrutiny, and more than that for action, by both regulators and lenders.

The HMDA analysis conducted here also finds a remarkably large number of cases in which Native American applicants are disadvantaged at statistically significant levels in credit markets. This is surprising because the relatively small number of Native American applicants in itself makes statistically significant results unlikely. Further steps should be taken to determine the extent of disadvantage of Native Americans in U.S. credit markets.

Recommendation Concerning Banking Umbrella Protections

The higher fees charged by large institutions to noncustomers for money orders suggests they may be trying to discourage non–account holders from purchasing services. If larger banks do price to discourage noncustomer use of the bank, then mergers will exacerbate the already troublesome problem of how consumers without bank accounts are be to served in our financial system. These are serious issues. The pattern of large banks' deposit-account and fee-generating practices should be given rigorous scrutiny in each proposed merger involving one or more large banks.

It must be kept in mind that government involvement in U.S. banking markets consists of more than simply provisions ensuring competitive markets and limiting market power. Government involvement also involves a trade-off: The performance of crucial social functions is demanded in exchange for the provision of certain unique public protections. The key protections are deposit insurance and the Federal Reserve safety net. These cushions provide depositors, lenders, and equity shareholders of the banking system with assurances that the credit money therein is "as good as gold"—or at least as good as U.S. dollars. Banking could not be conducted as it is today without these protections in place. The price of these protections is the performance of some crucial social functions—the provision of broad-based banking services, including access to credit and deposit instruments, at competitive prices. The Community Reinvestment Act is, from this perspective, merely an affirmation of the banking system's obligation to be socially as well as economically efficient. And as Alan Greenspan pointed out in June 1998, while banks may complain of regulatory costs, none have turned in their charters—suggesting that on balance, the net effect for banks of their protections and social responsibilities is positive.

Large merging banks' performance vis-à-vis this implicit quid pro quo is mixed. Large banks have performed very unevenly in providing access to credit, and very poorly in banking fees and costs. Their strategic focus increasingly centers on upscale customers and on packaging standardized services. For some customers this will bring more socially neutral treatment, but this outcome is not guaranteed. Large merging banks' CRA performance as measured here varies widely. Fair-share evidence clearly suggests that large merging banks are far less engaged in lower-income and minority neighborhoods, on average, than are other lenders. Probit evidence suggests that the loan decisions of large banks with in-state branches is less sensitive to minority and lower-income status, on average, than other lenders' decisions are. This in turn suggests that local circumstances, certainly including sustained community activism, have had some effect. Large banks without local branches, by contrast, show high levels of sensitivity to minority and lower-income status. This suggests that large U.S. banks are on a cusp: Do they *want* the engagement with lower-income and minority neighborhoods, with these areas' residents and businesses?

If large banks shift away from broad-based transaction accounts and broad-based credit instruments, there is no reason, a priori, to think that smaller banking institutions can both build deposit-customer and loan-customer bases with economic units cast aside by the large banks, and provide low costs on deposit accounts, decent returns on savings accounts, and low, competitive rates on loans to these households and small businesses. That is, if market segmentation goes too far, the banking system as a whole will not be able to justify its special protections by pointing to the practices and policies of small niche banks serving smaller-balance households and small businesses. These niche banks will be unable to both be competitively viable and provide broad-based banking services at competitive prices. This leads to a recommendation:

- Banks' special protections, deposit insurance and the safety net, should be limited to banks providing broad-based customer markets with instruments that increase access to credit and provide low-cost transaction accounts.

If large banks want to go head-to-head with investment banks and mutual funds in a competition for well-to-do clients and well-established firms, without satisfying the social responsibilities that justify banks' deposit insurance and lender-of-last-resort protection, then they should shed these privileges. If a withdrawal of these public protections from large merging banks is not advisable, then banking regulators and Congress should just say no to large bank mergers until it becomes clearer how the banking system as a whole can become more socially efficient, a mechanism for expanding equal opportunity to all, including lower-income and minority households.

3

Bank Mergers and Regulatory Policy from the 1960s to the 1990s

Merger Experience and Regulatory Policy, 1966–1981

Regulatory policy toward bank mergers and consolidation can be divided into three phases in recent U.S. history: 1966 to 1981; 1982 to the present; and a new regulatory phase, which is emerging now. This section describes the first regulatory regime; the next sections summarize some subsequent changes in banking and explore the second regulatory regime. Chapter 4 examines the emerging third regulatory phase.

The Clayton Act and the Federal Trade Commission Act of 1914, together with the Sherman Act itself, have defined U.S. antitrust policy. The Clayton Act in particular outlaws four specific practices: price discrimination that lessens competition; mergers that reduce competition; tie-ins and exclusive dealing that lessen competition; and interlocking directorates among competing firms. A burst of corporate reorganizations and mergers among banking firms in the 1950s led to the passage of the Bank Holding Company Act of 1956 and the Bank Merger Act of 1960. These acts required federal banking agencies to consider the probable effects on competition (that is, antitrust aspects) of proposed bank mergers. The 1963 *Philadelphia National Bank* (*PNB*) decision of the Supreme Court (United States Supreme Court, 1963) affirmed the applicability of antitrust law to banking.

The *PNB* decision confirmed the relevance of U.S. antitrust law, and hence the oversight of bank mergers by the Antitrust Division of the Department of Justice, by defining commercial banking as a unique line of business involving a specific cluster of products and activities—in particular, deposit-taking and credit creation. This line of argument implied that nonbanks not delivering the financial services encompassed in banks' line of business, such as thrifts and finance companies, did not constitute effective competition for banks; hence their presence in any banking market should not be factored in when considering the antitrust implications of any merger on market participation.[1]

Bank merger policy was further refined by the Bank Merger and Bank Holding Company Act of 1966 (U.S. Public Law 89–356, February 21, 1966). This act required bank regulators to deny mergers that substantially reduced competition unless "the anticompetitive effects of the proposed transaction are clearly outweighed in the public interest by the probable effect of the transaction in meeting the convenience and needs of the community to be served." The 1966 act created a two-step process for bank mergers: the Federal Reserve was first to approve or deny merger applications, then the Fed's decisions were to be reviewed by the Department of Justice pursuant to U.S. antitrust law.

The merger guidelines adopted in 1968 by the Department of Justice were based on then-conventional wisdom that concentrated markets allow excess profits, high prices, and reduced output through oligopolistic coordination. These guidelines developed formulas that emphasized market shares in given market areas. Under these rules, mergers could be blocked between banks with as little as 8 percent of market share in a given banking market area. The Herfindahl–Hirschman Index (HHI) used as the principal measure of market concentration generally rose (indicating more concentration) as the number of competitors dropped or as market share become more unevenly distributed among competitors.[2] The Warren court supported these guidelines in a series of cases defining bank markets and the allowable activities of bank holding companies (BHC).

The firmness of governmental commitment to limiting monopoly power was demonstrated in 1970 when Congress passed, and President Nixon signed, a series of amendments to the 1956 Bank Holding Company Act. Under the 1956 statute, the sole subsidiaries of banks with just one holding company could undertake any manner of business; according to Liang and Savage (1990), in 1970 the subsidiaries of one-bank holding companies were active in 276 Standard Industrial Classification (SIC) activity codes. But a surge of formations of one-bank holding companies by large banks in the late 1960s resulted in the passage of amendments in 1970 which extended nonbank activity regulation to all bank holding companies, not just multibank holding companies. Given this regulatory and legislative atmosphere, few mergers were approved in the 1966–1981 period.

Cracks Open in the New Deal Banking System, 1961–1979

U.S. banking was put under this system of antitrust oversight in the first stages of its transition from the segmented, restricted-competition system established in the New Deal to an integrated-market, free-competition model. The systemic insolvency of the banking system in early 1932, in the wake of the October 1929 Wall Street crash and of the subsequent Depression, forced drastic action by President Roosevelt and Congress in the first days of the New Deal. Over-competition by banks, and bank runs by fearful depositors, were blamed as the culprits for some banks' demise. The Glass-Steagall Act forced financial firms to choose between the conduct of wholesale and retail banking. This, taken together with the 1927 McFadden Act prohibition against interstate banking, reconstituted the U.S. banking system as one of segmented markets with tight restrictions on market entry.[3] Deposit insurance was provided to preclude bank runs, and deposit rates were capped under Regulation Q. These measures to stabilize banking clearly undercut market forces, and necessitated strong regulatory oversight. In the wake of all these changes, the aggressive business ethos of 1920s banking was replaced by the "prudent person" principle, according to which the bank manager's obligation was to manage her institution on behalf of depositors—that is, with safety and soundness foremost.[4]

The relatively prosperous years of the 1950s rekindled managerial confidence, especially at large banks. Money-center banks began shifting to liability management, an operating style in which managers first identify a loan target and then fund it with deposits and, if necessary, with purchased funds. In the 1960s, a combination of robust economic growth and increased interest rates brought further changes to the New Deal system. Market rates periodically climbed above maximum deposit rates, and threatened money-center banks with attrition from their deposit and borrowed-fund base—that is, with disintermediation. To counter this threat, these banks began issuing negotiable CDs in 1961. This precipitated a decade-long struggle with the Federal Reserve: The Fed fought to restrict large banks' access to funds, while large banks fought to create innovative sources of funds outside regulatory reach. The Fed backed off when the Penn Central bankruptcy touched off a commercial-paper crisis in May 1970. Large banks won unimpeded access to large deposits and to the Euromarkets.

In the 1970s the U.S. and global macroeconomic environments worsened further. The old system received a further blow when the Bretton Woods system of fixed-exchange rates broke down in August 1971. This, together with two substantial oil-price shocks, led to chronic exchange-rate depreciation throughout the 1970s, and in turn to two recessions and high levels of price inflation. The Euromarket, fueled by surplus funds from oil-exporting countries, exploded in size. One consequence of this distressed macroeconomic environment was unprecedented levels of nominal interest rates. High rates, in turn, triggered the creation of money-market mutual funds, which provided upper-income and even middle-income households with a liquid, interest-earning alternative to bank deposits. Disintermediation from banks of all sizes reached flood-tide levels by the late 1970s. Banks had to borrow at high rates to replace their lost deposits, while facing pressure from Euromarket-fueled international competitors.

These innovations and changes further compromised the integrated character of investment and savings under the segmented-market scheme of the New Deal system. The savings outflow to money-market mutual funds compromised banks' lending capacity, leading in short order to the establishment of robust, liquid corporate bond and paper markets. The "blue chip" corporations that had been the backbone of banks' commercial and industrial lending turned to these direct credit markets for most of their financing needs. Banks and thrifts were no longer alone at the center of a savings/investment process that rechanneled savings, created credit, and absorbed liquidity and default risk. The loans that remained with banks—especially mortgages and other long-term loans—often yielded less than it cost to carry them. Large banks in particular lost loan customers, and sought to replace them by opening new loan markets.

They turned in particular to less-developed countries in Latin America and to oil-patch loans in Texas and Oklahoma in the late 1970s and early 1980s. At the time, this appeared eminently rational, if also daring. The apparent messages of the early-1970s bouts of inflation and high interest rates were that oil resources would bring explosive growth in national (or regional) wealth, and that countries possessing important, nonexhaustible resources more generally would eventually find the way to prosperity. Underexplored overseas markets promised great riches to bankers willing to explore beyond the bounds of their traditional market terrains. Closer to home, loan opportunities in oil-patch areas of the U.S. beckoned. Walter Wriston of Citibank made his famous late-1970s remark that "Countries don't go bankrupt." The large banks whose Eurodeposit holdings were swelled with petrodollars jumped hardest for less-developed country (LDC) loans. Citibank and BankAmerica competed for first place in South American and Mexican lending volume. But many other banks followed along. Using the innovative method of loan syndicates assembled in money centers, many regional banks across the country participated in overseas loans as the 1970s gave way to the 1980s.

Community Reinvestment Concerns

Ironically, the emergence of the LDC lending trend slightly lagged behind another important 1970s trend in banking—the community reinvestment movement. The surge of African-American and Hispanic migrants to U.S. cities in the post-war era, combined with the opening of suburban developments and the new prosperity of the U.S. working and middle class, led to "white flight" from central-city neighborhoods. These trends had a class and a racial aspect. On the one hand, as central-city neighborhoods were thinned of some of their more prosperous households, their average income fell relative to the metropolis as a whole. On the other hand, members of racial and ethnic minorities found their way into numerous formerly all-white neighborhoods.

Banks often responded to these demographic shifts in ways that drew vociferous protests. In some places banks financed block-busting—a phenomenon in which the entry of a minority family into a neighborhood induced panic selling by white residents, followed by minority residents moving in as owners or renters. More commonly, banks seemed less willing to make loans in neighborhoods whose relative income was less, and whose racial composition was changing to include more minority residents. Residents of these neighborhoods, both minority and nonminority, noted banks' reduced willingness to make loans. A new term, "redlining," entered the national vocabulary in the early 1970s. Community activists such as Gail Cincotta, and soon the national press, used this term to characterize situations in which firms were reluctant to do business in lower-income or high-minority areas.

Investigations into bank practices by activist organizations suggested the existence of *bank* redlining, in which banks were making fewer loans in central-city—and hence lower-income and higher-minority—neighborhoods than elsewhere. It seemed likely that some banks were failing to serve their entire market areas uniformly; and it seemed possible that banks were discriminating against minority applicants (who were more likely than whites to seek home loans in minority areas). New legislation leveled the playing field over banking policy. The Equal Credit Opportunity Act of 1974 extended the reach of the Civil Rights Act of 1964 to credit markets, specifically disallowing credit-market discrimination. Subsequently, pressure on Congress by activist organizations and concerned citizens led to the passage of the Home Mortgage Disclosure Act (HMDA) of 1975. HMDA required insured lenders—primarily commercial banks, savings and loan associations, and credit unions—to report annually on the number and dollar volume of their residential loans in every census tract in which they had loans. This act thus provided the empirical evidence by which it could be determined whether banks' loan activity was higher in some portions of their market area than in others.

Preliminary evidence collected under HMDA suggested that bank redlining was indeed a significant problem. Continued community pressure on Congress then resulted in the passage of the Community Reinvestment Act of 1977. The CRA requires institutions to take affirmative steps to ensure that they identify and meet banking needs throughout the entire market area they serve; it also specifies that bank regulators will be responsible for determining the adequacy of bank CRA performance. Banks performing poorly under the CRA could be denied the right to open new branches, to close branches, or to expand into new geographic areas. Bank regulators did not jump to use HMDA results to aggressively enforce the CRA; but nonetheless a principle had been established, and a data source identified, which in future would allow continuing close analysis of and commentary on lender behavior.

Disintermediation and the Dynamics of Financial Competition

The community reinvestment movement, the HMDA, and the CRA all signaled rising public discontent with the performance of insured depository institutions just when many of these institutions were turning to new lending markets well outside their established market areas. It would seem on the surface that the rise of unmet credit needs in the city should obviously attract the loan business of banks that were losing portions of their customer base to outmigration and disintermediation. However, it did not play out this way.

Banks sought to follow their customer base to the suburbs. Those that could, under state laws, opened new suburban branches; those that could not made loans only in suburban locales. This market shift was costly in an era in which banks were already losing upscale customers on both their asset and liability sides. Further, many banks were confused about how to behave in light of urban demographic and social shifts. What determines the return to lending in any area is somewhat mysterious in the best of cases; it is safe to say that this return depends jointly on the inherent characteristics of the project and of the neighborhood. A bank watching its competitors abandon central-city areas and turn to new suburban tracts might fear that its own return on central-city loans would fall as overall credit flows in central-city areas lagged; and this would justify its own shift toward suburban markets—a phenomenon that would, in aggregate, bring about precisely the market flight from the inner city that had been feared. In times of great uncertainty, economic agents fall back on what they know; and what they know is where they live, who they work with, who they worship with. The city-suburban divide widened.

Regulatory Change and the Bank Merger Wave, 1980–1997

Figure 3.1 shows that commercial bank earnings were flat and trended downward through the 1970s. This figure also shows that banks' interest margin—their interest income relative to interest cost—deteriorated rapidly in this decade; that is, banks' principal formula for generating income, "borrow low, lend high," was jeopardized by a combination of macroeconomic adversity and regulatory strictures. Political leaders and industry regulators stepped in to save the reeling banking system. This salvation came in several separate steps. The first two substantially deregulated the nation's depository institutions.

With the federal government unable to tame inflation and credit growth, and banks and thrifts unable to check the surge of funds to money-market mutual funds, deregulation was inevitable. The Depository Institution Deregulation and Monetary Control Act of 1980 was signed into law by President Jimmy Carter in the waning days of his presidency. This act provided banks and thrifts with more freedom to compete with nonbank financial firms and eliminated deposit-rate limits over a period of years. Even as the provisions of this act took effect, one portion of the regulated banking system, the thrifts, came under special threat. The high inflation rates of this period resulted in high—and even double-digit—short-term interest rates. But the loan portfolios of savings and loans and mutual savings banks were stocked with long-term mortgages locked in at lower nominal interest rates. In consequence, many thrifts—and a smaller number of banks—tipped into technical insolvency and paid out more interest than they took in. A wave of thrift failures gathered force and threatened to swamp the resources of the once-impregnable savings and loan deposit insurance fund (the

Figure 3.1 **Commercial Bank Earnings Trends, 1966–1996**

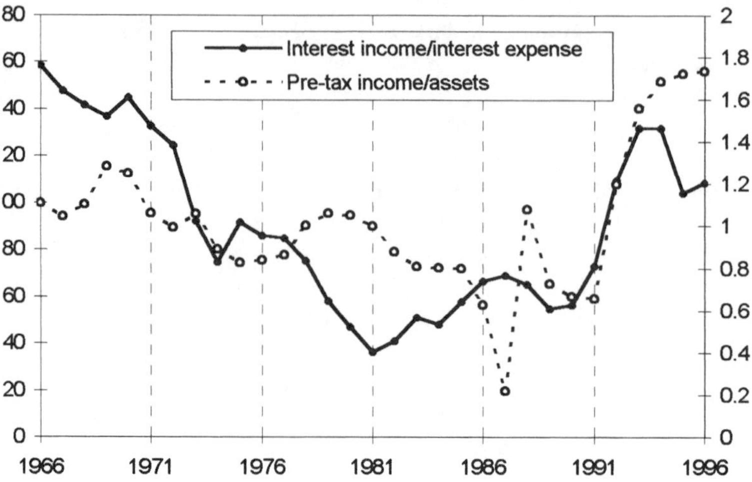

Source: FDIC.

Note: All figures in percentage terms. Interest income/interest expense shown on left axis, pre-tax income/assets on right axis.

FSLIC). This precipitated the Garn–St Germain Act of 1982, which focused on the deregulation of the thrift industry; it also triggered some state deregulation.

These acts, taken together, enhanced the flexibility of viable (solvent) depository institutions; for example, banks and thrifts were given more freedom to make loans, to purchase funds, to attract deposits, to buy and sell in financial markets, and even (in some states) to participate in underwriting and capital provision. Deposit insurance levels were increased, depositories were given more freedom to buy funds, and government guarantees for securitized home-mortgage debt were expanded. Meanwhile, the weak and insolvent depository institutions had to be disposed of. The sheer scale of failed thrifts (and later banks) appeared to be more than the resources of the deposit insurance fund(s) could absorb; so means were found wherein strong depository institutions could take over and absorb the weak.

In effect, market forces in banking were to be unleashed so that viable depository institutions could assist regulators in working out what to do with nonviable depositories. The turn toward market solutions meant a greater scope for market valuations, and a greatly enhanced role for equity markets in providing capital and support for bank strategies. Figure 3.2 depicts this shift. It shows that bank dividends as a percentage of banks' net income were flat until about 1982; after that, bank dividends have fluctuated wildly, demonstrating banks' increasing responsiveness to their equity owners.

Meanwhile, the banking system's surge in LDC lending was ingloriously

Figure 3.2 **Commercial Bank Dividends as a Percent of Net Income, 1966–1996**

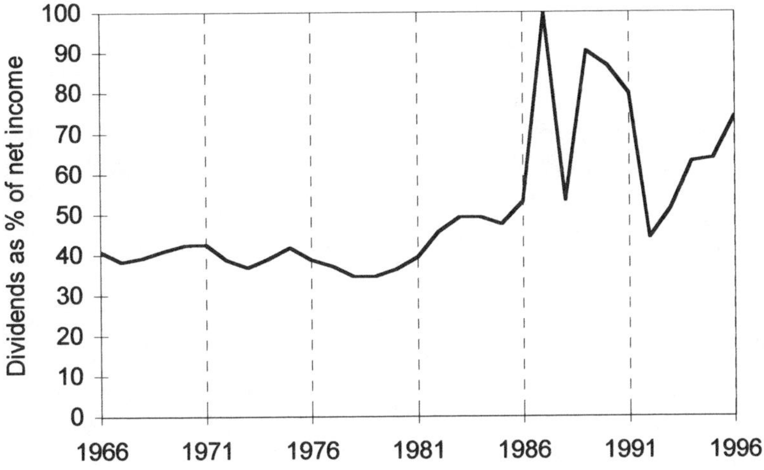

Source: FDIC.

aborted in August 1982 when Mexico defaulted on its current obligations. Billions of dollars of these loans went into arrears. Collapsing prices for crude oil and other commodities, combined with overambitious spending plans, brought on years of economic perversity in Latin America. The U.S. oil patch of Texas, Oklahoma, and Louisiana also tumbled. Continental Illinois and several large Texas banks failed, and the two megabanks most entrenched in Latin American lending, BankAmerica and Citibank, came near failure.

Changing Merger Guidelines: The Second Phase of Bank Deregulation

The Federal Reserve changed its merger guidelines in 1982 and in 1984 in accordance with these dramatic developments. The twin comprehensive deregulation acts of 1980 and 1982, in considerably expanding the allowable scope of bank activities and the range of permissible banking-market competition, themselves necessitated a rethinking of the appropriate guidelines for bank competition. These shifts became all the more important in light of the implicit strategy of drawing on strong banks' strength to help embattled deposit insurance funds handle the disposition of the weak and insolvent.[5]

The 1982 merger guidelines established new, significantly higher threshold levels of the HHI for permissible bank mergers. A banking market was considered unconcentrated if its postmerger HHI was below 1,000; it was considered moderately unconcentrated if its HHI was between 1,000 and 1,800; and it was considered highly concentrated at an HHI of 1,800 or more. The 1984 merger guidelines, in turn, "for the first time allowed the antitrust authority to consider efficiencies if convincing evidence existed that those gains would not be achieved but for the merger" (DeYoung, 1994a). These guidelines also loosened the notion of "banking market" as defined in the 1963 *PNB* decision.[6] Since thrifts were henceforth to make retail loans (and not just residential mortgages), the new guidelines took partial account of thrifts in determining the number and size of competitors in any given banking market. Specifically, thrift deposits were counted at 50 percent of commercial-bank deposits in calculating the total volume of bank deposits in a market. This reduced the degree of measured concentration, sometimes substantially, and thus opened the door to more bank concentration.[7]

Paralleling the shift from previous administrations to the Reagan administration was a shift in many economists' thinking. The prior consensus linking monopoly to excessive profits and welfare losses for consumers was challenged by a Chicago-based revision of industrial concentration theory known as the "new learning." This "new learning" argued that the degree of competition in a market is not properly measured by the number of competitors at any point in time; for monopoly could have arisen due to a super-efficient institution having crushed all its competition. Under this theory, effective competition requires only contestability—that is, that markets are open to entry by whatever competitors care to take on incumbent firms.[8]

What effect did the market-oriented Reagan administration and the "new learning" approach to market structure have on antitrust policy? One study, by DeYoung (1994a), has addressed this question. He finds no evidence that bank-merger regulatory policy concerning the degree of market competition changed significantly in the 1980s. He also finds that the shift to a larger benchmark score on the Herfindahl–Hirschman Index (1800, with merger increasing the score by at least 200) in 1985 was not an important determinant of the probability of bank-merger approval or denial. DeYoung does find, however, that the new majority of Reagan appointees on the Federal Reserve Board had a powerful effect on bank-merger approvals—tipping the balance toward approvals even for applications that previously would have been denied. Not until 1990 did the Department of Justice challenge a bank merger application under the new merger guidelines.

The Justice Department released Horizontal Merger Guidelines in 1992 that affirmed its acceptance of the "new learning" about market structure. These guidelines specified that the relevant antitrust market includes not just firms currently buying and selling in markets, but also "uncommitted entrants"—that is, firms likely to enter a given market, even if not now within it, in response to a "small but significant nontransitory increase" in the market price. The idea is that the *potential* threat posed by uncommitted entrants will in itself prevent firms already in the market from exercising their market power and raising prices.

The New Terrain of Bank Mergers and Operations

The changes described here have led step-by-step to a dramatic transformation in U.S. banking. As major problems afflicted overseas loans, oil-patch loans, and fixed-rate mortgage loans alike, bank and thrift failure rates climbed to levels not seen since the Depression. The responses to this wave of troubles—deregulation, new Fed appointees, new merger guidelines, and so on—have completely altered the terrain of bank operations, bank mergers, and bank oversight.

Bank operations have shifted dramatically as they became more exposed to market forces and entry pressures (see Figure 3.2). In part this means a retooling of bank strategy, discussed below. In part it means downsizing. Figure 3.3 shows that the number of bank branches has grown continually, reflecting the continuing struggle for market share in emerging markets; this trend is present even when the declining office total of savings institutions is added in. However, at the same time, the number of bank employees has trended downward after peaking in 1985 and 1986. This divergence in the trends for bank offices and bank employees is undoubtedly rooted in changing bank technologies and also in the rise of "supermarket branches." According to Radecki (1997), some 4,000 bank offices are supermarket branches, and more are on the way; he estimates that, when fully implemented, the adoption of this delivery method could reduce bank employment by about a tenth.

The wave of thrift and bank insolvencies in the 1980s and early 1990s in turn produced seismic changes in the shape of these industries. Table 3.1 provides the raw data for commercial banks, and Figures 3.4 to 3.6 interpret it. Figure 3.4 depicts the total number of U.S. commercial banks, 1966 to 1996. After 1985 the number of banks has fallen by 34 percent. If this linear trend continues, only about 5,400 banks will remain in the U.S. by 2010.[9] Figure 3.5 provides some details on the sources of reduction in the ranks of U.S. banks. Note that assisted mergers of failed banks were especially important in the late 1980s. In this figure the preference for market-assisted workout strategies as a means of handling failing banks is evident: the relative volume of assisted mergers far outweighs that of other failures. The outstanding feature of Figure 3.5, however, is the trend in unassisted (market) mergers. Until about 1980, unassisted mergers encompassed about 1 percent of the bank population every year; but they have grown in importance since then, until, by the mid-1990s, they now eliminate more than 5 percent of the bank population annually. Accompanying this pattern of rapid bank disappearance is a pattern of some entry into commercial banking. Figure 3.6 shows that a significant number of new entrants have continued to enter banking during this period. What is not clear in this figure is whether the improvement in the number of bank entrants in the past two years defines a new trend, or whether this represents just a temporary reversal in the post-1984 pattern of fewer new entrants.

These remarkable industrial shifts in banking in the 1980s and 1990s have

Figure 3.3 **U.S. Commercial Bank and Savings Institution Employees and Offices, 1966–1997**

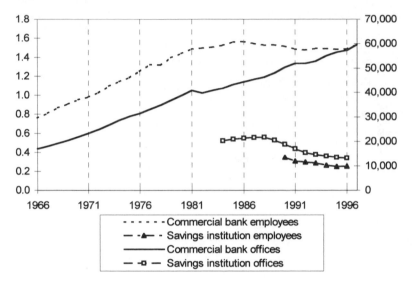

Source: FDIC.
Note: Employees in millions, left axis; offices, right axis.

provided fuel for the spread of the new thinking about the institutional core of U.S. intermediation. Bank regulators have relied heavily since the early 1980s on the notion that market forces themselves can be used to sculpt the evolving shape of this industry. Where statutory law differs from this approach, it is regarded as burdensome and anachronistic. Law and regulations of this sort have not entirely slowed regulators in their efforts to reshape banking markets. Indeed, the 1989 savings and loan "bailout" law—the Financial Institutions Reform and Regulatory Enhancement Act, or FIRREA—provided the Fed with a mandate for disposing of insolvent depositories under a "least cost to the taxpayer" criterion. The Fed took the opportunity to approve combinations it deemed appropriate, even when these contravened the letter or at least spirit of the McFadden and Glass–Steagall Acts.

Taken together, the easing of rules against interstate banking in the 1980s and the passage of the 1994 Riegle–Neal Interstate Banking Act have created a new dimension to the merger problem. Whereas horizontal mergers were previously the only available means of entering distant markets, branching is now more widely available. Indeed, mergers and intra- and interstate branching are alternative means of accomplishing similar ends. At this point, the expansion strategy of a large bank headquartered in a given county and state depends on the rules prevailing in this and in other states.[10] If this bank is able to branch statewide, it

Table 3.1 **U.S. Commercial Banks: Additions, Deletions, and Total Count, 1966–1996**

Year	Commercial banks at start of year	Additions: New charters	Additions: Conversions by nonbanks	Deletions: Unassisted mergers	Deletions: Distress mergers	Deletions: Other failures	Commercial banks at end of year
1966	13,544	99	24	121	6	2	13,538
1967	13,538	94	21	131	0	8	13,514
1968	13,514	82	19	125	3	0	13,487
1969	13,487	115	18	138	5	4	13,473
1970	13,473	178	13	146	2	5	13,511
1971	13,511	197	5	95	1	5	13,612
1972	13,612	236	4	118	0	1	13,733
1973	13,733	332	11	94	3	3	13,976
1974	13,976	364	6	113	3	0	14,230
1975	14,230	246	5	84	10	3	14,384
1976	14,384	161	6	125	13	3	14,410
1977	14,410	157	3	152	6	1	14,411
1978	14,411	149	2	165	5	1	14,391
1979	14,391	204	3	224	7	3	14,364
1980	14,364	205	1	126	7	3	14,434
1981	14,434	198	0	210	5	3	14,414
1982	14,414	317	8	256	25	7	14,451
1983	14,451	361	22	314	36	15	14,469
1984	14,469	391	49	332	72	9	14,496
1985	14,496	331	45	336	94	25	14,417
1986	14,417	257	31	341	120	34	14,210
1987	14,210	219	37	543	175	25	13,723
1988	13,723	229	3	598	203	17	13,137
1989	13,137	192	9	411	197	15	12,715
1990	12,715	165	24	393	150	14	12,347
1991	12,347	106	35	447	101	13	11,927
1992	11,927	72	11	428	87	29	11,466
1993	11,466	59	12	481	55	41	10,960
1994	10,960	50	17	548	11	16	10,452
1995	10,452	102	36	609	6	32	9,943
1996	9,942	146	46	554	5	45	9,530

Source: FDIC.

can do so freely when its financial capacity and market conditions permit; if not, it may engage in a merger strategy within the state to reach the same goal. Similarly, this bank's ability to penetrate other states' markets depends on the existing rules (these are summarized in Nesiba 1995, Tables 3.1, 3.2, 96–97). Some states allow bank holding companies headquartered elsewhere to acquire in-state banks, with or without reciprocity; others permit BHC acquisitions of

Figure 3.4 **Total Number of U.S. Commercial Banks and Savings Institutions, 1966–1996**

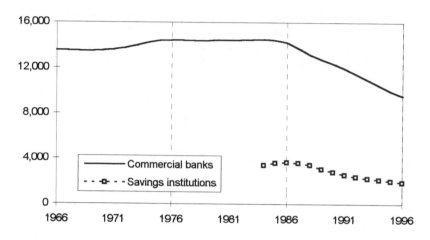

Source: FDIC

Note: Insured institutions only. Savings institutions include savings and loans and mutual savings banks. Pre-1964 data for savings institutions are not comparable.

Figure 3.5 **Causes of Reductions in Commercial Bank Population, 1966–1996**

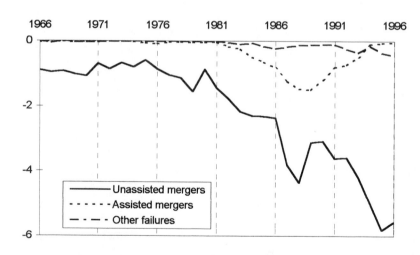

Source: FDIC.

Note: Figures depict percentage of bank population in previous year.

Figure 3.6 **Causes of Increases in Commercial Bank Population, 1966–1996**

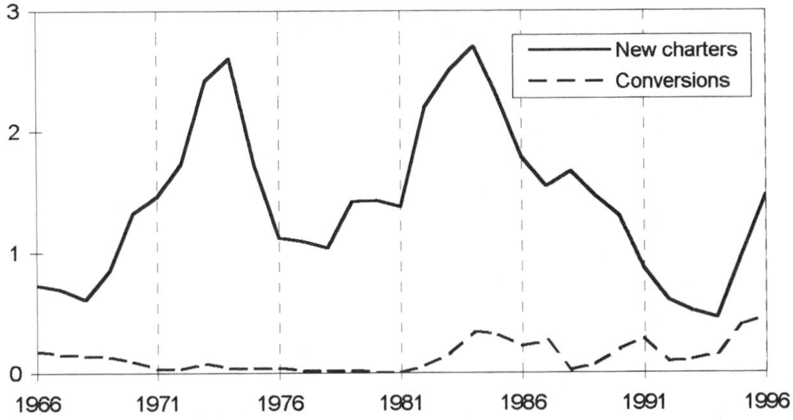

Source: FDIC
Note: Figures depict percentage of bank population in previous year.

in-state banks by banks headquartered in contiguous states (with reciprocity); still others allow interstate branching directly; and only Hawaii does not allow entry by out-of-state banks.

Case Studies of Recent Bank Mergers

Some case examples of the merger wave will illustrate the scope of its impact on the banking industry. This section reviews bank experience through the end of 1997. The events of 1998 are covered later in this volume.

The outstanding case is that of NationsBank, whose CEO, Hugh McColl, is pursuing a bank acquisition strategy as a means of becoming the nation's largest depository institution. As of the end of 1994, his NationsBank held the third position, with $170 billion in assets at year's end—a total ranking behind only Citicorp's $250 million and BankAmerica's $215 billion. Just seven years ago, NationsBank barely ranked in the top twenty-five in assets among U.S. banks. NationsBank has accomplished its rise with fifty bank acquisitions in the past thirteen years. McColl's rise was defined by his successful 1989 bid against Wells Fargo and Citicorp for First Republic Bank of Texas, a failed depository with $32.5 billion in assets. The deal doubled the size of NationsBank.

In a *Fortune* magazine cover story on August 1, 1995, McColl declared open season on banks. Within the next forty days, more than one bank a day was purchased, including a $1.6 billion takeover of Atlanta's Bank South by NationsBank. Two months later, *Fortune* assured its readers that these mergers were good for their savings accounts.[11]

NationsBank is not the only predator bank loose in the United States these days, merely the most active. Another major bank headquartered in Charlotte, First Union, used an acquisition strategy to become the nation's sixth biggest bank in 1995, and Banc One of Columbus, Ohio, used acquisitions to grow to seventh position in the same year.[12] Hostile takeovers generated such momentum that consensual takeovers have become very prevalent; many of these take the form of "mergers of equals"—First Chicago's joining with NBD Bancorp, the aborted bid of CoreStates Financial for Bank of Boston, and the successful 1997 merger of CoreStates with the aforementioned First Union of North Carolina.

The other remarkable growth story among U.S. banks has been that of BankAmerica. This bank nearly went under in 1985 in the wake of a ruinous lending competition with Citicorp to lend in Latin America in the late 1970s. BankAmerica shored up its business by taking on the management team of Wells Fargo, a competitor bank that (together with Citicorp's John Reed) defined the "upmarket" retail banking strategy. This involved a simple response to the invasions of banks' turf by nonbank competitors—eliminate cross-subsidies between less and more well-heeled customers. Henceforth, services would be provided at cost except for customers whose overall business volume or variety warrants special consideration. In effect, banks using this strategy eliminated or reduced cross-subsidies within product lines and instead used cross-subsidies strategically between product lines to retain and attract upscale customers.

BankAmerica was able to find its way back to recovery through modernization and through the virtues of its traditional strength—its massive retail base. At the same time, BankAmerica redefined its approach to this base by trying to go "upmarket," seeking out customers to whom it could sell a variety of financial services (portfolio management, credit cards, payments management, and so on), and distancing itself from customers who needed only basic financial services (Dymski and Veitch 1996a, 1996b). In 1994, it shored up its corporate banking business through the acquisition of Chicago's Continental Bank—another once-proud institution that had made billions in poorly monitored and ill-fated oil-patch loans in the early 1980s ("Friends for Life: Bank of America/Continental," *The Economist,* February 5, 1994: 79). The stock market richly rewarded BankAmerica's resurgence: Its stock price climbed from $39.50 in January 1995 to $54.87, nine times earnings, in August 1995; the stock went over $100 per share, thirteen times 1996 earnings, in December 1996.

Finally, per the expression "everything that rises must converge," the high-flying NationsBank and BankAmerica shocked the world with their agreement to merge in April 1998. The NationsBank merger with BankAmerica is both the largest bank merger in history, valued at nearly $60 billion in equity, and the boldest. It creates a bank with significant market share in twenty-four states, holding 8 percent of all U.S. bank deposits, whose span reaches from the Atlantic Ocean to the Pacific. With this merger, tomorrow has become today in U.S. banking. This episode and other recent developments in the bank merger wave are explored further in chapter 5.

Not surprisingly, widespread adoption of the growth-by-merger strategy has created substantial instability in the ranks of the biggest U.S. banks. For example, at the end of 1996 Citibank ranked as the largest U.S. bank, as it had for many years.[13] BankAmerica slipped to third after being passed by Chase Manhattan, whose deposit base grew by 88 percent ($75 billion) that year due to its merger with Chemical Bank. NationsBank itself ranked fourth; its consolidated deposit base grew by 7.9 percent ($10.1 billion) in 1996.[14] Meanwhile, Wells Fargo had moved into fifth position, thanks to acquisitions (largely First Interstate) that increased its deposit base by 94 percent ($36.8 billion). Other banks moved into the top ten due to acquisitions: PNC stood eighth, having increased its deposit base by $10.8 billion in 1996, a 43 percent increase; Fleet stood ninth, having grown in deposits by $29.4 billion, or 508 percent, in 1996; and Corestates stood tenth, having added $17.9 billion, or 107 percent, in 1996. Of the top twenty-five banks in deposit base as of December 31, 1991, only sixteen remained in the top twenty-five just five years later; of the top ten, only six remained (the newcomers were NationsBank, PNC, Fleet, and CoreStates). Predictably, the leader board has changed substantially since 1996. Table 9.1 in chapter 9 lists the largest U.S. banks as of June 30, 1998.

4

Explaining the Bank Merger Wave

Introduction: Three Approaches to Explaining Bank Mergers

Most explanations of the U.S. bank merger wave have emphasized operational efficiency. That is, they have argued that bank mergers can be explained by merging banks' desire to enhance safety and soundness and/or to boost their productivity in supplying financial services. Four distinct operating-efficiency explanations have been proposed: First, mergers enhance safety and soundness by allowing stronger banks to absorb weak or failing banks; second, mergers enhance safety and soundness by allowing diversification into new markets; third, mergers enhance productivity by allowing banks to exploit economies of scope; and fourth, mergers enhance productivity by allowing banks to attain greater economies of scale. The next several sections consider these four rationales in turn, considering the reasoning and evidence supporting each. This review of the evidence on operating-efficiency explanations for bank mergers concludes that these explanations are not sufficient to explain the sustained and continuing U.S. bank merger wave.

We then develop an alternative equity-market rationale for mergers. Equity-market rationales arise when mergers are expected to enhance bank equity value for owners and/or executive officers. This alternative approach rests on the insight that banks can increase their net profits without any enhancements in their operational efficiency: reducing the interest cost of their liabilities, increasing fees for depository services, increasing loan rates, reducing the likelihood of extraordinary costs, and increasing the revenues generated by fees. Banks may pursue mergers because they enhance banks' capacity to take these profit-increasing steps, and further because they increase stockholder value and enhance the position of bank executive officers—independent of any changes in operational efficiency per se.

We then discuss a third alternative explanation for bank mergers: They may be sought because they allow banks to redefine their role in financial markets, and thus to earn revenues in new ways from redefined customer bases. It should be noted at the outset that these various rationales are not mutually exclusive. More than one could be at work in any given case.

Mergers to Allow Least-Cost Absorption of Weak
or Failing Banks

Many mergers in recent years have involved the purchase of failing banks by prosperous ones. Throughout the 1980s, mergers of this sort were commonplace in the savings and loan industry; in particular, many expansion-oriented commercial banks picked up interstate banking assets by acquiring substantial portions of failing thrifts. These mergers were allowed under the "least cost to the taxpayer" criteria noted above. The underlying rationale was that managerial expertise in banking is scarce; thus, letting successful banks take over lemon banks in other markets spreads the benefits of strong management.

"Assisted" mergers of this type have also occurred between commercial banks. The downturn in the fortunes of the Texas oil patch accounted for many such mergers in the late 1980s. Figure 3.5 shows that this period marked the high-point of assisted mergers. The Texas banking crisis that accompanied the oil-patch crash led to state legislation in 1986 that permitted the purchase of in-state banks by out-of-state banks, and also loosened rules regarding in-state branching (Grant 1996). In 1987, Chemical Bank of New York took over Texas Commerce Bank, which then had $11.4 billion in assets. In that same year, Interfirst Bank, with $8.8 billion in assets, was taken over by RepublicBank Corporation. In 1988, First Interstate Bancorp of California took over Allied Bank of Texas ($4.9 billion); and with assistance from the FDIC, NCNB Corporation (NationsBank) purchased First RepublicBank, and Banc One of Ohio purchased MCorp.[1]

In some cases, bank takeovers have involved a strong bidder and a weak, but not yet insolvent, target; an example is the absorption of Security Pacific by BankAmerica in 1992. Another example, Wells Fargo's 1996 takeover of First Interstate, involved a stronger bidder and a weaker target, but not one near insolvency. It might seem that there is a continuum of weak target banks for strong banks to bid on—ranging from the insolvent to those whose growth rate is lower than that of more successful competitors. This impression is misleading, however. The stock prices of solvent targets of suitor banks almost invariably rise, creating capital-market inducements for takeovers even when the target banks' operating characteristics are sound. This theme is explored at length below.

Gains from Interstate Mergers

Mergers across state lines and interstate branching are substitute strategies—both expand their geographic range. Rhoades's 1996 study of bank mergers suggests that about half (3,255) of the 6,347 bank mergers in the period 1980–1994 were market-extension, not horizontal, mergers—suggesting that many mergers have indeed been oriented toward breaking into new geographic markets.[2] The pace of this activity increased in the mid-1980s: There were eight interstate bank acquisitions per year between 1980 and 1986, but forty-eight per year between 1986 and 1988 (Rose 1989, 10).

Because interstate branching per se was forbidden until the passage of the Riegle–Neal Interstate Banking and Branching Efficiency Act of 1994, mergers have been a favored route to interstate expansion. Numerous benefits have been claimed for banks that operate in more than one state. One is risk reduction, which implies greater safety and soundness. A given volume of bank loans of any type (say, construction loans for commercial real estate) made in just *one* location is riskier than the same volume of bank loans made in *two* locations with different economic fundamentals. Any given economic downturn ("shock") is unlikely to affect the two locations to the same extent—so the potential extent of loss from any one shock is less than when all loans are made in one or the other location. Calomiris (1990) points out, in addition, that banks with fewer branches are more susceptible to bank runs, since a more geographically diversified bank is less likely to be suspected of possible failure by its depositors.

Enhanced operating efficiency represents another potential benefit. At present, banks that operate in multiple states (such as NationsBank) must absorb duplicative operating costs; subsidiaries in states other than the home state require separate boards of directors, regulatory reports, examinations, audited statements, and also distinct support, control, and computer systems. Efficiency will also be enhanced insofar as payment processing involves a higher proportion of same-bank checks between payers and payees.

Benefits have also been claimed for markets, firms, and customers targeted by banks expanding interstate. The Bush administration's report on financial reform (U.S. Department of the Treasury, 1991, essay 17) argues that far-flung "home bank" networks may be more convenient for mobile consumers. Further, "The empirical evidence tends to support the argument that branching advances competition without diverting credit from local economies. Banks in statewide branching states have a lower return on assets and offer a broader array of consumer and business services than banks in restricted branching states." Elsewhere, Srinivasan argues (1991, 42) that banks taken over by out-of-state organizations may be better able "to attract capital to struggling local economies, to broaden their pool of management talent, to profit from improved stock prices for target banks, and to restore a customer base suffering from the departure of large business clients."

Some advantages from geographic expansion are indisputable. The potential for risk reduction from the geographic expansion of loan asset portfolios is real (Laderman and Pozdena 1991); so too are cost savings from eliminating redundant bank managements and boards. But geographic asset spreading can be accomplished through means other than mergers; and gains from more centralized administrative operations may be offset by the greater costs of larger-scale operations. Further, consumer advocates in numerous locales have charged for years that large banks often underserve the customers who are most dependent on the services offered by small community banks. Also, Rose's (1989, xii) study suggests the possibility of "credit droughts" as funds are withdrawn from some areas (such as Southwestern cities) to shore up money-center banks.

Mergers to Derive Benefits from Product-Line Diversification

Conducting two or more financial product lines leads to two potential benefits, independent of the returns on any one product line taken on its own: economies of scope and risk reduction. A rationale for mergers arises insofar as mergers allow acquiring banks to diversify into new lines of financial business.

Economies of scope exist in general when a firm can provide two activities more cheaply than it could provide either activity separately; they are explained by this firm's ability to use the same delivery mechanism to provide two separate services. The economies-of-scope rationale has been used (for example, in the 1991 Treasury Report) to support the elimination of the Glass–Steagall "firewalls" between commercial banking and investment activity. It also figures in some mergers, as in the BankAmerica purchase of Continental Bank mentioned above.

How important, in practice, are economies of scope in banking? Kim (1986) does find statistical evidence of small global economies of scope. But most studies (Mester 1987; LeCompte and Smith 1990) find that economies of scope are nonexistent in banking; and several, such as Cebenoyan (1998), have reported findings of scope diseconomies in banking.[3]

What about risk reduction from diversification? The argument here is similar to that for multiple geographic markets. The net earnings of firms active in different lines of business depend on outcomes in each line of business. The return in any one line of business may be low or negative due to an adverse shock. A firm engaged in that line of business receives benefits from diversification if that same shock has a smaller effect (or no effect) on returns in its other lines of business. So a banking firm can, in principle, reduce its risk by expanding into product lines whose returns are imperfectly correlated with those on the bank's existing products. Product-line expansion, in turn, can be accomplished by developing new products or by merging with firms that already deliver such products.

How important are diversification benefits? Wall, Reichert, and Mohanty (1993) conducted a comprehensive study of the portfolio effects of combining traditional bank activities with nonbank activities. These authors note that most studies find "limited potential for reducing portfolio risk by allowing banks to expand their investments in nontraditional activities" (2). Only Litan's 1986 study found diversification benefits from bank expansion into nonbanking activities. The authors use Litan's methodology and extend his data. Whereas Litan used 1981 IRS data, these authors obtained IRS data for the period 1971 to

1989. They find that while some pair-wise combinations of economic activities do decrease risk, just as many *increase* risk. Hence, whether any given bank's diversification into nonbanking activities reduces or increases risk depends on which activities it combines when, where, and how.

Interestingly, the pace of combinations between banks and nonbanking firms slowed in the last several years before 1998. By the late 1980s, the trend toward aggressive bank purchases of nonbank financial activities was being reversed (Rose 1989, 11–12). On one hand, it seemed that there was no halo effect and no real risk reduction either from bank mergers with nonbank financial firms. On the other hand, the megabanks most likely to push this envelope were universally badly damaged due to the successive adverse earnings shocks generated by the Latin American debt crisis, the collapse of oil-patch states' prosperity, and the bursting of the commercial real-estate bubble.

This trend was resoundingly reversed in 1997 and 1998, after several years of record profits had reflated banks' equity prices. Bankers Trust agreed on April 6, 1997, to buy Alex. Brown, a Baltimore investment bank, a move hailed as the practical end of the Glass–Steagall Act by *The Economist* (April 12, 1997). Both BankAmerica and NationsBank bought San Francisco investment-banking firms later in 1997: BankAmerica, Robertson, Stephens for $540 million; Nations-Bank, Montgomeries Securities for $1.2 billion. Prior to their merger, these banks ranked thirteenth and fourteenth in underwriting common stock, and now wanted to get into the booming business of underwriting and arranging mergers. Another nail was hammered into Glass–Steagall's coffin by the April 1998 merger of Citicorp and Travelers Group, the insurance giant, a $70 billion deal creating the world's largest financial services firm (*Wall Street Journal,* April 13, 1998).[4]

This rapid expansion by megabanks has been greeted with some skepticism in realms outside the superheated atmosphere of Wall Street in the late 1990s. *The Economist,* for example, wrote, "Many companies have tried, in various ways, to market both insurance policies and savings accounts, or to offer business customers both traditional bank loans and share underwriting. The success stories are few. Cross-selling motor insurance or emerging-market mutual funds to credit-card holders is easy in theory, but turns out to be extremely hard to do. . . . Or perhaps, not for the first time, the world's leading financiers are mistaking size for profitability" (April 11, 1998).

Mergers to Exploit Economies of Scale

The merger rationales discussed thus far are ultimately of only secondary importance. Episodes like Texas' banking collapse in the late 1980s do occur, but not predictably enough to figure in corporate expansion plans. Gains from product-line diversification or from interstate expansion per se can be attained via the expansion of existing banks, and do not require mergers. Also, as noted, the luster of nonbank activities has faded. Instead, the primary rationales offered for mergers is that the larger banks can deliver banking services more efficiently than smaller ones, and that mergers offer a more expeditious means of growing rapidly than incremental gains within established markets or the opening of branches in new or emerging markets.

To argue that banking is best conducted by a smaller number of firms is to argue that banking activities are subject to economies of scale. A long literature in economics has examined whether economies of scale exist in banking. Studies in this literature have taken two different approaches: the "profit" approach, which uses profits as a measure of whether small or large banks are more efficient; and the "cost" approach, which examines operating efficiency by bank size. We review these in turn.

Numerous authors have examined the relationship between profitability and bank size. Some studies have examined whether scale economies are a determinant of bank profitability. The most comprehensive study of this sort, by Berger (1995), finds that scale economies do not explain bank profits. Other studies take a more indirect approach—they examine whether large banks are more profitable, given an untested maintained hypothesis that larger banks are able to exploit scale economies unavailable to smaller banks. Most such studies come to the conclusion reached by Boyd and Graham (1991)—that bigger does not mean more profitable, either for all U.S. banks or for the largest. These authors find that very large and very small banks are not the most profitable—those in the middle are. Previous studies have found very small banks to be the most profitable; in any case, no studies have found that very large banks are systematically more profitable than smaller ones.

Most formal studies of economies of scale have taken the cost approach. All studies prior to 1982 consistently found that banks of all sizes exhibited increasing returns to scale. Subsequent studies (Humphrey 1990; DeYoung 1994a) have made clear that these findings were due to the use of the Cobb–Douglas functional form. When the more flexible translog specification was used, different results began to emerge.[5] Indeed, the first translog-based study, by Benston, Hanweck, and Humphrey (1982), found that banks attained optimal size between $10 and $25 million, with scale diseconomies setting in thereafter. These authors found economies at larger-asset sizes exclusively for large branch-banking organizations; and these banks' cost advantages disappeared after controlling for interdependencies among the number of offices and accounts. Subsequent translog studies found modest scale economies, which are exhausted below $100–200 million, after which scale diseconomies arise (see Clark 1988).[6]

Many studies of economies of scale in the late 1980s and early 1990s tested these conclusions. Rose (1989) used Functional Cost Analysis (FCA) data to establish that the optimal bank size for achieving scale economies is about $100 million in total assets.[7] Gropper's more recent study (1991) summarizes some empirical results for scale economies based on data drawn from the period

1979–1986. Most of these studies find scale economies are exhausted at small scales of output. Further, several other studies (including Berger and Humphrey 1990) have found diseconomies of scale for banking firms in the multi-million-dollar range. Among other studies, Noulas, Ray, and Miller (1990) found scale economies up to $3 billion in assets. Gropper himself finds evidence of scale economies at banks with over $500 million in assets; but the output economies he finds are modest in size. Evanoff and Israilevich (1991, 24) review the claim made in some studies that scale advantages exist "well beyond the $100-200 million range." These authors find that scale effects exist from $300 million to $50 billion; but as with smaller banks, these effects are relatively minor (varying by a factor of 5 percent). DeYoung (1994b) examines cost efficiencies in the provision of fee-based services. He finds that banks with large levels of fee-based services have been more cost-efficient than their peers over the past decade, but this efficiency advantage is small and does not significantly enhance profitability.

In sum, post-1980 studies have two basic findings: first, economies of scale in banking are achieved at modest asset volumes as low as $100 million; and second, even if economies of scale are to be had in specific financial activities, these confer relatively small cost advantages to larger banks. Very recent studies do not challenge these conclusions.[8]

Will technological change affect these conclusions? The most widespread example of technological change in banking is the automated teller machine (ATM). ATMs represent alternatives to bank branches; and whereas there were 40,600 bank branch offices and 2,000 ATMs in 1973, by 1993 there were 63,900 bank offices and 90,000 ATMs. The replacement of human tellers by machine processing, when introduced, brought the promise of a new level of efficiency in operation. However, a careful study by Humphrey (1994) concludes that "the expectation that ATMs would reduce bank costs has not been realized. Indeed, costs appear to be slightly higher." Humphrey points out that while every transaction costs less, customers' transaction patterns change toward more frequent, smaller transactions.

These findings cut two ways vis-à-vis merger policy. On the one hand, mergers could conceivably enhance overall banking efficiency insofar as they lead to the takeover of banking firms smaller than $100 million in size. On the other hand, since mergers increase bank size, but increasing bank size beyond $100 million cannot be expected to produce cost advantages, this empirical literature provides no consistent rationale for bank mergers. It is indeed the case that small banks have been eliminated by merger: Rhoades (1985) found that 93 percent of acquired banks in the period 1960–83 had assets less than $100 million. But examining the characteristics of 559 target banks during the 1981-1986 period, Hunter and Wall (1989) found little evidence that these target banks were weak performers (as the scale-economy argument for mergers would suggest). Indeed, these authors found that the most valued merger targets exhibited higher profitability and faster premerger growth in core deposits, and had proportionately more loans and more leverage.

Operating-Efficiency Rationales for Bank Mergers: A Summing Up

Two broad threads run through the various rationales we have examined in this chapter: One suggests that market forces are behind the merger wave; the other that government policy is driving the merger wave. According to the "market forces" arguments, the fundamentals of bank operations are leading the industry step by step toward consolidation. Economies of scale and scope will translate into profit advantages; in effect, gains and losses at the end of the proverbial business day will favor ever larger banks, forcing the demise or absorption of smaller banks in a longer run with an impatient arrival date. The evidence in the sections below pertains most directly to this line of thought. Before summing up the evidence for "market forces" arguments, we briefly consider the other thread—that government policy has defined the shape and pace of merger policy.

Does "Government Policy" Explain Mergers?

This line of thought asserts that the merger wave is occurring now because the government's flawed design for a banking system is coming apart. In effect, bad systemic architecture was a ticking time bomb whose demise has now been triggered, unleashing a string of failures, crises, and mergers.

The "bad architecture" argument runs as follows: The design of the United States' "New Deal" banking system had several interlinked design flaws that turned fatal in the midst of an adverse macroeconomic environment: barriers to entry, price rigidity and regulatory price ceilings, and maturity transformation. They were relatively inert as long as macroeconomic conditions were stable— that is, as long as price inflation remained within bounds and economic growth was fairly steady. Among depository institutions, savings and loan associations had the most acute potential for crisis, because their flawed regulatory structure gave them the most rigid product lines and led to worse maturity-transformation problems than commercial banks experienced. The onset of stagflation, as discussed above, weakened commercial banks, but it ripped the savings-and-loan structure asunder. This then led to more "bad architecture" in the form of several flawed early-1980s attempts to patch up the savings-and-loan industry by easing regulatory oversight and in turn allowing new activities. Then followed a series of banking crises: the crisis of loans to less-developed countries, especially in Latin America, which weakened the money-center banks; the crisis of oil-patch loans, especially in Texas, Louisiana, and Oklahoma; and then several smaller crises triggered by the collapse of speculative real-estate markets (especially Arizona and California in the West, and Massachusetts and New York in the

East). As an immediate consequence, some large banks were strengthened, and their appetites for expansion whetted; the Fed became more willing to accommodate; and the number of potential target banks expanded rapidly. As a further result, state rules on interstate banking were shuffled.

If the "flawed government policy" explanation holds, the character of regulation and deregulation will shape and channel bank and thrift merger activity, just as the regulatory structure shaped and channeled banking itself. Regulators' restrictions on what banks could do would dictate where banks were more likely to fail; government regulations, flawed or not, would dictate where mergers occurred by setting rules about what types of mergers could be undertaken. So, for example, banks in states with regional banking compacts would engage in mergers at a different pace and in different ways than banks in states with, say, strict rules against out-of-state banking entry. If this argument is right, then while the banking system may have some endogenous momentum toward consolidation, this momentum would be channeled and sculpted by government. Krozner and Strahan (1997) make precisely this argument. They argue that branching restrictions benefit small and inefficient banks in their competition with large and efficient ones. Until recent years, these small banks have used rent-seeking and political influence to maintain these protections until recent years. However, technological and financial innovations have removed the value of branching restrictions to small banks and tipped the balance against them. So small inefficient banks finally could not hide behind branching restrictions any longer, and the march of efficient larger banks resumed.

But the "flawed government" explanation does not stand up to scrutiny. Consider Krozner and Strahan's conception of branching restrictions as they affect inefficient small banks and efficient large banks. Would this argument have occurred to them in 1985 when BankAmerica, Citibank, and other large banks were barely surviving their lending blunders in Latin America, Texas, and Oklahoma? More importantly, Krozner and Strahan forget that regional banking compacts—that is, rent-generating restrictions on free bank entry—are responsible for the emergence of the super-regionals that are driving the process. The Southern banking compact forbade out-of-region mergers even as it facilitated in-region expansion by banks. This was hardly "survival of the fittest." It was regional protectionism. One further point this rebuttal demonstrates, and which becomes important in chapter 12, is that banking is invariably a creation of government and a creature of public policy in the modern age. The banking function is too complex, too sensitive, and too central to the economy's nerve center to be left to the market; and anyway, the momentum and structure of the market itself reflect government policy as in a mirror.

Table 4.1 provides more general evidence on the failure of the "flawed government" argument: summary information for every state on interstate expansion policies, merger activity, and changes in active commercial banks. States are divided into four groups in this table, based on their interstate expansion policies in 1989. Several aspects of Table 4.1 are of interest. First, states allowing no interstate expansion have lost as many operating banks, on average, as have states allowing entry with reciprocity. States that are completely open to interstate banking have lost twice as many banks, on average, in the period 1987–1993—a trend that can be traced to the extraordinary number of bank failures in four of these states (Alaska, Arizona, Oklahoma, and Texas). Second, a correlation is evident between interstate expansion policies and the extent of merger activity. Third, states permitting no interstate expansion have had a lower rate of new bank entry than have other states. Fourth, there is a remarkable amount of variation within each of Table 4.1's four state categories.

Table 4.1 suggests that state regulations and laws designed to limit interstate banking activities have had little effect. The real connection between regulatory structures and bank mergers is perhaps the different opportunities that different regulatory structures provide for using mergers to leverage a bank's strategic advantage. Table 4.2 demonstrates the point. This table sets out a schematic characterization of the eighteen states highlighted in this study. The vertical dimension classifies these states based on whether they are headquarters for one or more banks—banks that have established branch networks in other states. The horizontal dimension classifies states based on whether they have been active targets for expansion by out-of-state banks. Eleven states are targets for out-of-state bank expansion without serving as headquarters for any acquiring banks. Only two states (North Carolina and Massachusetts) serve as headquarters for acquiring banks without themselves having been targets for out-of-state acquirers. Only five states occupy other boxes. Two of these five—Minnesota and New York—have experienced weak entry threats by out-of-state acquirers (posed by Firstar and by Fleet and Keycorp, respectively).[9] Another two have recently received strong new entrants—First Union in the case of Pennsylvania, NationsBank and Norwest in the case of California. Only Georgia occupies an intermediate niche, home to both locally owned large acquiring banks and also a target for out-of-state acquirers; and since Nations Bank acquired Georgia's Bank South on February 1, 1996, Georgia's dual status is currently at risk.

Considered together, Tables 4.1 and 4.2 suggest the relative unimportance of regulations restricting bank expansion. The five states hosting rapidly expanding banks all fall into the expansion-with-reciprocity categories in Table 4.1. But only New York has operated under national reciprocity; and its banks' expansion has involved selected lines of financial business (credit-card lending, finance companies, and so on), not (for the most part) full-scale out-of-state branch networks. The other four states with acquiring banks have had regional reciprocity; but this has hardly restricted their forays into new banking markets—as illustrated by the expansion of Minnesota's Norwest into New Mexico and of California's Bank of America into Texas. Of course, these out-of-region forays have in many cases happened when systemic problems have emerged in portions of the banking system. But that is the point: Periodic state banking crises and the savings-and-loan "debacle" of the 1980s have created rifts in exclusionary rules.

Table 4.1 **Interstate Banking Policies and Bank Population Changes, by State and Cause, 1986–1993**

	Banks operating in 1986	Interstate Policy: 1989	Interstate Policy: 1993	Changes in # of banks	Intra-state mergers	Inter-state mergers	Bank fail-ures	Entry by new banks
				Changes, 1987-93, as Percent of 1986 banks				
States allowing no interstate expansion in 1989:								
IA	614	1	1	-13.7%	-4.2%	-8.3%	-2.1%	1.0%
KS	612	1	1	-19.9%	-6.2%	-11.8%	-4.1%	2.5%
MT	169	1	1	-30.8%	-25.4%	-4.7%	-4.1%	5.3%
ND	176	1	1	-19.9%	-13.6%	-9.1%	-4.5%	1.7%
NE	430	1	3	-16.3%	-5.3%	-10.2%	-1.9%	3.5%
NM	94	1	4	-13.8%	-7.4%	-3.2%	-5.3%	2.1%
Subtotal:	*2095*	*Group avg:*		*-17.9%*	*-7.7%*	*-9.3%*	*-3.2%*	*2.4%*
States allowing interstate expansion under regional reciprocity in 1989:								
AL	229	2	2	-6.6%	-10.5%	-6.6%	-0.9%	12.2%
AR	256	2	2	-0.4%	-2.0%	-2.0%	-1.2%	5.1%
CT	60	2	2	-23.3%	-16.7%	-8.3%	-33.3%	41.7%
DE	34	2	2	-5.9%	-17.6%	-11.8%	-2.9%	47.1%
FL	411	2	2	-7.1%	-15.8%	-12.4%	-7.3%	31.1%
GA	369	2	2	8.1%	-14.1%	-6.5%	-0.5%	28.5%
HI	10	2	2	-20.0%	-50.0%	0.0%	-10.0%	0.0%
MA	102	2	2	-41.2%	-37.3%	-2.0%	-15.7%	16.7%
MD	91	2	2	2.2%	-14.3%	-4.4%	-2.2%	19.8%
MN	727	2	2	-21.9%	-14.7%	-6.6%	-2.8%	2.2%
MO	610	2	2	-19.7%	-14.9%	-6.6%	-2.5%	4.4%
MS	141	2	2	-15.6%	-2.1%	-14.2%	-1.4%	2.1%
NC	64	2	2	9.4%	-1.6%	-26.6%	-3.1%	45.3%
NH	53	2	2	-58.5%	-26.4%	0.0%	-17.0%	13.2%
RI	14	2	2	-50.0%	-7.1%	-14.3%	-7.1%	7.1%
SC	73	2	2	8.2%	-5.5%	-9.6%	-1.4%	24.7%
TN	283	2	2	-12.0%	-13.8%	-10.2%	-0.4%	12.4%
VA	171	2	2	-3.5%	-8.8%	-7.0%	-3.5%	16.4%
WI	566	2	2	-23.0%	-19.1%	-6.4%	0.0%	2.7%
CA	445	2	3	-12.6%	-4.5%	-12.6%	-8.8%	13.5%
IL	1219	2	3	-21.5%	-18.2%	-6.7%	-0.7%	4.1%
IN	355	2	3	-33.2%	-24.5%	-8.2%	-1.7%	2.0%
LA	298	2	3	-27.2%	-5.7%	-7.0%	-19.1%	5.0%
PA	302	2	3	-13.2%	-15.2%	-10.3%	-0.7%	12.3%
VT	25	2	3	-20.0%	-16.0%	-4.0%	-8.0%	12.0%
WA	94	2	3	-6.4%	-4.3%	-24.5%	-2.1%	27.7%
CO	438	2	4	-27.9%	-20.8%	-8.4%	-8.9%	8.7%
NV	16	2	4	25.0%	0.0%	-12.5%	0.0%	37.5%
Subtotal:	*7456*	*Group avg:*		*-16.8%*	*-14.6%*	*-8.1%*	*-3.9%*	*10.3%*

(continued on next page)

	Banks operating in 1986	Interstate Policy: 1989	1993	Changes, 1987-93, as Percent of 1986 banks				
				Changes in # of banks	Intra-state mergers	Inter-state mergers	Bank fail-ures	Entry by new banks
States allowing interstate expansion under national reciprocity in 1989:								
KY	331	3	3	-6.6%	-6.9%	-4.8%	-0.6%	6.0%
MI	345	3	3	-39.7%	-37.1%	-7.2%	-0.3%	4.6%
NJ	117	3	3	-16.2%	-30.8%	-11.1%	-8.5%	33.3%
NY	195	3	3	-9.7%	-12.3%	-5.6%	-5.6%	13.8%
OH	304	3	3	-13.5%	-13.2%	-6.6%	-1.3%	7.2%
SD	134	3	3	-10.4%	-6.0%	-6.7%	-2.2%	6.7%
WV	211	3	3	-29.9%	-17.1%	-13.7%	-0.5%	1.4%
Subtotal	*1637*	*Group avg:*		*-19.2%*	*-18.0%*	*-7.5%*	*-2.0%*	*8.3%*
States allowing interstate expansion without reciprocity in 1989:								
AK	15	4	4	-46.7%	-13.3%	-13.3%	-33.3%	13.3%
AZ	54	4	4	-31.5%	0.0%	-20.4%	-29.6%	22.2%
ID	24	4	4	-12.5%	0.0%	-29.2%	0.0%	16.7%
ME	22	4	4	-4.5%	-13.6%	-9.1%	-4.5%	31.8%
OK	519	4	4	-28.5%	-5.2%	-10.8%	-15.2%	2.3%
OR	59	4	4	-23.7%	-3.4%	-18.6%	-1.7%	8.5%
TX	1972	4	4	-48.7%	-21.2%	-7.3%	-23.8%	3.9%
UT	50	4	4	-34.0%	-2.0%	-26.0%	-10.0%	6.0%
WY	106	4	4	-48.1%	-37.7%	-6.6%	-4.7%	0.9%
Subtotal	*2821*	*Group avg:*		*-43.2%*	*-17.5%*	*-8.9%*	*-20.6%*	*4.4%*
TOTAL	*14009*	*U.S. average:*		*-22.6%*	*-14.6%*	*-8.4%*	*-6.9%*	*7.7%*

Source: Nolle (Table A-18, 1995); state regulations.

Note: In columns 3 and 4, "1" signifies no entry by out-of-state-based banks permitted; "2" signifies that banks from within the region may enter as long as their home states return the favor; "3" signifies that banks from anywhere in the United States may enter if their home states return the favor; "4" signifies that any out-of-state bank may enter.

These rifts in turn have provided the means for acquisition-oriented banks to puncture these rules.

The eleven states clustered in the targets-without-headquarters box, by contrast, fall into each of Table 4.1's four interstate-banking policies. And four of these states are among the six U.S. states that have allowed no interstate expansion. In sum, regulatory policy has hardly affected, much less shaped, the path of interstate bank expansion.

Do "Market Forces" Explain Bank Mergers?

This leaves the "market forces" explanation for bank expansion. This argument too finds little support. Small banks have consistently outperformed large banks

Table 4.2 **Interstate Banking Patterns in States Included in This Study**

	State is major expansion target for out-of-state banks	State is minor expansion target for out-of-state banks	State is not an expansion target for out-of-state banks
States with banks expanding rapidly into other states		4 states (CA, MN, NY, PA)	2 states (MA, NC)
States with banks expanding moderately out of state		1 state (GA)	
States without banks expanding into other states	11 states (IA, ID, IN, MS, MT, ND, NJ, NM, TX, SD, WY)		

Note: Individual bank holding company expansion activities are discussed in chapter 8.

in terms of profitability, and small banks have been uninvolved in most recent commercial-banking disasters due to lending binges. These factors make it appear remarkable that large banks are expanding in the first place. Our review of the operational rationales for bank mergers does little to resolve this conundrum. Sporadic banking disasters do explain some recent mergers, but only in selected locations. Geographic expansion, which offers some risk-reduction benefits for banking firms, can be achieved either by interstate expansion or by merger—that is, it does not exclusively explain or justify mergers. Also, there is little evidence that mergers will allow acquiring banks to benefit from significant economies of scale or scope. In sum, the evidence reviewed here does not suggest that the bank merger wave stems from an industrywide lunge for enhanced operating efficiency.

Direct studies of the efficiency gains brought about by bank mergers are consistent with this conclusion. Rose (1987) undertook a comprehensive study of 591 federally and state-chartered financial intermediaries that changed ownership in the period 1970–1985. He found no statistically significant differences between merged and nonmerged firms with respect to various measures of profitability or with respect to asset growth; they did, however, increase their market share. Indeed, Rose found that of those banks citing economies of scope and scale as their major motivation in seeking merger, only 38 percent reported realizing such economies post-merger. Further, the research literature found "little evidence of return, risk, or efficiency advantages from interstate expansion" (Rose 1994, 1). In a more recent study, Srinivasan and Wall (1992) analyzed all bank mergers in the 1982–1986 period in which both participants had total assets of $100 million or more. They find no evidence that these mergers produce significant cost savings; to the contrary, noninterest expenses at these firms rose after mergers—as they did for the banking industry as a whole. Srinivasan (1992, 18) analyzed these data in more depth and found that while salaries were reduced at merging banks, these cost savings were more than offset by increases in other expenses, "suggesting that the banks did not achieve significant economies in consolidating back-office operations." Finally, DeYoung (1993) studied cost efficiency gains from bank mergers, for 348 mergers in 1987 and 1988. He found that while cost efficiency improved after most bank mergers, the gains were small and were unrelated to the acquiring banks' efficiency advantage over its target.

So if not operating efficiency per se, what explains banks' avid pursuit of mergers? Since the banking industry has been under intense competitive pressure from nonbank firms for the past two decades, it is implausible that this wave is due to owner and managerial irrationality. Whenever systematic market-driven shifts occur in a capitalist economy, it is safe to assume that someone expects to make money off the shift, or has already done so.

The Loose Relationship Between Operational Efficiency and Profitability

Simply because operational efficiencies are relatively small (or even nil) when large banks get larger does not mean that large banks cannot rationally pursue mergers in pursuit of increased profits and higher return on equity. This chapter demonstrates this point by constructing an alternative explanation of the bank merger wave. The argument proceeds in four stages. First, we show that banks can increase their net profits without any enhancements in their operational efficiency. Banks can accomplish this, in particular, by reducing the interest cost of their liabilities, increasing fees for depository services, increasing loan rates, reducing the likelihood of extraordinary costs, and increasing the revenues generated by fees. Second, we argue that mergers may be desirable from the banks' perspective in that they enhance banks' capacity to take these profit-increasing steps. Third, mergers may also be sought because they enhance the position of bank executive officers and because they increase value for bank shareholders— again, independent of any changes in operational efficiency per se. Fourth, mergers may be sought because they allow banks to redefine their role in financial markets, and thus to earn revenues in new ways from redefined customer bases.

Efficiency in economics is a poorly understood concept, not least because it is seldom carefully defined.[10] Operational efficiency is generally defined as how much output is produced per unit of input (that is, per dollar of cost). This seems straightforward. However, this generic definition takes on meaning only with respect to a particular economic unit or activity—and this is where the ambiguity creeps in. Just what constitutes banking efficiency is especially problematic, since it depends in part on what any analyst thinks that banks do. For example, the output-over-input definition may emphasize the size of the output-input margin, thus viewing the bank itself as a generator of profits. Alternatively, this definition can view input costs as variable, holding output fixed, thus viewing the bank as a locus of cost control. Further, Wheelock and Wilson (1995) contrast two views of banking—banks as producers of transaction services versus banks as intermediators between borrowers and depositors. These authors then provide empirical evidence that which banks are judged most efficient depends on what definition of banking is used.

The slippery links between bank profitability and operational efficiency are demonstrated with the help of Figure 4.1. This figure shows first that bank and owners' equity may differ for several reasons. Assuming it is publicly held, the bank obtains equity in the first instance by emitting equity shares to its owners. Over time, this bank's equity increases if it earns more in revenues than it pays out as dividends to its equity owners (equation b). The market's valuation of this bank's shares, however, depends on what market participants believe about the bank's future earning potential (equation c). As Wall Street grows more optimistic about this bank's future net profit flows, a gap between market and bank equity—between equations (b) and (c)—may open up. This gap is sometimes termed the "good faith" or "franchise value" of the banking firm.

The three illustrative efficiency measures shown as (h1) to (h3) in Figure 4.1 provide different interpretations of "operating efficiency," defined. The ability to generate output for any firm depends on objective circumstances in the markets it services, on the capabilities of its staff, and on its "X-efficiency"—that is, on that portion of its productivity that derives from employees' effort and teamwork.

Measures (h1) to (h3) highlight the ambiguity of the notion of efficiency; but at the same time they clarify the importance of efficiency for banking firms.[11] According to Berger, Hunter, and Timme (1993), cost inefficiencies on the order of 20 to 30 percent are common in commercial banks, and are far more important sources of profit leakage than the presence or absence of economies of scale or scope. These authors find that observed inefficiency is technical (over the use of all inputs), not allocative (over the wrong mix of inputs). Using comprehensive 1984 average cost data, Berger and Humphrey (1990) find that bank economies or diseconomies in operation are due more to efficiency of operation than to scale and scope economies per se.

So operating efficiency per se is a much more important factor than scale economies in bank performance. Figure 4.1 suggests two very different points about profitability and efficiency. First, an increase in efficiency (using any formula) will increase bank net profits, all other things held constant. But this said, bank profits and bank operational efficiency are only loosely correlated.[12]

A bank that operates with maximum efficiency may earn less than a more inefficient bank for a variety of reasons. As equation (d) suggests, bank net profits depend first on the presence or absence of extraordinary costs—that is, of precipitous losses such as the Latin American debt crisis and the commercial real estate collapse of the late 1980s. While such extraordinary "shocks" have afflicted large banks so regularly as to be merely ordinary, such "shock" events are

Figure 4.1 **Bank Efficiency and Bank Profitability**

Bank return on equity = (Net profits)/(Owners'equity)	(a)
Bank equity = (Shares issued)(Original auction price of shares)	
+ (Undistributed earnings)	
−(Reserves against expected loan losses)	(b)
Owners' equity = (Shares issued)(Market price of shares)	
≈ Bank equity + Expected future earnings	(c)
Net profits = (Revenues) - (Normal costs) - (Extraordinary costs)	(d)
where	
Revenues = (Fees from loan sales)(Loans made and sold)	
+ (interest earned on loans held)(Loans held)	
+ (Interest earned on securities)(Securities held)	
+ (Fees on deposit services) + (Other fees)	(e)
Normal costs = (Interest paid on liabilities)(Liabilities held)	
+ (Costs of facilities, services, and personnel)	(f)
≈ "Intermediation" costs) + ("Operating" costs)	
Extraordinary costs = (Loan losses absorbed) + (Other losses)	(g)
Some definitions of efficiency suggested by (a)—(g)	**(h)**
Operational efficiency(1) = Liabilities held /"Operating costs"	(h1)
Operational efficiency(2) = (Loans held + Securities held	
+ Liabilities held)/("Intermediation" + "operating" costs)	(h2)
Operational efficiency (3) = Revenues/Normal costs	(h3)

not taken into account as a component of normal costs. Second, a large bank may earn more than a small one even if it is less efficient in the sense of (h1) or (h2) because it has a large volume of fee-based income and loan sales. Third, a large bank may earn more profits than a more operationally efficient small bank if it is able to pay less for its liabilities or to earn more on its loans and securities. Fourth, a large bank may earn more than a more operationally efficient small bank by charging higher fees for deposit services.

Mergers may thus be desirable for banks if they are expected to enhance acquiring banks' capacity to increase profits, independent of the effect they may have, if any, on operational efficiency. Note that reducing rates paid to depositors and increasing borrowers' rates and depositors' fees are all related, at least potentially, to the degree of market power exercised by the banks in any given market. But is market power any longer important? As our discussion above noted, the "contestability" doctrine has argued that it is not. But rather than relying on theoretical speculation, we can turn for guidance to a recent study by Berger (1995). He conducts a thorough empirical analysis of competing hypotheses about the continuing relevance of the structure-conduct-performance paradigm for banking. His study tests two different explanations of the relationship between profits and market share: first, the view that this relationship stems from large firms' inappropriate exercise of market power; second, the view that this relationship stems from large firms' greater operational (scale) efficiency. Using a comprehensive dataset spanning the 1980s, and a gully specified model incorporating scale economies and other relevant factors, Berger concludes there is no support for the scale efficiency hypothesis; but there is support for the hypothesis that links market power and profits. This result suggests that banks may use mergers as a way of seeking out market power, so as to enhance their ability to generate net profits.

Equity-Market Motives for Mergers

If mergers may be sought to generate higher profits through increased market power or efficiency, they can also be sought because they enhance the bank's value for bank equity-owners and executive officers.

Several authors have suggested that bank takeovers may increase banks' franchise value for their shareholders. "Franchise value" consists of the returns from the banks' business activities, adjusted for a leverage factor, and adjusted further for value added from public subsidies. In the case of banks, these subsidies are of three major kinds: first, the value of deposit insurance—which makes bank customers unusually docile in reacting to changes in banks' fundamental financial position; second, the value of the too-big-to-fail guarantee that is implicitly provided to very large commercial banks; third, the value of the guarantees provided by the federal government or federal agencies to certain classes of bank asset (especially residential mortgages). Boyd and Graham (1991) and Hunter and Wall (1989) raise the possibility that banks seek to merge so as to become "too big to fail" and hence increase the value of uhe public guarantee against their liabilities.[13] Benston, Hunter, and Wall (1995) speculate that a bank planning to benefit from too-big-to-fail protection would exhibit risk-taking behavior. They postulate that banks could gain, alternatively from unloading low-risk securities and taking on more loans due to the risk-reduction associated with diversification in the wake of mergers. These authors analyze bid prices in the period 1981 to 1986 and find support for the latter (risk-reduction) but not the former (risk-taking) hypothesis. In particular, they find bid price varies negatively with relative size—a finding explained as due to the smaller expected gains from new-product introduction in the case of larger merger targets.[14]

We turn now to a second set of bank merger motives related to equity-market forces. To see this, refer again to Figure 4.1. Note that comparing any bank's performance with that of other banks or nonbank firms requires dividing its net revenues by owners' equity. Doing so, per definition (a), provides a measure of return on equity. Then as long as net profits are positive, increasing the scale of bank operations will enhance return on equity even if operating efficiency remains constant. For the bank's executive officers, increasing the bank's scale of operations increases its market share and enhances their own prestige and salaries.[15] While these twin motivations for mergers are magnified as operational efficiency increases, they are independent of it. Bank cash flows and cost efficiency are distinct and can be enhanced independently.

The ready access of some larger banking firms to Wall Street has an interesting implication for the distinction between expansion by merger and by branching. Branching emanates from the basic operations of the bank itself, and thus must ordinarily be supported by bank cash flows. Mergers, by contrast, can be supported either by bank cash flows or by obtaining financing in equity markets. So access to Wall Street is the key ingredient required to implement a merger-based strategy—and thus the key precondition for any bank requiring rapid growth.

Motivations of this sort may also be at work on the side of acquired banks. The owners of acquired banks' equity can expect to gain from selling their equity shares at a premium. This motive operates less for those poorly managed institutions for which mergers are needed to prevent insolvency than for the well-capitalized banks that are frequently targeted for mergers (as discussed above). The dynamic is one in which large, well-capitalized banks with ready access to integrated capital markets can raise the funds needed to take over, in the one case, nearly insolvent targets, and, in the other, well-capitalized smaller banks. In the latter case, acquiring banks pay a premium price for shares that enriches the owners of the latter even as they surrender control.

Wall Street Versus the Banking Industry?

More broadly, Wall Street can be thought of as having mounted a twofold, contradictory attack on the banking industry. On the one hand, its mutual fund managers have been taking deposit funds from banks for two decades; and on the other, its money and capital markets have been providing the credit needs for an ever-larger share of corporations. In consequence, Wall Street's success has occurred in part because of its capacity to take business from commercial banks and thrifts. The second prong of the attack has occurred from another quarter of Wall Street—the investment bankers and takeover specialists. The declining balance sheets of banks have created excess capacity, in Wall Street's view; so equity and loan capital to support the restructuring of the banking sector have been made available. Those banks deemed the most competitively fit are able to float equity issues on the Street, providing them with the cash needed to sweeten equity-plus-dollars offers for the equity shares of target banks. While the banking industry's stocks historically have relatively low price/earnings (P/E) ratios, surges of takeover activity boost prices and allow equity owners to unload their bank holdings at a premium (Serwer 1995).

Of course, stock-price undervaluation is a relative thing, as is the industrial vulnerability of banking. Since the Federal Reserve shifted to a cautiously expansionary policy in 1991, in the wake of a recession triggered in part by inappropriate monetary tightening, bank profits have recovered remarkably. The Fed's expansionary policy led to a low cost of funds, while the environment of stable inflationary expectations created a sizable margin on longer-term instruments. This situation, plus banks' shift toward safer loans in the wake of the LDC and commercial real-estate lending debacles of the 1980s, has created five successive years of record commercial-bank profits. Lost market share may be the rationale, but the lure has evidently been the record cash flows that accrue to firms in this line of business. Many bank stock prices have zoomed upward as much as 50 percent in 1995 in the heady atmosphere induced by merger mania. One fund, Invesco Industrial Income, bought Chase shares at $35 and then watched their value zip to $60 in the wake of the merger with Chemical (Egan 1995).

The competition for Wall Street equity is fierce, uneven, and unstable. For example, as of mid-1995, McColl's NationsBank was hobbled in its efforts to acquire another megabank by its relatively low P/E ratio. It had not delivered the 15 to 18 percent return on equity as had other large banks such as BankAmerica, Chase Manhattan, Chemical, Banc One, Barnett Banks, and Norwest. These banks' shares were trading at ten times earnings or more, versus NationsBank's eight times earnings. A low P/E is a message to the bank from Wall Street to steer clear of the mega-acquisition, for fear that this move would dilute the value of outstanding NationsBank shares.[16] Similarly, Wells Fargo's stock price fell markedly in 1997 after its hostile takeover of First Interstate in 1996 was followed by personnel problems, computer glitches, and customer unhappiness.

But what goes down in Wall Street usually comes up—the age-old formula that maximizes the brokerage fees on which financial exchanges feed. By 1996, NationsBank had climbed back into Wall Street's good graces and taken over Boatmen's Bancshares. Bank stock prices grew steadily through 1997 and 1998; bank megamergers became superheated, and Wall Street began betting on takeover gains. This surge is easily seen in the trend in the price-to-book-value ratios paid for bank mergers from the mid-1990s onward.

The stock prices of target banks often rise dramatically prior to a merger because of analysts' expectations that cash flows per equity share will be dramatically higher after the merger. This means that successful completion of the merger—that is, validation of the 1.5- to 2–times premium paid for acquired banks' stock—requires dramatic reductions in the staff and facilities of either the acquired bank, the acquiring bank, or both. From 1985 to the mid-1990s, banks have been acquired at an average of 1.5- to 2-times book value (Pouschine 1991).

In the mid-1995 to mid-1998 period, large banks' stock prices ran up at an especially heated pace. Large banks' price/earnings (P/E) ratios, which stood at 10 in mid-1995, had all climbed substantially by mid-June 1998: The stock prices of NationsBank, Citicorp, and First Union stood at a price/earnings ratio of approximately 20; the price/earnings of BankAmerica and Chase lagged just slightly at 19 and 18, respectively.

These rising stock prices are clearly linked to the intensifying pace of large banks' mergers in this period. In a September 6, 1997 article, *The Economist* documented the virtually linear increase in the price-to-book-value ratio for U.S. bank mergers: from 1.4 for the Chemical/Chase deal in August 1995, to over 2 in the Bank of Boston/BayBanks merger of December 1995, rising steadily to a price-to-book-value ratio of 3.99 in the NationsBank/Barnett deal of August 1997. First Union's purchase of Corestates for $16.1 billion in November 1997 involved a then-record price, and came at 5.39 times the book value of Corestates' stock. Even Wells Fargo's beleaguered stock price began to climb as of October 1997, as Wells was slowly put into play. Wells CEO Paul Hazen said in an interview with the *San Diego Union-Tribune* on December 5, 1997, "At these kinds of multiples, these kinds of prices, if somebody came to you with a story that would cause the currency of the combined company to appreciate, then I'm open to it." By June 1998, Wells Fargo's stock price represented remarkable multiples indeed—its price/earnings ratio stood at a remarkable 28.

The high bank stock prices of mid-year 1998 did not last the summer, with the consequence our argument would anticipate—a dramatic slowdown in bank merger activity. The late-1998 period is discussed at the end of chapter 5.

It is important to note that bank equity prices and bank merger activity are linked for all banks, not just the largest ones whose strategic moves draw the most media attention. In the mid-1995-to-mid-1998 period, many middle-sized banks have also experienced overheated equity prices and rising price-to-book-value multiples; and these trends, as with large banks, have often been merger related. It should be noted that the prices of middle-sized banks have been driven upward not just by Wall Street recognition of their earnings or earnings potential; independent of profit flows, these banks' stocks have become valued in part because their deposit bases may attract suitors seeking to enter new markets or to increase market share. For example, Regions Financial Corporation paid $2.7 billion in February 1998 to acquire First Commercial of Little Rock at four times book value. This purchase, combined with nine acquisitions in 1997, has made Regions the fifth-largest bank in the Southeastern states.

The Wall Street perspective on bank mergers permeates business press coverage.[17] The managements of expansionary banks are seen as dynamic elements moving banks forward; quotations by figures such as Hugh McColl of Nations-Bank to the effect that "when you stop growing, you start dying" are celebrated as a primal assertion of entrepreneurial zeal. By contrast, in the eyes of the press the managements of target banks are irrelevant. Takeover-target banks are instruments for achieving their owners' purposes; expansionary banks are instruments for achieving their managers' purposes. It is assumed that bank customers are best served by superior managers (implicitly, those at expansionary banks), and thus these managers should be given free rein in deciding where and when to expand. Business press accounts also assume that the activities of small banks with local owners will be fully replaced when larger banks displace these banks in far-flung market areas.

The bottom line in any drive to reduce excess capacity, of course, is corporate downsizing. This is one payoff that Wall Street and bank owners hope the bank merger wave will deliver.[18] Combinations of banks promise staff reductions from eliminating duplicate headquarters staff and duplicate line personnel. The closer in geographic market area and lines of business any two merging banks are, the more potential for job cuts there is. If the same revenues are generated by fewer staff—in terms of Figure 4.1, if an element of equation (f) is reduced while equation (e) remains relatively untouched—then net profits (equation d) and return on equity (equation a) will rise, pushing bank equity prices higher.[19]

The merger of Chemical and Chase, which brought together two money-center banks headquartered in New York, promised to save the new entity approximately $1.5 billion in costs through office closures and the furlough of 12,000 of its 73,000 employees. Driving the $10 billion merger of Chase and Chemical, which created the nation's then-largest bank, was the asserted rationale that "if they didn't combine, they both would have been taken over and massive firings would have taken place anyway" (Sloan 1995)—some 6 percent of Chase's shares having been bought before the merger by the Mutual Shares fund. While over 100 branches were targeted for closure, none of the combined thirty-six outside directors of either Chase or Chemical were eliminated. The effort to cut employees can lead to prolonged stress. By February 1998, for example, Chase was at 69,000 employees, up 1,200 from early 1997; and it announced plans to lay off a third of its 9,400-strong administrative staff (*Wall Street Journal,* February 6, 1998).

Many other mergers have resulted in downsizing initiatives, often greeted by surges in stock price. To cite some recent examples, in January 1997 Comerica announced cuts of 1,900 jobs—16 percent of its workforce—in an effort to reap benefits from its recent merger with a Detroit rival.[20] In late 1996, KeyCorp of Cleveland announced layoffs of 2,700 jobs and the closure of 280 branches; this move (viewed as making "tough choices today"), together with KeyCorp's share buyback led to a stock-price increase of $2.375, a 5 percent gain per share.[21] In October 1997, Citicorp moved to dismiss 9,000 of its 90,000 employees, taking a charge of $889 million against net income, in a move to make back-office operations more efficient. And the restructuring beat goes on.

Market-Shift and Bank Consolidation

The shift of banks across geographic borders, with larger banks rapidly taking market share from smaller ones, has deeper implications for banking markets and banking practices than just expanded opportunities for the assertion of market power by increasingly monopolistic providers. The ever-deeper penetration of large banks into U.S. banking markets is also associated with a redefinition of banking markets and even of banking itself by these same large banks.

This redefinition began in the 1970s, and has gathered ever more force since then, due to the same forces that triggered the deregulation and crisis of U.S. banking in these same years. As noted above, bank balance sheets came under dual attack in the 1970s. On the one hand, mutual funds took many wealthy and even middle-class depositors; on the other, many larger nonfinancial corporations began to borrow directly (and at lower costs) in the commercial-paper and corporate bond markets. Large banks especially were affected by the loss of their lowest-cost depositors and of their best blue-chip borrowers. The banking industry responded in several ways to this dual attack. One response, noted above, was to pursue higher-risk borrowers. Another response was a shift into "consumer banking"—that is, into the aggressive pursuit of upscale customers, in a strategy that might be more aptly termed "upscale consumer banking."

Pioneered by Citibank and Wells Fargo in the late 1970s, this strategic shift gathered force with banking deregulation in the mid-1980s. In the New Deal system, which effectively barred competition for depositors on the basis of price, competition took the form of the expansion of customer bases. This expansion was achieved by cross-subsidies on both sides of the balance sheet: High-balance, low-cost depositors received the same return on their deposit funds as did low-balance, high-cost depositors; and blue-chip borrowers received credit from local loan officers, just as mom-and-pop stores did. In the post-deregulation system, the locus of cross-subsidies has shifted. Instead of being between customer classes and within product lines (wealthy depositors to low-balance depositors, and blue-chip borrowers to mom-and-pop stores), cross-subsidies are now extended within customer classes and between product lines. The new banking is embodied in practices such as the use of fee waivers on deposit accounts to induce customers to maintain certain balances in their accounts, and an increase in costs for customers requiring only basic banking services.

The spread of fee-based services is linked to the growth of secondary loan markets, contingent loan commitments, and financial derivatives. DeYoung (1994b) shows that noninterest income is rising as a share of all income for banks of all asset sizes. But whereas noninterest income has risen only modestly for banks of under $100 million in assets, to approximately 20 percent, it has climbed substantially for banks with over $1 billion in assets to approximately 40 percent of earnings. This increasing dependence on fees and service charges, in lieu of earnings from intermediation per se (such as lending), represents a historic shift in the character of banking activities.

The shifts toward upmarket customers and to fee-based services are interlinked. Apart from the very wealthy, the customers most sought by banks are

targeted for the receipt of standardized financial services—credit cards, specialized deposit and investment accounts, and mortgage loans. Mergers are, in turn,
interlinked with these shifts in several ways. First, if banking can be redefined as
involving not idiosyncratic bank–customer relationships anymore but the distribution of standardized products to relatively homogeneous customers, by provider firms that were under continual competitive pressure to keep markups on
these products to an absolute minimum, then fewer providers might indeed be
needed. That is, the assumed redefinition of banking is a precondition of the
argument that the United States is overbanked. Second, mergers are an important
means of rapidly penetrating customer bases when the focal point of this entry is
the capture of the maximum number of desirable customers. As noted above,
bank expansion is accomplished more quickly via merger than via gradually
opening new branch offices in markets served by other competitors. As equation
(e) in Figure 4.1 makes clear, more transactions mean more revenue; and banks
that are quickest to capture the lion's share of transactions growth will not only
have the largest boost in cash flow; their equity shares will be most favored by
Wall Street, providing them with an edge in any competition for further equity-
financed expansion.

This strategic shift does not, however, mean that nonbank financial firms will
go quietly into the soft night. They have other plans; and these plans do not
necessarily involve purchasing banks so as to go head-to-head for banks' entire
retail base. Nonbanks' strategic emphasis was put bluntly by Tom Decker Seip,
the executive vice president of retail brokerage operations for Schwab, in an
interview with the *San Francisco Business Times:* "The banks would like to take
my customers. I don't want all of their customers. I just want the rich ones." This
has been nonbanks' game plan since Merrill Lynch came up with the money-
market mutual fund in 1972. Certainly, many firms in the wholesale and retail
brokerage and investment-banking businesses have experimented with many different combinations in an effort to find a lucrative mix capable of attracting and
holding an upscale customer base.

The most aggressive recent move toward realizing nonbanks' dream of a
selective raid on banks' turf was Morgan Stanley's purchase of Dean Witter,
Discover—the third-largest U.S. retail broker and a leading credit-card provider—in February 1997. *The Economist* (February 8, 1997) speculated that this
purchase laid "the ground for the kind of one-stop financial shop that big banks
have long aspired to build but have largely failed to. It seems improbable that
low-margin checking accounts have a place in this shop. Until now, the conventional wisdom had been that the commercial banks, rich after years of record
profits, would take the lead in creating consumer-finance conglomerates. Morgan Stanley's maneuver has raised the possibility that they may be left by the
wayside." This prose is rather breathless given the history of failed combinations
among nonbanks. Nonetheless, it is undoubtedly true that banks will face contin-

ued competition from nonbanks for their upscale customers. This will reinforce large banks' strategic shift toward customer-base segmentation, which was described above. And this shift takes commercial banks as a whole ever further from a social-efficiency ideal in which the ability to save and have access to credit is reinforced across all American households by a broad-based pool of bank customers.

5

The Ambiguous Basis for Regulating
Bank Mergers

Introduction: Three Regulatory Approaches

Our review of the rationales for banking mergers suggests that for acquiring and acquired banking firms, operational-efficiency and safety-and-soundness criteria are secondary. The central impetus behind mergers has instead been equity-market–based criteria—gains in asset values for equity holders and in market share for bank executive officers. The merger wave has been relatively independent of behavioral outcomes in the banking system.

Economists and policy-makers in the agencies that regulate banks have had three different responses to banks' merger wave. One view is that the merger wave solves the problem of excess capacity caused by the banking industry's secular slide in the past two decades. This view draws on the "new learning" approach to industrial structure, according to which market concentration will emerge due to the superior efficiency of successful competitors. A second view holds that regulators should remain hostile to market concentration, and hence to mergers. In this view, either the excess capacity in banking is overstated, or widespread mergers are not the best way to eliminate it. A third view is emerging among regulators. This view suggests a new basis for evaluating the advisability of mergers: the reaction of equity markets to bank actions. Like the first view, this third view anticipates the emergence of more market concentration and fewer banking firms. But unlike the "new learning" approach, it draws conclusions about bank behavior from equity-market reactions rather than from structural market studies. This chapter reviews these competing views in turn, as well as their implications for regulatory oversight.

**The Excess-Capacity Approach: The Market Is Dead,
Long Live the Market!**

In the business press, the rationale for the bank merger wave cited most commonly is the banking industry's excess capacity. But if economies of scale and scope are slim in banking lines of business, as suggested in chapter 2, in what sense is this industry burdened by excess capacity? Two answers have been suggested. One is summarized crisply by Tannenwald (1991). This author probes the reasons for the weak return-on-asset performance of New England banks since 1989. He attributes this primarily to secular regulatory, market, and technological shifts that have steadily increased banks' cost of funds and decreased the demand for traditional banking services. Banks' share of all financial assets has fallen by 15 percent since 1974, and their profitability has systematically declined. But, he adds, "commercial banks have responded to these secular pressures in shortsighted ways. . . . [T]hey have increased the proportion of their portfolios invested in commercial real estate loans . . . [leading to] problem loans. . . . [Further] commercial banks have responded to the competition for funds from MMMFs [money market mutual funds] and savings institutions by increasing the number of their branches" (Tannenwald 1991, 30–31). That is, banks have responded to their industry's secular slide with competitive strategies that have worsened excess capacity problems and reduced banks' cash flows. In effect, mergers are needed to save the banking industry from itself.

There is a second and complementary reason that mergers may help eliminate excess capacity in banking emerges from many analysts' redefinition of banking. If the traditional intermediation-and-depository interpretation is replaced by a view of banks as purveyors of standardized financial services, then a ready-made justification for mergers emerges: Standardized banking products can be delivered by firms near or far. The information revolution expands modern banking firms' market boundaries significantly beyond the narrow realm of their branch networks; similarly, it expands the set of banking firms with which customers (at least computer-linked customers) can transact. Many local banks can be replaced by a few large centralized banks. Banking is no longer a local activity. The local market is dead, the global market is here.[1]

Defenses of the Traditional Regulatory Approach

As we have seen, challenges to the structure-conduct-performance approach to bank oversight have been mounted since the 1970s. However, defenders of the "traditional" regulatory approach have challenged both the argument that mergers eliminate excess capacity and the argument that mergers are relatively inconsequential because banking now involves standardized activities for which location (and hence local market area) is irrelevant.

Boyd and Graham (1991) note, first of all, that banks' share of GNP has risen even though their share of financial holdings has fallen, since they derive fee-based income by servicing MMMFs and other "new" intermediaries. Tannenwald (1991), after setting out the secular-slide view of excess banking capacity, proceeds to criticize it. He argues that the extent of banking's secular slide has been overestimated for several reasons. For one thing, smaller banks' profitability has been unusually hampered by the reduced income of small businesses and farms in the wake of the severe 1982 recession. For another, larger banks' profitability was unusually affected, in turn, by the LDC debt crisis of the early 1980s, and by the mass delinquencies in commercial real estate lending in the later 1980s. In light of these considerations, a "dense" branch network may not be atavistic. It may reflect rigorous competition, not too little competition:

> The relatively large number of bank offices per capita in New England is not necessarily an indication that New England is overbanked. Rather, it may reflect a conscious strategy on the part of the region's banks to win customers by providing superior access and convenience.
> [T]he overhang of bad loans carried by NE's banking industry has made it unprofitable. . . . Once these extraordinary costs are eliminated, the underlying profitability of NE banking will reemerge (Tannenwald 1991, 43).

Rhoades (1992) provides further support for the local character of banking. He examines whether banking markets have become regional or national in scope by studying the behavior of mortgage loan rates in twenty cities. As he puts it, "If banking markets are nonlocal, then local supply and demand conditions would not be relevant in the evaluation of the competitive effects of any given merger" (1). He tests whether area effects such as the degree of local monopoly, market size, market growth, and per capita income matter. He concludes that they do:

> Local market conditions still make a difference. Moreover, . . . market concentration, as measured by the Herfindahl index, affects the prices charged in local markets for mortgages. This would appear to support the market-power explanation for the relationship of market structure to market performance rather than the Demsetz efficiency explanation. (11)

In other studies, Hannan (1989) and Berger and Hannan (1989) also found that local market factors, including concentration, were important in the levels of deposit interest rates and business loan rates.[2] Similarly, the 1988–1989 National Survey of Small Business Finances concluded that markets for small and medium-sized business firms (less than 500 FTE employees) "are generally limited to local commercial banks and, to a somewhat lesser extent, to local thrift institutions" (Elliehausen and Wolken 1990, 32). The same authors (1992) used the 1989 Survey of Consumer Finances to find that "financial services markets for consumers tend to be local."

One might object that banking is changing so quickly that conclusions about the local character of banking markets cannot be drawn for 1999 on the basis of a 1989 survey. Recent research by Federal Reserve economists, however, support the conclusions of these earlier studies. Kwast, Starr-McCluer, and Wolken (1997) use the 1992 Survey of Consumer Finances and the 1993 National Survey of Small Business Finances to show that banks remain the dominant providers of financial services for both households and small business, and local banks are by far the dominant providers of these services. Households' ties to local banks are especially strong for deposit services, not loans; small businesses' ties to local banks are even stronger, across a broader spectrum of financial services, including lines of credit. These authors find that "use of financial services has not changed as much in recent years as some observers have argued" (16).[3] The slow pace of change in consumers' banking habits includes households' adoption of electronic banking. Kennickell and Kwast (1997) use the 1995 Survey of Consumer Finances to show that very few households—primarily those that are upper-income, highly educated, older, and have substantial wealth assets—have adopted electronic means of conducting their financial business. The quip by Microsoft's Bill Gates, "Give me a piece of the transaction business and the banks are history" (Gates 1996), is apparently somewhat premature.

Taken together, these studies by Federal Reserve economists suggest first that banking remains a local activity even today. It follows, then, that the structure, conduct, and performance of firms in local market areas remain important in evaluating banks' merger and consolidation plans. Further evidence that banking-market concentration affects credit-market outcomes, which supports the idea that banking remains at least in part a localized set of activities, is provided in chapter 10.

Using Equity-Market Reactions to Evaluate Mergers

In the past several years, some researchers and regulators have begun to suggest that the criteria for evaluating both competition and efficiency in banking should be fundamentally redefined. Specifically, they argue that equity-market criteria should supplement or even displace operational criteria for evaluating bank efficiency and competition.

The underlying reason for this interest in equity-market criteria is the belief maintained by numerous Fed economists and officials that equity markets are efficient, and hence the equity market's judgment about firms is at least as meaningful as one derived from any inference from those firms' operational characteristics. Facilitating this view is the fact that stock-market prices of banking equities now vary more considerably than in the years before banking deregulation. This trend, in turn, has arisen because the return on banks' equity has become markedly more volatile since the mid-1980s (Brunner and English, 1993).[4]

The savings-and-loan debacle of the 1980s has also spurred the equity-market approach. Among market-oriented economists, explanations of this debacle center on the moral hazard induced by deposit insurance. The idea is that deposit insurance makes depositors indifferent to excessive riskiness in banks' asset selection and thus gives bank managers an incentive to engage in excess risk-taking.[5] Economists who prefer this explanation have drawn the lesson that avoiding such crises in the future necessitates market discipline of financial institutions. So interest in equity-market reactions to banking events as "rational" reactions has heightened.[6]

Rhoades's (1994) recent review of studies of the effects of bank mergers on efficiency signals the emergence of the new equity-market–oriented research. He found that these studies fall into two categories: traditional industrial-organization studies emphasizing bank operating performance, and "event studies" focusing on movements in banks' equity prices (and hence on returns to shareholders of affected firms) before and after mergers occur. He concluded that the nineteen operating-performance studies examined "indicate, with very few exceptions, that bank mergers do not yield improvements in efficiency or profitability and that in-market mergers do not have more favorable effects on performance than other mergers" (9). The twenty-one event studies indicate that stockholders of target firms gain, but there is only mixed evidence on returns to the stockholders of bidder firms.

Among the earliest studies emphasizing equity-market reactions are Born, Eisenbeis, and Harris (1988) and de Cossio, Trifts, and Scanlon (1987). These authors found that the announcement of bank acquisitions does not lead to "abnormal returns" in the case of interstate mergers, but does in the case of intrastate mergers. Both papers then conclude that interstate mergers do not lead to opportunities for excessive profit-making, but intrastate mergers often may.

In another paper of this sort, Laderman and Pozdena (1991) found that the larger the number of states in which bank holding companies are exposed to competition, the more their stock prices decline. They interpret this result, based on stock-market data for 174 bank holding companies over the period 1964–1989, as implying that "interstate banking tends to enhance potential and/or actual competition in state banking markets" (32). This assumes that the stock market is an accurate arbiter of whether increased interstate competition will enhance competition (through encouraging new entry) or discourage it (by encouraging more concentration).[7] These authors then estimate the effect of interstate banking legislation on bank stock performance, using data from 200 banking firms with traded shares. They find that stock returns are negatively affected by the passage of interstate branching legislation. They then conclude that this legislation has increased banking competition.

Whalen's event study (1994) of thirty-nine intracompany mergers of subsidiary banks by bank holding companies found that these mergers resulted in significant positive stock returns. Since bank holding companies operating banks across state lines are currently required to maintain separate boards of directors, Whalen interprets his results as implying that allowing the consolidation of interstate banking operations may well yield efficiency gains. As we have seen, this result is not supported by any results from the empirical literature on operational efficiency.

Finally, Demsetz and Strahan (1995) did a statistical-decomposition study of stock prices for bank holding companies which suggested that larger firms generate less risk than small ones. These authors found that large bank-holding companies in the period 1987–1993 were initially "riskier"—in the sense of having more variable stock prices—than small ones; but since 1993 large companies have been less "risky." The authors conclude that "diversification advantage of size has become apparent, and we have begun to observe an inverse relationship between size and risk" (13). These authors draw a conclusion about operational "risk" from empirical evidence about stock-market "risk."[8]

An Ambiguous Regulatory Response to Bank Mergers?

These competing and contradictory interpretations of bank mergers and consolidation explain the confused regulatory response to bank mergers. Prior to the current merger wave, regulators assumed that more concentration may lead to less competition and hence overpriced bank products. This logic has weakened considerably due to the influence of the "new learning"; the New Deal banking system is peculiarly susceptible to the "new learning" critique because of its severe limitations on market entry. The emergence of equity-market–based rationales for mergers has only generated more confusion.

This confusion is reflected in Fed evaluations of merger applications. As noted above, since the 1960s the Fed has set HHI (Herfindahl Hirschman Index) "trigger levels," above which merger applications will be evaluated closely for monopoly power. The HHI trigger levels were last reset (at a higher level) in the 1982 merger guidelines. In practice, however, regulators have been reluctant to apply even this higher bar in evaluating the advisability of mergers. In some cases, bank regulators are taking advantage of their flexibility under the Bank Holding Company Act to set aside traditional criteria and instead are using new criteria in evaluating the efficacy and advisability of bank mergers.[9] Holder (1993b) examines cases in which the HHI trigger level (1,800 postmerger HHI, plus a 200–point gain in the HHI due to the merger itself) was exceeded in the period 1982–1992. Of the 211 cases in which local markets' HHIs exceeded 1,800, only six cases resulted in merger denials—205 were approved.[10]

Further confusing the regulatory response is that the traditional approach has ambiguous implications for merger policy. This is because of the segmented character of banking markets in the New Deal system. Insofar as mergers allow banks to hurdle over regulatory barriers to entry, Srinivasan (1992) points out that the correlation between mergers and the reduction of effective competition may not hold: Mergers may enliven competition by allowing competent new players to challenge established market leaders.

Jeffrey A. Clark (1996) concludes from a policy perspective that small, specialized institutions might have difficulty competing with larger ones, but at some point any cost advantages associated purely with size disappear. This, he suggests, should put to rest any fears concerning the repeal of interstate banking prohibitions. Such repeals will not result in a small number of mammoth institutions, because the economies of scale are not there. This policy conclusion, however, assumes that (1) the size of banking institutions is governed by underlying economies in producing banking services; and (2) competitive processes will yield market outcomes that reflect these "fundamental" factors. Neither conclusion may be warranted. Institutional size may be partially the result of aggressive expansion plans, combined with advertising outlays; and competition among a few super-banks may lead these banks to strive for markets out of any proportion to the "true" economies that can be had by such expansion.

Thomas Hoenig (1996), president of the Federal Reserve Bank of Kansas City, succinctly pointed out the advantages of the "new learning" approach in a 1996 speech: "Instead of regulating to make institutions fail-safe, an alternative approach is to strengthen the stability of the financial system by . . . prevent[ing] large interbank exposures in the payments system and interbank deposits. Second, . . . require those institutions that engage in an expanding array of complex activities to give up direct access to government safety nets in return for reduced regulation and oversight" (5). Regulators would no longer have to attempt "expanded micromanagement" of individual institutions whose aggressive strategies would be better conducted outside the lender-of-last-return safety net. Large banks, in this argument, are participating in an expanding and increasingly global array of markets for credit provision and enhancement; and this in turn is due to "a technological revolution that has reduced the costs of information gathering, processing, and transmission" (6). Hoenig suggests that "the time may have come to sever the link between these institutions and the safety nets, making it feasible to significantly scale back regulatory oversight of their operations" (11).

This argument rests on two assumptions: first, that emerging, nontraditional banking activities are overwhelming traditional activities—a contention that is true for a small handful of large banks, but not for most other banks; second, that equity markets can perform risk-pricing and oversight responsibilities borne until now by regulators.[11] These assumptions are, respectively, unproved and untested. Nonetheless, they have been quickly embraced at the highest levels of regulatory decision-making.

Resolving the Ambiguities: Regulatory Oversight and Bank Megamergers

The ambiguity described here in regulatory oversight of bank mergers has arisen for a variety of reasons. For one thing, economists at the regulatory agencies continue to produce thorough and substantial research based on each of the three approaches described here; and this research often comes to conflicting conclusions on specific issues, as noted frequently in this volume. For another, while the "new learning" and equity market approaches are out of sync with the Glass–Steagall Act, that act remains the law. In any event, this ambiguity cannot persist in the face of the sort of industrywide push for change seen among banking firms in the 1990s. Decisions about merger applications must be made, and regulatory guidelines must be proposed and implemented. In the wake of these actions, either the bank merger wave rolls on, or it is stopped in its tracks. Two recent events have clarified the precise character of regulatory oversight at the present time, and thus resolved any ambiguity about precisely how the various regulatory criteria described above mesh in practice: the Federal Reserve's effort to change Regulation Y in 1996 and 1997, and its response to the rash of megamerger applications in 1998.

Regulation Y and "Fast-Track" Merger Approval

The Federal Reserve moved in the third quarter of 1996 to change Regulation Y, which governs the rules under which bank holding companies can pursue mergers and acquisitions. The Board's proposal suggested an "expedited action" arrangement, available to any lender meeting a number of screens. These expedited actions included provisions that the amount of acquired assets be less than 35 percent of holding-company assets in a twelve-month period, that the HHI increase by 200 points or less, and that banks holding 80 percent of the deposits controlled by the acquiring holding company have a satisfactory CRA record.

Both Fed chair Alan Greenspan and Fed member Susan Phillips spoke publicly about the rationale behind this change in Regulation Y. Greenspan, in an October 5, 1996, speech to the American Bankers Association, noted that the Fed should "avoid killing the goose that lays the golden egg." He argued that bank regulators should take a more passive approach to risk management, letting banks themselves develop and implement quantitative risk-management plans that may involve considerable risk-taking. He characterized Regulation Y as involving an area "still constrained by outdated and increasingly inefficient statutes." He noted, "If banks were unregulated, they would take on any amount of risk they wished, and the market would rate their liabilities and price them accordingly." Greenspan went on to observe that maximizing shareholder value is banks' highest objective. Phillips, in her November 25, 1996, speech in Washington, D.C., complemented Greenspan's remarks by suggesting: "Supervisory matters that are not significant to an organization's overall well-being or which are not related to a specific application under consideration are best addressed through other, more targeted supervisory actions."

It appears that the leadership of the Federal Reserve has bought into the idea that the equity-market criteria provide the ultimate test, and an efficient one, of whether bank performance is adequate or subpar. On February 21, 1997, the Board of Governors announced final changes in Regulation Y (12 CFR 225). These changes differed in some ways from those initially proposed in fall 1996. The Board noted that it had received 300 comments on its proposed regulatory change; representatives of bank holding companies, in particular, had supported its suggested streamlining of bank provision guidelines, while representatives of consumer groups had suggested maintaining the existing Regulation Y in place. The Board's decision states that it "largely incorporates the initiatives contained in its proposal," with some revisions designed to "improve public notice of acquisition proposals."

The new Regulation Y allows an expedited bank acquisition procedure when "the CRA performance rating of the lead insured institution and insured institutions with at least 80 percent of the assets of the acquiring bank holding company be [rated] satisfactory or better [under the CRA]." The new regulations further provide that the current waiting period for review (the "thirty/sixty-day" standard) remain in place if "a substantial written comment is received by the System during the public comment period"; and they state that a size limitation of $7.5 billion, or 15 percent of the consolidated total capital of the acquiring company, must be satisfied for any individual acquisition to qualify for the streamlined procedures. Proposed acquisitions that satisfy these criteria can receive System action as soon as fifteen to eighteen business days after the regulatory filing proposing the merger is first registered with the Federal Reserve System.[12]

The 1998 Megamergers

Days after the implementation of Regulation Y, First Bank System of Minnesota acquired U.S. Bancorp for $9 billion, or 3.4 times book value. This signaled a flurry of megamerger proposals, each outdoing the last, which occurred with no respite in 1997 and the first half of 1998. To cite just the largest: First Union and CoreStates; NationsBank and Barnett Banks; Citicorp and Travelers; Banc One and First Chicago NBD; BankAmerica and NationsBank; Wells Fargo and Norwest. In the realm of savings institutions, Washington Mutual acquired Great Western Bank and Home Savings, and Cal Fed merged with Golden State Bancorp. In 1997, a year of megamergers, five of the six largest deals involved financial services firms (*San Diego Union-Tribune,* September 16, 1997).

With the merger wave roiling into a tsunami, senior Federal Reserve officials were asked to explain the situation in several congressional hearings in spring 1998. In addition, Congress was in the process of considering H.R. 10, a comprehensive financial-services reform bill that sought to lift Glass–Steagall restrictions and make other far-reaching changes in banking law. So these hearings provide an opportunity for a full-scale understanding of the status of government regulatory policy vis-à-vis mergers and vis-à-vis banking law more generally. We begin by summarizing Federal Reserve Governor Laurence Meyer's April 1998 remarks before a House committee and then turn to Federal Reserve Chairman Alan Greenspan's comments in June before a Senate committee.

Meyer (1998) acknowledged that "the recent announcement of several large and interesting mergers" had triggered the session. He commented that the Fed was required by the Bank Holding Company Act to consider any merger proposal's competitive effects and also the record of the merging parties under the Community Reinvestment Act. When the proposed merger involves acquisition of a nonbanking company, the Fed must also consider whether the public will experience gains in efficiency, convenience, or competition that outweigh such adverse effects as "undue concentration of resources, decreased or unfair competition, conflicts of interests or unsound banking practices." He remarked that the Fed was compelled statutorily to approve any merger proposal satisfying all these statutory requirements. It cannot deny proposals because it "does not like this particular combination of firms."

Meyer did not portray megamergers as driven by economic necessity. He cited recent research finding scale economies in banking at levels up to $10 to $25 billion in assets—a far larger scale than recorded in the research covered here, but nonetheless a scale smaller than the size of the proposed megamergers. He admitted that small banks are profitable, and the "size does not appear to be an important determining factor even for international competition." He noted that efficiency gains have seldom been found from large bank mergers, and that efficiency gains are unlikely when merging banks' market areas do not overlap. Meyer also admitted that large banks' and out-of-state banks' higher fees are not easily explained.

Nonetheless, rather than taking a stance against megamergers because no compelling economic logic makes them necessary, he went on to defend mergers in three steps. First, he argued that such mergers would have little effect on the operational aspects of banking markets: "Recent mergers have not resulted in substantial adverse effects on the vast majority of consumers of banking services." He mentioned evidence that bank concentration has been, on balance, stable despite the merger wave. He asserted that bank mergers have not had an adverse effect on the availability of bank offices in lower-income and minority communities; that small business lending will not be harmed significantly by bank mergers after an initial transition period; and that large banks' CRA performance has often been exemplary.

Second, Meyer described megamergers as necessary and natural: "The recent wave of large bank mergers and merger announcements reflects to a large degree a natural response to new opportunities for geographic expansion and diversification as legal restrictions are removed." He cited as reasons for this wave "the search for cost economies [and] pressures brought by increased domestic and international competition," even after having argued that such factors are not relevant in this merger wave.

Third, Meyer reminded the committee that the Fed had the power to allow these mergers to go forward; and in any case, conflicts with Glass–Steagall would soon be eliminated by new legislation. The 1994 Riegle–Neal Act sets national and state-by-state concentration limits for interstate bank acquisitions of 10 percent and 30 percent, respectively—targets that even the huge NationsBank/BankAmerica combination meets (just barely). And he went on to argue that "even those deals that have already been announced cannot reach their full potential without legislation that broadens the ability of depository institutions to affiliate with insurance companies, securities firms and other financial services suppliers. Thus the Board . . . urges the Congress to pass H.R. 10."

Chairman Greenspan's testimony several weeks later (Greenspan 1998) marked an effort to induce quick Senate action on H.R. 10. Greenspan came prepared with an attachment making the point that Congress had tried unsuccessfully to repeal Glass–Steagall three times since 1984; and he pointed out that "the market will continue to force change whether or not Congress acts." He expressed support for H.R. 10's plan to keep the bank holding company structure intact, which he viewed as being more capable of supporting a viable banking safety net than the universal banking approach favored by Clinton's Treasury Department. Actually, apart from going through the various provisions of this proposal, Greenspan's comments focused on the question of how to maintain the safety net for banking after banks and nonbank financial firms were freer to combine as they choose. The chairman wants to limit the "subsidy implicit in the federal safety net [to] those activities that a bank can conduct directly." He noted that some have doubted the existence of the safety subsidy net of regulatory costs. We quote his rebuttal to this position at length because of its importance for chapter 12:

> The Federal Reserve has no doubt that the costs of regulation are large. . . . But no bank has turned in its charter in order to operate without the cost of banking regulation, which would require that it operate also without deposit insurance or access to the discount window or payments system. To do so would require both higher deposit and other funding costs and higher capital. It is also instructive that there are no private deposit insurers competing with the FDIC. For the same product offered by the FDIC, private insurers would have to charge premiums far higher than those of government insurance, and still not be able to match the certainty of unlimited payments in the event of default, the hallmark of a government insurer backed by the sovereign credit of the United States.

Greenspan goes on to describe the need to set up firewalls between the Tier-1 equity of the commercial bank subsidiary and any nonbank subsidiaries of a given holding company. He also argues that the Community Reinvestment Act will be strengthened through H.R. 10, in that a bank holding company wishing to maintain both a commercial bank and a variety of nonbank subsidiaries would be required to continuously demonstrate its compliance with CRA. He notes that a banking organization could engage in CRA-related activities through a holding company subsidiary. We return to the question of the future of community reinvestment and banking in chapters 11 and 12.

Global Financial Turbulence and the U.S. Banking Industry

The white-hot pace of bank mergers in 1997 and early 1998, which so captivated public attention, slowed dramatically after June 1998. In part this slowdown was related to the need of many large merging banks to digest their hastily chewed food. The speed with which bank megamergers had been declared left even the business press in doubt; for example, a June 13, 1998 article by the *Economist* argued that Norwest and Wells Fargo might have too little overlap and too disparate a strategic emphasis to represent a good fit. But concerns about strategic mismatch and organizational indigestion had hardly slowed the pace of merger events in the previous several years; and the challenge thrown out to their competitors by the merging BankAmerica and NationsBank would surely be expected to draw a like response. Yet as this book went to press, no such response had emerged, as either fact or rumor. Nor was there any indication that large banks had precipitously reconsidered their ongoing strategic reorientation.

What did change after June 1998 was the average level of bank stock prices, linked to a systemic downturn in bank earnings on a scale not seen since the early 1990s. At this time Wall Street equity prices generally began to slide from their historically high levels. For example, the Dow Jones Industrial Average (DJIA) peaked at just over 9,400, and the Standard and Poor 500 Index (S&P 500) at 1,190 in mid-July. The equity markets generally turned down in belated recognition of an unrelenting global financial and economic crisis. The first signs of trouble emerged in global financial markets with a run on several Southeast Asian currencies in August 1997, followed by the collapse of Korea's currency and market values at the end of 1997, a rapid decline in Japan's economic health and market prices in early 1998, and the Russian government's debt moratorium in mid-1998. On the last day of August, the DJIA fell to almost 7,400, a 20 percent drop, and then recovered to the 8,000 level before skidding again to 7,400 in early October. The S&P 500 experienced similar declines, as did almost all market indices. Subsequently, the markets staged a further rally; but the overall pattern has clearly turned from one of steady increase to one of turbulence punctuated by sudden price reversals.

Banks' stock prices have been disproportionately affected. The locus of global economic turbulence in financial assets and the revelation of large banks' involvement in various overseas financial difficulties caused a virtual flight from some bank stocks, even as market prices generally were falling. For example, BankAmerica stock peaked at just over 100 in mid-July and fell to a low of 53 in early September, a 47 percent drop; and Wells Fargo's stock price declined from a high of 394 in mid-July to 274 at the end of August, a 30 percent decline. As with financial market prices generally, bank stock prices did not stay at these depressed levels, but instead entered a roller-coaster period with a downward trend.

Propping up bank stock prices were two separate interventions by the Federal Reserve. On September 29, the Federal Reserve announced a reduction in the Federal Funds rate from 5.5 percent to 5.25 percent; and on October 15 a further drop of 25 basis points in the Federal Funds rate was announced and coupled with a cut in the discount rate from 5 percent to 4.75 percent. While these actions aimed at stabilizing financial market prices generally, they especially affected the banking sector, whose performance rests so heavily on interest rates.

Offsetting the Federal Reserve's actions, however, were a steady stream of revelations of large bank losses linked to their involvement in overseas markets. Just as the merger of NationsBank and BankAmerica was formalized, this organization announced that profits had fallen from $1.73 billion in the third quarter 1997 to $374 million in the third quarter 1998. Consequently, it was increasing its loan-loss reserves by $1.4 billion and setting aside $500 million as a reserve against continued global financial uncertainty (*Wall Street Journal,* October 14, 1998). While some $519 million of this decline in income was due to merger-related charges, the remainder was due to extraordinary losses suffered in overseas activities, including trading-related losses and a $200 million charge for a write-down on Korea's Koram Bank (*Wall Street Journal,* September 15, 1998). It was subsequently revealed that some $372 million in losses were due to BankAmerica's financing of what the *Wall Street Journal* (October 16, 1998) termed "its high-risk trading operation with D.E. Shaw," a hedge fund.

For many large banks, as for BankAmerica, earnings problems stemmed largely from their involvement in activities other than loan-making and deposit-taking, the traditional scope of banking; and when loan-making generated extraordinary losses, it often involved lending to hedge funds or others taking speculative positions in overseas financial assets. On October 8, 1998, the first day that its stock traded, Citigroup announced sharply lower quarterly earnings due largely to $700 million in hedge-fund and Russian losses by the Salomon Smith Barney group, which had been under the Travelers Group umbrella prior to Travelers' merger with Citicorp (*Wall Street Journal,* October 21, 1998).

Third-quarter earnings reports forced many other large banks to admit losses linked to hedge-fund exposure, trading losses, and exposure to Russian securities. These earnings reports drove some banks' stock prices downward, despite the Federal Reserve's interventions. Instability in bank stock prices ruled the day. First Union's stock price, for example, peaked at 66 in mid-July and fell as low as 43 in early October before recovering (at October's end) to 57. Chase Manhattan's stock price peaked at just under 78 on July 31 and fell to 37 in early October before rising by month's end to 55. And Wells Fargo's stock price continued its instability: From the end-of-August low of 274 mentioned above, it rose to 360 by the end of September, only to plummet to 300 in early October and then recover to just over 370 by month's end.

Weakened earnings and unstable, falling stock prices brought the period of weekly merger announcements to a sudden end. On July 20, SunTrust Banks announced the fifth-largest bank deal of 1998, its $9.8 billion purchase of Crestar Financial of Virginia. This merger continued the division of the Virginia banking market among several players, including Wachovia and First Union (both of which had entered by buying Virginia banks in mid-1997). Crestar CEO Richard Tilghman commented that his firm did not need to sell, but "we also have excess capital, and we are accumulating capital" so quickly that bank returns are weakening (*BankMergerFAX,* SNL Securities, July 27, 1998). The downturns in bank stocks and bank earnings soon solved the problem of excess bank capital differently from the way the bank mergers had. Tellingly, Crestar's stock price plunged from over $72 per share to $50 by the end of August 1998; and SunTrust's price dropped from $88 to $54 by the end of September. And since this merger by the nation's twentieth-largest bank holding company, no other merger by a large bank has gone forward.

The earnings prospects of the banking industry—and hence the prospects for bank stock prices and, per the argument of this book, for a continuation of the merger wave—are at best clouded at present. The current turbulence in bank stock prices has been brought about by many of these institutions' involvement in Asian and Russian lending and position-taking (possibly including their support of hedge funds) and by their trading losses. The potential for loss from these activities are now well known and reflected in banks' more modest share prices. But other warning signs abound. On June 23, the Federal Reserve issued large banks a letter warning them against undue lending to real-estate investment trusts (REITs). The market value of REITs has grown in the 1990s from under $20 billion to more than $140 billion, helping fuel the recovery in real-estate prices. Bank loans to REITs have risen just as REIT market prices have softened, leading the Federal Reserve to send banks a letter on June 23 warning against undue REIT exposure (*Wall Street Journal,* July 2, 1998). The vulnerability of the financial industry to market pressures in this area was illustrated by the failure on October 5, 1998, of Criimi Mae Inc., the largest buyer of commercial-mortgage-backed securities (*Wall Street Journal,* October 6, 1998). The problem stemmed not from the non-performance of the underlying mortgages, but from the downturn in these securities' market prices. Similarly, fears of credit risk have led large banks to back away from previous commitments to provide funding for pending mergers (*Wall Street Journal,* October 16, 1998).

In effect, large U.S. banks must now dance with the devil of market volatility, which has so well suited their own purposes until now. The consequences for bank operations are familiar. Citigroup announced 8,000 job cuts by the end of 1998, due both to their merger with Travelers and to the effects of global financial crisis (*Wall Street Journal,* September 18, 1998). Bankers Trust reported a third-quarter loss of $488 million, due largely to trading and securities losses, and then announced a program to shave 8 percent from its operating costs (*Wall Street Journal,* October 22, 1998). Thus weakened, Bankers Trust found itself the subject of takeover rumors involving Germany's Deutsche Bank AG.

6

Evidence on the Effects of Bank Mergers and Consolidation

Introduction: Another Armchair Sport or Big Brother?

The quickening pace of bank mergers has increased public concern over whether bank mergers, especially mergers creating huge megabanks, will adversely affect consumers and communities. Opinion has been split. *USA Today*'s Opinionline survey on April 17, 1998, collected recent editorial commentary on bank mergers. At one extreme was the *New York Times* editorial view that "Customers should now sit back and watch the games unfold, confident that they have nothing to fear from huge banks as long as there are other huge banks lurking in the same neighborhood." At the other was this opinion from the *St. Louis Post-Dispatch:*

> The purse strings of the local economy will become ever more remote and invisible and competition will decline and prices rise. . . . But, by that time, the old Fat Cat who ran the local bank will be almost as quaint and historical a figure as the local barber or sheriff. Citigroup, and the few remaining mega-financial services companies, will be as invisible, but ubiquitous, as Coca-Cola billboards. When economists asked about the new merger resorted to saying that it creates a Brave New World, they were right on the mark.

This chapter first reviews literature and studies that evaluate the effects of bank mergers and consolidation directly. It then reviews studies that shed light on the links between consolidation, lending patterns, small business lending, and bank branch locations. The chapter goes on to analyze data from Federal Reserve surveys of banking costs that contrasts the fees charged by different types of banks.

The Price and Efficiency Effects of Bank Mergers and Concentration

Several studies have evaluated the effects of bank mergers and consolidation on bank financial performance using a variant of the structure–conduct–performance approach. Peristiani (1996) finds that acquiring banks in the 1980–1990 period failed to improve managerial efficiency, but did experience some gains in scale efficiency and showed profitability gains. He finds that mergers in-market do not lead to as much efficiency improvement as might be expected.

A 1998 volume edited by Amihud and Miller features some empirical papers that come to uniformly skeptical conclusions about the efficiency effects of mergers. Berger's (1998) preliminary study of 1990s mergers finds that recent mergers have increased profits but not cost efficiency. Whereas acquiring banks were more efficient than acquirees in the 1980s, by the 1990s the two sides were more nearly equal; further, most gains Berger identifies are in mergers involving small banks as both acquirers and acquirees. Chamberlain (1998), in turn, finds that mergers have not substantially reduced expenditures; instead, cost savings in some areas have been offset by increases in others. Her research suggests little effect of bank mergers on profitability. Piloff and Santomero (1998) also see few gains for merging banks in terms of firm value.

If bank mergers have not increased efficiency per se, however, or resulted in cost savings at the level anticipated by Wall Street analysts (and bank CEOs), they have yielded more profits for merging banks. A study by Akhavein, Berger, and Humphrey (1997) finds that merged banks experience an increase averaging 16 percent in profit efficiency relative to other large banks. This improvement arises largely from increased revenues, not from cost efficiencies (as noted above). Indeed, the costs associated with bank megamergers can be prohibitive, as the winners seek to digest their new holdings; for example, NationsBank spent $1 billion on technology alone in 1997 (*Wall Street Journal,* April 13, 1998).

The importance of increasing revenues to banks' merger strategies has also been acknowledged in the business press. John McCoy, CEO and chairman of Banc One, commented to the *Wall Street Journal* in the wake of the Banc One/First Chicago deal that "people are seeing a need for scale. They are seeing a need to build revenue. . . . You can only get expenses down so much, and then you have to get more revenue" (April 14, 1998). Several weeks later, a *Journal* article on the Wells Fargo/Norwest merger remarked, "Big regional banks are finding that with revenue growth lackluster they are hoping to expand while slashing overhead through mergers" (June 8, 1998).

Aside from studies of the impact of mergers per se on banking markets, others have taken up the more general problem of the link between banking concentration and banking markets. Since the banking industry as a whole is undergoing consolidation and concentration, studies in this second category constitute reflections on the future of banking.

Shaffer (1994) reviewed the literature on the relationship between banking concentration and prices in banking markets. He concludes that most studies find high market concentration to be correlated with prices unfavorable to consumers. For example, the Berger and Hannan (1989) study cited above found that banks in the most concentrated markets paid twenty-five to 100 basis points less on money-market deposit instruments than were paid in the least concentrated markets. In a further study, Hannan (1991) found more evidence that small commercial loans are local in nature, and their pricing becomes less favorable to consumers as the level of banking concentration rises. Hannan and Prager (1996) examined "problem mergers"—those approved despite exceeding Department of Justice guidelines on allowable concentration—and found that both merging banks and their rivals in these concentrated markets lowered their deposit rates more than did banks in other markets.

Simons and Stavins (1998) also conclude that banking markets remain primarily local on the basis of their analysis of the 1992 Survey of Consumer Finances. They find that 68 percent of households use a local commercial bank as their primary provider of financial services, and another 24 percent, a local savings institution. Half of these are within two to three miles of home or work, and 75 percent are within twelve miles. Most households obtain credit within three to eight miles of home or work. Similarly, 84 percent of small businesses use a local commercial bank as their primary financial-services provider, and another 9 percent use a local thrift. Of thirteen categories of financial service, eight were obtained within four miles of the business site, and twelve of thirteen within seven miles (the exception is leasing services). The authors go on to analyze pricing trends, and conclude that "banks exercise market power in pricing money market deposits and CDs in their local markets. . . . [They] pay lower deposit rates in markets that are more concentrated. . . . Deposit rates are lower following a bank's participation in a merger for any level of market concentration."

Laderman (1995) reviewed sixty-five urban banking markets and found that concentration was rising even in markets with growing numbers of depository institutions—a phenomenon attributable to the increasingly unequal market share in these markets. Increasing concentration is not unique to the western United States Jayaratne and Hall (1996) document an increasing HHI (Herfindahl Hirschman Index) level in New York State cities between 1989 and 1994. These authors note that these increases were due more to thrift failures than to mergers in three of five markets; but they express concern that more merger-driven increases in HHI are all but certain in New York, especially New York City. Despite these worrisome results concerning market concentration, Federal Reserve economists have not yet documented a nationwide trend toward higher HHI scores. As in New York, it may be necessary for recent and proposed megamergers to be digested before the effects of the bank merger wave on deposit-market concentration across the nation are clear.

Rhoades (1995) considers the HHI a measure of market concentration and, in turn, of monopoly. While his study is designed as a purely statistical investigation of the HHI, it considers the Chicago School challenge to the HHI and market concentration itself as a measure of monopoly pricing. Of course, in the Chicago account (Landes and Posner 1981), a more efficient market might have a higher HHI (as better firms chased the weaker ones out of business), and the HHI itself might not have a significant relationship with monopolistic pricing.

Rhoades finds that the HHI remains a significant indicator of market concentration, and that market concentration varies inversely (in a sample of almost 1,700 banking markets) with bank profit levels—suggesting that the HHI remains an appropriate statistic for use in antitrust policy. Rhoades suggests that the HHI be supplemented by other measures, but his principal conclusion pertains not to the HHI but to the link between market concentration and monopoly pricing itself. And here he concludes: "In spite of deregulation, new secondary markets and financial instruments, and the adoption of electronic technology, there continue to be imperfections in local banking markets, which permit above-normal profits to persist" (1995, 673).

Rhoades (1996) goes on to argue that because market power remains important in local banking markets, small markets and small depositors are especially at risk from bank mergers. Since these markets and depositors constitute a large fraction of all banking assets, these effects should be weighted heavily in the formulation of merger policy.

More centralized banking markets may also be riskier. A report by Moore (1996) indicates that consumer credit, especially delivered through credit cards, has grown markedly at commercial banks; further, this trend is linked to a deepening level of household debt relative to income flows. Moore argues that this trend provides little reason to worry, since consumer debt is small relative to overall bank assets; but he admits that "Going forward, consumers' financial position may be somewhat vulnerable" (6). This is especially true because the aggregate statistics used in Moore's analysis mask the concentration of consumer credit-card debt in the hands of a relatively small number of banks, these in turn being linked increasingly to secondary markets for consumer-credit–backed securities. When bank profits depend on the volume of credit transactions alone, rather than on carrying any given volume through to maturity, and when third parties end up holding the debts so generated, lenders may fail to adequately consider the longer-term viability of the credits they authorize. This effect is offset by the reduction in risk that large banks enjoy when they make loans in different regions. This risk reduction follows from Nobel Laureate James Tobin's theoretical admonition not to "put all your eggs in one basket." When a loan portfolio includes loans reflecting different sets of regional economic conditions, a downturn in one bank lending market will have a smaller impact on the bank's entire loan portfolio than if the bank were undiversified.

Bank Consolidation and Lending Patterns

Some studies have directly or indirectly examined the impact of bank consolidation on lending patterns. One study, by Dunham (1986), examines overall patterns in credit flows. The author examines whether credit flows change after small independent banks are absorbed by larger out-of-state bank holding companies. She finds that small independent banks gather deposits and lend locally, with the funds raised exceeding their deposit base—resulting in fund outflows.

This pattern becomes more pronounced when the small bank affiliates with a larger bank holding company—so mergers and acquisitions do decrease credit flows in some communities. An analysis of loan growth by Furlong (1994) found that loan growth at banks owned out-of-state were not significantly different from that at other banks.

Several recent studies contrast the behavior of large banks not owned locally with that of small locally owned banks in the home-mortgage loan market. Studies of this sort shed light on how banking concentration might be expected to affect overall home-mortgage lending patterns. Kim and Squires (1995) run logit regressions for Milwaukee including some lender characteristics among their independent variables. Their regressions on HMDA-reported loans found that locally owned and operated banks did not perform better than other banks. Similarly, Williams and Nesiba (1994) find no difference in lending responsiveness for locally owned banks in St. Joseph County, Indiana; and my own studies of different aspects of lending in Los Angeles County (Dymski and Veitch 1994) have also suggested that small banks are no better than larger ones in inner-city lending.

Nesiba (1995) conducted his dissertation study on the relationship between community reinvestment and bank restructuring in St. Joseph County, Indiana. He considered whether small independent banks perform better than large banks in lower-income and minority neighborhoods, and whether bank mergers affected community reinvestment activity. He hypothesized that large merging banks should perform better post merger insofar as their growth strategy requires further mergers and acquisitions (48). In three cases in which acquiring banks took over local bank branches, he found that merging banks performed well in reinvestment terms. He attributed this to the products these banks had developed for use in reinvestment settings, and also to the pressure from advocates for lower-income and minority neighborhoods these banks had experienced in numerous cities.

A recent meeting of the Federal Reserve Board's Consumer Advisory Council suggests some effects not observed by Nesiba. Community and consumer group representatives to the Consumer Advisory Council reported at its spring 1997 public meeting on adverse results of bank consolidation that they experienced in attempting to persuade banks to develop new products and lending programs to serve lower-income people. The community and consumer group representatives attributed these difficulties to the increased size of banks after mergers and consolidation:

- Distant management was less likely to be familiar with conditions in their state or city;
- Longer lead time to develop new products reduced willingness to develop new products to serve needs in particular low-income communities;
- Options to develop loan and deposit products for the poor were reduced, because of a smaller number of major financial institutions to consider a proposed new program.

Bank Consolidation and Small-Business Lending

Several studies have explored the oft-voiced concern that continued shrinkage of the banking industry through mergers will lead to a shrinking volume of small-business credit, provided at higher prices.[1] Some formal studies lend support to this view. For one thing, the two Elliehausen/Wolken studies of small-business finances cited in chapter 5 find that small businesses depend on local commercial banks for their credit needs. This suggests that more distant lenders will be less able or willing to respond to small-business needs.

Keeton (1996) studied the effects of mergers on rural banks in the Tenth Federal Reserve District over the period 1986–1995. He found that business lending fell for several categories of bank merger. Turning first to rural banks, business loans fell by a cumulative average of 34 percent after three years for rural banks owned by urban organizations and acquired by out-of-state organizations. Keeton's regression analysis also suggested that farm loans fell substantially for this class of bank mergers (a 23 percent cumulative reduction after three years), and business loans also fell dramatically (by 21 percent) when urban holding companies acquired rural banks. His analysis of urban bank mergers, in turn, found that business loans fell substantially when the merged bank became a junior partner in a new organization; and this class of loan fell even more sharply when out-of-state organizations bought banks owned by urban organizations. Cumulative loan declines were similar to those for rural banks.

Nakamura (1992/1993) comes up with further indirect evidence that concentrated banking markets may be less hospitable to small-business credit needs. He finds that a small firm's checking account provides important information about its creditworthiness. Hence when small businesses maintain unified accounts with one lender, that lender is able to overcome information asymmetries with lower monitoring cost than otherwise. Insofar as small banks are more likely to use this monitoring method than are large banks, the disappearance of the former implies the loss of banks that provide relationship-based loans.

Recently, a series of empirical studies have shed additional light on the link between bank concentration and small-business credit. Some studies have found adverse effects. Small-business lending constitutes a much larger share of overall lending for small banks than for large banks; however, large banks provide a substantial overall share of small-business credit due to their sheer size in the marketplace. For example, Peek and Rosengren (1996) find that many large acquiring banks have not kept the small-business relationship-based loans that their acquired banks had maintained. They hypothesize that de novo entry opportunities will arise, but these are unlikely to fill the gap, in the short run at least.

Countering these "static" or point-in-time results is a series of even more recent studies arguing, first, that no net shift away from small-business lending has occurred because of the sheer size (if smaller relative commitment) of large merging banks; and, second, that new lenders will emerge to fill in any gaps left by large banks' absorption of smaller lenders. The most comprehensive analysis, by Berger, Saunders, Scalise, and Udell (1997), covers 6,000 mergers and acquisitions involving 10,000 banks. These authors find that the "static effects that reduce small business lending are mostly offset by the reactions of other banks and, in some cases, also by the refocused efforts of the consolidating institutions themselves."

The robust U.S. economy of the late 1990s is hardly the best environment in which to examine the possibility that bank concentration may tighten credit constraints on small business. Banks are seeking out creditworthy borrowers, and few small firms feel credit constrained. A recent assessment of bank loan growth (Gilligan 1997) found that growth rates in business loans under $100,000 were strongest at small banks and at the very largest banks. In the last recession period (1989–1991), banks' lending fell more to small businesses than to larger businesses; and it took longer to recover (Berger, Kashyap, and Scalise 1995). The next recession may give a clearer picture of the impact of bank consolidation on small businesses. In any event, if large banks are strengthening their commitment to small-business lending, they are lending in a different way. Jeep Bryant, First Union spokesman, commented to the *Wall Street Journal* (April 14, 1998) that his institution has doubled its commitment to small-business lending; in the process, "We have driven down the cost of providing small business loans by automating much of the underwriting process." This automation of underwriting is known as credit scoring, a topic discussed in chapter 11.

Bank Consolidation and Bank Branch Locations

One ongoing trend in banking is the realignment of bank branch networks associated with the reorganization of the industry. Branch densities in mature banking markets have declined because of consolidation (as branches are closed), the centralization of many banks' loan decision-making, and banks' orientation toward upper-income customers. Community Reinvestment Act considerations have, at the same time, led banks to maintain a presence in some lower-income and minority neighborhoods. Banks have opened, and continue to open, branches in emerging suburban and exurban markets, in an effort to capture the high-value-added customers who are purchasing homes in these new areas.

These shifts have bred controversy. On the one hand, community activists claim that bank branches are, in turn, systematically closed in inner-city neighborhoods, leaving have and have-not neighborhoods as the legacy of bank mergers. On the other hand, consider the testimony of Federal Reserve Governor Laurence Meyer before the House Committee on Banking and Financial Services:

> The issue of office closings is more complex than is frequently portrayed. Offices in markets served by both of the merging firms tend to be reduced. . . . Low- and moderate-income neighborhoods do not appear to be disproportionately

affected by such closings. Importantly, new entrants tend to partially offset the merger-induced reduction in banking offices, suggesting that, as new profit opportunities arise, other firms will come in. Moreover, the exploitation of such opportunities is much easier today than even two years ago before the full implementation of interstate banking. Put differently, if consumers demand locational convenience, banks of all sizes will need to, and are now able to, respond if they expect to remain viable competitors for retail customers. (Meyer 1998)

Meyer's carefully worded prose deserves some equally careful deconstruction. Studies have indeed found that merging banks do not disproportionately close offices in inner-city areas. At the same time, these areas had fewer branches per capita to begin with; so branch closings linked to mergers affect lower-income and minority areas more. Further, the surviving banks will continue to disproportionately open offices in prosperous and emerging suburban areas. Meyer's suggestion that bank offices will appear when consumers demand them is off the mark, however. No evidence supports this assertion. The fact is that there are banking customers and there are banking customers, as chapter 4 emphasized. Some figure more heavily in banks' plans than others; so some potential banking customers are more capable of registering an effective demand for banking services (to borrow Keynes's phrase) than are others.

Further, elsewhere in this volume I criticize the view expressed by Meyer that financial markets abhor a vacuum. Urban economic processes are nonlinear and path-dependent, with the consequence that market structures do not necessarily fill in empty spaces. Rather, market competitors tend to cluster in some areas while leaving others empty. Dymski and Veitch (1996a) show that bank closures in Los Angeles in the early 1990s occurred in geographic areas with relatively few bank branches, and bank openings were concentrated in areas in which a sizable number of bank branches were already present. Chang, Chaudhuri, and Jayaratne (1997) show that bank branches are spatially clustered in New York City, and that new bank branches' location can be described as rational herd behavior.

The reduced presence of banks in inner-city areas has, in turn, led to the growth of informal banking services provided by a diverse set of suppliers— check cashing stores, grocery and variety stores, liquor stores, and so on. John Caskey (1994, 1997) has analyzed the informal financial sector extensively. The research pulled together in his 1994 book found that bank branches and check-cashing stores often coexist in the same neighborhoods. This research indicated that check-cashers' prices were higher, but that this excess cost was accompanied by a more receptive—and often more language-friendly—environment for customers. Caskey's 1997 study, based on a survey of lower-income households, emphasized costs and account usage. This study found that lower-income households use informal-sector services much more frequently than do upper-income households, and pay much more (30 to 50 percent) for these services. The conclusions from Caskey's 1997 study are consistent with those from earlier nation-wide studies of check-cashing costs by the Consumer Federation of America (1988, 1989), which found check-cashing establishments charged high prices. A study of Los Angeles' informal sector by Dymski and Veitch (1996a, 1996b) found that check-cashing prices varied widely, and rose as income and economic resources declined. The Caskey and Dymski/Veitch studies encompass pawn-shops, which Caskey has characterized as "loan markets for the poor." Given the exorbitant loan rates charged by these firms, they are best regarded as "lenders of last resort," used primarily by those who must pledge their personal assets to meet cash-flow obligations.[2]

Mergers may also lead to a shift in the quality and quantity of branch services for two more reasons: First, the acquiring bank may not offer the entire range of services that were available in the target bank; second, as a condition of merger approval, the acquiring bank may divest itself of branches to other intermediaries offering only a partial range of banking services. This second reason was in evidence in the wake of the 1996 takeover of First Interstate Bank of California by Wells Fargo. Wells was forced to divest itself of sixty-one branches in se-lected market areas within California. These sixty-one branches were purchased by Home Savings, a large thrift institution headquartered in Chatsworth. This branch transfer had several deleterious implications for consumers. First, Home Savings planned to close twenty-seven of the sixty-one branches—making clear that it was interested primarily in the deposits these branches represent rather than the branches themselves. Second, Home Savings offers only selected bank-ing services. In particular, it makes no business or farm loans (except through the Small Business Administration), it has closed its affordable housing division, and it has withdrawn from making loans for multifamily housing (*California Reinvestment News,* Spring 1996, California Reinvestment Committee).

These geographic shifts in the location and number of banking offices are one of the factors behind the emergence of an "unbanked" sector among U.S. house-holds. There are others, of course: the emergence of more low-wage jobs, often filled by immigrant workers; and the strategic shift in banking, described in chapter 4. The size of this unbanked sector is poorly understood. The 1992 Survey of Consumer Finances found that approximately 12.5 percent of all households lacked checking accounts at banks—down from 14.9 percent in 1989. However, only 60 percent of families with less than $10,000 income had checking accounts.[3] This survey also found that saving and wealth levels de-clined precipitously for families with lower incomes. Huck and Segal (1997) recently obtained more troubling data about the dispersion of bank accounts from the 1996 Panel Survey of Income Dynamics (PSID). These authors found that whereas 78 percent of all households have bank accounts, only 47 percent of minority households and 54 percent of lower-income households do.

The shifts in large banks' office locations are ongoing, reflecting these firms' continuing search for optimal service delivery mechanisms; see Orlow, Radecki, and Wenninger (1996). Banks are experimenting with such mechanisms as the upscale branch, the child-friendly branch, and the coffeehouse branch (*Wall Street Journal,* October 22, 1997). Supermarket branches are, of course, another such mechanism. These authors and others argue that supermarket branches will help insure the broad geographic availability of retail banking services even as consolidation proceeds. This is partially true. However, grocery supermarkets are themselves going through a consolidation process, and are less likely to have spacious retail space in inner-city areas. Neighborhoods with disproportionately few bank branches are likely to have disproportionately few supermarkets.

Bank Consolidation and Banking Costs

Perhaps no dimension of banking change has drawn as much heat over America's kitchen tables as rising bank fees, and large merging banks are often the market leaders in this respect. A *Wall Street Journal* article on bank consolidation and banking consumers (April 14, 1998) found, for example, that Banc One began levying a $1 charge on its own customers to use its ATMs, with noncustomers paying $1.50; it also reported that several years ago First Chicago NBD began charging many of its customers $3 to transact business with a human teller if they could have conducted it electronically. BankAmerica stirred up controversy when it became the first West Coast bank to charge noncustomers for ATM use ($1.50 per transaction) in November 1996.[4]

One ongoing study of banking performance sheds particular light on banking consumer costs, especially in light of the ongoing process of banking consolidation: the Federal Reserve's annual survey of the availability and cost of banking services. This survey, required under section 1002 of the 1989 law FIRREA, has been conducted since 1989.[5] The levels of banking fees for different kinds of accounts are reported individually, and no overall index of trends in banking fees is developed. We analyzed this data for such trends. Some key results from this survey are reported in Tables 6.1 to 6.3 and in Figures 6.1 to 6.6.

Average costs for checking accounts of all kinds at commercial banks have been rising, in current dollars, since 1989; see Table 6.1. Even when adjusted for inflation, as Figure 6.1 demonstrates, the bank costs have been drifting upward since 1992. For example, the average monthly cost of a fee-only checking account has climbed from $3.32 in 1989 to $5.02 in 1996; in constant 1992 dollars, this is a jump from $3.75 in 1989 to $4.53 in 1996. Table 6.1 also presents data on average account costs at savings associations, as does Figure 6.2, allowing a comparison of costs at these two types of institution. These data clearly show that average costs are higher at commercial banks for every type of deposit account. In 1995, fee-only checking cost 21.5 percent more at commercial banks than at savings associations, while single-balance accounts cost 10.3 percent more and NOW accounts cost 24.6 percent more. This survey also found

Table 6.1 **Average Costs for Checking Accounts, Commercial Banks and and Savings Associations, 1989–1996**

Commercial Banks	1989	1990	1991	1992	1993	1994	1995	1996
(Current dollars)								
Single balance and fee checking	6.02	5.69	5.68	5.34	5.90	6.14	6.61	6.34
Fee-only checking	3.32	3.09	3.75	3.60	4.81	4.39	4.61	5.02
NOW accounts	7.05	7.67	7.84	7.32	7.78	8.02	8.49	8.15
(1992 dollars, using CPI-U)								
Single balance and fee checking	6.79	6.13	5.86	5.34	5.74	5.81	6.09	5.72
Fee-only checking	3.75	3.33	3.87	3.60	4.68	4.15	4.24	4.53
NOW accounts	7.96	8.26	8.09	7.32	7.56	7.59	7.82	7.36
Savings Associations	**1989**	**1990**	**1991**	**1992**	**1993**	**1994**	**1995**	**1996**
(Current dollars)								
Single balance and fee checking	4.70	4.73	5.53	5.46	5.50	5.58	5.95	5.75
Fee-only checking	4.29	4.14	3.60	4.02	3.51	4.28	4.04	4.13
NOW accounts	5.31	6.00	6.99	6.26	6.50	6.54	6.84	6.54
(1992 dollars, using CPI-U)								
Single balance and fee checking	5.30	5.09	5.70	5.46	5.35	5.28	5.48	5.19
Fee-only checking	4.84	4.46	3.71	4.02	3.41	4.05	3.72	3.73
NOW accounts	5.99	6.46	7.21	6.26	6.32	6.19	6.30	5.90

Source: Federal Reserve Board. See Hannan (1994) and Board of Governors (1996b, 1997).

Note: The CPI-U is the index of the Consumer Price Index for urban residents, computed monthly. July scores are used here, with the 1992 score set to 100. Single-balance and fee checking accounts are those in which a single fee is paid for unlimited use of a checking account as long as a required minimum balance is maintained. The NOW account and single-fee checking account costs denote amounts charged for low account balances. The fee-only checking cost listed reflects the average monthly cost of this account.

that large banks generally have higher fees than medium-sized banks, and in turn that medium-sized banks have higher fees and charges than small banks.

This survey also encompasses fees on a variety of consumer services and bank actions. Table 6.2 and Figures 6.3 and 6.4 summarize the results for commercial banks and savings associations. Perhaps the most striking result is captured in Figure 6.3: Even in constant dollar terms, fees for ATM use by noncustomers are rising steadily. Fees charged by banks included in the survey for most other services have remained about the same since 1989, in constant dollar terms, as Figure 6.4 shows.[6]

Two other findings in this Federal Reserve survey are of special interest. First, it compares the costs of banking accounts at small, medium, and large depository institutions as of 1995 and 1996. "Small" institutions include depository savings associations (thrifts) and commercial banks with less than $100 million in assets; "medium" institutions are those with more than $100 million but less than $1 billion in assets; and "large" institutions are those with more than $1 billion in assets. Table 6.3 and Figures 6.5 and 6.6 summarize the key result of this com-

Figure 6.1 **Checking Account Costs at Commercial Banks, 1989–1996**

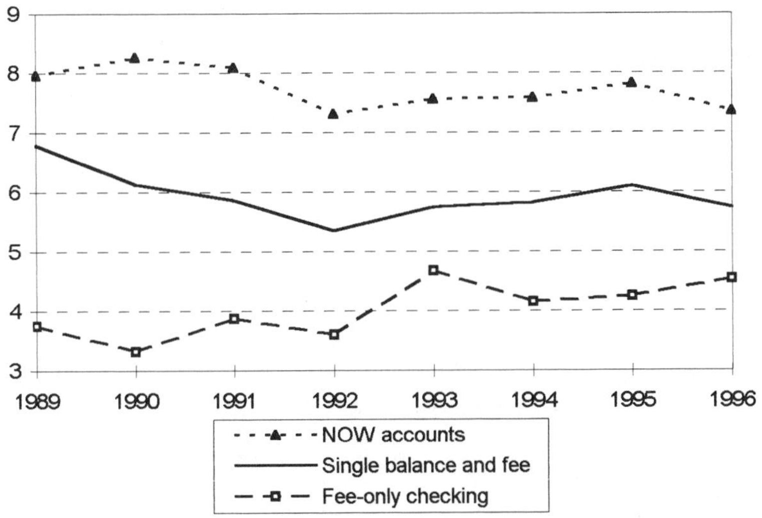

Source: Hannan (1994); Board of Governors (1996b, 1997).
Note: Figures denote average monthly costs in 1989 dollars.

parison: For most categories of banking fees and services charges, large institutions have the highest measured costs, while small institutions have the lowest costs. In Figure 6.5, this pattern holds for three categories of checking-account costs in 1995 and 1996. The same conclusion follows for the depiction, in Figure 6.6, of service charges for 1995. While not all institutions with over $1 billion are banks, most are; so this same result would be likely to hold if Federal Reserve analysts examined a stratified sample consisting only of commercial banks.

Second, fees charged by out-of-state banks are significantly higher on average than those charged by in-state banks. In both 1994 and 1995, out-of-state banks and thrifts charged monthly fees about 18 percent higher than did in-state banks and thrifts, while requiring substantially higher minimum balances to avoid fees. Out-of-state banks and thrifts also charge substantially higher fees for ATM use and insufficient-funds checks than do in-state banks and thrifts. The 1996 Federal Reserve report to Congress (Board of Governors 1996b) used regression analysis to determine whether this cost gap could be attributed to regional and market differences. It could not. Even after adjusting for such factors, a statistically significant gap remains.

Studies of bank and ATM fees have also been conducted by the U.S. Public Interest Research Group (PIRG) for several years. These studies conclude that bank-fee costs have risen much faster than is indicated in the Federal Reserve survey

Figure 6.2 **Checking Account Costs at Savings Associations, 1989–1996**

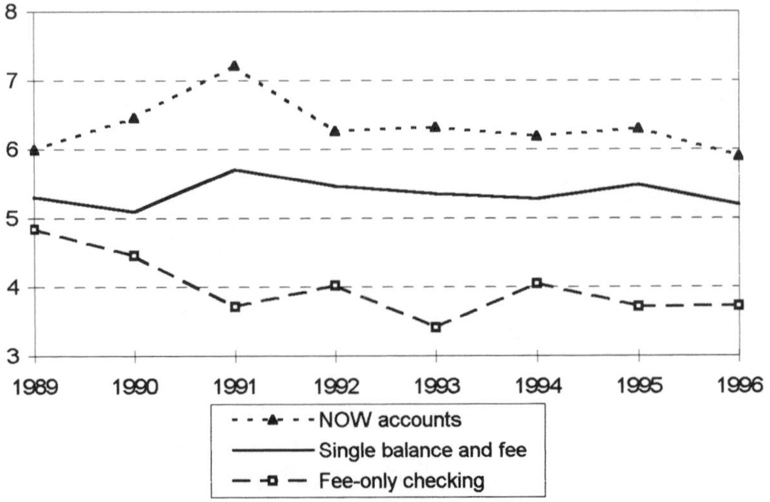

Source: Hannan (1994); Board of Governors (1996b, 1997).
Note: Figures denote average monthly costs in 1989 dollars.

discussed here. PIRG has reported that bank fees and bank minimum balances rose at twice the rate of inflation in the period 1993–1995. An April 1997 report of ATM fees found that surveyed 1997 fees on ATM use averaged $1.15, an increase of 18.6 percent from 1995; in April 1998, PIRG's survey found an average ATM fee of $1.23. Further, PIRG studies have documented the growth of numerous usage fees on bank accounts and especially the rise of ATM surcharges on noncustomers.

The higher rate of cost increases documented by PIRG in ATM use and in bank fees, compared with the Federal Reserve's own estimates, is due to these two organizations' differing methodologies: the Federal Reserve samples smaller banks more heavily, while the PIRG focuses on larger banks. In any event, both results are inconsistent with the notion of banking as a competitive industry subject to economies of scale. Either there are no economies of scale to be had in banking; or these economies exist but are not being transmitted to consumers because banking markets are not perfectly competitive. Neither interpretation finds evidence of mergers' widespread benefits for consumers.[7]

Summary: The Effects of Mergers and Consolidation

Taken together, the evidence reviewed in this chapter comes to several conclusions. First, there is little evidence that mergers systematically yield operating

Table 6.2 **Average Fees for Financial Services and Actions, Commercial Banks and Savings Associations, 1989–1996**

Commercial Banks	1989	1990	1991	1992	1993	1994	1995	1996
(Current dollars)								
Money orders for non-customers	1.96	2.21	2.37	2.01	2.27	2.39	2.47	NA
Checks returned	12.62	13.00	14.17	14.26	15.65	15.33	15.71	16.36
for insufficient funds								
ATM withdrawals, own customers	0.03	0.05	0.03	NA	NA	0.06	0.06	0.04
ATM withdrawals, non-customers	0.43	0.56	0.73	0.60	0.70	0.74	0.88	0.88
(1992 dollars, using CPI-U)								
Money orders for non-customers	2.21	2.38	2.44	2.01	2.21	2.26	2.27	NA
Checks returned	14.24	14.00	14.62	14.26	15.22	14.50	14.47	14.77
for insufficient funds								
ATM withdrawals, own customers	0.03	0.05	0.03	NA	NA	0.06	0.05	0.04
ATM withdrawals, non-customers	0.48	0.60	0.76	0.60	0.68	0.70	0.81	0.79
Savings Associations	**1989**	**1990**	**1991**	**1992**	**1993**	**1994**	**1995**	**1996**
(Current dollars)								
Money orders for non-customers	1.96	2.21	2.37	2.01	2.27	2.39	2.47	NA
Checks returned	13.23	14.25	15.41	14.95	16.36	16.30	17.06	17.62
for insufficient funds								
ATM withdrawals, own customers	0.09	0.12	NA	NA	NA	0.07	0.05	0.10
ATM withdrawals, non-customers	0.23	0.34	0.55	0.66	0.61	0.67	0.81	0.78
(1992 dollars, using CPI-U)								
Money orders for non-customers	2.21	2.38	2.44	2.01	2.21	2.26	2.27	NA
Checks returned	14.93	15.34	15.90	14.95	15.91	15.42	15.71	15.91
for insufficient funds								
ATM withdrawals, own customers	0.10	0.13	NA	NA	NA	0.07	0.04	0.09
ATM withdrawals, non-customers	0.26	0.37	0.57	0.66	0.59	0.64	0.74	0.70

Source: Hannan (1994); Board of Governors (1996b, 1997).
Note: See Table 6.1.

efficiencies for banking firms; at the same time, it is clear that merging banks experience gains in profits, largely by expanding their revenue streams. Second, bank mergers and consolidation have some effects that adversely affect consumer and nonfinancial business's interests. For one thing, bank customers pay higher fees at larger banks than at small ones, and higher fees at out-of-state–owned banks than at in-state–owned banks. For another, consumers earn lower rates in more concentrated banking markets.

Banking markets remain largely local markets; so if consolidation leads to increasing market concentration (and rising HHI scores), then monopolistic pricing will become a worry. Whether the bank merger wave will increase banking-market concentration is not yet clear; this effect depends in part on how banking and banking markets are defined in the brave new financial world.

Table 6.3 **Banking Cost by Depository Institution Size, 1995 and 1996**

	Small institutions	Medium institutions	Large Institutions
Checking account fees, 1995			
Single balance and fee checking	6.16	7.00	8.97
Fee-only checking	4.79	4.28	4.45
NOW accounts	8.25	8.65	10.81
Checking account fees, 1996			
Single balance and fee checking	6.13	6.49	7.59
Fee-only checking	5.04	4.96	5.19
NOW accounts	7.56	8.97	10.12
Selected services and actions, 1995			
Money orders for non-customers	2.17	2.93	3.78
Money orders for own customers	1.82	2.38	2.81
Checks returned for insufficient funds	14.56	17.99	20.03
ATM withdrawals, non-customers	1.01	1.05	1.18
Selected services and actions, 1996			
Checks returned for insufficient funds	15.05	18.97	20.29
ATM withdrawals, non-customers	1.11	1.07	1.24

Source: Board of Governors (1996b, 1997).
Note: See Table 6.1. Small institutions are banks and thrifts with $100 million or less in assets; medium institutions are banks and thrifts with more than $100 million and less than $1 billion in assets; large institutions are banks and thrifts with over $1 billion in assets.

Studies of bank consolidation and credit markets do not find that bank mergers have systematically reduced access to credit. Several studies with HMDA data suggest that large banks perform as well or better than small banks in reinvestment activity; more on this in chapters 8 to 10. Further, studies of small-business lending find some causes for concern in the bank merger wave. The disappearance of locally based banks engaged in relationship-based lending with small businesses may not lead to fewer small business loans; but it may lead to different small business loans, based on credit scoring and automated loan-making criteria. Some embrace this development because it implies that race-free and redlining-free criteria (see chapter 8) will dominate credit decision-making in the small business markets. Others are not so sure. Chapters 8 and 9 shed further light on the contrasting behavior of loans made by locally based and out-of-state banks.

Associated with the bank consolidation wave is a growth in the informal financial sector, which often charges higher rates for services than banks and other formal-sector intermediaries. And linked with this sector's growth is an unbanked portion of the U.S. population, whose members' ability to save and accumulate in the future is problematic because of holes in the financial services

Figure 6.3 **ATM Withdrawal Fees for Noncustomers, Commercial Banks vs. Savings Associations, 1989–1996**

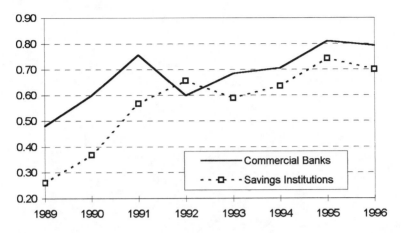

Source: Hannan (1994); Board of Governors (1996b, 1997).
Note: Average cost per withdrawal, 1992 dollars.

Figure 6.4 **Fees for Noncustomer Money Orders and NSF Checks, Commercial Banks vs. Savings Associations, 1989–1996**

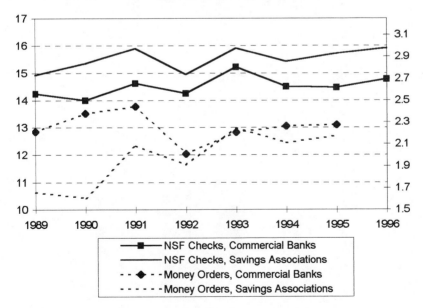

Source: Hannan (1994); Board of Governors (1996b, 1997).
Note: NSF checks are checks returned to payors for nonsufficient funds. Left axis depicts cost per returned check, 1992 dollars; right axis depicts cost per money order, 1992 dollars.

Figure 6.5 **Transaction Account Costs by Bank Size, 1995 and 1996**

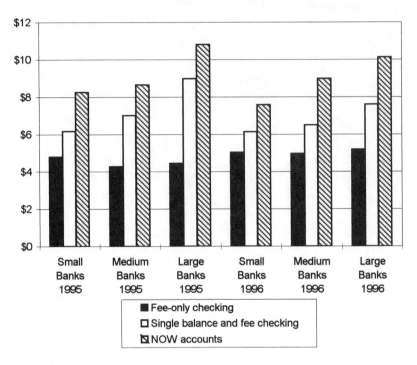

Source: Board of Governors (1996b, 1997).

Figure 6.6 **Service Charges by Banking Institution Size, 1995**

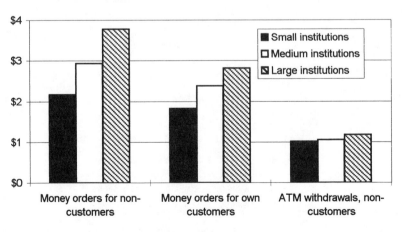

Source: Board of Governors (1996b).
Note: Figures depict cost per occurrence. Types of institution are not differentiated.

provided by informal financial firms. For example, recall the finding by Huck and Segal (1997) that minority households are much less likely, in the 1996 PSID, to have a bank account than are white households. These authors also find that only 18 percent of minorities have a prior relationship with the lenders to whom they apply for mortgages, compared with 38 percent of whites. This finding reinforces two of the recurring themes of the evidence on banking reviewed here—that banking remains primarily local, and it involves relationships over time.

In sum, the evidence reviewed here suggests that the *New York Times*'s editorial optimism about the benevolence of large banks is unwarranted; the caution and skepticism expressed by the *St. Louis Post-Dispatch* is more appropriate, as remote banks increasingly populate a land of households for most of whom banking remains largely a local affair.

7

Banking and Lending Structures

Do Regional Differences Matter?

Introduction: Operating, Competitive, and Social Efficiency

Underlying the studies reviewed in prior chapters is a conventional definition of operating efficiency as the difference between output volume and input cost. This conception has already been criticized as ambiguous. It is also an insufficient indicator of which banking firms over time will flourish and which will not. The simple concept of operating efficiency is flawed because it ignores the time dimension of banks' strategic problem. Operating efficiency per se implicitly focuses on the short-run problem of cost minimization, on the assumption that many asset commitments are locked in. But banking-firm survival depends at least as much on its *competitive* efficiency—its ability to generate stable, long-term growth by finding revenue-generating activities while avoiding or shedding excessive risks.

Competitive efficiency results from the combination of operating efficiency, which might be termed the short-term problem of maximizing revenues per dollar of cost, and longer-term risk management. The bank's short-term and longer-term problems lead to different criteria: The former could involve cutting costs by laying off staff, consolidating offices, and shedding high-cost customers; the latter might mean avoiding the possibility of catastrophic risk and taking steps to shed default risk. Longer-term banking efficiency is thus facilitated by the creation of secondary markets, the implementation of floating-rate interest-rate agreements with borrowers, and the extension of governmental and private guarantees against some categories of loan default.

Banks and banking markets have taken some of these steps toward operational and competitive efficiency in the past two decades, thereby increasing the value of banking franchises and opening the way to six straight years of record industry profits in the 1990s. This dual perspective on efficiency clarifies the logic behind the twofold equation for banking-system modernization envisioned by many economists and regulators: Allow competition for banking franchises while making banking franchises more valuable. It also clarifies the logic behind banks' shifting of risks and costs onto consumers: When consumers take on interest-rate risk by agreeing to variable-rate loans, they enhance banks' competitive efficiency; when they pay higher fees for checking accounts, they enhance banks' operating efficiency.

But the complementary lenses of operating and competitive efficiency are not the only ways of understanding efficiency. What if we began not with the welfare of the banking firm as a reference point, but instead with the welfare of the consumer household and the welfare of the community in which these households reside? Households, like firms, are threatened both by slowly acting forces in the economic sphere, as when revenues consistently fall short of outlays, and by rapidly unfolding catastrophic events such as job loss or stock-market collapse.

The financial efficiency of the consumer household can be understood by adapting the terminology intended originally for banking firm efficiency. From a short-term perspective, a household is most efficient when its costs of conducting transactions and carrying debt are at a minimum relative to its cash flow. As in the case of banks discussed above, this short-term perspective is ambiguous. Short-term efficiency could refer to how cheaply a household can conduct the banking (credit and transactions) activities associated with a certain level of income and wealth, or to whether a household is able to maximize its income margin by making use of banking services. Clearly, the simultaneous search for short-term efficiency by banks and households involves some aspects of a zero-sum game, wherein one's gain is the other's loss.

It is more interesting to consider a household-sector analogy to the notion of longer-term or systemic efficiency. In the case of banks, this means examining the factors that might jeopardize the viability of the banking industry as a whole. In the case of households, the property of longer-term or systemic efficiency refers to the viability and sustainability of the communities within which people live. Admittedly, consumer households are not members of communities in the sense that banks are members of the banking system. No matter where a given bank operates, it always remains within the banking system; but this is not the case for consumers, who often shift from community to community in the course of their income-earning members' careers. But while individual mobility creates a chronic free-rider problem for most communities, the fact remains that nearly all consumer households live in and depend on the services provided in *some* community at every point in their lifespan.

How well does the individual household function? This depends both on its own capacities, efforts, and wealth assets, and on the integrity of the social fabric in the community that surrounds it. A community can be defined as socially efficient insofar as it permits households residing within it to make full use of their capacities, efforts, and assets; insofar as it protects households residing within it from being disadvantaged due to factors unrelated to their capacities, efforts, and assets; and insofar as it facilitates the attainment of new capacities and assets by those households seeking to accumulate wealth.

This brings us to a novel approach to efficiency, which informs the analysis of the next four chapters—the notion of social efficiency. A set of arrangements is said to be "socially efficient" insofar as it allows a higher proportion of households to fully utilize their financial, physical, and human assets; insofar as it facilitates a higher proportion of households to attain a secure and nourishing home environment; and insofar as it protects all households from economic disadvantage due to noneconomic factors. The concept is qualitative and inherently social. It is also designed so that social efficiency can be ranked on a continuum—say, as a proportion of the population measured from 0 to 1 for each of the three dimensions set out here. The "social efficiency" of the banking sector (or of any other sector) at any point in time depends on whether that sector is contributing to, or deterring, the attainment of social efficiency in the community. While some communities are well supplied with public and private facilities that will facilitate the full economic functioning households, others are not. Hence, it is important to begin any investigation of "social efficiency" in real-world communities by comparing their basic institutional characteristics—their different financial histories and differences in their financial structures and credit-market patterns.

The task undertaken in the next four chapters is to identify salient aspects of financial structure in different communities, especially comparative credit-market outcomes, and to explore the implications of these different financial structures for the social efficiency of the banking sector in these different places. This investigation will, in turn, give us a basis for evaluating the social-efficiency effects of the consolidation and merger wave in banking.

In this chapter, we first develop an argument that local financial structures remain important in credit-market outcomes even in the contemporary cybernetic, borderless world. We then examine financial structures in sixteen Eastern and Western cities in depth: We compare financial infrastructures and lending flows in cities that have had different experiences with bank mergers and consolidation. Chapter 8 then introduces a regression model of the residential credit market and applies it to the sixteen Eastern and Western markets analyzed in chapter 7.

The East/West contrast developed in these two chapters permits us to evaluate whether place matters in financial structures and credit-market outcomes. We find that it does. This leads to chapter 9, which looks more systematically at the differential characters and behaviors of urban financial structures in different regions of the United States. Chapter 9 contrasts several Southwestern cities with cities in the Mountain/Great Plains states, in the Midwest, in the Northeast, and in the Southeast. This contrast centers on whether the same financial institutions play the same roles in different areas, with special attention to a comparative analysis of credit-market disadvantage. Chapter 10 then confronts the problem of whether banking-market structure affects credit-market outcomes. Data for California cities' banking-market structure is used to conduct an econometric test of whether banking-market concentration affects access to credit.

Local Financial Structure in the Globalizing World

In the efficient-markets view, financial structure is understood as passive and purely reactive in economic dynamics because information is uniform and readily available, and because relatively complete market opportunities allow agents to achieve optimal balance sheets and asset portfolios. In the alternative view developed here, financial structure is among the elements shaping (and being shaped by) economic dynamics. Market opportunities are incomplete, and information is heterogeneous and idiosyncratic. Because agents operate under fundamental uncertainty, they will have different understandings of what constitutes information and what it means. Because agents have different levels of economic power (and power is relational), one cannot "read" their market options by simply describing their objective circumstances.

An economy's financial structure as defined here consists of two elements: local financial infrastructures that meet the demand of households and businesses for credit and for the means of making monetary transactions; and the pattern of credit flows, that is, the level of capital and credit demanded and obtained by different segments of the household and business sectors. As emphasized in chapters 4 and 6, local financial infrastructures and credit flows fit tightly together: The local financial infrastructure creates and channels most credit flows in any local area. Because of new lending technologies and banking strategies, a growing share of credit flows in any area may originate with financial intermediaries lacking branches and offices there. How does financial structure influence the development and continued growth of urban space? How might these links be changing? This section expands on the argument in chapter 1, that the character of access to credit depends not simply on how efficiently and readily lenders can identify pre-given opportunities, but also on the two-way interaction between a structure of financial firms and an environment that these firms both construct and enable.

Why Local Financial Structure Matters: Access to Credit and Structures of Opportunity

The economic act of creating any new urban space involves the precommitment of financial resources. This new space can be planned well or haphazardly, depending on the extent of planning and the depth of these resources.[1] So financial structure always "comes first" in spatial development, and "matters" insofar as all urban communities work to maintain a vital historical capital base, strive to recreate it, or struggle to overcome a historical legacy of underinvestment. The trajectory of an established urban area depends on financial structures in several ways.

The number and type of financial-intermediary offices matter for economic growth and for credit flows. A community benefits in several ways from having a significant number of formal bank offices. For one thing, this reduces transaction costs and enhances security for local businesses. For another, the very presence of local branches indicates competition for that community's financial business. This ensures localized competition for customers, and signals that this community's economy and assets are valued. For smaller financial institutions whose charters and business franchises are local, maintaining a healthy local economy and asset base by meeting local credit and transaction needs is a matter of survival. The relationship between local bank soundness and local economic growth is, indeed, two-way. Samolyk (1992) provides evidence that regional economic health is affected by regional bank performance—sounder local banks lead to sounder local economies; and clearly locally chartered banks can be important "engines" of local or regional growth.[2]

The number and type of financial-intermediary offices matter insofar as urban growth in particular takes on a "boom and bust" character, which can be more formally described as nonlinear and path dependent. Growth in localized areas can be increasingly nonlinear and path dependent as strategic interactions among banks and nonbank lenders become more important in governing a given area's growth; and these strategic interactions certainly depend on the configuration of offices and historical credit flows in local areas.

Credit Patterns and Information Structures

Local financial structures also matter because of the link between information and uncertainty. If financial markets were efficient, information would be uniform and uniformly interpretable. But given that information is costly to obtain and obtained under conditions of uncertainty, different lenders will acquire different kinds of information about loan applicants; and even when they acquire the same information, they may interpret it or use it differently in evaluating creditworthiness. Further, the more lenders that are active in a given locale, the more diverse is the information collected and the ways in which this information is interpreted.

At the heart of chapters 8 to 10 is a model of lenders' decisions in home-loan markets across the country. This model illustrates the importance of information structures in the relationship between financial institutions and credit-market outcomes. This model investigates, in effect, whether lenders use different informational variables, and how they use them, in credit-market decisions. It does so on the basis that home-purchase loans are relatively uniform contracts—a problematic assumption that is discussed at the beginning of chapter 8. Given contractual uniformity, if lenders evaluate information as per the efficient market hypothesis, there should be little variation from one lender type to another in the use of information to evaluate creditworthiness. If all lenders active in a given area know that a certain list of variables conveys information about creditworthiness, and if all lenders understand these variables in the same way, then the variables included in our empirical test of the determinants of loan approval rates should either be found insignificant or significant by every lender subgroup— and if significant, they should all have the approximately the same level of significance. But suppose instead that the variables in this model of loan approval have widely varying degrees of significance, as indeed we find below for race and lower-income variables. This suggests an environment in which the informational postulates needed for financial-market efficiency are violated, and hence an environment in which local financial structures—how lenders read signals, and which signals they read—matter. This brings us to our next questions: What are these differences, and what do they mean?

What kinds of information do lenders collect and evaluate as they peer through the lens of an uncertain world? Figure 7.1 suggests some possibilities. Information can be understood as flowing to lenders through either public or private channels. A lender accesses a public information channel when it seeks out data about borrowers that is emitted at low cost by applicants, uniformly measured and capable of being audited, collected at a centralized point by a third party, and rankable in a numerical order clearly related to creditworthiness. By contrast, information is carried through private channels when it is either costly to emit or costly to collect, difficult to audit, heterogeneous and not readily rankable, or not centrally collected by any third party. The difference between these channels is a matter of degree, not type. When private information channels connect lenders and borrowers, borrowers have an informational advantage over lenders—they know more about their personal circumstances.[3] Counterbalancing this, however, are two sources of advantage for lenders: They control the scarce resource—credit—needed by the borrower, and they have access to information about borrower populations whose characteristics are similar to those of any given applicant.

Two types of asymmetric information present difficulties for lenders: missing information about borrower type, which creates ex-ante adverse selection problems; and missing information about borrower intentions and effort, which creates ex-post moral hazard problems. Signals can be used to divide borrowers into "good" and "bad" types, but signals also may be good (appropriate) and bad (unfair). Good signals are, among other things, behavioral—they are based on actions emitted (and hence at least partially controlled) by applicants. Bad or inappropriate signals are, by contrast, not behavioral but presumptive—they assume that agents in particular categories fall into different creditworthiness classes without checking this assessment against agent behavior. Figure 7.1 distinguishes between behavioral and presumptive signals, and in turn between information about applicants and information about applicants' communities.

Figure 7.1 **Public and Private Information Channels in the Credit Market**

	Public information channels (ex ante signals of "type")	**Private information channels (may also pertain to ex post performance)**
Information about applicants		
Behavioral signals	Applicant rankings using behavioral information revealing creditworthiness (e.g., income, loan/income ratio, credit report)	Behavioral information relevant to applicants' likely effort (e.g., "character," experience, track record in meeting obligations)
Presumptive signals	Statistical rankings of applicants using categorical information (e.g., race, gender, age)	Ascriptive aspects of applicants presumed relevant to effort (e.g., race, gender)
Information about applicant communities		
Behavioral signals	Behavioral indicators of community asset values (e.g., new building, home sales and refinancing, average incomes)	NA
Presumptive signals	Statistical indicators of neighborhood "quality" (e.g., neighborhood racial composition, financial office branches)	Ascriptive characteristics of neighborhood residents (e.g., neighborhood racial composition)

Figure 7.1 includes some suggestive examples of these different types of information. Generally, public information channels can be collected at any point in time—and because of their characteristic low cost, they can be collected for loan applicants in a given community by lenders without local branches there. Information collected via private channels, by contrast, is often relational, requiring the commitment of resources over time; so information of this type is most likely to be collected by banks with local branches in place.

This contrast suggests, in turn, that financial intermediaries making loan decisions at a distance try to differentiate, in advance, between "good" and "bad" borrower types; and this can be done using appropriate (behavioral) signals or inappropriate (presumptive) signals. Lenders drawing on local branch structures to make loan decisions, by contrast, are likely to augment public information with privately obtained information. Indeed, as advances in computer and communications technology increase the breadth and depth of public information channels, local institutions' survival may depend on their ability to nurture the private channels they have built up over time. Nonetheless, the matrix of possibility is complex: the information channels open in any community depend on how many intermediaries are active, how many maintain branches there, community diversity, and so on.

Standard microeconomic theory suggests that the emergence of bank and nonbank lenders active in numerous regions will weaken the links noted here between financial structure and local economic growth. The idea is that when financial resources are scarcer in capital-starved regions, those regions' return to financial investment will be higher than elsewhere; hence as financial resources flow more easily among geographic markets, those regions should receive inflows of external funds until risk-adjusted regional returns are equalized. The arguments developed here about path dependence and information channels suggest, to the contrary, that such equalization will not occur; indeed, locales with weak informational channels may be left further behind those with stronger channels and more robust financial infrastructures.

Eastern and Western Banking Market Areas:
An Overview

If local market structures matter in financial markets, how do they matter? The remainder of this chapter begins to answer this question. We investigate financial structures and outcomes in different geographic markets, with special attention to any possible correlation between interstate bank entry, market share, and one measure of credit-market performance, the fair-share index. The cities included here are grouped into western and eastern clusters: The western cluster includes Los Angeles, California; Albuquerque, New Mexico; Billings, Montana; Boise, Idaho; Des Moines, Iowa; El Paso, Texas; Fresno, California; and Sioux Falls, South Dakota. The eastern cluster includes Minneapolis/St. Paul, Minnesota; Ft. Wayne, Indiana; Lancaster, Pennsylvania; Newark, New Jersey; Springfield, Massachusetts; Savannah, Georgia; Wilmington, North Carolina; and Jackson, Mississippi.

As Table 7.1 shows, two of these eight Western cities are located in states that have been completely open to interstate expansion, three in states permitting no interstate entry in 1989, and three in states allowing entry with reciprocity. By contrast, seven of these eight Eastern cities are in states with regional reciprocity policies; the other, Newark, is in a state with national reciprocity policies in place.

Our interest in these sixteen cities' financial structures centers on these questions:

- Do out-of-state and in-state lenders differ significantly in their local lending behavior?
- Do commercial banks and nonbank lenders differ in lending behavior?

Table 7.1 **Basic Statistics on Population and Banking for Sixteen U.S. Metropolitan Areas.**

	MSA population in 1990	Minority population, pop. 1990	1989 state policy on interstate banking	Changes in banks, 1987-93: Total	Due to mergers
Eight cities west of the Mississippi River					
Los Angeles, CA	3,198,742	2,006,526	Regional reciprocity	-12.6%	-17.1%
Albuquerque, NM	589,131	267,247	None permitted	-13.8%	-10.6%
Billings, MT	113,419	7,126	None permitted	-30.8%	-4.7%
Boise, ID	295,851	23,639	Open	-12.5%	-29.2%
Des Moines, IA	392,928	28,189	None permitted	-13.7%	-12.5%
El Paso, TX	591,610	439,726	Open	-48.7%	-28.5%
Fresno, CA	729,780	342,364	Regional reciprocity	-12.6%	-17.1%
Sioux, Falls, SD	123,809	3,699	National reciprocity	-10.4%	-12.7%
Eight cities east of the Mississippi River					
Minn./St. Paul, MN	2,464,124	210,078	Regional reciprocity	-21.9%	-21.3%
Newark, NJ	1,824,321	649,303	National reciprocity	-16.2%	-41.9%
Ft. Wayne, IN	363,811	40,090	Regional reciprocity	-33.2%	-32.7%
Lancaster, PA	422,822	29,071	Regional reciprocity	-13.2%	-25.5%
Springfield, MA	436,941	36,667	Regional reciprocity	-41.2%	-39.3%
Jackson, MS	395,396	171,804	Regional reciprocity	-15.6%	-16.3%
Wilmington, NC	942,091	197,241	Regional reciprocity	9.4%	-28.2%
Savannah, GA	242,622	91,590	Regional reciprocity	8.6%	-20.6%

Note: Figures in the last two columns are calculated as a percentage of 1996 commercial banks.

- Are there differences between the lending behavior of large merging banks located in-state and those without in-state offices?

Data Sources and Definitions

For each city, Home Mortgage Disclosure Act (HMDA) data for three years (1992, 1995, and 1996) are used. HMDA data are collected by federal regulatory agencies from virtually all lenders that make residential loans in the United States. These data are divided into several subgroups by lender type: small in-state commercial banks, large commercial banks with branches in-state, large commercial banks without in-state branches, savings and loan associations, and mortgage companies. These subgroups exclude credit unions and smaller banks without in-state branches.

The term "large bank" here refers to thirty-six bank holding companies meeting at least one of the following three criteria: first, the commercial banks they operate are among the top twenty in total assets as of December 31, 1997;

second, bank-holding-company asset size exceeded $50 billion as of December 31, 1997—a hurdle met by twenty-seven companies; third, they have made significant acquisitions in two or more of the states included in this study. These banks, listed in Table 9.1 in chapter 9, are termed "merging banks" in this study because, as a group, they have grown in part by actively acquiring other bank and nonbank firms. The term "small in-state bank" refers to all other banks whose bank-holding-company headquarters is located within a given state. This narrow approach to what constitutes a "large bank" captures the very largest banks at the heart of banking consolidation; but because this term is so narrow, the "small in-state banks" category includes some relatively large institutions.

For the thirty-six large banks singled out here, loans attributed to any registered banks or mortgage companies within these institutions' holding-company umbrella are attributed to these holding companies per se. This seems appropriate because large U.S. banks have remarkably complex and often very different organizational structures. Managers of the banks so classified may disagree with this unified characterization; indeed, some acquiring banks have striven to maintain the "local responsiveness" and even managers of institutions they have purchased in new market areas. Nonetheless, Norwest Iowa differs from, say, the East Des Moines National Bank in a fundamental way: the former is part of a multistate entity that exerts control over its component parts; the latter is answerable only to itself. The definition of large bank used here, then, permits us to test precisely whether centrally owned, ig geographically dispersed, institutions behave differently than banks that are geographically dispersed without being centrally owned.[4]

Data on bank branch offices and on nonbank financial offices have been taken from the ProCD SelectStreet and SelectPhone listings for 1996.[5] The data on nonbank financial offices allows us to compare the number of bank branches with the total offices operated by thrifts and credit unions, by "informal sector" firms such as check-cashing stores and pawnbrokers, and by loan brokers, including mortgage and finance companies.

Market Share and Approval Rates, East Versus West

The most obvious contrast between residential lending markets in Eastern and Western cities is that commercial banks' market share is much higher in the East. Figure 7.2 illustrates that commercial banks made 47.8 percent of all 1996 home purchase loans in the eight Eastern cities, but only 27.8 percent in seven Western cities (excluding Los Angeles). This difference arises primarily because mortgage companies have a 15 percent higher market share in these Western cities. Mortgage companies account for the same share of Western home-purchase loans in 1996 as do banks in Eastern markets. Figure 7.2 also indicates that market share is higher in the East for each commercial-bank category—small banks, large banks in-state, and large banks out-of-state.

Figure 7.2 **Home-Purchase Market Share by Lender Type in Sixteen Eastern and Western Cities, 1996**

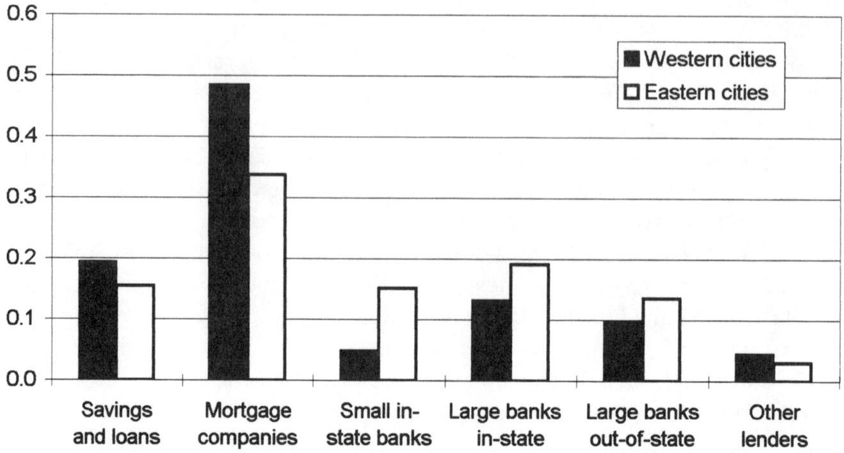

Source: Author's calculation, 1996 HMDA data.

East and West also differ in loan approval patterns. Figure 7.3 shows that Western cities' approval rates are consistently 5 to 10 percent lower than Eastern cities'. This gap holds up for every lender group. The devil is in the details, however; and to these we now turn.

Eight Western Cities

This section discusses aspects of financial structure in Los Angeles and the other seven cities west of the Mississippi listed in Table 7.1.[6] Los Angeles is included because of its remarkable size and diversity. The other seven cities are medium-size metropolitan areas (MSAs) without major cities nearby; they differ dramatically in their states' interstate-banking policies and in the makeup of their human and banking populations. In Los Angeles, Albuquerque, and El Paso, half or more of all residents are minorities; in the other five cities, the overwhelming majority of residents are white. As Table 7.2 shows, Los Angeles, Albuquerque, and El Paso also stand out because they have substantially fewer bank branches and other financial offices, measured by population per branch, than do the other cities analyzed here—with the exception of pawnbrokers and check-cashers.

Los Angeles

The vast majority of Los Angeles's bank branches are offices of in-state–owned banks. This is hardly surprising, given California's reciprocal-entry policy to-

Figure 7.3 **Home-Purchase Loan Approval Rates by Lender Type in Sixteen Eastern and Western Cities, 1996**

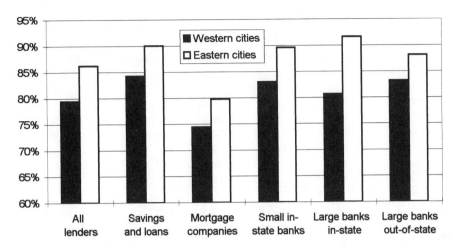

Source: Author's calculation, 1996 HMDA data.

ward interstate banking—that is, banks headquartered in a given state can branch into California as long as California's banks have the same privilege in return—and the aggressive expansion policies of several California banks. As of mid-1996, 38 percent of Los Angeles's bank branches were operated by Bank of America, Wells Fargo, and First Interstate.[7]

Los Angeles's home-purchase and refinancing loan market shrank by 49 percent in application volume between 1992 and 1996, caused by both the low-interest-rate–driven refinancing wave of 1992 and the subsequent stagnation of the Southern California home-purchase market in the mid-1990s.[8] The domination of Los Angeles's banking market by California institutions is not reflected in its residential loan patterns. As Table 7.3 shows, 21 percent of all applications were taken by commercial banks in 1992, and 27 percent in 1996. Large merging banks accounted for 57 percent of all bank applications in 1992, and for 78 percent in 1996—with most of this difference due to large banks without in-state branches. The middle portion of Table 7.3 demonstrates that the proportion of minorities in the applicant pool grew across the board between 1992 and 1996. Merging banks as a whole had a lower proportion of minority applicants in both years than did other lenders; however, large banks with in-state branches had a substantial jump in minority applicants between 1992 and 1996, with minorities constituting half of all their 1996 applicants.

Table 7.2 **Financial Offices per 100,000 Population in Selected Western and Midwestern Cities, 1996**

	Bank, Thrift branches	Credit union offices	Invest- ment offices	Mortgage, finance companies	Pawnshops check- cashers	Total fin- ancial offices	1990 Metropolitan Population
SOUTHWEST							
Fresno, CA	19.6	3.2	4.9	14.9	4.7	47.3	729,780
Los Angeles, CA	19.5	5.1	8.4	10.8	7.7	51.4	3,198,742
Modesto, CA	36.3	7.1	9.1	33.3	9.1	94.8	198,336
Albuquerque, NM	15.3	2.9	6.5	32.8	6.8	64.2	589,131
Sante Fe, NM	27.6	9.4	17.4	33.4	5.1	92.8	137,895
El Paso, TX	8.6	3.0	8.6	26.9	12.5	59.7	591,610
SW Average	18.7	4.5	8.0	16.8	7.7	55.7	
MOUNTAIN/GREAT PLAINS							
Billings, MT	22.9	8.8	21.2	19.4	12.3	84.6	113,419
Boise, ID	26.0	7.1	11.2	37.9	7.1	89.2	295,851
Sioux Falls, SD	45.2	13.7	30.7	13.7	5.7	109.0	123,809
Casper, WY	9.8	6.8	12.1	6.8	6.8	42.2	132,600
MTN Average	25.8	8.6	16.7	24.0	7.7	82.8	665,679
MIDWEST							
Des Moines, IA	38.7	8.9	14.0	10.4	5.1	77.1	392,928
Dubuque, IA	31.3	20.8	26.6	10.4	6.9	96.1	86,369
Ft. Wayne, IN	20.2	8.5	9.3	15.8	2.2	55.9	366,485
Gary, IN	6.6	3.1	0.5	5.8	1.5	17.5	604,526
Terre Haute, IN	22.9	2.4	5.7	8.6	2.4	41.9	209,978
Indianapolis, IN	34.2	10.4	9.8	26.5	5.2	86.1	634,408
Minneapolis, MN	30.0	5.8	17.6	24.4	3.9	81.6	1,768,985
Rochester, MN	29.4	8.5	17.0	21.8	3.8	80.5	105,620
MW Average	26.8	6.8	12.4	18.8	3.7	68.6	

Source: 1996 ProCD SelectPhone database and 1990 Census data.

Fresno, Albuquerque, and El Paso

The three middle-size Western cities in our sample have substantial minority populations. While New Mexico disallowed interstate branching (as of 1993), Albuquerque's banking structure shows deep penetration by out-of-state–owned banks; only thirty-seven (25 percent) of Albuquerque's 149 bank branches are operated by New Mexico–owned banks. Almost all the rest are owned, as of mid-1996, by four out-of-state principal banks—BankAmerica of California,

Table 7.3 **Market Share in Eight Western Cities, Home-Purchase and Refinancing Loans, 1992 and 1996**

	1992 Market Share (Applications)			1996 Market Share (Applications)		
	All commer- cial banks	Merg- ing banks	Merging banks with in-state branches	All comm- ercial banks	Merg- ing banks	Merging banks with in-state branches
All applicants (Percent of all applications)						
Los Angeles, CA	20.2	8.4	7.7	26.6	14.0	6.8
Fresno, CA	28.5	17.8	13.4	32.6	5.3	3.8
Albuquerque, NM	35.4	9.8	6.4	28.0	23.6	16.5
El Paso, TX	27.3	8.1	7.6	21.3	4.6	4.6
Billings, MT	50.3	28.9	28.7	37.8	34.1	27.9
Boise, ID	56.0	34.9	23.1	39.0	23.5	9.7
Sioux Falls, SD	71.3	16.2	16.1	56.2	4.4	3.2
Des Moines, IA	53.9	14.1	5.9	40.6	30.9	18.8
Minority applicants (Percentage share of all applications)						
Los Angeles, CA	37.5	32.7	36.1	43.1	40.4	46.6
Fresno, CA	22.4	22.1	23.8	35.8	42.6	46.6
Albuquerque, NM	28.2	30.5	34.0	40.6	40.8	41.4
El Paso, TX	55.0	48.8	49.4	64.8	58.9	58.3
Billings, MT	2.3	2.6	2.6	3.0	4.0	3.4
Boise, ID	2.2	2.1	2.1	8.0	8.5	8.2
Sioux Falls, SD	0.5	1.2	1.2	1.8	0.8	1.1
Des Moines, IA	3.1	2.9	3.8	6	5.4	5.8
Applicants under $50,000 income (Percentage share of all applications)						
Los Angeles, CA	30.2	30.0	33.3	29.7	27.9	39.6
Fresno, CA	47.8	45.4	49.0	56.4	64.0	70.8
Albuquerque, NM	57.2	58.5	57.4	59.6	60.5	62.7
El Paso, TX	66.6	67.5	69.3	64.5	50.9	50.4
Billings, MT	61.5	60.8	60.6	64.9	66.5	63.9
Boise, ID	50.6	49.0	41.4	62.4	63.3	63.4
Sioux Falls, SD	64.9	63.4	63.7	67.8	53.4	54.7
Des Moines, IA	51.6	50.4	43.7	56.5	61.4	59.5

Source: 1992 and 1996 HMDA data.
Note: "Merging banks" includes all banks classified as large in this study; see chapter 9.

Boatmen's Bancshares of Missouri (which owned Sunwest in 1996, and was subsequently bought by NationsBank), First Security of Utah, and Norwest of Minnesota. At the other extreme is Fresno, in which out-of-state holding companies operated no bank branches as of 1996. On the other hand, two in every three Fresno bank branches are operated by large banks headquartered in either San Francisco or Los Angeles. El Paso is midway between these extremes. In the wake of Texas's out-of-state bank-purchase legislation of 1986 (see chapter 3),

49 percent of the commercial banks registered in Texas in 1987 disappeared by 1993. Some 48 percent of El Paso's forty-four bank branches are operated by bank holding companies owned out of state.[9]

In these cities, as in Los Angeles, commercial banks accounted for less than a third of home-mortgage loans in both 1992 and 1996 (Table 7.3). Large banks constituted a relatively small part of banks' portion of Albuquerque's market in 1992, but a dominant portion by 1996. Surprisingly, large merging banks' share of the El Paso and Fresno markets shrank between 1992 and 1996, suggesting that other banks are doing more of this lending in these two cities. In Fresno, for example, half the loan applications taken by commercial banks originated with the four large in-state banks at that point in time—BankAmerica, Wells Fargo, Security Pacific, and First Interstate. However, by 1996 these banks (now including only BankAmerica and Wells Fargo) accounted for just 25 percent of commercial-bank applications; banks owned out-of-state and without local branches had become the dominant subgroup among commercial banks. In Albuquerque, by contrast, the banking portion of the home-loan market has been increasingly dominated by large institutions operating in-state but owned out-of-state.

Minority applicants grew dramatically as a share of all applicants in each of these three cities—from about one-quarter in 1992 to over 40 percent in 1996 in both Fresno and Albuqerque, and from just over half to 75 percent in El Paso. The Los Angeles pattern of merging banks having lower proportions of minority applicants than other lenders does not hold up in these cities. This uniform shift toward higher minority proportions was accomplished in different ways. In Fresno, the minority applicant pool declined slightly (7 percent) from 1992 to 1996, but white applicants were down 62 percent. In Albuquerque the white applicant pool grew 70 percent, but the minority pool grew 274 percent. El Paso's white applicant pool shrank 20 percent while its minority pool grew 83 percent. Furthermore, in each of these cities the percentage of applicants earning less than $50,000 grew significantly for most categories of lender shown in Table 7.3 between 1992 and 1996. So the residential loan market as a whole moved "downstream" rather dramatically in these three cities; by 1996, about 60 percent of applicants at banks, and at least two-thirds of applicants at nonbank lenders, fell below the $50,000–income benchmark.

Billings, Boise, Sioux Falls, and Des Moines

The remaining Western cities are relatively small and largely white. The banking infrastructures of these four market areas differ considerably, reflecting these states historical interstate-banking policies (Table 7.1). Reflecting Montana's long-standing policy of excluding entry by out-of-state banks, 76 percent of all bank offices in Billings are branches of in-state banks. Also, all of the credit union offices in the city are Montana-owned. Iowa, too, has historically barred entry by out-of-state banks. And while two large banks owned out-of-state have established branch networks in Des Moines—Boatmen's Bancshares (now NationsBank-owned) and Norwest, only seventeen (23 percent) of Des Moines' seventy-four bank branches are operated by these two out-of-state holding companies. Sioux Falls, in a state (like California) that has historically allowed entry with reciprocity, has a higher percentage of branches owned by large out-of-state bank holding companies—41 percent of its fifty-one bank branches as of 1996 were operated by Norwest and First Bank of Minnesota. Finally, in Idaho, which has been open to out-of-state bank entry, some 47 percent of Boise's seventy bank branches were operated by bank holding companies headquartered out of state as of 1996.

Table 7.3 shows that commercial banks' share of the home-purchase and refinancing loan market shrank by 12 percent or more in each of these four cities; by 1996, banks made more than half this market only in Sioux Falls. Merging banks have widely varying shares of these four markets. The bank portion of Billings' home-loan market has been consistently dominated by large banks, whereas these lenders have been relatively unimportant in Sioux Falls; and merging banks have taken an increasing share of Des Moines' market, but a declining share in Boise.

Home-loan applications grew by more than 40 percent in both Billings and Boise between 1992 and 1996, but declined by 15 percent in Des Moines and by 29 percent in Sioux Falls. Merging banks have been increasing market share in the two growing home-loan markets, but decreasing their share in the two declining ones. Minority applicants have been growing rapidly in absolute numbers in all four cities—increasing just over 60 percent between 1992 and 1996 in Sioux Falls and Des Moines, by 155 percent in Billings, and by 282 percent in Boise. The volume of white applicants grew by about 40 percent in Billings and Boise, but declined in the other two cities. Further, the proportion of applicants with incomes under $50,000 grew in all four cities. The lower portion of Table 7.3 shows that banks have fewer applicants with incomes under $50,000 than do nonbank lenders.

Fair Share in Eight Western Cities

So in all eight Western cities, lower-income individuals and minorities comprise a growing share of the home-loan market. In general, banks take proportionately more applications from upper-income and white applicants than do nonbanks. These same trends are found in data on loans made, which are not displayed here. Among banks, market-share statistics suggest no consistent differences between all banks, all merging banks, and merging banks with in-state branches.

What about communities—do some lenders make fewer loans in lower-income and high-minority areas than others? And how satisfactorily do lenders as a whole treat lower-income and high-minority areas compared with upper-income and lower-minority areas? A good test of lenders' commitment to lower-income and high-minority areas is the "fair share" measure developed by Shlay (1989). This measure tests whether the levels of loan applications and loan flows differ substantially in areas of different types within any given metropolis. Redlining is *suspected* when lower-income or high-minority areas have systematically lower loan flows, given application levels. And as chapter 3 suggests, redlining is *found* when loan flows differ systematically among areas due to social, not economic, differences among these areas. It may result from lenders' discrimination, lenders' unfamiliarity with redlined areas, lenders' marketing strategies, and so on. Fair-share analyses are open-ended: they identify geographic differences but say nothing about the forces leading to these differences.

Shlay's fair-share approach first divides a metropolis—Chicago, in her 1989 article—into suburban, gentrified, and "neighborhood" areas. Loan flows in these different areas are divided by the number of owner-occupied units, and then compared. A "neighborhood" area is considered not to have a fair share of the residential loan market if its loan flows, adjusted for eligible units, are significantly fewer than those elsewhere. This diagnostic then indicates the need for heightened reinvestment scrutiny. Shlay's 1989 study, and many others using this or a similar technique, have found that loan flows vary negatively with minority population.

Fair share is defined differently here. Shlay's method requires a prior division of any given metropolitan area into different subareas based on multiple quantitative and qualitative criteria. Chicago is huge, and is also the national test tube for redlining and reinvestment activism and analysis; so dividing Chicago into subareas proceeds along well-worn pathways. Most of the metropolitan areas included here, however, are much smaller than Chicago, and thus harder to subdivide. We need a method of differentiating subareas that does not rely on prior research and can be applied uniformly in metropolitan areas with very different income levels and racial compositions. This method must be able to encompass both Los Angeles and Boise.

We propose a method of subdividing metropolitan areas in Tables 7.4, 7.5, and 7.6. We first identify the census tracts in every metropolitan area with the highest proportion of minority residents, without regard to the proportion of minorities in this metropolis's population. We next identify those census tracts with the lowest median incomes, again without concerning ourselves about the relative median incomes of different cities. These two groups of tracts could overlap because of the high inverse correlation between minority status and income in most cities. To avoid a perfect overlap between high-minority and lower-income tracts, we select 25 percent of every metropolis's tracts as its high-minority areas, and 33 percent of every metropolis's tracts as its lower-income areas.

These tables contain the results of our fair-share analysis of the eight Western cities. Table 7.4 characterizes 1992 and 1996 results for the residential credit market as a whole. The first two columns of this table present the ratio of

Table 7.4 **Fair-Share Scores for Residential Credit Flows in Eight Western Cities, 1992 and 1996**

Census tracts with the largest proportion of minorities (25% of total)

	Applications in minority areas as percent of those in other areas		Loans made in minority areas as percent of those in other areas	
	1996	1992	1996	1992
Los Angeles, CA	*19.7*	28.7	*16.6*	24.8
Fresno, CA	36.8	34.4	32.8	*19.1*
Albuquerque, NM	69.3	*22.1*	35.7	*18.6*
El Paso, TX	*11.5*	*8.3*	*8.0*	*6.8*
Billings, MT	289.9	42.7	50.3	44.1
Boise, ID	*23.8*	*24.8*	*19.1*	27.6
Sioux Falls, SD	44.8	38.7	27.5	31.1
Des Moines, IA	*27.6*	*25.7*	24.3	26.7
Eight-city median	32.2	27.2	25.9	25.7

Census tracts with the lowest 1990 median income (33% of total)

	Applications in lower-income areas as percent of those in other areas		Loans in lower-income areas as percent of those in other areas	
	1996	1992	1996	1992
Los Angeles, CA	*39.9*	60.4	*34.5*	*46.1*
Fresno, CA	*46.5*	*47.3*	*39.5*	51.0
Albuquerque, NM	112.9	*40.2*	*48.3*	*32.8*
El Paso, TX	69.7	*22.0*	*25.9*	*24.2*
Billings, MT	329.3	66.0	50.3	58.1
Boise, ID	*38.1*	*35.1*	*28.3*	*34.1*
Sioux Falls, SD	55.6	*49.6*	*34.2*	*40.8*
Des Moines, IA	*37.8*	*31.7*	*31.2*	*30.1*
Eight-city median	51.1	*43.7*	*34.4*	*37.5*

Note: All raw figures are adjusted for 1990 owner-occupied units, as explained in the text. Scores not meeting fair-share benchmarks are italicized. This benchmark is 33.3 for minority areas, since 25%/75% = 33.3, and 50% for lower-income areas, since 33%/67% = 50.

home-purchase loan applications in minority areas to those in nonminority areas, expressed as a percentage. The next two columns present this same ratio for loans made. In each column, the number of applications (and loans) in each census tract is divided by that tract's total number of 1990 owner-occupied homes. This adjusts for the uneven distribution of homes eligible for purchase within metropolitan areas—in virtually every city, lower-income and minority areas have proportionately fewer owner-occupied homes and more apartments than other areas.[10] Once these supply adjustments are made, then if loan applications and loans are distributed equally across census tracts, we should find ratios of 33 percent (25/75, in percentage terms) for minority areas and 50 percent (33/67) for lower-income areas. These are our fair-share benchmarks.

In 1996, only two of the eight Western cities met the minority fair-share benchmark for loans made: Albuquerque and Billings. El Paso's scores are especially bad. In 1992, only Billings passed the loans-made benchmark. Performance was somewhat better for applications taken. The eight-city median fair-share score for minority areas improved for loan applications between 1992 and 1996, from 27.2 percent to 32.2 percent; the median score for loans made remained steady at just over 25 percent.

The fair-share benchmark for the lower-income areas shown in the lower portion of Table 7.4 is 50 percent. In 1996 every city's loan applications satisfied this benchmark level—indeed, the eight-city median suggests that just over half of all applications were registered in lower-income areas, up from 43.7 percent in 1992. However, the median percentage of loans made in lower-income areas is substantially less, 34.4 percent in 1996, down from 37.5 percent in 1992. So while applications have shifted toward lower-income areas, loan approvals have not. Three cities—Des Moines, Boise, and El Paso—failed to meet the 33 percent benchmark level for loans made in 1996; three also failed this benchmark in 1992, including El Paso and Des Moines.

Table 7.5 contrasts the fair-share performance of commercial banks with that of nonbank lenders, again for home-purchase loans only. Numerous credit market shifts occurred between 1992 and 1996. In 1992, commercial banks' proportion of loan applications in minority areas was the same or somewhat more than was nonbank lenders' proportion; and the same held true for loans made. But by 1996, commercial banks' share of applications and loans made in minority areas was substantially below that of nonbank lenders, except in Des Moines. Indeed, commercial banks did not meet the fair-share benchmark of 33 percent in six of these eight Western cities.

In lower-income areas, nonbank lenders again perform better than do commercial banks. Again, commercial banks had about the same median share of applications in lower-income areas as did nonbanks in 1992; but their median share dropped slightly by 1996, while nonbank lenders' median share rose. Both banks and nonbanks had similar medians in 1992 and 1996 for loans made; commercial banks' median score failed the fair-share benchmark in both years. By 1996, commercial banks failed to meet the lower-income fair-share benchmark in seven of the eight cities; nonbank lenders failed this benchmark in three.

Overall, Table 7.5 suggests that commercial banks perform more poorly than nonbank lenders on fair-share criteria. This table also includes fair-share figures for banks that were operating in 1992 and closed by 1996. In some cities, such as Billings and Des Moines, these closed banks performed uniformly better than commercial banks as a whole (in the comparison year of 1992) on all four

Table 7.5 **Fair-Share Scores for Bank and Nonbank Lenders, Home-Purchase Loans in Eight Western Cities, 1996**

	1996 Applications		1996 Loans		1992 Loans Commercial banks		
	Commercial banks	Other lenders	Commercial banks	Other lenders	All	Closed by 1992	Other lenders
Census tracts with the highest proportion of minorities (25% of total)							
Los Angeles, CA	15.1	21.2	12.2	18.1	21.3	18.1	25.6
Fresno, CA	32.5	38.7	29.3	34.3	18.6	3.9	19.1
Albuquerque, NM	44.1	76.5	30.2	37.8	20.4	17.3	18.0
El Paso, TX	14.0	11.0	6.9	8.4	12.2	12.2	4.6
Billings, MT	24.7	450.6	20.9	67.9	33.4	60.8	57.1
Boise, ID	19.9	26.4	17.8	20.0	27.8	32.9	27.4
Sioux Falls, SD	34.6	57.3	24.9	32.4	35.4	36.1	17.2
Des Moines, IA	30.1	26.1	25.9	23.3	26.6	33.6	26.7
Eight-city median	27.4	32.6	22.9	27.8	23.9	25.5	22.4
Census tracts with the lowest 1990 median income (33% of total)							
Los Angeles, CA	31.8	42.6	27.4	37.0	36.6	23.7	48.5
Fresno, CA	36.4	51.6	28.9	44.6	25.0	16.9	58.5
Albuquerque, NM	67.0	127.8	42.7	50.4	28.8	19.1	34.3
El Paso, TX	30.4	82.3	19.4	28.2	19.2	56.4	26.5
Billings, MT	36.0	510.1	32.7	86.3	46.4	68.8	72.7
Boise, ID	29.4	44.0	24.1	31.5	31.5	40.2	36.9
Sioux Falls, SD	44.1	70.0	32.8	36.7	43.3	49.1	31.8
Des Moines, IA	38.2	37.6	32.0	30.5	30.4	36.9	29.8
Eight-city median	36.2	60.8	30.5	36.9	31.0	38.6	35.6

Note: All figures depict the ratio of loans or applications in lower-income (high-minority) census tracts to loans or applications in other tracts, adjusted for 1990 owner-occupied units; see text. Scores not meeting fair-share benchmarks are italicized. This benchmark is 33.3 for minority areas (25%/75% = 33.3) and 50% for lower-income areas (33%/67% = 50).

fair-share criteria; in others, closed banks performed worse than other banks. The median fair-share figures for closed banks in these eight cities are, however, uniformly better than those for all banks—on average, closed banks performed better in fair share terms.

Table 7.6 wades deeper into this water by evaluating the fair-share performance of different types of commercial banks: small in-state banks, large banks headquartered in-state, large banks owned out-of-state but with in-state branches, and large banks without in-state branches. There is again considerable variation from city to city. On balance, small in-state banks perform best for both applications and loans made in minority areas; and large banks without in-state branches perform worst. Large banks as a whole perform relatively poorly, especially in the loans-made category: these banks' minority-area fair-share scores do not meet the 33 percent benchmark in fifteen of sixteen cases. The results for the lower-income fair-share tests are somewhat different. Large banks without in-state branches perform better than small in-state banks in the applications index; but this large-bank group falls to worst in the loans-made index, while small in-state banks again outperform large banks. Large banks fail to meet the fair-share benchmark of 50 percent in every case for loans made.

In sum, our fair-share analysis of lending patterns for minority and lower-income areas suggests that the commercial-banking sector as a whole performs more poorly than nonbank lenders; among banks, large merging banks—especially those without in-state branches—perform more poorly than small in-state banks. However, there is considerable city-to-city variation.

Eight Eastern Cities

Our investigation of eight banking markets east of the Mississippi begins with the tale of two large metropolitan areas, Minneapolis-St. Paul, Minnesota; and Newark, New Jersey; the former has a minority population of just 8.5 percent, versus 36.5 percent in the latter (Table 7.1). Then come three smaller Northern cities—Fort Wayne, Indiana; Lancaster, Pennsylvania; and Springfield, Massachusetts, with minority populations ranging from 7 percent to 11 percent. Finally, we take a turn through the South: Savannah, Georgia; Jackson, Mississippi; and Wilmington, North Carolina.

Minneapolis–St. Paul and Newark

In-state banks operate almost all bank branches in Minneapolis; the sole significant exception is Firstar Bank, headquartered in Milwaukee, which operates thirty-two local branches (6 percent of the 1996 commercial bank and thrift total). This bank and Minnesota's two large in-state banks, First Bank and Norwest, together operate 168 (that is, 31.6 percent) of the area's 530 bank and thrift branches. This proportion is almost identical to that for BankAmerica and Wells Fargo/First Interstate branches in Los Angeles. Minneapolis-St. Paul is amply stocked with formal financial institutions. As Table 7.2 demonstrates, this city has high per-capita levels of bank branches, investment offices, and mutual fund offices; however, it has relatively low levels of credit-union branches, pawnbrokers, and check-cashing stores.

Newark's financial structure offers a study in contrast to Minneapolis: it has substantially fewer offices of every type, as Table 7.7 shows. Newark contains 54.7 financial offices of all kinds per 100,000 residents, versus 81.6 in Minneapolis. These two cities' banking backbones also differ in that only a minute

Table 7.6 **Fair-Share Scores by Type of Commercial Bank, Home-Purchase Loans in Eight Western Cities, 1996**

	1996 applications				1996 loans			
		Large	Large out-of-state:			Large	Large out-of-state:	
	Small	merging	with	without	Small	merging	with	without
	in-state	in-state	branches	branches	in-state	in-state	branches	branches
Census tracts with the highest proportion of minorities (25% of total)								
Los Angeles, CA	*18.2*	*15.5*	*18.0*	*13.5*	*14.2*	*11.2*	*20.6*	*11.1*
Fresno, CA	70.1	50.0	*0.0*	*28.6*	51.4	30.7	*0.0*	*28.8*
Albuquerque, NM	37.6	NA	42.9	50.2	38.8	NA	*31.4*	*21.5*
El Paso, TX	*13.4*	NA	*14.0*	*8.4*	*7.9*	NA	*10.3*	*0.2*
Billings, MT	*20.7*	NA	*23.2*	91.7	*18.3*	NA	*21.3*	*22.6*
Boise, ID	NA	NA	*29.7*	*19.9*	NA	NA	*22.0*	*17.8*
Sioux Falls, SD	*26.5*	NA	39.9	62.3	*25.9*	NA	*25.8*	46.1
Des Moines, IA	33.2	NA	*31.6*	*14.3*	32.7	NA	*26.1*	*11.0*
Eight-city median	*26.5*	*32.7*	*26.4*	*24.3*	*25.9*	*21.0*	*21.7*	*19.6*
Census tracts with the lowest 1990 median income (33% of total)								
Los Angeles, CA	*47.1*	*27.9*	*30.7*	*27.8*	*39.8*	*20.3*	*34.8*	*24.6*
Fresno, CA	73.5	56.5	*27.5*	*23.6*	*49.4*	*38.6*	*35.2*	*24.5*
Albuquerque, NM	84.8	NA	59.2	80.8	92.2	NA	*43.8*	*26.5*
El Paso, TX	*17.9*	NA	*19.7*	57.8	*9.9*	NA	*12.8*	*8.5*
Billings, MT	*40.7*	NA	*31.8*	110.7	*40.2*	NA	*30.0*	*42.6*
Boise, ID	NA	NA	*40.3*	*30.2*	NA	NA	*29.6*	*22.8*
Sioux Falls, SD	*34.9*	NA	51.0	56.7	*31.5*	NA	*38.1*	*34.7*
Des Moines, IA	*40.7*	NA	*38.5*	*29.5*	*37.2*	NA	*31.3*	*23.9*
Eight-city median	*43.9*	*42.2*	*31.8*	56.7	*40.0*	*29.4*	*34.8*	*24.6*

Note: All figures depict the ratio of lower-income (high-minority) tracts to other tracts, adjusted for 1990 owner-occupied units. Scores not meeting fair-share benchmarks are italicized. This benchmark is 33.3 for minority areas (25%/75%) and 50 for lower-income areas (33%/67%).

number of Newark's branches are operated by large banks—twenty-five of its 418 branches (6 percent) are Chase Manhattan branches.

The number of home-purchase and refinancing loan applicants fell significantly in both Minneapolis and Newark between 1992 and 1996, by 37 percent and 42 percent, respectively; with even higher declines in the white applicant total. Interestingly, in both markets commercial banks took a larger share of applications in 1996 than in 1992, as Table 7.8 shows; and the share of applications at merging banks doubled. As in the West, the percentage of applicants with incomes below $50,000 increased for all categories of lender between 1992 and 1996.

Table 7.7 **Financial Offices per 100,000 Population in Selected Eastern Cities, 1996**

	Bank, Thrift branches	Credit union offices	Invest- ment offices	Mortgage, finance companies	Pawnshops, check- cashers	Total fin- ancial offices	1990 metropolitan population
NORTHEAST							
Erie, PA	20.0	11.2	9.1	10.5	1.5	52.3	275,572
Lancaster, PA	18.7	4.0	5.9	12.5	0.9	42.1	422,822
Philadelphia, PA	45.0	6.3	13.5	26.6	12.4	103.7	2,062,886
Newark, NJ	24.0	4.0	8.7	15.2	2.7	54.7	1,738,572
Trenton, NJ	26.4	4.6	12.0	12.3	1.8	57.1	325,824
Brockton, MA	21.0	9.8	4.2	15.4	1.4	51.7	143,005
Lowell, MA	13.6	2.2	3.7	7.0	0.4	26.9	271,167
Springfield, MA	8.2	2.6	5.3	4.6	4.3	24.9	586,302
NE Average	28.9	5.1	9.7	17.2	5.9	66.8	
SOUTHEAST							
Athens, GA	65.1	3.4	16.0	51.4	27.4	163.3	87,594
Savannah, GA	26.3	5.5	12.4	38.7	14.8	97.7	216,935
Biloxi, MS	53.5	12.3	6.6	42.6	26.5	141.4	211,403
Hattiesburg, MS	34.4	5.1	12.2	40.5	20.3	112.4	98,738
Jackson, MS	21.0	3.8	8.9	33.1	10.9	77.6	395,396
Asheville, NC	50.7	13.7	21.1	50.7	13.7	149.9	94,706
Fayetteville, NC	56.7	8.5	21.3	107.7	72.3	266.4	70,576
Greenville, NC	33.4	4.6	13.9	17.6	4.6	74.1	107,924
Wilmington, NC	31.0	7.0	13.4	38.0	7.6	97.0	171,153
SE Average	35.8	6.7	12.0	41.1	17.7	113.3	

Source: 1996 ProCD SelectPhone database and 1990 Census data.

Fort Wayne, Lancaster, and Springfield

These three cities have remarkably low population-weighted levels of financial offices. Fort Wayne has a modest per-capita level of financial offices (Table 7.2); its financial infrastructure closely resembles Newark's. It has an especially low level of pawnbrokers and check-cashing stores and few investment and mutual fund offices. Springfield is located in a state with regional reciprocity rules for interstate branching and a long tradition of locally based savings institutions. It is thus surprising that Springfield has the fewest financial offices of any city examined here; its 24.9 offices per 100,000 residents constitute just one-half the average found even in the low-infrastructure cities of the Southwestern region. Springfield has extremely low levels of every type of financial office

Table 7.8 **Market Share in Eight Eastern Cities, Home-Purchase and Refinancing Loans, 1992 and 1996**

	1992 Market Share (Applications)			1996 Market Share (Applications)		
	All commer- cial banks	Merg- ing banks	Merging banks with in-state branches	All comm- ercial banks	Merg- ing banks	Merging banks with in-state branches
All applicants *(Percent of total applications)*						
Minneapolis, MN	43.2	22.0	19.0	50.4	45.4	31.7
Newark, NJ	38.9	11.6	6.1	43.9	24.4	7.1
Ft. Wayne, IN	46.5	4.6	3.5	39.5	24.1	18.2
Springfield, MA	81.9	10.6	6.9	66.5	20.1	8.7
Lancaster, PA	62.1	14.5	5.2	65.2	23.1	7.5
Wilmington, NC	65.3	26.8	26.0	49.4	28.3	11.7
Savannah, GA	57.3	47.6	22.2	42.8	29.0	13.5
Jackson, MS	66.5	1.2	0.0	51.6	8.7	0.0
Minority applicants *(Percentage share of total applications)*						
Minneapolis, MN	3.0	3.2	3.3	7.6	7.8	8.1
Newark, NJ	13.8	15.7	18.8	20.5	23.4	25.7
Ft. Wayne, IN	4.6	2.5	2.6	5.4	5.4	5.8
Springfield, MA	4.1	5.5	3.9	13.3	21.4	31.1
Lancaster, PA	3.5	6.6	7.9	7.2	7.8	5.7
Wilmington, NC	7.8	7.1	7.2	7.8	10.1	5.2
Savannah, GA	16.0	14.2	12.8	18.1	17.6	17.1
Jackson, MS	14.2	5.2	NA	22.9	23.5	NA
Applicants under $50,000 income *(Percentage share of total applications)*						
Minneapolis, MN	45.5	45.2	46.3	51.0	50.7	49.9
Newark, NJ	21.8	22.8	19.9	25.4	26.3	27.6
Ft. Wayne, IN	60.9	54.7	50.8	68.2	71.5	68.4
Springfield, MA	51.9	49.1	46.2	62.6	69.0	82.3
Lancaster, PA	61.1	60.9	61.2	68.2	73.2	69.5
Wilmington, NC	51.7	26.8	26.0	50.7	56.3	45.9
Savannah, GA	56.4	56.6	56.2	56.2	57.9	49.4
Jackson, MS	51.4	43.7	NA	57.0	70.3	NA

Source: 1992 and 1996 HMDA data.
Note: "Merging banks" includes all banks classified as large in this study; see chapter 9.

except pawnbrokers and check-cashers. None of its bank branches are out-of-state owned. Lancaster, in turn, has the second lowest level of financial offices, next to Springfield. Every type of office is represented at a below-average level, with check-cashing stores and pawnbrokers being especially scarce.

As in Minneapolis and Newark, the number of home-loan applicants in all three cities declined between 1992 and 1996, with the number of white applicants falling by 13 percent in Fort Wayne and by 47 percent or more in Lancaster and Springfield, and the number of minority applicants increasing. In Fort Wayne, 21 percent of the 1992 applications and loans were made by banks that subsequently closed before 1996; in the other Eastern and Western cities considered here, this percentage fluctuated between 2 percent and 7 percent. These three banks' market-share experiences fall into two distinct patterns. In Lancaster, as Table 7.8 shows, commercial banks accounted for just under two-thirds of all applications (and loans) in both 1992 and 1996. An increasing percentage of all applications, 14.5 percent in 1992 and 23.1 percent in 1996, were taken by large—usually out-of-state—banks. Springfield's market-share statistics are almost identical to Lancaster's, except that nonbank lenders had an even smaller market share in 1992. In Fort Wayne, by contrast, nonbank lenders had a market share of 53.5 percent in 1992, which increased to 60.5 percent in 1996. In 1992 almost all bank loan applications were taken by small banks; but by 1996, merging banks accounted for over half of all bank applications, and 75 percent of these were filed at large banks operating in-state.

The share of applications filed by minorities increased substantially between 1992 and 1996 in Springfield, from 6.7 percent of the total to 15.5 percent. While large banks had a below-average share of minority applicants in 1992, by 1996 their share was considerably higher than even the higher average level. In Fort Wayne and Lancaster, by contrast, the share of minorities in the applicant pool grew, but more modestly. Table 7.8 also demonstrates that, as elsewhere, the share of applicants with incomes below $50,000 increased substantially in each of these three cities, with this increase distributed among all lender types.

Wilmington, Savannah, and Jackson

These three cities are in states that are long-standing members of the Southern regional banking compact, which has allowed intraregional interstate entry. Wilmington's financial infrastructure is more robust than those examined in the Midwest and Northeast, primarily because of its large pool of mortgage brokers and finance companies. Some nineteen of Wilmington's fifty-three bank branches are owned by North Carolina's three large banks—NationsBank, First Union, and Wachovia. Savannah's financial infrastructure closely resembles Wilmington's. It is relatively well endowed with bank branches (Table 7.2), with very high population-weighted levels of mortgage brokers, finance companies, pawnbrokers, and check-cashers. Just 18 percent of Savannah's bank branches are maintained by large out-of-state banking firms (Wachovia of North Carolina), and another 11 percent by a large in-state institution, Bank South, now owned by Nationsbank of North Carolina. Jackson, by contrast, has a modest financial infrastructure: The population-adjusted levels of every category of financial office place Jackson somewhere between the patterns for Southwestern and Mountain/Great Plains cities. None of Jackson's bank branches as of mid-1996 were owned by out-of-state bank holding companies.

In contrast to the other Eastern cities, these three cities' home-loan markets grew between 1992 and 1996—by 79 percent in Wilmington, 28 percent in Savannah, and 21 percent in Jackson. In all three Southern cities, as Table 7.8 shows, nonbank lenders' market share grew from just over a third in 1992 to half or more in 1996. In both Wilmington and Savannah, the applicant market share of merging banks with in-state branches fell by about 50 percent between 1992 and 1996; in Jackson, large banks' market share was relatively small in both years. Commercial banks had lower percentages of minorities in their applicant pools than did nonbank lenders in all three cities in 1996; and merging banks with in-state branches had lower percentages of minorities than did commercial banks as a whole in all three cities. As elsewhere, the proportion of applicants with incomes under $50,000 rose markedly in every city and for nearly every class of lender, between 1992 and 1996. In 1996, about three-quarters of all applicants had incomes below $50,000 at nonbank lenders, versus just over 50 percent at commercial banks (and just under 50 percent at merging banks in-state).

Fair Share in Eight Eastern Cities

Overall, lower-income individuals and minorities comprised a larger share of the home-loan market in 1996 than in 1992, in these eight Eastern cities; as in the West, the proportion of applications in minority and lower-income areas also rose. Tables 7.9 to 7.11 present fair-share measures for the eight Eastern cities. As Table 7.9 shows, overall fair share ratios for loans made fell below the 33 percent benchmark for high-minority areas in five Eastern cities in 1996, and in five somewhat different cities in the same year. Performance was somewhat worse for lower-income fair share: In both 1992 and 1996, only one city's lenders exceeded the 50 percent benchmark for loans made. Application totals rose significantly for minority and lower-income areas, between 1992 and 1996; but no such trend appears for loans made.

Table 7.10 shows that commercial banks and nonbank lenders have similar fair-share averages, but very different scores city by city. In 1996, the score for nonbank lenders fell below the 33 percent minority-area benchmark in all eight cities, while the score for commercial banks failed the benchmark five times; and similarly for the lower-income benchmark. On average, the 1992 minority-area fair-share scores for banks open in 1992 but closed by 1996 are lower than for other lenders (including other banks) for high-minority areas; but in that same year, closed-banks' lower-income fair-share scores exceed those for other lenders.

The fair-share data shown in Table 7.11 for the different types of commercial bank *do* yield two clear conclusions. First, merging banks headquartered in-state have higher fair-share scores than other bank types. Large banks with in-state headquarters perform well on both minority and lower-income fair-share benchmarks in the four cities in which they operate. Second, small in-state banks come in second in average fair-share performance, soundly beating large banks headquartered out-of-state, whether or not these banks have in-state branches. This

Table 7.9 **Fair-Share Scores for Residential Credit Flows in Eight Eastern Cities, 1992 and 1996**

Census tracts with the largest proportion of minorities (25% of total)

	Applications in minority areas as percent of those in other areas		Loans made in minority areas as percent of those in other areas	
	1996	1992	1996	1992
Minn./St. Paul, MN	32.9	32.0	29.7	23.8
Newark, NJ	35.7	36.1	33.6	27.7
Ft. Wayne, IN	18.1	16.4	14.6	14.5
Lancaster, PA	50.2	43.7	38.7	40.3
Springfield, MA	50.0	40.9	39.5	46.5
Wilmington, NC	33.5	19.9	19.3	51.1
Savannah, GA	8.5	6.7	6.6	3.5
Jackson, MS	7.7	6.9	5.5	9.6
Eight-city median	33.2	25.9	24.5	25.7

Census tracts with the lowest 1990 median income (33% of total)

	Applications in lower-income areas as percent of those in other areas		Loans in lower-income areas as percent of those in other areas	
	1996	1992	1996	1992
Minn./St. Paul, MN	41.1	38.6	36.2	30.4
Newark, NJ	49.9	54.3	46.8	28.8
Ft. Wayne, IN	28.8	25.3	21.8	21.5
Lancaster, PA	71.3	59.1	56.6	47.5
Springfield, MA	44.2	51.3	39.7	46.5
Wilmington, NC	44.5	24.2	29.5	56.2
Savannah, GA	32.2	23.1	22.3	6.7
Jackson, MS	22.9	15.4	11.7	14.3
Eight-city median	42.7	31.9	32.8	29.6

Note: All raw figures are adjusted for 1990 owner-occupied units, as explained in the text. Scores not meeting fair share benchmarks are italicized. This benchmark is 33.3 for minority areas, since 25%/75% = 33.3, and 50% for lower-income areas, since 33%/67% = 50.

second pattern is observed strongly in the Northeastern cities included here. In Fort Wayne and in the three Southern cities, small in-state banks perform less well; in particular, in-state banks have extremely low minority fair-share scores in the three Southern cities.

Summary

In both the Western and Eastern cities examined here, minority applicants and lower-income applicants are growing rapidly as a share of the market, as are

Table 7.10 **Fair-Share Scores for Bank and Nonbank Lenders, Home-Purchase Loans in Eight Eastern Cities, 1996**

| | 1996 Applications | | 1996 Loans | | 1992 Loans Commercial banks | | |
	Commercial banks	Other lenders	Commercial banks	Other lenders	All	Closed by 1992	Other lenders
Census tracts with the highest proportion of minorities: (25% of total)							
Minn./St. Paul, MN	34.1	31.6	*29.8*	*29.6*	34.3	*11.5*	*22.0*
Newark, NJ	43.2	30.8	42.7	*27.2*	*27.2*	*11.1*	36.9
Ft. Wayne, IN	*15.9*	*19.4*	*12.4*	*15.9*	*18.5*	*22.8*	*16.9*
Lancaster, PA	44.8	59.9	43.6	*29.4*	43.2	52.7	43.0
Springfield, MA	52.3	45.1	45.7	*27.2*	37.7	141.0	80.3
Wilmington, NC	*22.4*	43.2	*17.0*	*22.4*	*24.0*	46.6	220.9
Savannah, GA	*9.8*	*7.5*	*8.0*	*5.1*	*6.4*	*17.8*	*4.7*
Jackson, MS	*7.3*	*8.1*	*4.2*	*6.9*	*10.6*	*11.8*	*23.5*
Eight-city median	*28.2*	*31.2*	*23.4*	*24.8*	*25.6*	*20.3*	*30.2*
Ratio of lower-income area to other-area loans among purchase loans							
Minn./St. Paul, MN	*40.3*	*41.9*	*36.1*	*36.3*	*42.1*	*41.2*	*28.7*
Newark, NJ	*45.0*	57.4	54.9	*40.8*	*35.9*	*17.0*	*26.6*
Ft. Wayne, IN	*27.3*	*29.6*	*20.7*	*22.4*	*34.6*	46.6	*19.0*
Lancaster, PA	66.9	79.4	61.9	*46.6*	*48.0*	49.7	55.7
Springfield, MA	*43.4*	*45.9*	*38.6*	*42.2*	*41.9*	153.8	62.2
Wilmington, NC	*35.0*	52.6	*29.1*	*29.9*	*24.9*	55.0	245.2
Savannah, GA	*34.9*	*30.0*	*28.6*	*16.0*	*10.6*	*15.7*	*8.5*
Jackson, MS	*18.5*	*27.5*	*9.6*	*14.1*	*16.1*	*13.9*	*36.3*
Eight-city median	*37.6*	*43.9*	*32.6*	*33.1*	*35.3*	*43.9*	*32.5*

Note: All figures depict the ratio of loans or applications in lower-income (high-minority) census tracts to loans or applications in other tracts, adjusted for 1990 owner-occupied units; see text. Scores not meeting fair-share benchmarks are italicized. This benchmark is 33.3 for minority areas (25%/75% = 33.3) and 50% for lower-income areas (33%/67% = 50).

applications filed in minority and lower-income neighborhoods. The fair-share gaps found for high-minority and lower-income areas are thus of central importance in overall access to credit in urban credit markets.

In the fair-share analysis conducted here, racial and income fair-share gaps are common in both 1992 and 1996; on average, all lenders' racial fair-share performance is worse than lower-income fair-share performance. In the Western cities, commercial banks' performance is worse on average than that of nonbank lenders; but in the Eastern cities, the average performance of banks and nonbanks is not notably different in fair-share terms. Among banks, in the West small in-state banks perform best on average in fair-share measures; in the East, merging banks headquartered in-state do best, followed by small in-state lenders. Merging banks without in-state branches perform fairly badly in both East and West.

The evidence reviewed here suggests that regional variation in credit-market processes and financial structures is important. So are differences in lender type. But the descriptive evidence assembled here, including that for denial gaps and

Table 7.11 **Fair-Share Scores by Type of Commercial Bank, Home-Purchase Loans in Eight Eastern Cities, 1996**

	1996 applications				1996 loans			
		Large	Large out-of-state:			Large	Large out-of-state:	
	Small	merging	with	without	Small	merging	with	without
	in-state	in-state	branches	branches	in-state	in-state	branches	branches
Census tracts with the highest proportion of minorities (25% of total)								
Minn./St. Paul, MN	29.2	38.1	33.9	*23.1*	45.7	35.0	29.6	*23.7*
Newark, NJ	91.8	NA	*18.5*	*17.2*	101.8	NA	*14.6*	*11.9*
Ft. Wayne, IN	*11.1*	NA	*19.0*	*13.8*	*9.8*	NA	*15.0*	*12.0*
Lancaster, PA	51.5	67.1	*17.5*	43.6	46.5	62.7	*15.0*	41.5
Springfield, MA	44.1	78.8	NA	58.3	47.9	50.7	NA	*19.4*
Wilmington, NC	*18.0*	*31.6*	NA	27.6	*14.4*	27.1	NA	*17.6*
Savannah, GA	*3.2*	NA	*6.6*	20.5	*3.7*	NA	*5.8*	17.3
Jackson, MS	*7.8*	NA	NA	*2.5*	5.0	NA	NA	*2.1*
Eight-city median	23.6	52.6	*18.5*	*21.8*	30.0	42.8	*15.0*	17.5
Census tracts with the lowest 1990 median income (33% of total)								
Minn./St. Paul, MN	52.0	*43.7*	*28.1*	*29.5*	60.5	*42.6*	*22.0*	32.7
Newark, NJ	104.5	NA	*35.4*	*28.0*	113.9	NA	*39.3*	*20.9*
Ft. Wayne, IN	*29.3*	NA	*24.8*	*24.5*	*26.3*	NA	*16.8*	*19.7*
Lancaster, PA	70.0	80.5	*33.8*	66.7	63.5	70.4	*30.1*	59.5
Springfield, MA	*40.9*	*48.7*	NA	*32.5*	*37.5*	69.8	NA	35.3
Wilmington, NC	*30.6*	54.4	NA	*29.7*	28.5	45.2	NA	23.2
Savannah, GA	*45.2*	NA	*29.8*	44.6	55.2	NA	25.6	29.3
Jackson, MS	*16.6*	NA	NA	35.2	*9.8*	NA	NA	*9.5*
Eight-city median	43.1	51.6	*29.8*	31.1	46.4	57.5	25.6	26.2

Note: All figures depict the ratio of lower-income (high-minority) tracts to other tracts, adjusted for 1990 owner-occupied units. Scores not meeting fair-share benchmarks are italicized. This benchmark is 33.3 for minority areas (25%/75%) and 50% for lower-income areas (33%/67%).

fair-share gaps, cannot be used to pinpoint structural regularities more exactly. And even if we were to examine more finely differentiated data of the sort presented here, a further problem would remain. No matter what differences we find among lender types or among cities and years, we cannot rule out the possibility that factors unique to these different cities or to different lenders' borrower pools lie behind any differences we might observe. Fortunately, we can control at least partially for factors of this sort by using appropriate econometric models. This is the task of the next three chapters.

Appendix 7

Which Loans to Count? Conventional Versus Nonconventional Home-Purchase Loans

The two types of loan used to finance the acquisition of most single-family homes, conventional and Federal Housing Administration (FHA), have very different characteristics. FHA loans carry substantially lower down payments than do conventional loans, 5 percent versus a minimum of 20 percent. Further, FHA loans are available primarily to first-time home buyers with small amounts of savings, whereas conventional loans are often taken out and retired multiple times by home-owning households. Finally, virtually all FHA loans are backed by governmentally sponsored insurance, whereas conventional home loans have such insurance only if the homeowners or lenders involved make special arrangements.

The question then arises whether these differences lead to a very different borrower-lender relationship for these two types of home loan. The answer would appear to be yes. When making an FHA loan, the lender functions as a conduit for a transaction that is only indirectly risky.[11] When making a conventional loan, the lender functions as an intermediary interested in the riskiness of its own portfolio, since it often retains responsibility for losses due to loan default. In effect, FHA loans provide an "out" for lenders that are irrationally unwilling to extend conventional loans to some classes of borrowers. Bradford (1979) presented evidence that FHA lending could even be a factor contributing to inner-city neighborhoods' decline.

These considerations then lead to the question for this analysis of whether to perform analysis with conventional loan data only, or with combined conventional and nonconventional loan data.[12] The differences between these loan types are undoubtedly important in the marketplace. The question of whether FHA loans provide an opportunity for lenders to meet the letter but not the spirit of antidiscrimination and reinvestment laws should be investigated extensively.

However, FHA loans are included with conventional loans in most analyses conducted here, for several reasons. First, FHA loans often comprise an important share of the market for single-family home-purchase loans; to exclude them would significantly limit the scope of our analysis. Second, differences between conventional and FHA applications do not arise systematically in all the cities evaluated here. In research not shown here (available from the author on request), the market-share, denial-gap, and fair-share analysis of this chapter was conducted separately for conventional and nonconventional loans. This analysis found no consistent differences in the patterns of FHA and conventional loans for all the cities east or west of the Mississippi; nonconventional home-purchase loans sometimes comprise a very large share of the minority and lower-income market, and sometimes an insignificant share. Third, since this study examines many cities' financial structures without going into depth on any one, it is not possible here to differentiate cases in which FHA loans are being used appropriately to encourage first-time homeowners from cases in which lenders are using FHA loans to avoid risks they associate with certain classes of borrowers. Thus, it seems best to use the widest available pool of loans for most analysis conducted here, except when the differential risk of conventional and nonconventional loans might be important for the conclusions we draw.

8

Differential Access to Credit, East and West

Introduction: Probit Analysis of Access to Credit

At the heart of our inquiry into credit-market patterns are these core questions: Do banks that have acquired other banks and extensive branch networks behave "better" or "worse" than other banks in their treatment of minority borrowers and neighborhoods? Are these banks "better" or "worse" than other banks in their treatment of low-income borrowers and neighborhoods? Are nonbank lenders "better" or "worse" than banks?

These questions are about patterns in lending markets and credit flows, not about specific individuals at specific points in time. Consequently, to distinguish "better" from "worse" means identifying patterns in a large number of cases for which we possess only limited information. Judgments have to be made about how to group data and assess outcomes; these are inescapably difficult and often controversial.

The simple descriptive statistics of lending patterns and financial infrastructures in sixteen cities suggested that lower-income borrowers and minority applicants have less chance of succeeding in credit applications than do other applicants. They also suggested that lower-income and high-minority areas often do not receive a fair share of loan flows. It also appeared that some lender types were less likely to make loans in lower-income and high-minority areas than others, and more likely to deny minority and lower-income applicants. Finally, credit-market patterns and financial infrastructures differed from West to East. These conclusions raise some questions: How much does lower-income and racial status matter? And how differently do these factors behave from one place to another?

Community activists have produced descriptive statistics of the sort reviewed in chapter 7 since Home Mortgage Disclosure Act data first became available two decades ago. However, statistical gaps of just this sort, while lauded by inner-city residents as telling the truth they live, have been greeted with suspicion by regulators and banks. Simple descriptive statistics may mislead because they are partial. Factors not explicitly considered may account for observed patterns, so that conclusions drawn on the basis of these patterns are spurious. For example, banks' and nonbanks' loan denial rates for minorities may differ because they attract minority applicants with very different levels of financial risk; in this case an apparent racial lending gap reflects a racial financial-risk gap.

Descriptive statistics per se, then, do not pass the "what if" and "all else equal" tests that a skeptic might pose. The "what if" test involves questions like these: What if an income level that is low in one locale is perfectly adequate in another? What if different regions have different definitions of what constitutes a "neighborhood with a significant minority population"? Place-to-place comparisons are hampered by the very diversity in size, population, and so on, that make them different. Place-to-place comparisons must then control for differences among places.

But even when some controls for place-to-place variation are included, as in the lower-income and high-minority area measures used in chapter 7, finding that two subgroups differ leads to "all else equal" questions. Why, for example, do minority loan applicants often have twice the probability of loan denial as white applicants? Why do fair-share gaps arise? To respond to such questions, one must account for the influence of multiple differences among subgroups. Then, one can ask whether the variable of interest still matters, all else being equal.

Responding to the "all else equal" challenge requires moving from descriptive statistics to more refined statistical methods. In chapters 8 to 10, we conduct probit analysis of credit-market outcomes. Probit analysis is a form of regression analysis. Regression methods test whether factors (independent variables) that *may* plausibly be said to cause an outcome of interest (the dependent variable) do in fact explain the observed instances of this outcome. For example, one might ask whether the average income and proportion of homeowners in a given area *determine* the level of loan flows there. Probit analysis is a specialized form of regression in which the dependent variable is a probability that an event of interest might occur.[1] Probit analysis can be done on HMDA data collected since 1990 because the information collected includes the action taken on each reported loan application; thus these data can be used to evaluate the probability that applicants will be approved for home-loan credit.

A word of warning is in order. Regression and probit analyses provide only tentative answers to the "what if" and "all else equal" challenges. Even a successful result that a set of independent variables significantly determines a given dependent variable depends on the architecture of the model used—which variables are included and which excluded, what time frame and geographic area are encompassed, what functional form is used, and so on. No regression or probit model is definitive, because including one set of variables and adopting one functional form necessarily precludes other variables and functional forms. Nonetheless, while probit and regression analysis are imperfect, they are informative.[2]

A caveat concerning our home-purchase loan results should be acknowledged before we proceed. The model developed here assumes that home-purchase loans are relatively uniform contracts in their terms and conditions. This is not true in practice. Many journalists and community activists have documented that the terms and conditions of mortgage loans vary for different lenders, borrowers, and areas. Loan terms can be especially exploitative in the murky realm of subprime lending, which often involves second and third mortgages for un-derinformed homeowners. The relevant questions for our purpose are how fre-quently do exploitative terms occur in home-mortgage markets, and how wide are these observed differences? By all accounts, subprime lending in the residen-tial credit market occurs primarily on refinancing and fix-up loans.

With this problem in mind, the probit analysis conducted here uses only home-purchase loans. This should screen out most exploitative terms. Within the class of home-purchase loans, how wide are differences in terms? The author's own investi-gation (reported in Dymski, Veitch, and White 1991) of Los Angeles home-purchase loans in the 1987–1989 period found no systemic differences in average loan matu-rity and interest rates among different areas of Los Angeles or among different borrower classes. In their study of 1996 Panel Survey of Income Dynamics (PSID) data, Huck and Segal (1997) find that minority and low-income households pay somewhat higher mortgage rates than other households. However, the differences they observe are relatively small; for example, for original mortgage loans, minority households have an average rate of 8.1 percent, versus 7.9 percent for whites. These authors find much wider differences for refinanced mortgages, which are not used in this study's probit equations. Undoubtedly some of the results reported here would change if it were possible to control for loan terms and conditions.

Regression and Probit Analyses of Residential Credit Markets: An Evolving Tradition

Community activists have argued for years that banks violate the Community Reinvestment Act and the Equal Credit Opportunity Act and contribute to inner-city decline by leaving good credit risks unfunded. Banks' defenders have re-sponded that banks cannot afford uneconomic loans in the competitive post-deregulation era; and anyway, the market abhors a vacuum—so nonbank lenders attuned to neglected neighborhoods will keep financial markets efficient by meeting any financial needs that banks no longer serve.

Both sides in this debate have been served by HMDA data, the existence of which is due to years of agitation by an energetic community-based movement. This debate has had two phases, corresponding to the two phases of bank report-ing under HMDA since its passage into law in 1975. One model has predomi-nated during each phase.

The Redlining Model

From the late 1970s to the end of the 1980s, social scientists, regulators, and community activists developed the redlining model. This regression model pro-vided a rigorous empirical test of the existence of fair-share–type gaps for inner-city neighborhoods around which lenders may have drawn a "red line."

Community activists themselves had done the first analyses of residential lending flows, often by simply counting the number of loans of different kinds that were made in their neighborhoods and pointing out that this number was very low. Banks' and thrifts' rejoinder to such charges was a variation of "compared to what?" The redlining model per se was developed by analysts interested in a more neutral and defensible method of ascertaining whether lending flows in different areas were indeed disparate. These models focus not on explaining lender behavior per se, but rather on identifying neighborhood-specific factors that lenders might plausibly use as lending yardsticks. The idea is to have some factors that are legitimately associated with the economic character of the neighborhood, and also some factors that should ideally have no systematic relationship to this economic character. If it can be established that the latter were significant, and in the right direction, then redlining has been found.

Technically, the redlining model became feasible in the late 1970s because lenders reported the number and dollar volume of their loan flows under HMDA at the census tract level. Numerous economic, housing, and social variables are reported at the census tract level in the decennial census conducted by the federal government. So an appropriate dependent variable is readily constructed by dividing through the sum of loans in a given census tract by the number of (say) owner-occupied homes in that census tract. Independent variables can then be selected from the long list of census variables. Redlining models take this form:

$$\text{Detrended reported} \atop \text{mortgage flows} = f \left(\text{Area economic} \atop \text{variables,} \quad {\text{Area social variables} \atop \text{[including area race]}} \right) \qquad (8.1)$$

When equation 8.1 is run as an ordinary least-squares regression, it estimates whether variables appearing on the right-hand side of this equation—that is, the independent variables—affect the level of the dependent variable on the left-hand side. The coefficients for significant independent variables provide some insight into the magnitude of these variables' effect on the dependent variable. If economic fundamentals drive loan-making decisions, then area economic variables should affect housing value, and hence mortgage flows; but area social variables, including neighborhood racial composition, should be insignificant. Redlining can be alleged when areas that differ socially in some significant way from others receive lower loan flows than their economic fundamentals would suggest are appropriate. These "social differences" could refer to area racial composition, area location (inner city versus suburb), and so on.

The area social variables in equation 8.1 can be estimated in two different ways—either by dividing census tracts on the basis of predefined community boundaries, or by dividing census tracts on the basis of a neutral criterion such as median-income level or proportion of minority residents. Versions of equation 8.1 estimated both ways have concluded that redlining exists and is significant. An example of the community-boundary method is the study by Bradbury, Case, and Dunham (1989), which grouped Boston's census tracts into sixty "neighborhood" areas; an example of the neutral criterion method is the study of Los Angeles by Dymski, Veitch, and White (1991).[3]

Redlining studies based on equation 8.1, while widely used, have been roundly criticized. One problem was the limitations in HMDA data. Until 1990, only depository institutions—commercial banks, credit unions, mutual savings banks, and savings and loan associations—were required to report their loans. Mortgage companies were not required to report their residential loan activity. Further, home-purchase and refinancing loans could not be evaluated separately. Finally, nothing about applications or about loan-recipients' characteristics was reported.

Some criticism focused on the redlining model itself. Benston (1981), for example, pointed out that redlining studies do not test for whether lower loan flows in minority areas are due to lower loan demand in those areas. These studies also do not control for the possibility of greater lending risks in redlined areas, due to greater residential turnover and a higher proportion of renters (Canner 1981) or to market failure (Guttentag and Wachter 1980).[4] More fundamentally, the redlining model focuses entirely on structural area factors, while ignoring individual behavioral factors. This limitation is relatively unimportant for community activists seeking remedial policies for structural inequalities. However, it is a critical problem for social scientists—including most economists—who understand any market's outcomes on the basis of the motivations and qualifications of individual firms and households on that market's supply and demand sides. A more satisfactory model of the urban credit market would have to incorporate, at a minimum, some detail about individual applicants' demand patterns and creditworthiness. But this was not possible with the HMDA data of the 1970s and 1980s.

The Mortgage Discrimination Model

The key problem with the redlining model from the perspective of many economists, then, is that it completely ignores individual loan applicants; and incorporating information about individual loan applicants could be accomplished only if more detailed data were collected under the Home Mortgage Disclosure Act. Some studies using specialized data from different cities—especially the *Atlanta Constitution's* Pulitzer Prize–winning "Color of Money" series (Dedman 1988)— showed that such detailed data might indeed reveal patterns of racial and geographic bias. The opportunity for procuring better HMDA data came in 1989 when the Bush administration and Congress put in place the savings and loan "bailout" act eventually known as FIRREA. One provision written into this act was a requirement for enhanced HMDA reporting.

HMDA reporting requirements were expanded as of 1990 to require lenders to collect selected data on an application-by-application basis, with some detail about individual applicants—including applicant race, gender, and income. Further, mortgage companies were included. The new HMDA data contained several variables that in themselves permit more in-depth investigations of credit markets. The key difference, however, is in the fundamental unit of analysis—instead of the volume of loans in a census tract, banks now report on what action was taken in the case of every application. This allows econometric investigations of the determinants of the lender's loan decision itself. Researchers could consider whether minority applicants, for example, were more or less likely to be approved for a loan than white applicants; and the factors included as independent variables could include data about both the area in which applicants wished to finance a home and about applicants themselves. That is, it became possible to investigate the possibility of discrimination against applicants of certain types, using equations that capture aspects of a lender's decision on a loan application:

$$
\begin{array}{l}
\textit{Probability of loan} \\
\textit{approval for a given} = f \\
\textit{applicant pool}
\end{array}
\left(
\begin{array}{cccc}
\textit{Individual} & \textit{Individual} & \textit{Area} & \textit{Area} \\
\textit{economic} & \textit{social} & \textit{economic} & \textit{social} \\
\textit{variables,} & \textit{variables,} & \textit{variables,} & \textit{variables}
\end{array}
\right) \quad (8.2)
$$

Formally, the shift from equation 8.1 to equation 8.2 involves a change from ordinary least-squares models to logit and probit models. Substantively, this shift in data availability relegated equation-8.1 models to the sideline. However, a redlining test can easily be embedded into equation 8.2, creating a joint test for both discrimination against individuals and redlining against areas.

Numerous studies using a variant of equation 8.2 have been done with 1990s HMDA data. The shift in focus from redlining to discrimination, and the increased richness of the data, have spurred many more academic and government economists to do studies of home-loan markets. Incorporating loan demand and some aspects of application creditworthiness have not satisfied critics of empirical work on urban credit markets; to the contrary, the new data have heated up the debate even more. The reason for increased controversy is that equation 8.2 invites the researcher to design a model that captures personal discrimination—that is, differential treatment of minority applicants in credit markets based *only* on their race and not on their economic characteristics. This is a narrow interpretation of discrimination—for example, it leaves out structural discrimination, wherein whites and minorities have different average levels of income and/or wealth. And in any event, the focus on personal discrimination makes missing-variable bias a chronic problem: Whatever set of variables is included, other excluded variables may be correlated with applicant race.

A high point among these discrimination-model studies is a 1992 study by the Federal Reserve Bank of Boston (Munnell et al. 1992) of 1990 home loans in Boston. What made this study so special was that Boston bank lenders gave Boston Fed researchers complete access to their case files on 1990 home-mortgage applicants. This allowed the construction of models of applicant creditworthiness using the same information as had the banks themselves. The Boston Fed researchers found that even when they included this comprehensive list of variables pertinent to applicant creditworthiness, African-American applicants had a 60 percent greater chance of loan denial than equally creditworthy whites. For many analysts and policy-makers, this result was the statistical "smoking gun" showing that banks do discriminate by race.[5]

However, some critics have challenged even this seemingly complete model of credit-market outcomes. The main attacks have challenged the adequacy of equation 8.2 itself. First, it has been pointed out that obtaining a home loan is just one step in a multistep process of home acquisition: The applicants must also choose a prospective area, obtain information from real-estate brokers, receive an appraisal on their old and new homes, obtain insurance, and so forth. Equation 8.2, because it focuses on just one source of discrimination in the home-acquisition process, may thus cast blame on lenders that should properly rest with others (such as realtors, assessors, and so on). Second, critics have observed that the loan applicant–lender relationship itself involves a series of actions and decisions: The applicant selects a lender; the lender selects a specific mortgage product; the lender approves or denies the application; approved applicants decide whether to accept; after funding is received, the borrower decides whether to repay or default.[6] In this view, only a simultaneous-equations approach can accurately depict this process, not a single-equation approach such as equation 8.2. One-equation models are likely to overestimate lender discrimination. Third, some critics argue that equation 8.2 is irrelevant because banks make loan decisions based on expected default rates.[7] These various criticisms have been answered by several authors.[8]

A reasonable conclusion is that the use of equation-8.2–type models, as per the Boston Fed study, and the subsequent debate over these models have both advanced and confused affairs in empirical studies of reinvestment. In Boston and elsewhere, rigorous studies of discrimination against minority loan applications, incorporating results for redlining, have been implemented. The failure of the Boston study to convince hard-core skeptics of the existence of discrimination in loan markets is a caution; for more thorough study of the bank loan decision than occurred for the 1990 Boston data is unlikely.[9] Researchers without complete access to bank files, as in the Boston Fed study, cannot claim to have definitively established the existence of racial discrimination because they cannot defend themselves against the charge of omitted-variable bias.

Where does this leave things? It depends on the analyst's starting point. For economists who believe markets work and that only definitive tests to the contrary have any merit, empirical studies of credit-market outcomes using HMDA data are rendered pointless.[10] This reaction seems too extreme; for economists who understand that social and economic factors can intermingle in market processes, studies of this sort remain valuable. For one thing, as Stengel and Glennon (1995) have pointed out, while equation-8.2 models are useful in determining when personal discrimination *may* be present, even they are not definitive in this respect. For another, personal discrimination is not the only social variable that can affect loan-market outcomes, nor is it even the only form of discrimination—as mentioned, structural discrimination may exist and contribute to the significance of variables in an equation-8.2 model. Having said this, it has to be acknowledged that sorting out the precise contribution of personal and structural discrimination factors in an equation-8.2 model is difficult or impossible in most cases; in effect, the researcher must either live with some interpretive ambiguity or abandon her empirics.

Model 1: A Probit Approach to Comparative Access to Credit

The purpose of the regression model developed here is twofold: to examine whether outcomes in different credit markets differ significantly in social efficiency terms, and to probe whether different lenders behave differently in distinct markets in social-efficiency terms. The notion of social efficiency adopted here focuses on whether individuals and areas are at a disadvantage in gaining access to homeownership because of racial minority status or because of lower-income status. Racial minority status is measured for both individuals and neighborhoods. The model asks whether loan-market applicants in four distinct racial categories—Native American, African-American, Asian-American, and Hispanic—have a statistically different chance of being approved for a loan than do other applicants (respectively, non-Native American applicants, non-African-American applicants, and so on). The model then uses a one/zero dummy variable to ask whether applications for homes in census tracts with relatively high proportions of minority residents are less likely to receive credit than do applications for homes in other census tracts. The model also uses a one/zero dummy variable to ask whether applications for homes in lower-income areas—the one-third of all census tracts with the lowest 1990 median incomes—are at a disadvantage relative to applications for homes in other areas.

Finally, the model asks whether applicants with lower incomes in any market are at a disadvantage relative to the other applicants in that market. This lower-income variable is constructed in this way: For applicants placed in the lower third of all applicant incomes, their income levels are multiplied by one; and other applicants' incomes are multiplied by zero. This last effect is of special interest because the model also uses every applicant's income, and their loan-income ratio, as independent variables. Thus, the model asks whether the fact that one is in the lower third of applicants' incomes *also* affects loan-approval probability, *even after* one's income and loan-income levels have been taken into account.

In effect, this model tries to achieve some of the purposes of both redlining and discrimination analysis, and thus strives for a compromise between equations 8.1 and 8.2. This model is described fully, with some technical discussion, in the appendix to this chapter, but its design and central results are summarized here. This model adopts the same type of format as with discrimination equations of the 8.2 sort. It accounts for several economic characteristics of each individual applicant, most notably income and loan/income ratio. It also includes a dummy variable for every applicant's relative loan size and loan/income ratio (measured against the pool of all other applicants in any given market). While these four characteristics of borrowers will arguably be most important in determining loan approval or denial, many other characteristics may come into play.[11]

This means that the account of individual effects is open-ended. The racial and lower-income variables described above denote individual applicants who are either minorities or among the one-third of all applicants with the lowest incomes. These variables will pick up both the specific effect of race and lower-income status per se, plus the effect of other variables that may both be relevant for the loan decision and differ by applicant race. These other variables could include economic characteristics of individual applicants that vary systematically by race, other than income level, the loan/income ratio, loan rank, and loan/income rank. They could also include social characteristics of individual applicants that vary systematically by race. So any finding that a given applicant race variable is statistically significant could mean

- individual minority applicants have different income-earning prospects than white applicants, as these are assessed by lenders;
- individual minority applicants hold different average levels of financial and nonfinancial wealth assets than do white applicants;
- individual minority applicants have different histories of credit problems, bankruptcy, job problems, layoffs, or unemployment than do white applicants;
- individual minority applicants may differ systematically from white applicants in terms of social criteria that do not translate strictly into economic factors, but which lenders use in their loan decision-making;
- individual applicants who are racial minorities face personal discrimination, in that their applications are processed, coded, or evaluated differently from those of white applicants.

The first three factors are arguably related to economically rational discrimination by lenders—sometimes termed "statistical" discrimination. The last two factors should not come into play in an economic calculation and can be considered social.[12] Obviously, a finding of statistical significance for individual race could mean that any of these five factors matter. The tests run here cannot differentiate which of these five apply in a given case. In fact, even the distinction between economic and social factors blurs: A racial difference in wealth levels in any one period—clearly an economic difference—may result in part from the existence of personal discrimination in an earlier period. The pure effects of skin color or cultural (or, for that matter, gender) bias in any one period will ossify into structural differences in future periods.[13] So while our approach entails some explanatory ambiguity, it also creates a broad-brush racial variable, the overall degree of significance and magnitude of which suggests when more detailed analysis is warranted.

The model estimated here differs from most equation-8.2-style studies conducted with the new HMDA data in that it investigates the magnitude of area effects without prejudging whether differences by area *should* exist. Most such studies ignore geographic variations in lending flows, or view them as justified due to local variations in risk correlated with racial residential patterns. For example, Carr and Megolugbe (1993) characterize the "locational risk characteristic of the underlying collateral" as one of the "legitimate risk factors" in the lender's decision (280). Several studies have tried to show that the correlation between area racial composition and lending flows disappears when more variables accounting for risk and economic fundamentals are included.[14] No presumption is made here that area effects are capturing some other unmeasured, legitimate risk factors. The central point here is to determine whether area matters at all in different places, and in turn whether it matters less or more for different classes of lenders. Area variables are not used here to control for neighborhood "quality"; and since no established methodology exists for measuring neighborhood "quality," none is used here.

Two variables accounting for some economically relevant differences among areas are incorporated explicitly into the model used here: residential density and the percentage of owner-occupants. The model also includes variables measuring the number and dollar value of purchase-loan transactions in these various areas. These variables are used to allow an examination of the character of lender competitive behavior, a topic discussed in chapter 10. The dummy variables used here for minority area and lower-income area are then open-ended. If found to be significant, they capture otherwise unmeasured differences in economic and social structure. Geographic differences of this sort could arise due to any number of factors that lenders think may influence applicants' creditworthiness, including

- structural gaps between areas due to the aggregated effects of individual bias *given* the concentration of some classes of individuals in this area;
- structural gaps between areas due to historical differences in the resources, wealth, and income levels of the households living there;
- structural gaps between areas due to historical differences in the amount of such community resources and assets as public schools, health facilities, commercial and industrial enterprises, and physical infrastructure;
- expected growth in structural gaps due to the prospective widening of geographic resource and wealth gaps in the future;
- differences in the racial composition of different areas, independent of all other factors.

Some studies assume that geographic differences in loan flows are unjust only if they are triggered solely by the last factor. However, the other four factors may also lie behind geographic differences in loan flows that are unjust, if one remembers that structural geographic differences at any point in time may arise at least in part because of prior episodes of bias against individuals and areas. As above, finding that the minority or lower-income area variables matter does not prove bias against minority or lower-income areas per se—that is, it does not prove redlining exists. But it does indicate that one or more of the above factors may be at work, and hence geographic factors should be more carefully investigated in these markets.

In sum, the model used here is, by design, broadly similar to the equations that economists and sociologists have developed to test for race and income effects in HMDA lending. At the same time, the specification has been made economical, thus allowing its ready application to a wide variety of geographic market areas. Because the model is economical, it is not complete. Thus, one cannot claim that a variable capturing minority status constitutes an adequate measure of whether lenders discriminate by race in making loan decisions. While this caveat restricts the interpretive use of this model, it must be kept in mind that *any* open-ended model is similarly restricted; and, as noted, experts have not reached agreement that any closed-ended model has yet been produced.

In any event, the coefficients estimated in Model 1 for individual race measure the *cumulative differences between minority and nonminority individuals in credit-market outcomes, including both individual discrimination and structural economic differences.* Model 1 does not differentiate *among* these various aspects of minority/nonminority difference; it sums across all these differences and captures the total difference in mean circumstances. Similarly, the Model 1 coefficients for lower-income individuals measure the *cumulative differences between lower-income and other borrowers in credit-market outcomes.* And its coefficients for area race and area income capture the *cumulative differences between minority and nonminority areas, as well as those between lower-income and other areas.* None of these coefficients reflect the specific influence of personal discrimination; they reflect the sum of the circumstances that distinguish applicants in one section of the market from another. These summed circumstances are not separated into portions for which banks may be responsible, and those for which they are not responsible—this model does not identify "perpetrators" of racial or income-based injustice. The model does, however, indicate the width of the divide between different constituents within the population of applicants for home-purchase loans.

Modeling Caveats

Apart from the issues discussed above, three further limitations in the empirical work conducted here should be acknowledged. None of these limitations make the results unreliable; rather, they suggest caution in interpreting the results obtained.

The first limitation arises because the dependent variable used here is the probability of loan approval. This dependent variable is discontinuous—it can be only a "yes" or a "no," a "1" or a "0." For this reason, as discussed above, probit analysis must be used, not regression analysis per se. Probit techniques have some drawbacks: they have questionable statistical properties, and they are volatile and potentially explosive.[15] To offset this last set of drawbacks, large amounts of data—thousands of cases—must be deployed. Using probit denies us the ability to look at the characteristics of behavior in small or even medium market areas; the demands of estimation instead require that smaller places be combined into larger pools. And even then answers are not guaranteed—any one estimation may fail due to peculiar characteristics of either the data or the search algorithm.

Second, the model estimated here takes the form of a one-equation "reduced form" model. This is controversial. Galster and Keeney (1988), among other authors, have pointed out that economic outcomes in urban environments reflect many intersecting, time-phased processes. While a one-equation approach cannot hope to capture the nuances of such interaction, it is used here. For one thing, the caution suggested by Galster and Keeney pertains with special force to closed-ended explanations designed to identify the magnitude of specific factors. That is not the purpose of the estimation conducted here. For another thing, a one-equation model may be appropriate given the implicit interpretation of the credit market adopted here. What is being modeled is the outcome of the lending decision. And while outcomes over time in an urban environment flow from a variety of interacting factors, the lending decision reflects at best a moment-in-time response to this complex structural situation. Further, the agent whose behavior is being modeled here is the lender. The discussion of the credit market in chapter 7 suggests that credit is typically rationed in the credit market. The rationing of credit is, in turn, a situation in which supply is less than demand at the observed market outcome. In effect, the factors impinging on the agent demanding credit can be set aside insofar as what governs the observed flow of credit is not these demand factors but instead whatever factors determine the lender's supply-side response to credit demand.

A third key limitation of this estimation is that all coefficients in probit analyses are model-specific. In a somewhat different model, one would likely get a somewhat different coefficient. One test of the reliability of any estimate in a given model is indeed to re-estimate the equation with different sets of variables. When the coefficient for a given variable fluctuates relatively little from model to model—and is normally statistically significant—that result is called robust. Most of the coefficients reported throughout this study, if statistically significant, are robust—a side effect of the large sample sizes required for the equations estimated here. Nonetheless, because of the model-specific character of coefficients reported here, any given coefficient should be taken with a grain of salt. For one thing, one must keep in mind that multiple factors could be at work, as discussed in the previous subsection. For another, changing the model will almost certainly change the coefficient, if only at the margin. The best interpretation of statistically significant coefficients is as a signpost, an indicator of the order of magnitude of different effects in a given sample.

Modeling Strategy

The purpose of creating Model 1 is to put in place a portable, efficient model that incorporates some of the key elements found in contemporary redlining and discrimination equations. This representative model can then be used as a vehicle for running a series of "horse races" among lender types. That is, separate equations are run for different groups of lenders, to check on whether these different lender groups have reacted differently to the racial and income-related characteristics of an applicant pool. This is a much more modest goal than testing for the presence of personal racial discrimination, but it is appropriate given the focus of this study.

Separate probit equations are run for the following lender groups in chapters 8 to 10: all lenders, savings and loan associations, mortgage companies, small banks chartered in-state, large merging banks with in-state branches, large merging banks without in-state branches.

This division of lenders highlights whether lenders of different types indeed perform differently in residential credit markets. Note that commercial banks are separated into three distinct categories; this allows us to focus specific attention on intra-industry differences in credit-market behavior.

East, West, and Differential Access to Credit

Table 8.1 contains the results of probit equations for seven of the eight Western cities discussed in chapter 7 (leaving out Los Angeles). Table 8.2 contains results for probit equations for the eight Eastern cities. For every equation in each table, the number of observations used is first shown, followed by the proportion of loans approved. Three numbers are shown at the bottom of every equation. The first, the log likelihood for normal, provides some insight into whether the normal distribution can be used to categorize variables by their degree of significance; the greater the absolute value of this number, the more assured we can be that this assumption is warranted. The third number, the likelihood ratio test, measures goodness of fit: if an equation fits well, this ratio test should have a value equal to 1 or only slightly less than 1.[16] The second number, the Pearson chi-square, tests for the reliability of coefficient scores; the closer to 0 this score is, the more reliable. Throughout this study, the coefficients for any equation with a likelihood ratio score of 0.75 or more are typically not reported; neither are the coefficients for any equation whose Pearson score exceeds 0.33.

Table 8.1a **Probit Results for All Lenders and Nonbanks in Seven Western Cities, All Home-Purchase Loans, 1996**

Variables:	All Lenders, banks and non-banks		Savings and loan associations		Mortgage Companies	
	Estim.	Std. Err.	Estim.	Std. Err.	Estim.	Std. Err.
Intercept	-1.176	(0.101) ***	-0.697	(0.227) ***	-1.661	(0.147) ***
Applicant characteristics						
Native American	-0.447	(0.044) ***	-0.390	(0.117) ***	-0.404	(0.054) ***
African-American	-0.251	(0.045) ***	-0.482	(0.098) ***	-0.171	(0.063) ***
Asian-American	0.064	(0.052)	0.200	(0.126)	0.058	(0.071)
Hispanic	-0.161	(0.017) ***	-0.181	(0.040) ***	-0.162	(0.022) ***
Female	0.040	(0.015) ***	0.052	(0.033)	0.015	(0.020)
Loan/Income ratio	-0.028	(0.008) ***	-0.020	(0.014)	-0.005	(0.013)
Log(Applic. Income)	0.502	(0.023) ***	0.451	(0.049) ***	0.475	(0.033) ***
Loan rank (4 levels)	0.106	(0.011) ***	-0.001	(0.024)	0.179	(0.016) ***
Loan/income rank	0.194	(0.010) ***	0.136	(0.021) ***	0.170	(0.014) ***
Lower-income	-0.027	(0.006) ***	-0.023	(0.014) *	-0.024	(0.008) ***
Census tract characteristics						
Residential density	-0.009	(0.002) ***	0.013	(0.009)	-0.015	(0.003) ***
Owner occupants	0.077	(0.059)	-0.160	(0.155)	0.143	(0.078) *
High-minority	-0.059	(0.020) ***	-0.117	(0.047) **	-0.018	(0.028)
Lower-income	-0.078	(0.021) ***	-0.130	(0.048) ***	-0.058	(0.029) **
High-loan activity	0.025	(0.016)	-0.065	(0.039) *	0.070	(0.023) ***
High loan amounts	0.044	(0.016) ***	0.107	(0.037) ***	0.020	(0.022)
No. of observations	66,185		12,772		32,089	
Proportion of approvals	0.788		0.841		0.734	
Log likelihood for normal	-29030		-5197		-15639	
Pearsn Chi-Sq: Pr>Chi-Sq	0.000		0.000		0.000	
L.R. Chi-Sq: Pr >Chi-Sq.	1.000		1.000		1.000	

*** denotes significance at the 1% level, ** at the 5% level, * at the 10% level.

Note: Standard error terms are shown in parentheses to the right of each coefficient. Cities included here are Albuquerque, Boise, Billings, Des Moines, El Paso, Fresno, and Sioux Falls. Dummy variables were used for each city in this analysis. These equations were also run for conventional loans only, with results very similar to those shown here for conventional and FHA/VA loans.

In the middle rows for every equation, the coefficients for every variable included in the probit are shown in three separate clusters. These coefficient values, taken as a whole, together led to the lowest sum of squared errors for the equation as a whole. So each coefficient has a dual character: it suggests the specific contribution of a given variable to the probability of loan approval, but it also reflects the values assigned to every other variable in this equation.

The coefficients estimated for independent variables convey reliable informa-tion only when they are statistically significant. An independent variable is sig-

Table 8.1b **Probit Results for Commercial Banks in Seven Western Cities, All Home-Purchase Loans, 1996**

Variables:	All commercial banks Estim.	Std. Err.	Small in-state banks Estim.	Std. Err.	Large merging banks in-state Estim.	Std. Err.	Large merging banks out-of-state Estim.	Std. Err.
Intercept	-0.454	(0.202) **	-0.492	(0.487)	-0.910	(0.348) ***	0.904	(0.340) ***
Applicant characteristics								
Native American	-0.397	(0.112) ***	-0.209	(0.364)	-0.267	(0.173)	-0.438	(0.163) ***
African-American	-0.262	(0.086) ***	-0.357	(0.184) *	-0.254	(0.193)	-0.485	(0.132) ***
Asian-American	0.026	(0.100)	-0.089	(0.241)	0.165	(0.202)	0.068	(0.157)
Hispanic	-0.133	(0.035) ***	-0.069	(0.097)	-0.140	(0.064) **	-0.085	(0.059)
Female	0.101	(0.031) ***	0.154	(0.077) **	0.140	(0.055) **	0.074	(0.050)
Loan/Income ratio	-0.066	(0.019) ***	-0.129	(0.056) **	0.013	(0.031)	-0.244	(0.048) ***
Log(Applic. Income)	0.521	(0.044) ***	0.635	(0.108) ***	0.608	(0.075) ***	0.112	(0.074)
Loan rank (4 levels)	0.042	(0.022) *	-0.063	(0.053)	0.003	(0.040)	0.084	(0.036) **
Loan/income rank	0.225	(0.020) ***	0.209	(0.053) ***	0.195	(0.035) ***	0.169	(0.038) ***
Lower-income	-0.034	(0.012) ***	0.028	(0.030)	-0.043	(0.022) **	-0.039	(0.019) **
Census tract characteristics								
Residential density	0.007	(0.006)	0.006	(0.011)	-0.006	(0.015)	0.000	(0.011)
Owner occupants	-0.321	(0.128) **	-0.202	(0.314)	-0.301	(0.244)	-0.307	(0.205)
High-minority	-0.096	(0.042) **	-0.028	(0.099)	-0.134	(0.076) *	-0.182	(0.072) **
Lower-income	-0.160	(0.044) ***	-0.264	(0.103) **	-0.023	(0.078)	-0.130	(0.070) *
High-loan activity	0.031	(0.032)	-0.026	(0.073)	0.068	(0.061)	0.012	(0.055)
High loan amounts	0.053	(0.034)	-0.0003	(0.080)	0.115	(0.060) *	0.155	(0.054) ***
No. of observations	20,579		3,194		8,718		6,472	
Proportion of approvals	0.850		0.879		0.823		0.841	
Log likelihood for normal	-7630		-1046		-3466		-2561	
Pearsn Chi-Sq: Pr>Chi-Sq	0.000		0.391		0.000		0.286	
L.R. Chi-Sq: Pr >Chi-Sq.	1.000		1.000		1.000		1.000	

*** denotes significance at the 1% level, ** at the 5% level, * at the 10% level.
Note: Standard errors are reported in parentheses next to coefficients.

nificant when its values change systematically—either negatively or positively—with the pattern of loan approvals and denials. Significance is highest at the 1 percent level of confidence; following statistical convention, significance is also measured at the 5 percent and 10 percent level. Coefficients that do not meet at least the 10 percent test should be ignored as statistically insignificant and hence not reliably different from zero. For statistically significant independent variables, a positive coefficient means that variable takes on higher values more frequently for loan applications that are approved; a negative coefficient means that an independent variable takes on higher values for applications resulting in loan denials. In effect, statistical significance for a variable means that knowing its value conveys an advantage in whether any particular application was approved or denied. The size of coefficients also matters. For example, as the negative coefficients for minority applicants become larger, one can infer that minority applicants are more relatively disadvantaged in being approved for loans.

Consider first the results for seven Western cities, shown on Table 8.1a. The

Table 8.2a Probit Results for All Lenders and Nonbanks in Eight Eastern Cities, All Home-Purchase Loans, 1996

Variables:	All Lenders, banks and non-banks		Savings and loan associations		Mortgage Companies	
	Estim.	Std. Err.	Estim.	Std. Err.	Estim.	Std. Err.
Intercept	-1.775	(0.081) ***	-0.357	(0.170) **	-2.520	(0.138) ***
Applicant characteristics						
Native American	-0.314	(0.086) ***	-0.473	(0.198) **	-0.111	(0.134)
African-American	-0.289	(0.021) ***	-0.392	(0.047) ***	-0.153	(0.030) ***
Asian-American	0.037	(0.041)	-0.007	(0.083)	0.138	(0.067) **
Hispanic	-0.077	(0.035) **	-0.288	(0.074) ***	0.000	(0.057)
Female	0.052	(0.014) ***	-0.006	(0.031)	0.058	(0.021) ***
Loan/Income ratio	-0.003	(0.004)	-0.004	(0.006)	0.043	(0.013) ***
Log(Applic. Income)	0.602	(0.020) ***	0.287	(0.041) ***	0.710	(0.034) ***
Loan rank (4 levels)	0.076	(0.010) ***	0.058	(0.022) ***	0.118	(0.017) ***
Loan/income rank	0.220	(0.008) ***	0.076	(0.018) ***	0.270	(0.014) ***
Lower-income	-0.019	(0.005) ***	-0.035	(0.012) ***	0.003	(0.008)
Census tract characteristics						
Residential density	-0.004	(0.002) **	0.006	(0.005)	-0.007	(0.004) *
Owner occupants	0.126	(0.031) ***	-0.060	(0.071)	0.241	(0.052) ***
High-minority	0.001	(0.020)	-0.114	(0.049) **	0.063	(0.030) **
Lower-income	-0.061	(0.019) ***	-0.004	(0.044)	-0.079	(0.028) ***
High-loan activity	-0.087	(0.016) ***	0.001	(0.037)	-0.129	(0.025) ***
High loan amounts	0.116	(0.015) ***	0.1825	(0.033) ***	0.102	(0.022) ***
No. of observations	132,556		20,412		44,533	
Proportion of approvals	0.862		0.901		0.798	
Log likelihood for normal	-45501		-6015		-17841	
Pearsn Chi-Sq: Pr>Chi-Sq	0.000		0.000		0.000	
L.R. Chi-Sq: Pr >Chi-Sq.	1.000		1.000		1.000	

*** denotes significance at the 1% level, ** at the 5% level, * at the 10% level.

Note: The cities included here are Minneapolis-St. Paul; Newark; Springfield, MA; Ft. Wayne; Lancaster; Wilmington, NC; and Savannah. Dummy variables were used for cities. These equations were also run for conventional loans only, with results similar to those shown here for conventional and FHA/VA loans.

first column contains the estimates from a probit model for all 1996 home-purchase loans in these seven metropolitan areas. Some 78.8 percent of the 66,185 applications included in this estimation were accepted. This model fits well: it passes the likelihood-ratio test, and fourteen of the seventeen variables shown are significant at the 10 percent level or better. In this equation for the overall home-purchase loan market, the four variables accounting for economic characteristics of individual applicants (loan/income ratio, the logarithm of applicant income, loan rank, and loan/income rank) fit well and have coefficients whose

Table 8.2b **Probit Results for Commercial Banks in Eight Eastern Cities, All Home-Purchase Loans, 1996**

Variables:	All commercial banks		Small in-state banks		Large merging banks in-state		Large merging banks out-of-state	
	Estim.	Std. Err.	Estim.	Std. Err.	Estim.	Std. Err.	Estim.	Std. Err.
Intercept	-1.112	(0.110) ***	-1.465	(0.190) ***	-0.543	(0.185) ***	-0.398	(0.208) *
Applicant characteristics								
Native American	-0.419	(0.112) ***	-0.620	(0.201) ***	-0.294	(0.166) *	-0.739	(0.193) ***
African-American	-0.425	(0.030) ***	-0.503	(0.050) ***	-0.360	(0.054) ***	-0.367	(0.050) ***
Asian-American	-0.047	(0.053)	0.001	(0.092)	-0.085	(0.075)	-0.035	(0.068)
Hispanic	-0.094	(0.045) **	-0.055	(0.078)	-0.045	(0.074)	-0.167	(0.075) **
Female	0.066	(0.019) ***	0.126	(0.035) ***	0.070	(0.031) **	0.042	(0.032)
Loan/Income ratio	-0.025	(0.008) ***	-0.001	(0.007)	-0.063	(0.018) ***	-0.192	(0.034) ***
Log(Applic. Income)	0.489	(0.026) ***	0.654	(0.045) ***	0.316	(0.042) ***	0.322	(0.050) ***
Loan rank (4 levels)	0.064	(0.013) ***	-0.047	(0.023) **	0.095	(0.021) ***	0.118	(0.026) ***
Loan/income rank	0.151	(0.011) ***	0.095	(0.018) ***	0.122	(0.019) ***	0.235	(0.025) ***
Lower-income	-0.022	(0.007) ***	-0.013	(0.013)	-0.011	(0.012)	-0.022	(0.012) *
Census tract characteristics								
Residential density	-0.002	(0.002)	0.003	(0.005)	-0.010	(0.005) **	0.000	(0.004)
Owner occupants	0.064	(0.041)	0.117	(0.093)	0.135	(0.066) **	0.001	(0.071)
High-minority	-0.014	(0.028)	0.007	(0.053)	-0.029	(0.044)	-0.094	(0.049) *
Lower-income	-0.076	(0.026) ***	-0.024	(0.046)	-0.106	(0.042) **	-0.126	(0.045) ***
High-loan activity	-0.023	(0.021)	0.023	(0.037)	-0.011	(0.033)	-0.068	(0.039) *
High loan amounts	0.068	(0.020) ***	0.0869	(0.035) **	0.098	(0.034) ***	0.049	(0.034)
No. of observations	66,124		19,973		25,308		17,857	
Proportion of approvals	0.8911		0.8955		0.9162		0.8815	
Log likelihood for normal	-20280		-6054		-6478		-5786	
Pearsn Chi-Sq: Pr>Chi-Sq	0.000		0.000		0.000		0.000	
L.R. Chi-Sq: Pr >Chi-Sq.	1.000		1.000		1.000		1.000	

*** denotes significance at the 1% level, ** at the 5% level, * at the 10% level.
Note: Standard errors are reported in parentheses next to coefficients.

signs are in the expected direction (–, +, +, and +). Similarly, the equation's measures of area all fit well.

We focus our attention here on the variables measuring the effect of race and lower-income status for applicants and neighborhoods. Negative and significant coefficients are obtained for three of the four minority-applicant categories: –0.447 for Native American applicants, –0.251 for African-American applicants, and –0.161 for Hispanic applicants. How should these coefficients be interpreted? The Hispanic coefficient of –0.147, for example, implies that Hispanics in this applicant pool have a 14.7 percent lower probability of loan approval than non-Hispanic applicants, holding constant the other variables included in this equation. African- American applicants, in turn, have a 25 percent lower probability of loan approval relative to non-African-Americans; and so on. As discussed above, these gaps may represent personal discrimination, structural discrimination, unmeasured economic factors that differ by race, or some combination of all three. In effect, significant minority-applicant variables reflect an implicit functional relationship of the following sort:

Minority borrower status = f (Lender overt discrimination, lender procedural discrimination, labor-market differentials, individual wealth differential, family wealth differential, differential in prior credit-market experience)

The coefficients for lower-income applicants are also significant and can be similarly interpreted: −2.7 percent for applicants whose incomes place them in the bottom third of applicant incomes; −5.9 percent for applications on homes in minority areas; −7.8 percent for applications on homes in lower-income neighborhoods. The lower-income coefficient is of special interest, since Model 1 tests separately for the significance of income, loan/income ratio, and lower-income status. The effect of every applicant's income on loan approval is estimated separately from this lower-income variable; so finding a negative and significant lower-income variable means that lower-income applicants are being penalized *both* for having incomes that are low *and* for being among those applicants with lower incomes.

So race and lower-income status matter in these Western cities; what about the eight Eastern cities included here? Table 8.2a contains the raw results for these cities. In the all-lenders probit, significant negative coefficients are attached to three of the four minority-applicant variables, while the Asian-American coefficient is statistically insignificant. The coefficients for lower-income applicants and neighborhoods, −0.019 and −0.061, respectively, are close to those for Western cities, but the high-minority area variable is insignificant.

Figure 8.1 depicts the all-lenders results for Eastern and Western cities visually. This figure shows that Native American and Hispanic applicants are at a greater disadvantage in the West, while African-American applicants have a slightly higher disadvantage in the East. Overall, Native Americans' negative coefficients have the largest magnitude, followed by African-Americans and then Hispanics. Lower-income coefficients are significant but small in both West and East; and minority and lower-income area effects are more important in the West. Overall, the footprint left by racial and lower-income effects in residential credit markets is clearly larger and deeper in the seven Western cities than in the eight Eastern ones.

The magnitude of the coefficients found for both Eastern and Western cities is striking. The chances of home-loan approval would appear to be very slim for applicants who fall into certain categories and seek homes in certain neighborhoods. Suppose an African-American applicant whose income places him among the bottom third of all applicants seeks a home in one of our Western cities, in a neighborhood that has a large proportion of both minority residents and lower-income residents. The first column of Table 8.1a suggests that his disadvantage

Figure 8.1 **Race and Lower-Income Coefficients from All-Lender Probits for Fifteen Eastern and Western Cities, 1996**

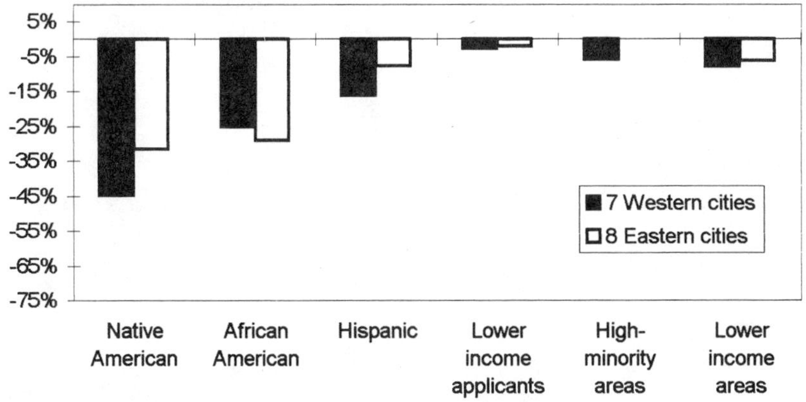

Source: Model 1 probit equations using 1996 HMDA data.
Note: These figures show estimated effects on loan approval.

relative to non-African-American applicants with higher incomes seeking homes in nonminority, upper-income neighborhoods is given by the sum −25.1 percent + −2.7 percent + −5.9 percent + −7.8 percent = −41.5 percent. An applicant with this same profile in one of our Eastern cities would face a cumulative disadvantage of −28.9 percent + −1.9 percent + −6.1 percent = −36.9 percent.

These cumulative effects are overstated, however, for two reasons. First, statisticians have found (see Long 1997) that coefficient values for variables of the sort used here tend to be overstated in probit models. No simple adjustment is possible, because coefficients in probit models cannot be interpreted independently of the model that generates them. For example, the African-American coefficient of −.251 derived here is not model-independent; a different probit model would generate a different coefficient. On the other hand, the magnitude and high degree of statistical significance of this variable in this model suggest that this variable will indeed be significant in other specifications. Empirical experiments by the author confirm this.

A second reason for overstated cumulative effects is that the independent variables whose coefficient values have been added together are co-related. That is, an African-American applicant may have a higher probability of being lower-income than a non-African-American applicant; and a home in a minority neighborhood may have a higher probability of being in a lower-income neighborhood. So the probability of being both African-American and lower-income is higher than that of *not* being African-American and *not* being lower-income; and similarly for the neighborhood example. We asked above what is the disadvantage in gaining loan approval for an applicant who is African-American *and* lower-income *and* wanting a home in a neighborhood that is both lower-income *and* high-minority.

Since the disadvantage associated with this special status is interpreted as a reduced probability of loan approval, we want to know the effect on the probability of loan approval of an applicant's being African-American *and* lower income *and* seeking a home in a lower-income *and* minority neighborhood. It can be shown that this equals:[17]

(Effect on loan-approval probability of being African-American)

+ (Effect on loan probability of being lower income)

+ (Effect on loan probability of seeking a home in lower-income neighborhood)

+ (Effect on loan probability of seeking a home in a minority neighborhood)

− (Probability of being African-American given that one is lower-income and seeking a home in a lower-income, minority neighborhood) (Probability of being lower-income given that one is seeking a home in a lower-income, minority neighborhood) (Probability of seeking a home in a lower-income neighborhood given that it is also a minority neighborhood) (Probability that a home for which one has applied is in a minority neighborhood).

This last term provides a useful way of understanding the associations among different characteristics in the applicant pool; it simply equals the probability of being African-American *and* lower income *and* seeking a home in a lower-income *and* minority neighborhood.[18] This is a small probability, just 0.15 percent in our Western applicant pool and 1.23 percent in our Eastern applicant pool. So the net effect on loan approval of being African-American *and* lower income *and* seeking a home in a lower-income *and* minority neighborhood, compared to applicants not in each of these categories, is −(41.5 percent−0.15 percent) or −41.0 percent in our Western cities, and −(36.9 percent −1.2 percent) or −35.7 percent in our Eastern cities.

This adjustment is required because the independent variables in our probit equation are not truly "independent" in a probabilistic sense. Indeed, for the Western and Eastern applicant pools used in Tables 8.1 and 8.2, the correlations among the variables mentioned in this discussion (African-American, lower-income, lower-income area, and minority area) are as shown on page 157.

The existence of these correlations among the variables that predict the probability of loan approval explains the adjustment needed when considering how several independent variables jointly affect a typical applicant. For example, the effect on loan approval of being African American and lower-income in our Western cities equals (−25.1 percent−2.7 percent), adjusted for the joint probability of being both African-American and lower-income, 0.66 percent: taken together, −27.1 percent.

	Western cities	Eastern cities
African-American and lower-income	−0.011	−0.107
African-American and lower-income area	0.007	0.14
African-American and minority area	0.006	0.221
Lower-income and lower-income area	0.209	0.21
Lower-income and minority area	0.622	0.179
Lower-income area and minority area	0.189	0.459

Results for Different Lender Types, West and East

In practice, all loans are made by specific types of lender—commercial banks, savings and loans, and mortgage companies. How do these different lenders perform, East and West? Is the West/East difference for all lenders in Figure 8.1 present in every lender sector? These questions are answered empirically in the remaining columns of Tables 8.1a and 8.1b, and Tables 8.2a and 8.2b. These columns distribute the observations used in the "all lenders" probit into several subcategories—savings and loan associations, mortgage companies, and all commercial banks; and within the commercial bank category, small in-state banks, merging banks in-state, and merging banks out-of-state. Model 1 was run separately for each lender subgroup, for both Eastern and Western cities.

All these equations pass the goodness-of-fit tests. The patterns of coefficient significance and insignificance change as one moves from equation to equation. Since each equation fits the data reasonably well, these shifts in coefficient significance can be interpreted as indicating behavioral differences among the various lender groups. For example, among the seven Western cities, the African-American coefficient is negative and significant for every lender group, but its magnitude is largest for merging banks out-of-state (−.485) and smallest—indeed, insignificant—for merging banks in-state (0.0). This suggests that merging banks out-of-state in these cities were least likely to approve applications from African-Americans, and merging banks in-state most likely, all else being equal. Since the same data are used for both probits, this in turn suggests either that the African-American applicants applying to merging banks out-of-state have very different economic characteristics than African-Americans applying to merging banks in-state; or that African-American applicants are being evaluated very differently by these two distinct sets of large banks; or both.

Figures 8.2 and 8.3 compare commercial banks as a whole with savings and loans and mortgage companies in these Eastern and Western markets. In Figure 8.2 for Western cities, the coefficients for these three groups are remarkably similar; overall, mortgage companies have a somewhat lower level of estimated race and lower-income disadvantage than the other two lender types. Figure 8.3 shows that mortgage companies also have lower levels of race and lower-income disadvantage in Eastern cities; in this figure, mortgage companies have signifi-

Figure 8.2 **Race and Lower-Income Coefficients by Lender Type from Probits for Seven Western Cities, 1996**

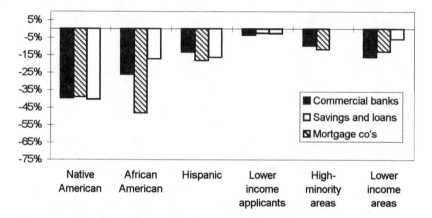

Source: Model 1 probit equations using 1996 HMDA data.
Note: These figures show estimated effects on loan approval.

Figure 8.3 **Race and Lower-Income Coefficients by Lender Type from Probits for Eight Eastern Cities, 1996**

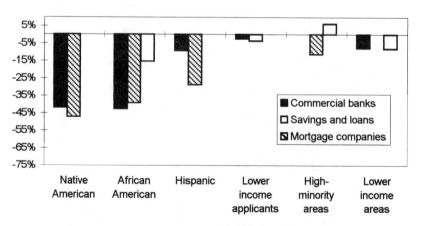

Source: Model 1 probit equations using 1996 HMDA data.
Note: These figures show estimated effects on loan approval.

cant negative coefficients only for one minority applicant group—African-Americans. Interestingly, commercial banks, savings and loan associations, and mortgage companies have surprisingly similar race and lower-income coefficients in both the Western and Eastern probits.[19]

Figures 8.4 and 8.5 contrast the coefficients of the three subcategories of commercial bank. In the Western cities probit (Figure 8.4), small in-state banks have significant coefficients only for African-American applicants and lower-income areas. Merging banks with in-state branches have just three significant coefficients among the six tested, and these are all relatively small in magnitude. Merging banks without in-state branches stand out as having the highest estimated race and lower-income disadvantage, in terms of both the number and size of significant coefficients. A very similar story is told in Figure 8.5 for the Eastern probit: Small in-state banks have only two significant coefficients—those for Native American and African-American applicants. Three coefficients are significant for merging banks in-state, and these all have relatively small magnitudes. By contrast, large banks without in-state branches have significant negative coefficients for all six race and lower-income categories, and these are often sizable.

Summary of Probit Results

These equations for the determinants of the probability of loan approval in Western and Eastern markets suggest four tentative conclusions. First, they provide solid evidence that racial minority and lower-income applicants, as well as minority and lower-income areas, are at a disadvantage in residential credit markets East and West. Second, for 1996 data this disadvantage is significant in both the Western and Eastern markets examined here. Third, different lender types behave very differently in the home-purchase loan market with respect to race and lower-income variables. In both West and East, mortgage companies appear less sensitive to race and lower-income variables than are banks and savings and loan associations; and among commercial banks, large banks without in-state branches appear systematically more sensitive to race and lower-income variables than are small banks and large banks with in-state branches. Fourth, there is some indication that regional differences may be important in credit-market outcomes, even given that different lender types have similar race/lower-income coefficient patterns in both West and East.

These results for lenders' sensitivity to minority and lower-income factors extend the conclusions from chapter 7 by sacrificing some of the detail in the descriptive statistics reviewed there. Chapter 7 came to few definite conclusions about credit-market patterns regarding minority and lower-income applicants and areas, largely because of the place-to-place diversity evident in the data. The analysis in this section has yielded much more definite results about the sensitivity of different lender types to race and lower-income largely by bundling different cities' data together and ignoring this place-to-place diversity.

Figure 8.4 **Race and Lower-Income Coefficients by Bank Type from Probits for Seven Western Cities, 1996**

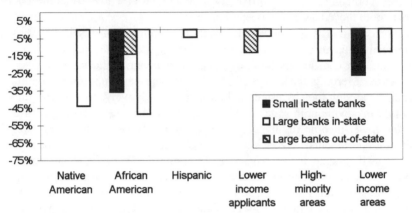

Source: Model 1 probit equations using 1996 HMDA data.
Note: These figures show estimated effects on loan approval.

Figure 8.5 **Race and Lower-Income Coefficients by Bank Type from Probits for Eight Eastern Cities, 1996**

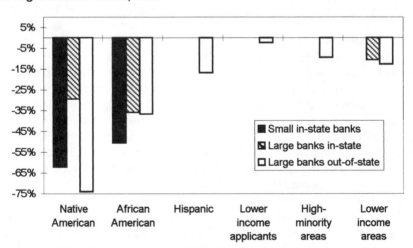

Source: Model 1 probit equations using 1996 HMDA data.
Note: These figures show estimated effects on loan approval.

Probit analysis provides some gain, then, in determining whether and how much social factors such as minority and lower-income status affect access to credit. The diversity of place-to-place statistics in chapter 7 provides a provocative contrast with the uniformity of conclusions drawn here. Further decomposition of U.S. credit markets is warranted; running probit equations for cities in different regions will provide more insight into whether the uniformity found in chapter 7 or the diversity found in chapter 8 is the more fundamental result.

Sorting Out Differences in Financial Infrastructure

The first step in further decomposing U.S. credit markets is to add more cities. Tables 7.2 and 7.8 contain a roster of thirty-five cities whose financial infrastructures as of mid-1996 have been analyzed for this study. In these tables, these cities' data on financial offices is organized into five regions: Southwest, Mountain and Great Plains, Midwest, Northeast, and Southeast. These cities were chosen so as to have large and small metropolitan areas in every region. Appendix 8B demonstrates that this regional grouping is superior to other methods of grouping financial infrastructures (in particular, by city size or proportion of minority residents).[20]

These cities were also chosen because they are located in states whose niche in the U.S. banking market is of interest here. For example, California is a state dominated by a small number of locally chartered and controlled banks that have implemented aggressive expansion strategies elsewhere; and California's cities have very few branches of out-of-state banks. But other states closely resemble California, as Table 4.2 made clear: Minnesota, Pennsylvania, New York, Massachusetts, and North Carolina. The other states are all "target" states: some, such as Mississippi and New Jersey, are served by numerous and well-established in-state banks; others, such as Idaho and New Mexico, have a decreasing number of in-state banks and are largely served by local affiliates of out-of-state–owned bank holding companies.

The regional division used in Tables 7.2 and 7.8 is crude but serviceable. Texas may seem out of place in the Southwest; but with its large Hispanic and Asian-American populations, Texas more resembles California demographically than it does Mississippi. The population-adjusted averages for each region tell an interesting story. The Southwestern cities, on average, have relatively low numbers of financial offices, especially compared with the Mountain/Great Plains cities. These latter cities are well supplied, in per-resident terms, with both formal and informal financial offices. The Midwestern cities, in turn, are well supplied with formal offices—banks and thrifts, credit unions, and investment and mutual fund offices—but have relatively low levels of informal financial offices. The Southeastern cities are very well supplied with bank offices and have exceptionally high numbers of informal financial offices—mortgage brokers, finance companies, pawnbrokers, and check-cashers. These cities have only modest numbers of investment and mutual fund offices, however, and relatively few credit unions. The Northeastern cities vary most widely, but on average fall somewhere in the middle.

These tables suggest that the financial infrastructures in U.S. cities have different regional profiles. Indeed, statistical analysis of the data in these two tables suggests that there are three distinct financial-infrastructure "types"—the Southwestern, the Mountain/Great Plains, and the Southeastern.[21] These are depicted in Figure 8.6. The Southwestern financial infrastructure, in a word, is lean. Note that the Southwest averages fewer formal and informal financial offices of every type, on a population-weighted basis, than any other region. This region has fewer than half the number of banks, thrifts, and loan brokers that the Southeast cities included here have. The Mountain/Great Plains pattern is very different: Its cities have relatively few pawnbrokers and check-cashers—almost as few as the Southwest, on a population-weighted basis. However, this region has significantly higher numbers of every other type of financial office, from credit unions and investment offices to banks and loan brokers. The Southeastern cities have about the same number of financial offices per capita as do the Mountain/Great Plains cities; but these offices are distributed differently. The Southeast has an exceptionally large number of informal financial offices of all kinds, and the highest relative number of bank branches. Compensating for this surplus of offices relative to the Mountain/Great Plains region is the Southeast's relatively small numbers of credit union branches and investment offices.

There is a story to be told here. The older industrial parts of the country appear to be the best supplied with credit unions. This makes sense, for not only are credit unions the prototypical membership-only, locally based financial intermediaries, they are often associated with well-organized, large-scale employment sites. Large unionized industrial plants are the most likely candidates for credit unions of this type. Some credit unions' membership is rooted in cultural or national identity; and here, too, the Northeast and Midwest have had important inflows of immigrants from particular European countries during the early part of this century. By contrast, the Southeast and Southwest are typically open-shop states with little history of taking in large numbers of European immigrants in the early decades of this century. Further, the current immigrant wave, while it is centered on the Southwest and accompanied by rapidly growing ethnic banks, has not generated a large outpouring of new credit unions.

Also intriguing is the relatively large number of informal offices in the Southeast. We might speculate further that this plethora of loan-brokers, check-cashers, and pawnbrokers is so large today because of the South's history—the chronic poverty that characterized much of this region through this century, and more importantly, the legacy of the Jim Crow era. Access to formal banks may have been problematic for many, both because "separate but equal" laws would have kept African-Americans off bank lobby floors (except to sweep them) and because African-Americans and poor whites often had jobs with little security

Figure 8.6 **Financial Offices per 100,000 Population, City Averages in Different U.S. Regions, 1996**

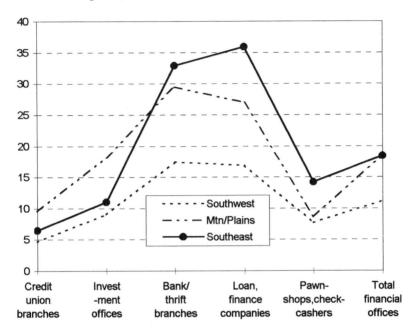

Source: Author's calculations using ProCD database.
Note: Figures depict offices of each type per 100,000 residents.

and low wages. In this climate, which persists in some corners even in today's New South, a set of transaction-oriented institutions would spring up parallel to the formal banking sector, as would a set of credit-market institutions focused on asset-based lending.[22]

Summary

This chapter opened with a brief review of the extensive empirical literature on the social efficiency of urban credit-market outcomes. Since the late 1970s, social scientists, policy-makers, and activists have used several techniques to evaluate this social efficiency, and in particular the sensitivity of loan flows and loan approvals to minority and lower-income applicants and areas. A formal probit model was then developed for use in this study; and this model was used to generate econometric evidence on access to capital in urban markets west and east of the Mississippi, with special attention to racial and income divisions in the applicant pool. This econometric evidence suggested that mortgage companies are more sensitive to minority and lower-income variables than are other lenders, and that merging banks without in-state branches are more sensitive than other lenders. Given the diverse cities included, the equations run for Western and Eastern cities were remarkable: both equations proved very robust statistically, and both generated surprisingly similar conclusions for the different lender subgroups. The uniformity of these probit results presents an intriguing contrast with the diverse results for the city-by-city analysis done in chapter 7. The question is whether diversity or uniformity is the more fundamental pattern.

The next step is a more extensive econometric analysis. A logical way to proceed is to investigate U.S. urban credit markets on a regional basis. The next chapter extends the model developed here to several regions and numerous states.

Appendix 8A

A Probit Model of
the Residential Credit Market

The starting place in any estimation effort involving HMDA data is a behavioral model of the residential credit market. Every transaction made or forgone in this market involves three separate steps. First, on the demand side, potential homeowners apply for credit from specific lenders. On the supply side, lenders must decide to approve or deny these borrowers' applications. Finally, approved applicants must decide whether to accept lenders' offers.

The first step in this process cannot be observed using HMDA data, and will be ignored here. Putting this step aside allows us to abstract from the property seller and from the housing market on which the residential-credit market rests. The third step, in turn, is of only minor significance for home-purchase loans—most applicants approved for credit take it. Hence our focus will be on the lenders' decision to lend or deny credit.

The lending decision emerges from the interplay of three factors: the viability of the potential homeowner as a borrower; the circumstances of the lender; and the condition and location of the property for which the buyer seeks a mortgage loan. Prior to widespread securitization, the circumstances of the lender figured heavily in this equation: that is, the financial position and liquidity of the prospective lender were important determinants of how many loans could be made. In the current era of securitized housing finance, these factors have faded in importance; the intermediaries making loans typically bundle them and sell them off to nonintermediary portfolios. Hence what comes to the fore are the characteristics of the borrower and of the property.

The property sought by any applicant has two salient characteristics that contribute to its overall market value: its inherent physical features, and the physical and social amenities offered by the area surrounding it. The characteristics of the surrounding neighborhood can be divided into economic features such as the average income level of neighborhood residents, the percentage of owner-occupied homes, and residential density; and social features such as the neighborhood's racial composition. The loan applicant in turn has economic characteristics such as current income level and household size and composition;

and social characteristics such as race and gender. The idea behind this economic/social distinction is that the economic factors should, in principle, guide decisions, while social factors such as applicant race and neighborhood racial character should be unimportant.

So in deciding whether to make a home mortgage loan, the lender evaluates the bundle:

Creditworthiness = f [Applicant (economic characteristics, social characteristics), Property(inherent characteristics, neighborhood, economic characteristics, social characteristics)].   (8a.1)

The idea of empirical tests of phenomena such as racial redlining and racial discrimination is precisely to incorporate as many economic variables as possible into specifications like 8a.1, along with social variables of interest. In principle, the economic variables should explain all the variance in the data, leaving purely social variables without explanatory power.

Suppose that every applicant for residential credit is subjected to a creditworthiness screening as per equation 8a.1. When an applicant's characteristics are satisfactory they can be graded as a "+"; when unsatisfactory, they are graded as a "−." Focusing here on racial difference, let "W" denote white, "M" minority, and "E" any racial composition. Then racial discrimination occurs when an applicant evaluated as:

Creditworthiness = f [Applicant (+, +, W), Property (+),
Neighborhood (+, E)]

is granted credit, while at least some applicants with the following profile

Creditworthiness = f [Applicant (+, +, M), Property(+),
Neighborhood (+, E)]   (8a.2)

are not. Racial redlining, in turn, would arise if applicants with characteristics evaluated as

Creditworthiness = f [Applicant (+, +, E), Property(+),
Neighborhood (+, W)]

were approved for credit, while at least some applicants with the following profile

Creditworthiness = f [Applicant (+, +, E), Property (+),
Neighborhood (+, M)]   (8a.3)

were not.

Clearly both racial discrimination and redlining might be at work whenever minority applicants seek credit for homes in minority neighborhoods. The idea in both 8a.2 and 8a.3 is that all *economic* factors are approximately the same for both white and minority borrowers (or for properties in both white and minority neighborhoods), so that *racial* difference alone explains why more white borrowers (or properties in white neighborhoods) are approved for credit.[23]

Empirical estimations equations based on equation 8a.1 take the form:

Probability of loan approval = f [Applicant (economic characteristics, social characteristics), Neighborhood (economic characteristics, social characteristics)].　　　　　　　　　　　(8a.4)

As warned in the text, equation 8a.4 has interpretive limits. It does not incorporate information on the characteristics of the properties sought by applicants; it has only a partial roster of applicants' economic characteristics; and it measures only some of the economic and social characteristics of neighborhoods that might influence borrowers' preferences and lenders' decisions. While these limitations are regrettable, the best should not become the enemy of the good in empirical estimation—for if it did, empirical work in economics would become nearly impossible. Empirical studies on this or on any topic fill in portions of a matrix of explanatory possibility; if never definitive, they can shed suggestive light on processes in the real social world.

Further, the residential-loan regression analysis developed in this case sidesteps the central limitations of this approach. That is, we are comparing the results from a given specification for one set of lenders with those from that same specification for a different set of lenders. Attention thus centers on the relative magnitude of specific variables for different lender groups.

A Model of the Probability of Loan Approval

The model developed for this study represents an empirical embodiment of equation 8a.4. At the same time, because this study ranges widely over many geographic locales, an economical specification incorporating readily available explanatory variables is desirable. The model estimated thus represents a compromise between economy and explanatory depth:

Model 1:

Probability of loan approval in 1996 = Intercept term, (V1)

Individual economic characteristics
[Applicant's loan/income ratio, (V2)
Log of applicant's annual income, (V3)
Size rank of applicant's loan relative to all MSA loan
applications, (V4)
Rank of applicant's loan/income ratio relative to the loan/income

ratios of all applicants in the same MSA, (V5)
Variable equal to the annual income for those 25 percent of
applicants in every MSA with the lowest income levels, and equal
to zero otherwise], (V6)

Individual social characteristics
[Dummy variable for Native American applicants, (V7)
Dummy variable for African-American applicants, (V8)
Dummy variable for Asian-American applicants, (V9)
Dummy variable for Hispanic applicants, (V10)
Dummy variable for female applicants], (V11)

Neighborhood economic characteristics
[Residential density (the census tract's population per residential
unit), (V12)
Proportion of owner occupants (relative to all census tract residential
units), (V13)
Dummy variable for areas with high loan volumes (those 50 percent
of census tracts with the largest number of 1995 loans), (V14)
Dummy variable for areas with high loan values (those 50 percent of
census tracts with the highest average 1995 loan values)], (V15)

Neighborhood social characteristics
[Dummy variable for low-income areas (those 33 percent of MSA
census tracts with the lowest 1990 median-income levels), (V16)
Dummy variable for high minority areas (those 25 percent of MSA
census tracts with the highest proportion of minority residents)],
(V17)

Dummy variables take on the value "1" when a given characteristic is present,
and "0" otherwise. They provide a way of asking whether the characteristic in
question—for example, a loan application being registered in a high-minority
area—significantly affects the dependent variable (here, the probability of loan
aqproval).

Model 1 has seventeen variables, including the intercept variable (V1). The
logarithm of applicant income (V2) is used rather than applicant income because
the logarithm compresses the values of applicant incomes to values close to 1,
which improves the efficiency of the probit estimation procedure. Beyond the
raw measures of loan/income ratio and income for each applicant (V2 and V3),
we also include measures of how these values for each applicant compare with
the remainder of the MSA applicant pool (V4 and V5).

We test explicitly whether applicants with low incomes (V6), minority applicants (V7 to V10), and female applicants (V11) are at a disadvantage relative to
all other applicants in lenders' applicant pool. In general, we account for every

racial-minority category separately; this allows us to evaluate lender sensitivity to different minority categories separately.

The next set of regressors measures the influence of neighborhood economic factors on loan decisions—for every census tract, the average number of residents per household (V12) and the proportion of owner-occupied residences among all housing units (V13). Two geographic variables in Model 1 (V16 and V17) then test whether neighborhood social characteristics—their residents' income levels and racial composition—affect lenders' decisions. These variables are constructed by singling out the 33 percent of tracts with the lowest median incomes, and the 25 percent of tracts with the highest proportion of minority residents, in every metropolitan area included here. This section also incorporates two other area-related variables: We calculate the total number of loans, and the average dollar-value of loans, in every census tract; and then we single out that half of census tracts with the highest values of each (V15 and V16). These last two variables measure whether lenders' decisions are sensitive to other lenders' actions; that is, whether there is a strategic coordination aspect to residential loan-market decisions.

Comments

Some comments on the modeling method used here are appropriate for those interested in more detailed aspects of the estimation reported in chapters 8, 9, and 10.

1. The probit model used here is one of the family of qualitative response models used in econometric analysis. It is designed for situations with two responses that can be interpreted as the probability of a given event. Six actions are recorded for loan applications under HMDA: loan approved and made; loan approved but not made; loan denied; loan withdrawn by applicant; loan application incomplete; and other or not available. To create the binary (yes/no) responses required for probit analysis, all applications that were withdrawn, left incomplete, or not specified were discarded. The two loan-approved categories were then combined, on the assumption that whether a loan will be taken does not affect banks' decisions. While this assumption is debatable, the loans approved but not taken usually amount to no more than 5 percent of the loans made and taken.

2. Logit models are sometimes used to estimate the probability of loan approval in credit markets. It is well known among statisticians that the results derived from probit and logit models are virtually indistinguishable when the dependent variable is specified the same way. As a test of model consistency, some markets' data was estimated using both logit and probit methods. As expected, no significant differences were found.

3. The results reported in chapters 8 to 10 encompass a huge number of individual estimations. For the sixteen distinct market areas analyzed, estimations

are done separately for all lenders and for several subcategories of lenders. Separate runs have been done for 1992, 1995, and 1996 data. Even reproducing these results in the concise format of Tables 8.1 and 8.2 would require more than 100 pages. Consequently these raw results are not reproduced here. Those interested in these detailed results may contact the author.

4. Since discussion in the text focuses on a subset of the variables estimated, results for many variables in Model 1 are neither presented or discussed. Some brief comments about the estimation results for these variables are thus in order. In these equations, the economic variables for individuals and geographic areas are usually significant, and the coefficients of these variables usually take on the anticipated signs: The probability of loan approval improves as the borrower's income rises and as the borrower's loan/income ratio falls, as the proportion of owner-occupied homes rises, as residential density falls, and as census-tract loan activity rises. There is a remarkable degree of consistency in these variables, given the geographical diversity of the market areas included in these estimations.

For the estimated variables not discussed in the text, two surprising results stand. First, the variables for applicant loan rank and for applicant loan/income rank are consistently positive. Second, the female borrower variable, when significant, usually takes on a positive coefficient. These surprising results deserve further study.

5. Goodness-of-fit is problematic at best for probit models, due to these models' sensitivity. Failure to pass diagnostic tests does not indicate that the estimated coefficients are misleading; nor does passage of these tests imply that a given model is correct and its coefficients believable. Using a large number of observations, as is done here, is one means of ensuring that reliable results are obtained; but this is by no means foolproof.

6. The results shown for this study were generated using version 6.12 of SAS for Windows 95, under license to the University of California, Riverside. Those interested may communicate with the author concerning his SAS programs.

Appendix 8B

A Method for Classifying
Financial Infrastructures

Is it appropriate to group U.S. financial markets by region? The grouping of the thirty-five cities shown in Tables 7.2 and 7.7 by region may not best capture their similarities and differences. Two other possibilities suggest themselves. First, financial infrastructures may differ primarily by metropolitan size. Figure 8B.1 depicts this possibility: It groups metropolitan areas with 1.5 million or more residents, 500,000 to 750,000 residents, 400,000 to 450,000 residents, and under 300,000 residents. This schematic depiction immediately suggests that metropolitan size and financial infrastructure have no unique relation, for the city size with the highest population-adjusted level of financial offices is the smallest one, but in second place is the grouping for cities of over 1.5 million.

Another possibility is that financial infrastructures are organized according to the racial composition of the metropolitan population. Here, the thirty-five cities are divided into three groups, as follows: largely white (11 percent or fewer minority residents); some minorities (more than 11 percent to 28 percent minority residents); many minorities (more than 28 percent minority residents). Figure 8B.2 illustrates the financial infrastructures of cities classified by proportion of minority residents. Similarly, no unique relation between financial infrastructure and minority population is evident in this figure.

The question is whether the metropolitan-size or minority-population groupings of these thirty-five cities are superior to the regional-difference grouping shown in Figure 8.6. The following method is used to answer this question. For each of these three methods of grouping the thirty-five cities' financial infrastructure, group means are computed. The difference between every city and each group average was then computed and summed by city and grouping, as explained in footnote 21. These differences were then squared, summed by region, and contrasted with differences obtained by the other grouping methods. It was also determined how many local infrastructures were properly categorized using each method in turn. Table A8.1 records the results of these tests. The second column shows how many local infrastructures were accurately categorized for each grouping method. Of thirty-five local infrastructures tested, no more than twenty

Figure 8B.1 **1996 Financial Offices per 100,000 Population, by Size of Metropolitan Area in 1990**

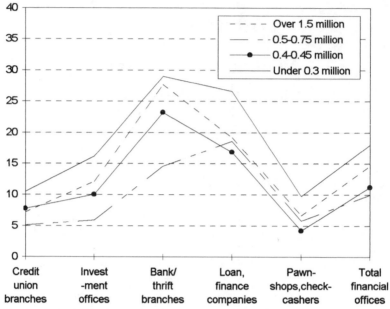

Source: Calculations by author using ProCD database.
Note: Figures depict offices of each type per 100,000 residents.

Table 8B.1 **Measures of Financial Infrastructure Similarity**

Infrastructure grouping by:	Number of local infrastructures closest to this grouping method	Sum of squared differences for this grouping method
None	35	18,122.7
Geographic region	17	11,375.1
Population size	18	13,078.3
Proportion of racial minorities	20	11,992.6

Source: ProCD data on financial offices, 1996, U.S. Census, 1990
Note: Average figures for the number of financial offices per 100,000 are computed for each grouping—geographical region, population size, and proportion of minority residents. A sum of squared differences (s.s.d.) is then computed for each of the thirty-five cities, using each computed average in turn. When a city's s.s.d is smallest for its own grouping, it counts as one in column two. Column three records the overall s.s.d. for each method when every city is assigned to its own grouping.

Figure 8B.2. **1996 Financial Offices per 100,000 Population by Minority Population Proportion in 1990**

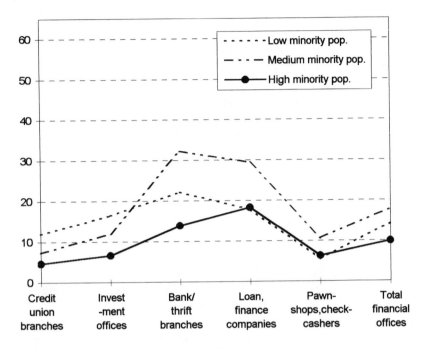

Source: Calculations by author using ProCD database.
Note: Figures depict offices of each type per 100,000 residents.

(for the racial-minority method) best fit any given grouping. The total score for the sum of squared differences for each method is recorded for each grouping method in the third column of Table A8.1. This column reports the result of the following calculation: For each of the six components of every city's infrastructure, the difference between the average population-adjusted number of financial offices and this city's population-adjusted financial offices is computed. This difference is then squared, and the resulting scores are summed. Note that the total sum of squared differences in the absence of any method of grouping cities' infrastructures equals 18,123; this sum is derived by comparing every city's financial-office pattern with the average for all thirty-five cities taken as a whole.

When groupings by region, city size, or minority population are done, the total sum of squared differences is reduced considerably. This reduction indicates how much the fit of every city's data is improved by each grouping technique. The regional grouping yields the best improvement in the total sum of squared differences, with a score of 11,375. Hence this grouping most accurately captures the similarities among different cities.[24]

9

Regional Patterns
in Credit-Market Disadvantage and
Financial Structures

Introduction: Cities and Lenders

This chapter builds on chapter 8 in two ways. First, it reports on probit estimations for seventeen separate market areas, covering eighteen states and 120 separate metropolitan areas. Second, it deepens the financial infrastructure analysis of chapter 8 by analyzing banking and other financial offices in thirty-five cities spread around these eighteen states.

Most of the probit equations run here combine several metropolitan areas in a given state. This method precludes detailed results for individual cities, but provides enough observations that equations can be run for subsets of lenders as well as for all lenders. Specifically, probit equations were run for each of the following seventeen geographic areas:

Southwestern Cities

(1) Los Angeles County*
(2) Southern California cities—Orange County, Riverside–San Bernardino, San Diego, San Luis Obispo, Santa Barbara, Ventura County
(3) Inland California cities—Bakersfield, Fresno*, Merced, Modesto*, Sacramento, Stockton
(4) Northern California cities—Oakland (East San Francisco Bay), San Francisco, San Jose, Santa Cruz, Santa Rosa
(5) New Mexico—Albuquerque*, Las Cruces, Santa Fe*
(6) Texas—Amarillo, Austin, Dallas, El Paso*, San Antonio

---

*The thirty-five cities whose financial infrastructures are examined in this chapter are indicated with asterisks in the above listing.

Great Plains/Mountain Cities

(7) Boise*, ID; Billings* and Great Falls, MT; Bismarck, Fargo, and Grand Forks (ND only), ND; Sioux Falls* and Rapid City, SD; Casper* and Cheyenne, WY

Midwestern Cities

(8) Iowa—Cedar Rapids, Davenport, Des Moines*, Dubuque*, Iowa City, Sioux City, Waterloo

(9) Indiana—Bloomington, Elkhart, Evansville, Ft. Wayne*, Gary*, Indianapolis*, Kokomo, Lafayette, Muncie, South Bend, Terre Haute*

(10) Minnesota—Duluth, Grand Forks (MN only), LaCrosse (MN only), Minneapolis*, Moorhead, Rochester*, St. Cloud

Northeastern Cities

(11) Pennsylvania—Allentown, Altoona, Erie*, Johnstown, Lancaster*, Philadelphia*, Pittsburgh, Reading, Scranton, Sharon, State College, Williamsville, York

(12) New York—Albany, Binghamton, Buffalo/Niagara Falls, New York City, Nassau County (Long Island), Rochester, Syracuse

(13) New Jersey—Atlantic City, Bergen-Passaic, Jersey City, Middlesex-Somerset-Huntingdon, Monmouth-Ocean, Newark*, Philadelphia (NJ only), Trenton*, Vineland-Millville-Bridgeton

(14) Massachusetts—Barnstable-Yarmouth, Boston, Brockton*, Fall River, Fitchburg-Leominster, Lawrence, Lowell*, New Bedford, Pittsfield, Springfield*, Worcester

Southeastern Cities

(15) North Carolina—Asheville*, Charlotte-Gastonia-Rock Hill, Fayetteville*, Goldsboro, Greensboro-Winston-Salem-High Point, Greenville*, Hickory-Morganton, Jacksonville, Raleigh-Durham-Chapel Hill, Rocky Mount, Wilmington*

(16) Georgia—Albany, Athens*, Atlanta, Augusta, Columbus, Macon, Savannah*

(17) Mississippi—Biloxi-Gulfport-Pascagoula*, Hattiesburg*, Jackson*, Memphis (MS only)

Large Merging Banks

Table 9.1 lists the thirty-four institutions classified as large merging banks in this study. At the core of this list are twenty-five of the top twenty-six bank holding companies by asset size as of December 31, 1997; ABN AMRO is excluded because it made no mortgage loans as of that date. Another seven bank holding

Table 9.1 **Bank Holding Companies (BHCs) Designated as Large Merging Banks**

	Head-quarters	BHC assets ($ Mil.) (1)	Asset rank 12/97	6/98	Branches in these states (2)	Post-1995 acquisition by:
Banks headquartered and with branches in states included in this study:						
Chase Manhattan	NY	366,995	1	1	NJ, TX	
Citicorp	NY	330,751	2	2	CA	
NationsBank (3)	NC	307,985	3	3	GA, TX	BankAmerica
BankAmerica (3)	CA	263,885	5	5	ID, TX	NationsBank
First Union	NC	228,996	6	6		
Wells Fargo (4)	CA	93,200	10	11	TX	Norwest
Norwest (5)	MN	93,153	11	12	IN, IA, MT, NM, ND, SD, TX, WY	Wells Fargo
Fleet Bancshares	MA	100,817	12	10	NJ, NY	
PNC Bank Corporation	PA	75,918	13	14	IN	
First Bank System (6)	MN	73,750	15	16	MT, SD	
Suntrust Banks, Inc.	GA	61,393	20	20	NJ	
Mellon Bank	PA	47,602	26	23	NJ	
Corestates	PA	NA	24	NA	NJ	First Union
Bank South	GA	NA	NA	NA	MS	NationsBank
First Interstate	CA	NA	NA	NA	ID, MT, NM, WY	Wells Fargo
Banks headquartered in included states, without branches in other included states:						
J.P. Morgan and Co.	NY	280,777	4	4		
Bankers Trust	NY	173,311	7	7		
BankBoston	MA	70,498	16	17		
Wachovia	NC	64,818	17	18		
Bank of New York	NY	63,003	19	19		
Republic NY Bancorp	NY	59,919	21	21		
BayBanks	MA	NA	18	NA		BankBoston
Banks with branches in included states, headquartered elsewhere:						
Banc One (7)	OH	124,781	8	8	TX	
First Chicago NBD (7)	IL	119,781	9	9		BancOne
Keycorp	OH	75,677	14	15	IN, NY, WY	
Comerica	MI	35,196	28	26	CA	
Southtrust	AL	34,668	31	27	MS	
Firstar	WI	19,983	43	43	MN	
First Security Bank	UT	19,360	49	44	MT, NM	
Boatmen's Bancshares	MO	NA	NA	NA	NM, TX	NationsBank

(continued on next page)

Banks with neither headquarters nor branches in included states:

National City Corp.	OH	81,258	23	13	
Barnett Banks	FL	NA	25	NA	NationsBank
Bank IV	KS	NA	NA	NA	Boatmen's
NBD	MI	NA	NA	NA	First Chicago

Notes: (1) As of June 30, 1998. (2) As of December 31, 1997, for states included in this study only. (3) These institutions' merger was effective after June 30, 1998. (4) Wells's merger with Norwest was effective after June 30, 1998. (5) Includes Sunwest Bank of NM and TX. (6) Renamed U.S. Bancorp in 1997. Assets for holding companies acquired after 1995 are shown only if they reported balance sheets separately as of June 30, 1998. (7) These institutions' merger was effective after June 30, 1998.

companies are on this list because of their extensive branch networks in states included in this study. Of these seven, three—Bank South, Boatmen's Bancshares, and First Interstate—have merged with other institutions on this list. The other four—Comerica, Southtrust, Firstar, and First Security—are holding companies in the top fifty nationwide with branch networks in at least two of the states included in this study. Finally, two banks—NBD and Bank IV—are included because they are large holding companies absorbed by larger bank holding companies on this list. More details on large banks' acquisition histories appear below.[1]

These holding companies fall into four categories. The largest number, fourteen, are headquartered in states included in this study and have branches in at least one of the other states listed above. Eight institutions are headquartered in included states, but have no branches in any of the other states included here. Another eight are holding companies that have branches in one or more of the included states, but are headquartered in other states. And four have no branches in included states and are headquartered elsewhere.

The terms "large" and "merging" are used synonymously to refer to the institutions on this list. It is not strictly true that all these institutions are actively pursuing other banks as targets; however, without access to privileged corporate information, there is no way to differentiate large bank holding companies with active acquisition agendas from those without such agendas. Since all the holding companies on this list are aggressively managed whether or not they seek to take over other banks, the simple expedient is to treat "large" and "merging" as interchangeable.

Multidimensional "Disadvantage" in Credit Markets

At the very heart of this study are comparisons of the behavior of different lender groups in different market areas. Of special interest in these comparisons are four distinct aspects of minority and lower-income difference. Such place-to-place and lender-to-lender comparisons create several analytical problems. First, how can the multiple dimensions of minority and lower-income difference be squeezed to one or two? Second, what adjustments can be made for the large differences in the number of racial minorities in different places? Unless these questions are answered, overall assessments of social efficiency in residential credit markets cannot be made.

This section develops a "disadvantage" method which permits an overall assessment of access to credit for minority applicants, for applicants seeking loans in minority areas, for lower-income applicants, and for applicants seeking loans in lower-income areas. Results for this disadvantage index are presented in Tables 9.2 and 9.3, on the basis of the Model 1 coefficients reported in Tables 8.1 and 8.2. The construction of the numbers shown in these tables is best described with the help of an example.

With the Western and Eastern probit results in mind, consider the following thought experiment. Suppose there are 1,000 loan applicants in a hypothetical credit market. How many of these 1,000 applications would be inappropriately set aside due to applicants' minority or lower-income status, independent of other factors? To answer this question, we must approximate the magnitude of race and lower-income effects, including only those effects that are statistically significant when other factors impinging on creditworthiness are taken into account. Fortunately, the statistically significant coefficients for race and lower-income variables in Tables 8.1 and 8.2 provide precisely this approximation of minority or lower-income "disadvantage."

The Native American coefficient from the all-lenders equation for the seven Western cities, shown in Table 8.1a, suggests that Native Americans face a 44.7 percent lower probability of loan approval than other applicants, all else being equal. The coefficient for African-American applicants suggests a 25.1 percent lower probability of loan approval, and that for Hispanics a 16.1 percent lower probability. All these coefficients are significant at the 1 percent level; the coefficient for Asian-American applicants is not statistically significant.

The social significance of these coefficients depends on how many prospective borrowers fall into these minority categories. Suppose that our pool of 1,000 hypothetical applicants includes 100 members of each minority group—that is, 100 Native Americans, 100 Asian-Americans, 100 African-Americans, and 100 Hispanic-Americans. One way of interpreting the $-.447$ coefficient for Native American applicants is to imagine that 44.7 of these 100 Native American applicants are arbitrarily discarded from the applicant pool, while the remaining applicants remain in this pool, on equal footing with non-Native American applicants. This ignores the likelihood that *every* Native American applicant is a candidate for personal discrimination or structural difference; but it does represent one way of measuring the size of these cumulated differences. Similarly, 25.1 and 16.1, respectively, of the 100 African-American and 100 Hispanic applicants are discarded. So 86 of the 400 minority applicants in our hypothetical pool (21.5 percent) are effectively discarded due to cumulative racial difference.

A similar calculation can be done for lower-income borrowers. If there are 333 lower-income applicants in a loan pool of 1,000, as Model 1 implies, the all-lender coefficient of −0.087 in Table 8.1a implies that 9 applicants—2.7 percent of 333 lower-income applicants—are discarded. What about minority and lower-income areas? While one in three census tracts in every market are defined as lower-income and high-minority areas, we hypothesize that one in six applications are registered for homes in each of these areas. This adjusts in a crude but uniform way for the lower relative pool of owner-occupied homes in these areas and for demand effects. The coefficients of −0.059 for high-minority areas and of −0.078 for lower-income areas suggest that if 167 applications are registered in each area type, approximately 10 applications will be discarded in high-minority areas and another 13 in lower-income areas.

Adding up the figures from these race and lower-income effects for our applicant pool of 1,000 suggests a total disadvantage of about 118. That is, the effective size of this applicant pool is 882 instead of 1,000 because of its racial and lower-income composition. Most discarded applications, 96, can be traced to racial disadvantage, the remaining 22 to lower-income disadvantage.

This procedure is followed throughout Tables 9.2 and 9.3, with one modification. When a coefficient has a significance level of 5 percent, its disadvantage score is multiplied by 0.95; when its significance level is 10 percent, its score is multiplied by 0.90. This adjustment makes some allowance for the degree of confidence we have in different coefficients.[2] Note that a given population's estimated "disadvantage" can be positive, as in the case of mortgage companies' applications in minority areas in the seven Western cities. As with negative disadvantage figures, these positive coefficients could reflect a variety of factors—higher wealth and service levels, lender marketing strategies, and so on. We include these positive coefficients for individual variables, and then report "net" disadvantages for minority and lower-income status. So negative "disadvantage" scores imply the "subtraction" of applicants; positive scores, the effective "addition" of applicants.

The Elements of Credit-Market Disadvantage

The severity of disadvantage in any given market area can be traced to two factors. One is the extent of disadvantage, on average, for every minority applicant, for every lower-income applicant, and for every applicant for a home in a minority or lower-income area. This element is captured by the size and significance of probit coefficients. The second and equally important element in disadvantage, however, is the size of the applicant pool affected. For example, the larger the proportion of minorities in an applicant base, the higher the disadvantage score and the social significance of minority status, all else being equal. The same holds true for lower-income status and for the two area effects. The definitions of lower-income applicant and of minority and lower-income areas used here largely control for this size effect; but variability in minority applicants remains of paramount importance in interpreting disadvantage in these credit markets.

Two methods are available for handling this "size" problem. The first of these has been discussed just above. That is, we can construct a fictitious population with an arbitrary number of individuals in exposed categories. The 100–100–100–100–1,000 or "equiproportional" approach assumes that minorities are a large share of the overall applicant pool (40 percent). It also assumes that no one minority's disadvantage is more or less important than another's; in effect, every group's weight is the same (10 percent of the hypothetical applicant pool).

A second approach to the problem of "size" is to use the demographic composition of an actual applicant pool to compute the social significance of disadvantage. The bottom portion of Tables 9.2 and 9.3 demonstrate this approach by using the "own" characteristics of each applicant pool. In the seven Western and Eastern cities examined here, the home-purchase loan pool contains, for every 1,000 applicants:

	Seven Western cities	Eight Eastern cities
Lower-income individuals	355	342
Applications in lower-income areas	216	155
Native American applicants	11	4
African-American applicants	21	80
Asian-American applicants	22	24
Hispanic applicants	256	26
Applications in minority areas	187	108

The impact of regional variation on the extent of disadvantage is clear from these figures. One in four applicants in the Western cities is Hispanic, but the proportion is only one in forty in the Eastern cities. And conversely, the Eastern applicant pool contains four times the proportion of African-Americans the Western pool does. Also, more lower-income applications are also filed in the West than in the East, as are more applications for minority areas.[3]

East, West, and Credit-Market Disadvantage

What does our metric of disadvantage tell us about the Western and Eastern cities highlighted in chapters 7 and 8? First consider equiproportional disadvantage. Western cities' disadvantage is larger for savings and loans and for mortgage companies than Eastern cities'; but all three disadvantage scores for commercial banks are higher in Eastern cities than in the West. The Western cities' all-lender disadvantage is larger than in the East primarily because such a large proportion of Western applications are filed at mortgage companies. Note that about 86 percent of the 36.4–point gap between West and East is due to the West's higher level of racial disadvantage, relative to that measured for Eastern cities.

Comparisons among lender subgroups are of interest, as are overall scores. In the Western cities, savings and loans and large banks out-of-state have the highest disadvantage scores by a considerable margin. Next in line, in the West, are mortgage companies and small in-state banks. The best performance, which discards the fewest overall hypothetical applicants, is by large banks in-state. In the Eastern cities, a slightly different story emerges. There, large banks out-of-state and savings and loans again perform worst in overall disadvantage; next come small in-state banks and large banks in-state; and the best performance in Eastern cities is by mortgage companies.

The "own market" method depicted in the lower portions of Tables 9.2 and 9.3 generate lower total disadvantage scores for every lender group except one— large banks in-state in the Western cities. In the Western cities, disadvantage shrinks to about three-quarters the level measured under the equiproportional method, and in Eastern cities it shrinks to about half. None of the lender types change position, but the gaps between lender types change significantly. This demonstrates graphically the sensitivity of performance measures to the composition of the applicant pool.

This summary of disadvantage scores for Western and Eastern cities again suggests, as did chapters 7 and 8, that regional and inter-lender differences matter in credit markets. The remainder of this chapter reports on a more detailed examination of regional and inter-lender difference in financial structures and credit-market outcomes. For selected states in five regional areas within the United States, the remainder of this chapter presents summary information about merger activity, focusing on the large banks enumerated above; summary loan-market characteristics, including loan denial rates and market-share statistics; and results of estimations of Model 1.

Southwestern Cities

In the Southwestern cities examined here, mortgage companies have the largest share of the home-purchase market, about 45 percent in 1996. Further, mortgage companies' and commercial banks' market share has been growing at the expense of savings and loans, as Figure 9.1 shows. These shifts do not mean that savings and loans' loan volume is shrinking: Figure 9.2 demonstrates that the market volume of home-purchase loans in covered cities is growing rapidly. And while commercial bank volume doubled between 1992 and 1995, mortgage companies' volume almost tripled.

Chapter 8 pointed out a distinctive "Southwestern" pattern for population-adjusted financial offices. This pattern is demonstrated clearly in Figure 9.3.

(text continued on p. 186)

Table 9.2 **A Standardized Measure of Borrower Disadvantage in Seven Western cities, 1996**

	All lenders	Small in-state banks	Large banks w/in-state branches	Large banks w/no in-state branches	Savings and loans	Mortgage com-panies
Equiproportional borrower characteristics						
Income-related disadvantage						
Lower-income applicants	-9.0		-14.3	-13.0	-7.7	-8.0
Lower-income areas	-12.7	-44.1		-43.3	-21.7	-9.7
Total income disadvantage	-21.7	-44.1	-14.3	-56.3	-29.4	-17.7
Minority disadvantage						
Native American disadv.	-44.7			-43.8	-39.0	-40.4
African-American disadv.	-25.1	-35.7		-48.5	-48.2	-17.1
Asian-American disadv.						
Hispanic disadvantage	-16.1		-14.0		-18.1	-16.2
Minority area disadv.	-13.4		-7.2		-19.5	
Total minority disadv.	-99.3	-35.7	-21.2	-92.3	-124.8	-73.7
Total disadvantage	*-120.9*	*-79.8*	*-35.5*	*-148.6*	*-154.2*	*-91.4*
States' own borrower characteristics						
Income-related disadvantage						
Lower-income applicants	-9.6		-15.3	-13.8	-8.2	-8.5
Lower-income areas	-16.4	-57.0		-28.1	-28.1	-12.5
Total income disadvantage	-26.0	-57.0	-15.3	-41.9	-36.2	-21.0
Minority disadvantage						
Native American disadv.	-5.1			-5.0	-4.4	-4.6
African-American disadv.	-5.2	-7.4		-10.0	-9.9	-3.5
Asian-American disadv.						
Hispanic disadvantage	-41.3		-35.8		-46.3	-41.5
Minority area disadv.	-15.0		-11.0	-34.0	-21.9	
Total minority disadv.	-66.5	-7.4	-46.8	-49.0	-82.6	-49.6
Total disadvantage	*-92.5*	*-64.4*	*-62.1*	*-90.9*	*-118.8*	*-70.6*

Note: "Equiproportional" disadvantage assumes there are 100 members of each minority (Native American, African-American, Asian-American, and Hispanic) represented in a hypothetical set of 1,000 borrowers; that 167 of these borrowers will apply for home loans in high-minority areas; that 333 of these individuals are lower-income; and that 167 of these 1,000 individuals will apply for homes in lower-income areas. The figures for states' own borrower characteristics assume these minority and lower-income categories occur in this fictitious population of 1,000 individuals in the same proportions as among actual borrowers.

Table 9.3 **A Standardized Measure of Borrower Disadvantage in Eight Eastern Cities, 1996**

	All lenders	Small in-state banks	Large banks w/in-state branches	Large banks w/no in-state branches	Savings and loans	Mortgage companies
Equiproportional borrower characteristics						
Income-related disadvantage						
Lower-income applicants	-6.3	-4.3		-7.3	-11.7	
Lower-income areas	-10.2		-17.7	-21.0		-13.2
Total income disadvantage	-16.5	-4.3	-17.7	-28.4	-11.7	-13.2
Minority disadvantage						
Native American disadv.	-31.4	-62.0	-29.4	-73.9	-47.3	
African-American disadv.	-28.9	-50.3	-36.0	-36.7	-39.2	-15.3
Asian-American disadv.				13.8		
Hispanic disadvantage	-7.7	-5.5		-16.7	-28.8	
Minority area disadv.				-15.7	-19.0	10.5
Total minority disadv.	-68.0	-117.8	-65.4	-129.2	-134.3	-4.8
Total disadvantage	*-84.5*	*-122.1*	*-83.1*	*-157.6*	*-146.0*	*-18.0*
States' own borrower characteristics						
Income-related disadvantage						
Lower-income applicants	-6.5	-4.4		-7.5	-12.0	
Lower-income areas	-9.5		-16.4	-19.5		-12.2
Total income disadvantage	-16.0	-4.4	-16.4	-27.1	-12.0	-12.2
Minority disadvantage						
Native American disadv.	-1.3	-2.5	-1.2	-3.0	-1.9	
African-American disadv.	-23.2	-40.3	-28.9	-29.4	-31.4	-12.3
Asian-American disadv.				3.3		
Hispanic disadvantage	-2.0	-1.4		-4.3	-7.5	
Minority area disadv.				-10.2	-12.3	6.8
Total minority disadv.	-26.4	-44.3	-30.0	-43.6	-53.1	-5.5
Total disadvantage	*-42.4*	*-48.7*	*-46.5*	*-70.7*	*-65.1*	*-17.7*

Note: See notes to Table 9.2.

Figure 9.1 **Average Market Share in Selected Southwestern and Midwestern Cities, Home-Purchase Loans, 1992, 1995, and 1996**

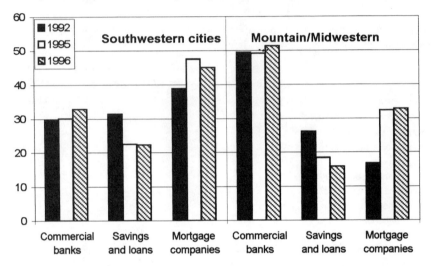

Source: All home-loan figures in this chapter are based on HMDA data.
Note: All figures depict market share in percentage terms.

Figure 9.2 **Market Volume in Selected Southwestern and Midwestern Cities, Home-Purchase Loans Made, 1992 and 1995**

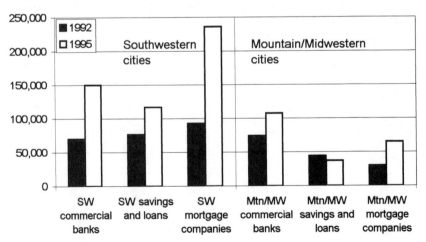

Figure 9.3 **Financial Offices per 100,000 Population in Selected Southwestern Banking Markets, 1996**

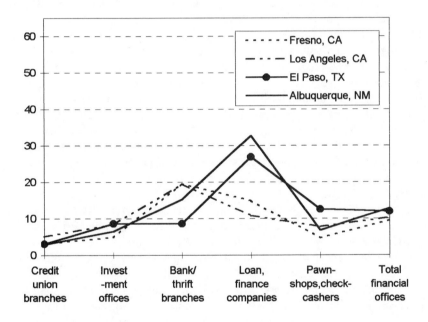

Source: All figures showing financial offices in this chapter are based on the author's calculations using the ProCD database.

Note: Figures show financial offices of each type per 100,000 residents.

There are *extremely* low numbers of credit union and investment offices, relatively few bank and thrift branches, and a modest number of pawnbrokers and check-cashing stores operating in the four cities surveyed. The sole significant difference comes in loan brokers: the two California cities, Los Angeles and Fresno, have much lower population-adjusted levels of these offices than do El Paso and Albuquerque.

Acquiring Banks and Merger Activity

California's banking markets have been largely controlled by California-head-quartered banks. Exceptions are few: Citicorp has had a network of nondepository loan-production offices in place for over a decade; and Comerica recently began California operations after its 1992 takeover of the Bank of Industry and its November 1996 acquisition of Metrobank.[4]

In the meantime, California's two merging banks have been active elsewhere in this region. BankAmerica (BoA) has purchased numerous banks, including Security Pacific National Bank in April 1996, Sandia Federal Savings Association of New Mexico in March 1991, Seafirst Corporation of Washington in January 1996, and Continental Illinois in September 1994. In the wake of these and other purchases, BoA has established branch networks in a range of states including New Mexico, Washington, Florida, Arizona, Nevada, and Oregon. The growth of Wells Fargo National Bank, California's other remaining acquiring bank, has unfolded very differently. Where BoA has been incorporating market areas steadily and incrementally, Wells has expanded its range in a couple of decisive leaps. Wells Fargo bought the Bank of North Texas in January 1995, Texas National Bank in July 1995, and First Interstate in April 1996. Since First Interstate had an established network of affiliated banks outside California, this last acquisition gave Wells branches in many Western states.

Merging banks headquartered outside the Southwest have also acquired market share in Southwestern markets outside of California. Norwest, as noted in chapter 7, has a branch network in New Mexico, due to its 1993 acquisition of Rocky Mountain Bankshares. Boatmen's Bancshares of Missouri was an active acquiring bank before its 1996 acquisition. Boatmen's entered Texas via acquisition in 1988.[5] Its most significant acquisition was that of Bank IV, Kansas' largest commercial bank; but this came in October 1996, less than a year before NationsBank purchased Boatmen's in June 1997. The most spectacular merger in American banking history was announced in spring 1998: the "merger of equals" between BoA and NationsBank, with Charlotte designated as the new bank's headquarters.

Denial Rates, Market Share, and Fair Share

What patterns in denial rates and market share are found in Southwestern residential-credit markets? Figure 9.4 presents data on overall denial rates by market area for 1996 home-purchase loans, and also detailed results for the three subsets of commercial banks.[6] New Mexico and Texas have overall denial rates almost double those in all the California market areas included. As discussed above, this difference arises in part because mortgage companies have much higher denial rates in these two states than in California. Figure 9.4 shows that in the three coastal California market areas, denial rates are tightly bunched for all bank types. However, in the inland California, New Mexico, and Uexas cities included here, merging banks in-state have high denial rates relative to the average, while small in-state banks are lower than the average.

Market-share data for home-purchase applications in Southwestern markets are displayed in Figures 9.5 and 9.6. Figure 9.5 shows that mortgage companies have a disproportionately high share of applications in lower-income areas in all these urban clusters; that merging banks without in-state branches have disproportionately low market shares in lower-income areas in all these clusters except for Los Angeles; and that savings and loans have disproportionately low market shares in four of the six market areas shown. The same pattern is found for high-minority areas. A similar pattern is found in the market shares for minority and lower-income applicants. Figure 9.6 depicts lender proportions of minority applicants for 1996 home-purchase loans. Mortgage companies have a higher-than-average share of minority applicants, and savings and loans a below-average share, in all six market areas. Merging banks without in-state branches have below-average shares of minority applicants everywhere except the two Southern California market areas.

Fair-share statistics for loans made in these Southwestern cities are presented in Table 9.4; unlike in chapter 7, no figures for applications are shown. In high-minority areas, nonbank lenders have consistently higher fair-share scores than do commercial banks. Among banks, small banks consistently outperform merging banks. Merging banks consistently have scores below the fair-share benchmark level of 25 percent for minority areas; and among these banks, banks headquartered out-of-state perform far worse on average than banks headquartered in-state—their scores often total less than half those of other lenders. The scores for Northern California cities often fall very near or below the minority-area benchmark. But the Texas scores are remarkably low; no lender group meets even half the fair-share standard, with merging banks without in-state branches performing worst. The bottom portion of Table 9.4 contains fair-share statistics for lower-income areas. The patterns for lower-income areas are virtually identical to those for high-minority areas. Nonbanks outperform banks; among banks, small in-state banks perform well, while merging banks headquartered out-of-state perform worst. Northern California's lenders as a whole skirt the fair-share benchmark of 33 percent, but Texas's lenders universally fall well short of it, especially large out-of-state banks.

(text continued on p. 192)

Figure 9.4 **Denial Rates by Lender Type in Selected California and Southwestern Cities, Home-Purchase Loans, 1996**

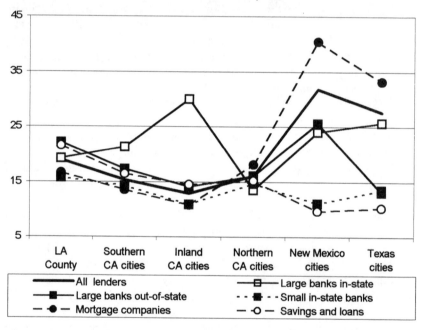

*Note:*Figures depict denial rates as percentage of approved and denied loans only.

Figure 9.5 **Market Share in Lower-Income Areas of Selected California and Southwestern Cities, Home-Purchase Loans, 1996**

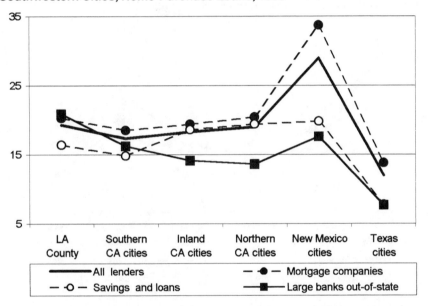

Note: Lower-income areas are defined as the third of every city's census tracts with the lowest 1990 median incomes. Figures denote percentages of all loan applications.

Figure 9.6 **Minorities in the Applicant Pool of Selected California and Southwestern Cities, Home-Purchase Loans, 1996**

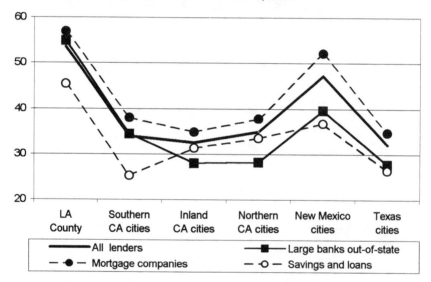

Note: Figures denote percentage of all race-identified applicants.

Table 9.4 **Fair-Share Scores by Lender Type for Loans Made, Purchase Loans in Western and Midwestern Cities, 1996**

	All lenders	Non-bank lenders	All commer-cial bks	Small in-state banks	Large in-state banks	Large out-of-state banks with branches	Large out-of-state banks without branches
Ratio of minority-area to other-area loans among purchase loans							
California cities							
Los Angeles CA	28.9	28.6	29.8	36.4	*14.0*	20.6	30.0
Southern Cal cities	33.6	35.5	28.9	46.1	20.0	31.2	22.8
Inland Cal cities	31.0	32.6	24.8	34.7	22.8	13.0	20.4
Northern Cal cities	25.5	27.1	22.1	33.2	27.1	13.4	18.2
CA cities median	**30.0**	**30.6**	**26.8**	**35.5**	**21.4**	**17.0**	**21.6**
Other Southwestern cities							
New Mexico cities	33.8	36.6	26.6	33.7	NA	23.1	18.5
Texas cities	11.1	10.9	11.5	14.5	NA	10.6	6.1
SW cities median	**22.4**	**23.7**	**19.1**	**24.1**		**16.9**	**12.3**
Mountain and Midwestern cities							
Mtns/Plains cities	28.9	37.5	*21.1*	*20.7*	NA	26.6	23.6
Iowa cities	24.7	22.6	27.7	33.5	NA	24.1	12.5
Minnesota cities	31.9	33.1	30.9	26.2	34.1	32.2	21.2
Indiana cities	31.9	39.8	23.1	21.8	NA	24.8	16.8
Plains/MW median	**30.4**	**35.3**	**25.4**	**24.0**	**34.1**	**25.7**	**19.0**
Ratio of lower-income area to other-area loans among purchase loans							
California cities							
Los Angeles CA	54.3	54.3	54.5	73.6	*24.8*	34.8	53.9
Southern Cal cities	60.5	60.4	60.9	81.5	*41.3*	30.1	59.2
Inland Cal cities	40.0	42.8	29.3	34.6	28.2	11.0	27.1
Northern Cal cities	35.4	36.8	32.6	42.8	36.3	15.7	28.7
CA cities median	**47.2**	**48.5**	**43.6**	**58.2**	**32.3**	**22.9**	**41.3**
Other Southwestern cities							
New Mexico cities	44.6	46.5	39.7	72.2	NA	32.7	25.1
Texas cities	20.0	20.7	18.3	23.7	NA	16.0	11.7
SW cities median	**32.3**	**33.6**	**29.0**	**48.0**		**24.4**	**18.4**
Mountain and Midwestern cities							
Mtn/Plains cities	50.0	51.5	48.5	84.0	NA	41.7	69.8
Iowa cities	32.6	33.3	31.7	34.5	NA	29.3	26.7
Minnesota cities	37.1	38.6	35.8	41.9	39.5	27.1	23.8
Indiana cities	37.6	47.1	27.3	29.2	NA	29.9	26.1
Mtn/MW median	**37.4**	**42.9**	**33.8**	**38.2**	**39.5**	**29.6**	**26.4**

Note: All ratios are adjusted for available owner-occupied units in every census tract. Italicized ratios fall below the fair-share benchmarks of 33 for minority areas and 50 for lower-income areas. The methodology used here is introduced in chapter 7.

Probit Analysis

Model 1 probit equations were run for four different California market areas, for New Mexico's three metropolitan areas, and for the five Texas metropolitan areas listed on page 174. For each area, equations were run first for all lenders; and also for mortgage companies, savings and loans, and three categories of banks—small in-state banks, merging banks with in-state branches, and merging banks without in-state branches. The large number of estimations conducted here make it impractical to report detailed results as per Tables 8.1 and 8.2. The only variables whose coefficients are reported comprehensively are those for minority and lower-income applicants and those for high-minority and lower-income neighborhoods.[7]

The coefficients estimated for minority applicants in Southwestern cities are reported in Tables 9.5a and 9.5b. First consider the "all lenders" column. In all six city clusters estimated, African-American loan applicants are at a statistically significant disadvantage relative to nonblack applicants.[8] Native American applicants are at a disadvantage in four of six city clusters. However, while Hispanic applicants are at a disadvantage in three city clusters, they have a statistically significant advantage in the other three. Asian-American applicants are statistically indistinguishable from other loan applicants in four city clusters; in the remaining two, Los Angeles and Texas, they have an advantage.

The remaining columns contain probit results for different lender types. For both bank and nonbank lenders, African-American and Native American loan applicants consistently have significant negative coefficients. The other minority coefficients, however, are extremely variable. Asian-American applicants have no statistically significant differences from other applicants in inland California and New Mexico cities; but in the other city clusters they have both advantages and disadvantages with different sets of lenders—in the same market areas. Sign-reversal—the occurrence of both significant positive and negative coefficients—also occurs for Hispanic applicants in the four California markets.

Table 9.6 presents coefficients for minority neighborhoods, which demonstrate the degree of disadvantage for applicants seeking homes there. In the all-lender probits, minority neighborhoods are at a disadvantage in three city clusters, and at an advantage in one, Texas. For the five lender subgroups estimated, applications for homes in minority neighborhoods are at a disadvantage for between one and three of the lender groups—except for inland California and New Mexico, in which the minority neighborhood variable is invariably insignificant. Coefficients for lower-income applicants (those with the one-third of all applicants with the lowest incomes) and for lower-income neighborhoods are presented in Table 9.7. Lower-income applicants and areas are often at a statistical disadvantage; but again there is substantial variability among markets and within markets.

(text continued on p. 197)

Table 9.5a **Coefficients for Applicant Race, Probit Equations for Home-Purchase Loans in Selected California Cities, 1996**

	All lenders	Small in-state banks	Large banks w/in-state branches	Large banks w/no in-st. branches	Savings and loans	Mortgage companies
Los Angeles County						
Native American	-0.139	-0.186	-0.442	0.163	-0.410	-0.196
	(0.07)**	(0.388)	(1.410)	(14.0)NR	NR**	(0.102)*
African-American	-0.210	0.032	-0.355	-0.282	-0.496	-0.156
	(0.018)***	(0.089)	(0.390)	(3.59)NR	NR***	(0.026)***
Asian-American	0.067	-0.037	0.541	-0.105	0.126	0.017
	(0.015)***	(0.063)	(0.251)**	(2.76)NR	NR	(0.024)
Hispanic	0.064	0.198	-0.098	0.008	-0.156	0.112
	(.012)***	(0.062)***	(0.254)	(2.50)NR	NR***	(0.018)***
Southern California Cities						
Native American	-0.260	-0.426	-0.44	-0.284	-0.349	-0.165
	(0.048)***	(0.426)*	(0.209)**	(0.239)	(0.123)***	(0.071)**
African-American	-0.247	-0.213	-0.526	-0.450	-0.412	-0.158
	(0.020)***	(0.125)*	(0.117)***	(0.126)***	(0.052)***	(0.028)***
Asian-American	-0.016	-0.246	0.332	-0.138	-0.018	0.002
	(0.016)	(0.085)***	(0.072)***	(0.074)*	(0.034)	(0.026)
Hispanic	0.032	0.099	-0.147	-0.219	-0.107	0.099
	(0.011)***	(0.062)	(0.056)***	(0.069)***	(0.027)***	(0.016)***
Inland California Cities						
Native American	-0.100	0.015	-0.672	-0.549	0.045	-0.025
	(0.082)	(0.326)	(0.45)NR	(0.043)	(0.237)	(0.122)
African-American	-0.264	-0.549	-0.138	-0.482	-0.420	-0.191
	(0.032)***	(0.117)***	(0.21)NR	(0.222)**	(0.075)***	(.046)***
Asian-American	0.026	0.071	0.199	0.013	-0.046	0.043
	(0.030)	(0.122)	(0.13)NR	(0.208)	(0.057)	(0.047)
Hispanic	0.041	-0.071	-0.136	-0.068	-0.056	0.071
	(0.019)**	(0.079)	(0.08)NR*	(0.137)	(0.043)	(0.28)**
Northern California cities						
Native American	-0.149	-0.159	-0.203	-0.067	-0.138	-0.186
	(0.261)	(0.600)	(0.277)	(0.182)	(7.55)	(0.10)*
African-American	-0.360	-0.877	-0.464	-0.292	-0.343	-0.310
	(0.094)***	(0.181)***	(0.082)***	(0.070)***	(2.33)	(0.038)***
Asian-American	-0.004	0.102	0.064	0.136	-0.016	0.070
	(0.053)	(0.093)	(0.045)	(0.034)***	(1.220)	(0.024)***
Hispanic	-0.152	-0.198	-0.122	-0.136	-0.309	0.08
	(0.068)**	(0.124)	(0.052)**	(0.053)**	(1.680)	(0.028)***

(Table 9.5 continues on the next page)

Table 9.5b **Coefficients for Applicant Race, Probit Equations for Home-Purchase Loans in Southwestern Cities, 1996**

	All lenders	Small in-state banks	Large banks w/in-state branches	Large banks w/no in-st. branches	Savings and loans	Mortgage companies
New Mexico cities						
Native American	-0.512	0.074	-0.433	-0.239	-0.573	-0.422
	(0.049)NR***	(0.630)	(0.17)**	(0.251)	(0.14)***	(0.056)NR**
African-American	-0.466	-0.956	-0.153	-0.483	-0.439	-0.336
	(0.072)NR***	(0.313)***	(0.255)	(0.260)*	(0.165)***	(0.094)NR**
Asian-American	-0.109	-0.482	0.133	0.182	-0.203	-0.106
	(0.084)NR	(0.445)	(0.314)	(0.409)	(0.205)	(0.104)NR
Hispanic	-0.302	-0.095	-0.213	-0.096	-0.344	-0.269
	(0.020)NR***	(0.110)	(0.065)***	(0.080)	(0.051)***	(0.024)NR***
Texas cities						
Native American	-0.151	-0.028	0.014	NA	-0.202	-0.152
	(0.060)**	(0.247)	(0.028)		(0.166)	(0.082)*
African-American	-0.223	-0.301	-0.374	-0.447	-0.235	-0.258
	(0.017)***	(0.066)***	(0.048)***	(0.080)***	(0.047)***	(0.025)***
Asian-American	0.161	-0.035	-0.152	0.452	0.144	0.155
	(0.031)***	(0.123)	(0.081)*	(0.146)***	(0.069)**	(0.050)***
Hispanic	-0.095	-0.065	-0.165	-0.280	-0.112	-0.112
	(0.012)***	(0.051)	(0.040)***	(0.070)***	(0.031)***	(0.017)***

*** denotes significance at a 1% confidence level, ** significance at 5%, * at 10%.
Note: Standard errors are shown in parentheses below each coefficient. Coefficients for Texas and for savings and loans in Los Angeles are taken from probits for 1995 data.

Table 9.6 **Coefficients for Minority Neighborhoods, Probit Equations for Home-Purchase Loans in Western and Midwestern Cities, 1996**

	All lenders	Small in-state banks	Large banks w/in-state branches	Large banks w/no in-st. branches	Savings and loans	Mortgage companies
Los Angeles	-0.044	-0.069	-0.03	-0.023	0.005	-0.069
	(.018)**	(0.087)	(0.392)	(3.60)NR	NR	(.027)***
Southern Cal. cities	-0.039	-0.11	-0.14	-0.138	-0.047	-0.049
	(0.013)***	(0.074)	(0.066)**	(0.081)*	(0.032)	(0.019)**
Inland Cal. cities	-0.001	-0.011	-0.082	-0.006	-0.009	-0.007
	(0.020)	(0.074)	(0.094)NR	(0.145)	(0.045)	(0.029)
Northern Cal. cities	(0.138)	0.079	-0.081	-0.168	-0.12	-0.133
	(0.057)	(0.114)	(0.048)	(0.041)***	(1.400)	(0.024)***
New Mexico cities	-0.048	-0.052	-0.013	-0.102	0.040	-0.047
	(0.034)NR	(0.192)	(0.110)	(0.150)	(0.092)	(0.041)
Texas cities	0.034	-0.082	-0.084	-0.061	0.011	0.053
	(0.018)*	(0.069)	(0.053)	(0.117)	(0.048)	(0.025)**
Great Plains cities	-0.010	-0.247	-0.082	0.017	-0.179	0.008
	(0.027)	(0.116)**	(0.089)	(0.097)	(0.057)***	(0.042)
Iowa cities	0.057	0.137	-0.019	-0.166	0.039	0.033
	(0.046)	(0.124)	(0.114)	(0.142)NR	(0.107)	(0.079)
Indiana cities	0.061	0.089	0.013	-0.171	0.002	0.108
	(0.023)***	(0.062)	(0.061)	(0.090)NR*	(0.059)	(0.037)***
Minnesota cities	0.091	0.053	0.01	-0.138	-0.017	0.160
	(0.032)***	(0.084)	(0.050)	(0.077)*	(0.070)	(0.058)***

*** denotes significance at the 1% level, ** at the 5% level, * at the 10% level.

Note: NR means an equation is statistically unreliable. Minority neighborhoods consist of the one quarter of census tracts in every metropolitan area with the highest proportion of minority residents.

Table 9.7 **Coefficients for Lower-Income Applicants and Neighborhoods, Probit Equations for Home-Purchase Loans in Southwestern Cities, 1996**

	All lenders	Small in-state banks	Large banks w/in-state branches	Large banks w/no in-st. branches	Savings and loans	Mortgage companies
Los Angeles County						
Lower-income applicants	-0.036	-0.016	0.014	-0.021	-0.035	-0.041
	(.004)***	(0.018)	(0.073)	(0.73)NR	NR	(.0055)***
Lower-income areas	-0.058	0.073	0.059	-0.035	-0.104	-0.041
	(.016)***	(0.082)	(0.351)	(3.19)NR	NR	(.024)***
Southern California cities						
Lower-income applicants	-0.021	-0.011	-0.024	-0.030	-0.008	-0.026
	(0.003)***	(0.020)	(0.016)	(0.493)	(0.008)	(0.005)***
Lower-income areas	-0.081	-0.218	-0.005	-0.069	-0.112	-0.012
	(0.014)***	(0.074)***	(0.062)	(2.10)	(0.032)***	(0.021)
Inland California cities						
Lower-income applicants	-0.015	-0.007	0.003	0.028	0.001	-0.035
	(0.006)**	(0.025)	(0.03)NR	(0.045)	(0.014)	(0.009)***
Lower-income areas	-0.013	-0.004	0.101	-0.044	-0.074	0.047
	(0.023)	(0.097)	(0.09)NR	(0.170)	(0.050)	(0.033)
Northern California cities						
Lower-income applicants	-0.018	-0.055	0.001	-0.023	-0.017	-0.018
	(0.160)	(0.030)*	(0.013)	(0.011)**	(0.380)	(0.007)***
Lower-income areas	-0.053	0.126	0.013	-0.056	-0.057	-0.063
	(0.059)	(0.124)	(0.049)	(0.044)	(1.440)	(0.025)**
New Mexico cities						
Lower-income applicants	-0.012	0.104	-0.061	-0.149	-0.050	0.011
	(0.01)NR	(0.046)**	(0.028)**	(0.037)***	(0.021)**	(0.01)NR
Lower-income areas	0.068	-0.106	-0.150	-0.056	-0.183	0.106
	(0.03)NR	(0.200)	(0.110)	(0.145)	(0.087)**	(0.04)NR**
Texas cities						
Lower-income applicants	-0.043	-0.004	-0.022	-0.028	-0.025	-0.033
	(0.004)***	(0.016)	(0.013)*	(0.022)	(0.010)**	(0.006)***
Lower-income areas	-0.066	0.088	-0.045	-0.124	-0.101	-0.053
	(0.017)***	(0.067)	(0.053)	(0.111)	(0.045)**	(0.023)**

*** denotes significance at a 1% level, ** significance at 5%, * at 10%.
Note: Standard errors are shown in parentheses below each coefficient.

The variability found in race and low-income coefficients for Southwestern cities supports the core points made in chapter 7 about the ambiguities of information formation and use in credit markets with small borrowers. To restate these points: First, lenders do not simply make credit-market decisions based on a standardized set of information with well-known statistical properties; instead, different lenders use different kinds of information, and interpret similar informational bits differently. Second, lenders may use behavioral signals, presumptive signals, or both, in assessing creditworthiness. Race and lower-income status are clearly candidates for presumptive signals. Third, the kind of information generated by a given lender depends in part on that lender's own efforts, programs, and institutional structure. In sum, the variation in sign and magnitude of race and lower-income coefficients suggests that different lenders construct information about the same objective circumstances differently, and have divergent assessments of the significance of these factors. Thus, it is only to be expected that these coefficients will vary substantially. The results in Tables 9.5 to 9.7 and elsewhere in this chapter resoundingly support the idea that financial structure matters in credit markets: How efficiently these markets work depends in part on what kind of financial intermediaries are in place, on what they do, on what they consider information, and on how they collect this information.

The nonuniformity that pervades Tables 9.5 to 9.7, for both city clusters and lender subgroups, is itself of central importance for our investigation. Recall that the purpose of Model 1 is to compare the behavior of different lender subgroups—especially merging banks versus other banks—using an economical and yet representative model of loan approval. Partitioning lenders into subgroups sets up an analytical "horse race" for lender groups, permitting us to assess their relative performance vis-à-vis minority and low-income applicants and areas. The disadvantage method introduced above provides a means for figuring out who wins this race, since it converts a multidimensional assessment of lender behavior into one score.

Whether any systematic comparison of one lender's race and lower-income coefficients with another's, as in our "horse race," is valid, lenders depend on one key assumption: that the variation between the subgroups being tested—say, between African-American applicants and other applicants—is greater than the variation within the members of this subgroup from one lender type to another. To state this less formally, the "horse race" is legitimate if African-American borrowers who file applications with different lender types have more in common with one another in economic terms than does every lender type's African-American applicants with the nonblack applicants with that lender type. The econometric literature on discrimination in credit markets, reviewed in chapter 8, suggests that this assumption *is* allowable. So comparisons across lender types within common market areas are appropriate.[9]

Table 9.8 reports disadvantage scores for Southwestern cities. Both lower-income and minority disadvantage scores are computed, following the method introduced on page 178; these are combined into a total disadvantage figure for every lender subgroup in every city cluster. The disadvantage calculation for the all-lenders probit, displayed in the far left column, finds New Mexico with the highest total disadvantage, and the inland California cities and Los Angeles with the lowest. There is again considerable city-to-city and lender-to-lender variability, due largely to the use of only statistically significant coefficients in disadvantage calculations. Figures 9.7 to 9.12 are designed to facilitate interpretation of these Southwestern-cities results by depicting disadvantage scores graphically. Each figure presents disadvantage scores as calculated using the "uniform proportions" method; recall that a *negative* disadvantage score indicates a lesser chance of loan approval, all things being equal. For ease of interpretation, these figures depict disadvantage scores on an inverted scale. So any column extending upward from zero represents disadvantage; conversely, a column extending downward indicates advantage. To facilitate comparison, all disadvantage figures use a uniform y-axis, which varies from −190 to 50.

Taken as a whole, these six figures contain relatively low disadvantage levels across lender groups—that is, relatively low skylines—in Los Angeles (Figure 9.7) and the inland California cities (Figure 9.9). By contrast, the highest across-the-board disadvantage and a Manhattan-like skyline is found in southern California cities (Figure 9.8) and New Mexico (Figure 9.11). The best way of determining sector-by-sector performance is to look across the results for the six city clusters. First consider mortgage companies. In five of the six cities, this sector's disadvantage profile is remarkably similar—a small amount of lower-income disadvantage and a slightly higher level of racial disadvantage, adding up to a smaller total disadvantage score than for most other lender types. The exception is New Mexico, where mortgage companies have a new lower-income advantage but a very high level of racial disadvantage. The savings and loan sector is characterized by minimal lower-income disadvantage and extremely high racial disadvantage in four of the six city clusters. The exceptions are northern California, where thrifts register a zero disadvantage score, and Texas, where their disadvantage level is equivalent to that of mortgage companies.

Merging banks without in-state offices have the same disadvantage pattern everywhere but Los Angeles County: a high overall level of disadvantage, driven especially by very high net racial disadvantage. Merging banks with in-state offices have the same approximate pattern in four of these five cities. In inland California, large banks in-state have the lowest disadvantage scores of any sector. In Los Angeles, large banks out-of-state register lower-income advantage and zero racial disadvantage; but large banks in-state register relative high disadvantage scores. Small banks have a complex pattern: In Los Angeles, small banks register zero lower-income disadvantage and positive racial advantage; in every other California probit, small banks have the worst disadvantage performance of any sector, led by racial disadvantage. In New Mexico and Texas, small banks' disadvantage performance is somewhat better than average.

(text continued on p. 203)

Table 9.8 **Borrower Race/Lower-Income Disadvantage in California and Southwestern Cities, 1996**

	All lenders	Small in-state banks	Large banks w/in-state branches	Large banks w/no in-st. branches	Savings and loans	Mortgage com-panies
Equiproportional borrower characteristics						
Los Angeles County						
Lower-income disadv.	-21.7	0.0	0.0	26.4	0.0	-20.2
Minority disadv.	-28.1	19.8	-51.4	0.0	-104.2	-31.6
Total disadvantage	-49.8	19.8	-51.4	26.4	-104.2	-51.8
Southern California Cities						
Lower-income disadv.	-20.2	-36.4	0.0	0.0	-18.7	-8.7
Minority disadv.	-54.0	-82.1	-98.2	-100.1	-86.8	-29.3
Total disadvantage	-74.2	-118.5	-98.2	-100.1	-105.5	-38.0
Inland California Cities						
Lower-income disadv.	-4.7	0.0	0.0	0.0	0.0	-11.7
Minority disadv.	-22.5	-54.9	-13.6	-45.8	-42.0	-12.4
Total disadvantage	-27.3	-54.9	-13.6	-45.8	-42.0	-24.0
Northern California Cities						
Lower-income disadv.	0.0	-16.5	0.0	-7.3	0.0	-16.0
Minority disadv.	-73.6	-87.7	-70.2	-56.6	0.0	-55.0
Total disadvantage	-73.6	-104.2	-70.2	-63.9	0.0	-70.9
New Mexico Cities						
Lower-income disadv.	11.4	32.9	-19.3	-49.6	-44.9	16.8
Minority disadv.	-125.7	-95.6	-62.3	-43.5	-135.6	-102.6
Total disadvantage	-114.3	-62.7	-81.6	-93.1	-180.5	-85.8
Texas Cities						
Lower-income disadv.	-25.3	0.0	-6.6	0.0	-23.8	-19.4
Minority disadv.	-25.2	-30.1	-51.1	-27.4	-21.0	-26.8
Total disadvantage	-50.6	-30.1	-57.7	-27.4	-44.9	-46.2
States' own borrower characteristics						
New Mexico cities						
Lower-income disadv.	-83.7	-36.7	-21.5	-55.3	-69.6	-30.1
Minority disadv.	-129.0	-3.1	-90.7	-1.4	-146.6	-114.0
Total disadvantage	-212.7	-39.8	-112.2	-56.7	-216.2	-144.1
Texas cities						
Lower-income disadv.	-22.5	0.0	-6.7	0.0	-19.5	-17.3
Minority disadv.	-29.4	-8.0	-38.5	-58.4	-26.0	-22.6
Total disadvantage	-51.9	-8.0	-45.2	-58.4	-45.6	-39.8

Source: Author's probit equations using 1996 HMDA home-purchase loans.
Note: Methodology is explained in the text.

Figure 9.7 **Residential Lending Disadvantage in Los Angeles County, 1996**

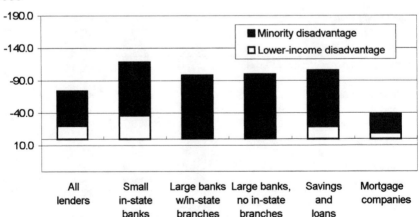

Note: All disadvantage figures shown in this chapter depict disadvantage per 1,000 hypothetical borrowers using the equiproportional method for Model 1 probits.

Figure 9.8 **Residential Lending Disadvantage in Southern California Cities, 1996**

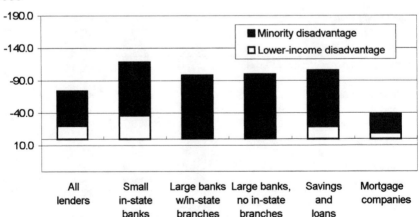

Note: Disadvantage is shown per 1,000 hypothetical borrowers.

Figure 9.9 **Residential Lending Disadvantage in Inland California Cities, 1996**

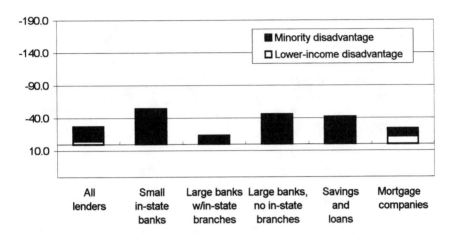

Note: Disadvantage is shown per 1,000 hypothetical borrowers.

Figure 9.10 **Residential Lending Disadvantage in Northern California Cities, 1996**

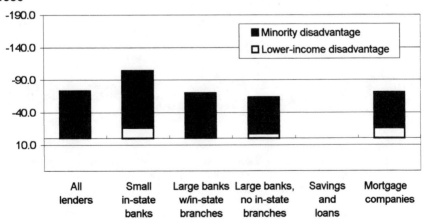

Note: Disadvantage is shown per 1,000 hypothetical borrowers.

Figure 9.11 **Residential Lending Disadvantage in New Mexico Cities, 1996**

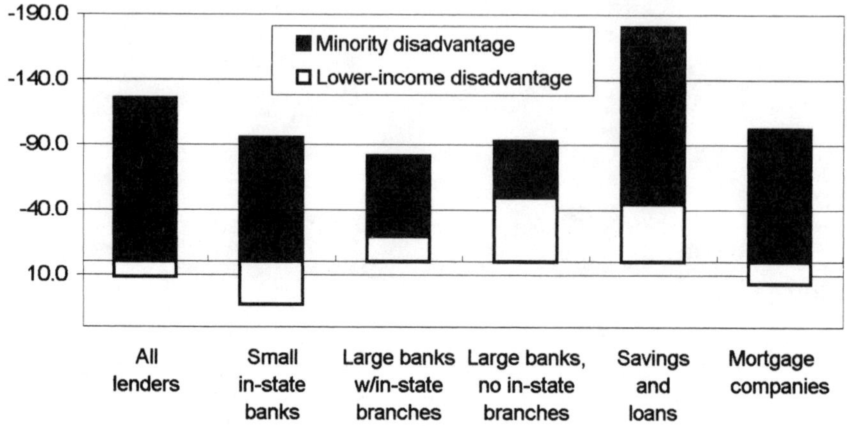

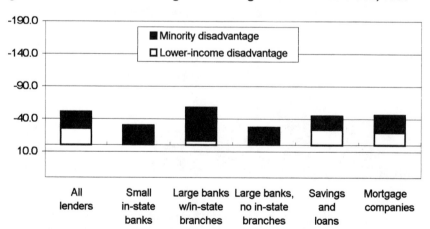

Note: Disadvantage is shown per 1,000 hypothetical borrowers.

Figure 9.12 **Residential Lending Disadvantage in Five Texas Cities, 1996**

Note: Disadvantage is shown per 1,000 hypothetical borrowers.

We might hypothesize that this scattershot performance by small banks reflects their adaptive role in urban credit markets. The niches they fill depend in part on the climate created by other, larger financial intermediaries, and in part on local circumstances. For example, the stellar Los Angeles performance is due in large part to the presence of numerous ethnic banks serving minority (especially Asian-American) client communities.

Summary

Taken together, this fair-share and probit analysis of minority and lower-income disadvantage in Southwestern home-purchase markets suggests several conclusions. Overall, nonbank lenders perform better than do banks, for both fair-share and disadvantage indices; and among nonbanks, mortgage companies outperform thrifts. This conclusion that mortgage companies are performing relatively well in racial and lower-income terms should be interpreted cautiously. As discussed above, some investigations have found that the lightly regulated nonbank lending sector, including some mortgage companies, has exploited minority borrowers and inner-city communities by imposing onerous terms on loans that banks will not make. It is not possible to confront this finding here due to data limitations; however, of relevance here is this study's finding (based on an analysis of denial rates) that mortgage companies compete head-to-head with banks in some places, and function as residual lenders elsewhere. This may also hold true within any sizable metropolitan area—so mortgage companies' strong fair-share performance may reflect their willingness to meet credit demands overlooked by others, *as well as* some mortgage companies' exploitation of poorly informed, vulnerable households in underserved neighborhoods.

Banks' overall performance is not good in the fair-share and disadvantage analysis conducted here. Small banks perform well in fair-share terms, but poorly in disadvantage. Merging banks, whether in-state or out-of-state, have poor results in our fair-share test and mediocre to bad results in our disadvantage test (with several exceptions).

Mountain/Plains and Midwestern Cities

The Mountain/Plains and Midwestern urban markets for home-purchase loans are dominated by commercial banks, which control about half the market (Figure 9.1). As in the Southwest, mortgage companies' market share has been growing, primarily at the expense of savings institutions. Figure 9.2 shows that these Mountain/Midwestern markets have grown much more slowly in recent years than have Southwestern markets.

Figures 9.13 and 9.14 present summary measures of financial infrastructure. The Mountain/Plains states have high population-adjusted levels of credit union branches, investment offices, and bank branches; by contrast, their informal

financial sectors are extremely small. The Midwestern cities examined here generally have population-adjusted levels of credit-union branches, investment offices, and bank branches higher than in the Southwest, but lower than in
Mountain/Plains cities. Interestingly, the two largest Midwestern cities in Figure
9.14 have financial infrastructures better, on average, than this region's smaller
cities. Terre Haute and Gary, Indiana, have the weakest financial infrastructures
of the cities included here.

Acquiring Banks and Merger Activity

In the Mountain/Great Plains states, two banks owned out-of-state have stood out
as important market players—Norwest and First Interstate. Norwest Bank entered Montana by purchasing the Montana Bank in April 1991 and Bank of
Montana in February 1995. It has been operating in North Dakota since January
1988 pursuant to a regional banking compact. Norwest entered Wyoming
through the acquisition of Wyoming National Bank in November 1988, and it
has had long-standing operations in South Dakota. And as mentioned above,
First Interstate has operated as a franchise bank for many years in Montana and
Wyoming, among other states. A third important out-of-state bank is First Security Bank of Utah, which has had a presence in Idaho for two decades, and it
established the First Security Bank of Idaho in June 1996. It also purchased three
Wyoming banks in the period 1990–1994 and established the First Security Bank
of Wyoming in November 1997.

   The Midwestern states included here have been battlegrounds of interstate
bank acquisition activity. Minnesota's Norwest and U.S. Bancorp (formerly First
Bank System) have been active acquirers, while Indiana and Iowa have been
frequent targets. We have already mentioned Norwest's presence in the Moun-
tain/Great Plains states. In June 1997, First Bank System of Minnesota acquired
Colorado National Bank; two months later, it bought U.S. Bancorp of Oregon,
which had established a market presence throughout the Northwest.[10] First Bank
changed its corporate name to U.S. Bancorp in August 1997 and acquired Piper
Jaffray, a Midwestern retail brokerage, in December 1997. These acquisitions
have made U.S. Bancorp the fourteenth largest commercial bank in the U.S.
Clearly its Northwestern U.S. strategy puts it on a collision course with Norwest.

   Meanwhile, Norwest is in competition with other acquiring banks in the Mid-
west per se. Norwest now operates a branch network in Indiana, headquartered in
Fort Wayne, and in Iowa. Banc One of Ohio also operates a commercial banking
operation in Indiana in 1988, thanks to its takeovers of First American National
Bancorp and American Fletcher National Bank. NBD Bank of Detroit acquired
Indiana National Bank's Hoosier State operations in 1993, and then was itself
acquired by First Chicago. And in October 1998, Banc One bought out First
Chicago NBD Bank. Keycorp of Cleveland entered Indiana by merging with
First Citizens Bancorp of Indiana in December 1994.

Figure 9.13 **Financial Offices per 100,000 Population in Selected Mountain/Plains Banking Markets, 1996**

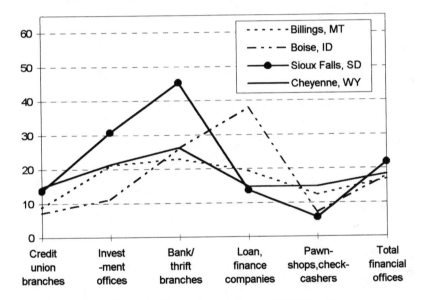

Note: Figures show financial offices of each type per 100,000 residents.

Figure 9.14 **Financial Offices per 100,000 Population in Selected Midwestern Banking Markets, 1996**

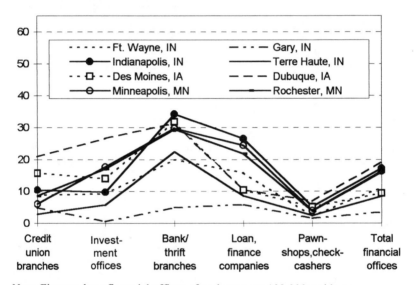

Note: Figures show financial offices of each type per 100,000 residents.

Iowa, which like Indiana has a long tradition of community banking, has also figured in the acquisition plans of out-of-state banks. As mentioned, Norwest has a branch network in this state, as does Firstar of Milwaukee. Firstar has also acquired banking operations in Illinois and Minnesota (the latter through acquiring American Commercial Bank in July 1996).

Denial Rates, Market Share, and Fair Share

Figure 9.15 sets out data on 1996 denial in the Mountain/Midwestern states, which are substantially lower than in the Southwest (Figure 9.4). This figure also shows that in the Mountain/Midwestern cities selected here, as in New Mexico and Texas, mortgage companies have the highest denial rates, followed by merging banks without in-state branches. The lowest denial rates are found at savings and loan associations, but small banks and merging banks with in-state branches also have low rates.

Market share statistics for lower-income areas are shown in Figure 9.16. Two patterns stand out in this figure. First, mortgage companies have the highest average market shares in lower-income areas, while savings and loans have below-average shares. Second, among commercial banks, small in-state banks consistently have higher market shares in lower-income areas than do both sets of merging banks. Fair-share calculations for these cities, shown in Table 9.4, demonstrate that nonbank lenders perform better than banks for both lower-income and high-minority areas. All categories of commercial bank lenders perform badly in the minority fair-share measure. In the lower-income fair-share test, small in-state banks perform better than both merging bank categories in every city cluster except Indiana.

Probit Analysis

The results for Mountain/Plains and Midwestern probit estimations using 1996 home-purchase loan data are presented in Tables 9.7 to 9.10. Table 9.7 demonstrates that lower-income applicants are at a statistically significant disadvantage only in Minnesota; and homes in lower-income areas have a disadvantage in loan applications only in the Mountain/Plains and Minnesota city clusters. These results for lower-income applicants and areas, and for minority areas, contrast with those for the Southwestern cities, in which these variables were chronically significant and usually negative.

Table 9.9 presents coefficients for applicant race. Minnesota's cities have the largest number of significant negative coefficients for every minority category. In the Mountain/Plains probits, Native American and Hispanic applicants are chronically at a disadvantage in the residential credit market; in Indiana and Iowa, African-American applicants are most likely to be at a disadvantage. Among lender subgroups, small in-state banks have the largest

(text continued on p. 212)

Figure 9.15 **Denial Rates by Lender Type in Selected Mountain and Midwestern Cities, Home-Purchase Loans, 1996**

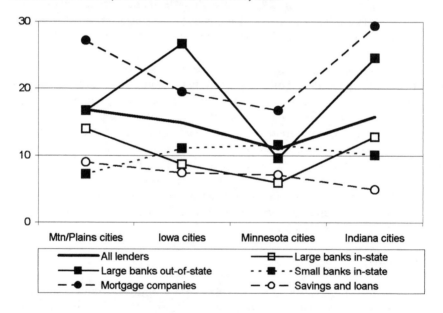

Note: Figures depict denial rates as percentage of approved and denied loans only.

Figure 9.16 **Market Share in Lower-Income Areas of Selected Mountain and Midwestern Cities, Home-Purchase Loans, 1996**

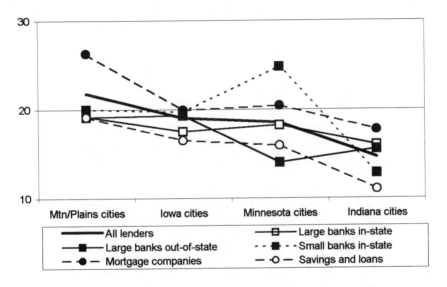

Note: Lower income areas here are the third of every city's census tracts with the lowest 1990 median incomes. Figures denote percentage of all applications.

Table 9.9 Coefficients for Applicant Race, Probit Equations for Home-Purchase Loans in Mountain and Midwestern Cities, 1996

	All lenders	Small in-state banks	Large banks w/in-state branches	Large banks w/no in-st. branches	Savings and loans	Mortgage com-panies
Mountain/Plains cities						
Native American	-0.346	-0.097	-0.249	-0.334	-0.382	-0.353
	(0.084)***	(0.402)	(0.217)	(0.254)	(0.177)**	(0.129)***
African-American	-0.240	-0.314	-0.401	0.049	-0.406	-0.206
	(0.117)**	(0.388)	(0.341)	(0.361)	(0.225)*	(0.201)
Asian-American	0.106	-0.002	0.491	NA	0.294	0.040
	(0.098)	(0.500)	(0.401)		(0.239)	(0.142)
Hispanic	-0.270	-0.295	-0.179	-0.375	-0.391	-0.214
	(0.042)***	(0.201)	(0.146)	(0.128)***	(0.083)***	(0.068)***
Iowa cities						
Native American	-0.207	0.11	-0.337	-0.203	0.065	-0.571
	(0.170)	(0.428)	(0.438)	(0.315)NR	(0.386)	(0.329)*
African-American	-0.406	-0.707	-0.312	-0.471	-0.512	-0.228
	(0.078)***	(0.202)***	(0.227)	(0.267)NR*	(0.177)***	(0.125)*
Asian-American	0.104	-0.064	0.207	-0.027	0.217	0.218
	(0.104)	(0.251)	(0.270)	(0.252)NR	(0.241)	(0.196)
Hispanic	-0.092	-0.427	-0.122	0.251	0.208	-0.02
	(0.075)	(0.202)**	(0.179)	(0.197)NR	(0.174)	(0.137)
Indiana cities						
Native American	-0.238	0.069	-0.415	0.386	-0.487	-0.219
	(0.11)**	(0.267)	(0.358)	(0.327)NR	(0.275)*	(0.176)
African-American	-0.134	-0.435	-0.002	-0.188	-0.493	0.067
	(0.030)***	(0.079)***	(0.077)	(0.106)NR*	(0.075)***	(0.046)
Asian-American	-0.013	-0.010	-0.060	-0.099	0.084	-0.060
	(0.074)	(0.179)	(0.178)	(0.306)NR	(0.202)	(0.122)
Hispanic	0.106	-0.239	0.141	-0.082	-0.202	0.31
	(0.047)**	(0.129)*	(0.116)	(0.166)NR	(0.113)*	(0.071)***
Minnesota cities						
Native American	-0.325	-0.715	-0.311	-0.59	-0.620	-0.065
	(0.116)***	(0.288)**	(0.183)*	(0.232)***	(0.228)***	(0.220)
African-American	-0.346	-0.226	-0.531	-0.541	-0.668	-0.196
	(0.053)***	(0.178)	(0.070)***	(0.113)***	(0.112)***	(0.099)**
Asian-American	0.049	0.076	-0.157	-0.041	-0.008	0.212
	(0.059)	(0.171)	(0.082)*	(0.116)	(0.113)	(0.107)**
Hispanic	-0.180	-0.595	-0.067	-0.563	-0.363	-0.233
	(0.071)**	(0.206)***	(0.111)	(0.162)***	(0.154)**	(0.130)*

*** denotes significance at a 1% confidence level, ** significance at 5%, * at 10%.
Note: Standard errors are shown in parentheses below each coefficient.

Table 9.10 **Coefficients for Lower-Income Applicants and Neighborhoods, Probit Equations for Home-Purchase Loans in Mountain/Midwestern Cities, 1996**

	All lenders	Small in-state banks	Large banks w/in-state branches	Large banks w/no in-st. branches	Savings and loans	Mortgage com-panies
Mtn/Plains cities						
Lower-income applicants	-0.006	-0.045	-0.016	0.012	0.005	-0.010
	(0.008)	(0.032)	(0.250)	(0.027)	(0.017)	(0.012)
Lower-income areas	-0.114	-0.055	-0.043	-0.232	-0.105	-0.060
	(0.027)***	(0.124)	(0.086)	(0.092)**	(0.057)*	(0.042)
Iowa cities						
Lower-income applicants	0.018	-0.004	-0.028	-0.005	0.016	0.059
	(0.018)*	(0.316)	(0.030)	(0.028)NR	(0.025)	(0.017)***
Lower-income areas	-0.054	-0.129	-0.110	-0.009	-0.110	-0.023
	(0.034)	(0.099)	(0.095)	(0.086)NR	(0.076)	(0.055)
Indiana cities						
Lower-income applicants	-0.005	0.015	-0.020	0.029	-0.005	0.0004
	(0.006)	(0.016)	(0.017)	(0.021)NR	(0.015)	(0.010)
Lower-income areas	-0.013	0.030	-0.065	-0.065	-0.060	0.015
	(0.024)	(0.061)	(0.062)	(0.083)NR	(0.060)	(0.037)
Minnesota cities						
Lower-income applicants	-0.021	-0.012	-0.016	-0.004	-0.028	0.001
	(0.009)**	(0.022)	(0.014)	(0.019)	(0.018)	(0.015)
Lower-income areas	-0.059	-0.111	-0.146	-0.036	-0.004	-0.026
	(0.028)**	(0.065)*	(0.049)***	(0.067)	(0.065)	(0.048)

*** denotes significance at a 1% confidence level, ** significance at 5%, * at 10%.
Note: Standard errors are shown in parentheses below each coefficient.

average disadvantage for minority applicants, followed by savings and loans and then by large banks with no in-state branches. Table 9.10 shows that location in a high-minority neighborhood conveys a disadvantage in loan approval in Mountain/Plains cities, but an advantage in Indiana and Minnesota to mortgage-company applicants. Otherwise, minority neighborhood status has no effect in these largely white city clusters.

The disadvantage scores for Mountain/Midwestern cities are presented in Table 9.11, with graphical depictions shown in Figures 9.17 to 9.20. These figures display a remarkable degree of intraregional diversity in disadvantage performance. The disadvantage skylines from the Southwestern cities (Figures 9.7 to 9.12) are relatively uniform in height compared with those found here. No evidence of lower-income disadvantage is found in Iowa and Indiana, but racial disadvantage is prominent in each city cluster. In three figures, merging banks with in-state branches have zero disadvantage scores. In the fourth, Minnesota, a sizable disadvantage score is registered. Minnesota (Figure 9.20) stands out from the other city clusters because of its consistently high skyline of primarily racial disadvantage, a pattern broken only by its mortgage companies' zero score. Savings and loans, small in-state banks, and merging banks without in-state branches all have positive disadvantage scores in all four city clusters. Mortgage companies have zero and negative scores in Minnesota and Indiana, but positive scores in the other two city clusters.

Northeastern Cities

Commercial banks dominate the market for home-purchase loans in the Northeast even more than in the Midwest. As Figure 9.21 shows, commercial banks' market share has remained in recent years at approximately 55 percent. Savings and loans' market share has eroded only slightly since 1992, in contrast to the other regions (see Figure 9.1). Mortgage companies have their regional market share, less than 30 percent. The Northeastern market, like the Southwestern, has a huge annual volume, as Figure 9.22 shows. This volume grew 42 percent between 1992 and 1995—almost identical to the 41 percent growth of the Mountain/Midwestern states, and much slower than the Southwestern city clusters' growth of 110 percent.

Financial infrastructures in eight Northeastern cities are portrayed in Figure 9.23. Philadelphia is better provisioned with offices of all types, on a population-weighted basis, than other cities. Two patterns emerge in financial infrastructures. The Massachusetts cities of Brockton, Springfield, and Lowell all have exceptionally low levels of every type of financial office except for credit union branches, which are plentiful. The remaining cities, all outside the Bay State, have a similar infrastructure pattern: relatively plentiful credit union branches; averages for investment offices and bank branches equal to the Mid-

(text continued on p. 218)

Table 9.11 **Borrower Race/Lower-Income Disadvantage in Mountain/Great Plains and Midwestern Cities, 1996**

	All lenders	Small in-state banks	Large banks w/in-state branches	Large banks w/no in-st. branches	Savings and loans	Mortgage com-panies
Equiproportional borrower characteristics						
Great Plains cities						
Lower-income disadv.	-19.0	0.0	0.0	-36.8	-15.8	0.0
Minority disadv.	-84.4	-39.2	0.0	-37.5	-140.3	-53.2
Total disadvantage	-103.4	-39.2	0.0	-74.3	-156.1	-53.2
Iowa cities						
Lower-income disadv.	5.4	0.0	0.0	0.0	0.0	19.6
Minority disadv.	-40.6	-111.3	0.0	-42.4	-51.2	-71.9
Total disadvantage	-35.2	-111.3	0.0	-42.4	-51.2	-52.3
Indiana cities						
Lower-income disadv.	0.0	0.0	0.0	0.0	0.0	0.0
Minority disadv.	-15.8	-65.0	0.0	-42.6	-111.3	49.0
Total disadvantage	-15.8	-65.0	0.0	-42.6	-111.3	49.0
Minnesota cities						
Lower-income disadv.	-16.0	-16.7	-24.4	0.0	0.0	0.0
Minority disadv.	-69.0	-127.4	-95.2	-187.2	-163.3	6.3
Total disadvantage	-85.0	-144.1	-119.6	-187.2	-163.3	6.3
States' own borrower characteristics						
Great Plains cities						
Lower-income disadv.	-23.8	0.0	0.0	-46.1	-19.8	0.0
Minority disadv.	-12.3	-15.0	0.0	-11.2	-25.8	-9.3
Total disadvantage	-36.1	-15.0	0.0	-57.3	-45.6	-9.3
Iowa cities						
Lower-income disadv.	5.7	0.0	0.0	0.0	0.0	20.6
Minority disadv.	-7.8	-21.5	0.0	-8.1	-9.8	-5.8
Total disadvantage	-2.1	-21.5	0.0	-8.1	-9.8	14.8
Indiana cities						
Lower-income disadv.	0.0	0.0	0.0	0.0	0.0	0.0
Minority disadv.	0.1	-31.1	0.0	-27.6	-35.6	19.0
Total disadvantage	0.1	-31.1	0.0	-27.6	-35.6	19.0
Minnesota cities						
Lower-income disadv.	-18.1	-19.2	-28.0	0.0	0.0	0.0
Minority disadv.	-0.6	-9.8	-19.0	-39.5	-24.2	18.7
Total disadvantage	-18.6	-29.0	-47.0	-39.5	-24.2	18.7

Source: Author's probit equations using 1996 HMDA home-purchase loans.
Note: Methodology is explained in the text.

Figure 9.17 **Residential Lending Disadvantage in Mountain/Great Plains Cities, Home-Purchase Loans, 1996**

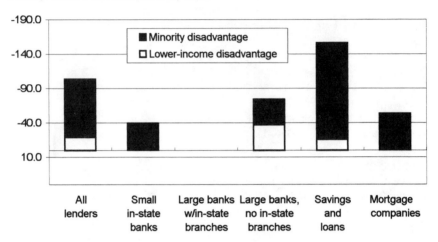

Note: Disadvantage is shown per 1,000 hypothetical borrowers.

Figure 9.18 **Residential Lending Disadvantage in Iowa Cities, Home-Purchase Loans, 1996**

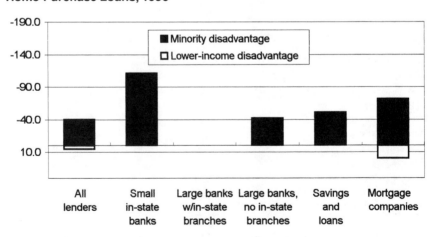

Note: Disadvantage is shown per 1,000 hypothetical borrowers

Figure 9.19 **Residential Lending Disadvantage in Indiana Cities, Home-Purchase Loans, 1996**

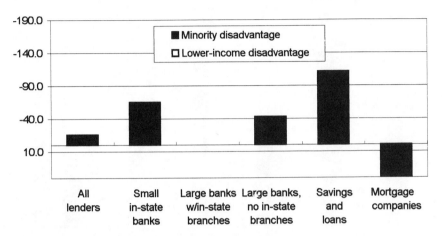

Note: Disadvantage is shown per 1,000 hypothetical borrowers.

Figure 9.20 **Residential Lending Disadvantage in Minnesota Cities, Home-Purchase Loans, 1996**

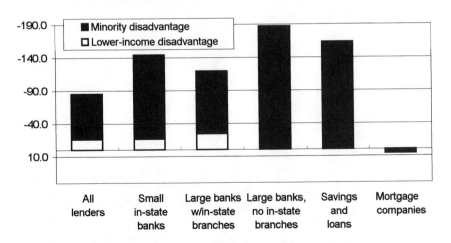

Note: Disadvantage is shown per 1,000 hypothetical borrowers.

Figure 9.21 **Average Market Share in Selected Eastern Cities, Home-Purchase Loans, 1992, 1995, and 1996**

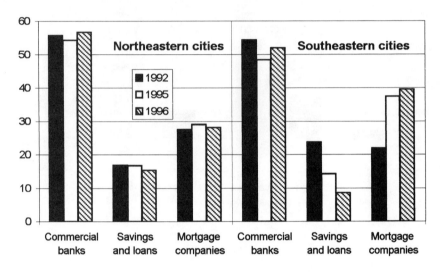

Note: Figures depict market share in percentage terms.

Figure 9.22 **Market Volume in Selected Eastern Cities, Home-Purchase Loans Made, 1992 and 1995**

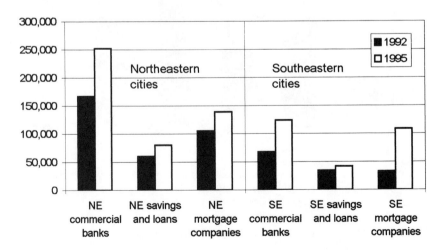

Figure 9.23 **Financial Offices per 100,000 Population in Selected Northeastern Banking Markets, 1996**

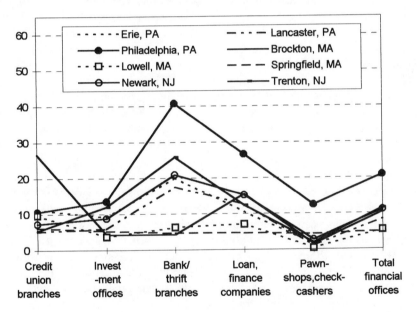

west (and higher than the Southwest); and very low relative numbers of informal financial offices.

Acquiring Banks and Merger Activity

The Northeastern states included here fall into several categories vis-à-vis acquisitions and mergers. New York, Pennsylvania, and Massachusetts resemble California. All are home to major banks that have consolidated their hold on in-state deposit markets without building up extensive bank-branch networks in other states, and none have (to this point) experienced major penetration by out-of-state banks.[11] New Jersey, by contrast, has been a target for acquiring banks headquartered in other states, much like Indiana or New Mexico. New York has been rife with acquisition activity, which we describe here only briefly. Any list of acquisition-oriented retail banks in New York is topped by Citibank and Chase (see Table 9.1). Interestingly, while Citi was among the originators of "upscale retail banking," it has not pursued a NationsBank or Norwest-like strategy of regional branch building to pursue this aim. Instead, Citi runs a diverse network of nonbank offices throughout the nation, which focuses on selling products and services via multiple delivery channels, not on collecting deposits. Chase Manhattan Bank has been acquiring other New York banks for many years. These mergers include two former money-center banks, Manufacturers Hanover Trust Company in June 1992 and Chemical Bank in July 1996. This latter merger gave Chase market position in Texas; as noted in chapter 4, Chemical Bank took over Texas Commerce Bank in 1987. Chase may be initiating a market-expansion strategy, as evidenced by its November 1997 conversion of its San Francisco–based trust company operation into a commercial bank. Marine Midland Bank has been pursuing an aggressive merger strategy in upstate New York, but has not ventured out-of-state since its travails two decades ago.

In Pennsylvania three key players have emerged. CoreStates Bank grew out of the old First Pennsylvania Bank, headquartered in Philadelphia, in 1990; it has subsequently acquired many community banks in-state. It entered Delaware with the 1996 purchase of Delaware Trust Company, and New Jersey with the 1996 purchase of New Jersey National Bank (which itself had been acquiring in-state community banks since the 1960s). Now CoreStates' further evolution will be blended with that of First Union of North Carolina, with which it merged in early 1998. PNC Bank Corp. of Pittsburgh has been involved in a more far-flung acquisition strategy reminiscent of Norwest. It acquired Chemical Bank's New Jersey holdings in October 1995. PNC commercial banks operate in Indiana, Delaware, Kentucky, and Massachusetts. The third important Pennsylvania bank, Mellon Bank of Pittsburgh, has expanded into Delaware, Maryland, New Jersey, and Virginia via acquisitions since 1994; and it has acquired community banks throughout Pennsylvania. Interestingly, Mellon fought off an unsolicited takeover bid by Bank of New York in the spring of 1998.

Massachusetts has seen the same pattern of acquisition as have New York and Pennsylvania. Fleet Bank, originally headquartered in Rhode Island, merged with Bank of New England of Massachusetts in January 1991, giving it an extensive Massachusetts market share. It then merged with Shawmut National of Connecticut in December 1995, and has also made acquisitions elsewhere in the New England region. New Jersey, as mentioned, has been a target for acquiring out-of-state banks. Among the large acquiring banks identified here, at least four—Mellon, CoreStates, Suntrust, and Chase Manhattan—have branches in New Jersey. Despite this, New Jersey retains numerous in-state community banks, so evidently it will retain its target status for the foreseeable future.

Denial Rates, Market Share, and Fair Share

Figure 9.24 shows that denial rates are more uniform for different lender types in Northeastern urban markets than anywhere else in the United States except California cities. Given this uniformity, two patterns found elsewhere emerge here—mortgage companies have higher-than-average denial rates, and savings and loans lower-than-average denial rates. Repeating another pattern found in other regions, in every city cluster mortgage companies have a disproportionately large share of home-purchase loan applications in lower-income areas, and savings and loans a disproportionately small share (Figure 9.25). Small in-state banks have a relatively low market share in lower-income areas; merging banks' share varies from city cluster to city cluster. As Figure 9.26 shows, mortgage companies also have a generally high proportionate share of minority applicants, while savings and loans and small in-state banks invariably have a relatively small number of minority applicants. In a unique trend, however, merging banks with in-state branches invariably have relatively high numbers of minority applicants.

How do these market share patterns map into fair-share terms? Table 9.12 provides fair-share statistics for 1996 home-purchase loans made. Unlike any other region, both the minority and lower-income benchmarks of 25 percent and 33 percent are generally met. For three of the four states, large banks with in-state branches have the highest median fair-share scores for minority areas, while merging banks without in-state branches and small in-state banks have the lowest scores. New Jersey's pattern is different: there, small in-state banks do best, with a minority score almost double the fair-share benchmark. The same pattern is found in the analysis of lower-income fair share at the bottom of Table 9.12. Note that merging banks with in-state branches have remarkably high fair-share scores in many markets, a pattern that could reflect either reinvestment focused on the residents of impacted areas or gentrification (with upper-income households moving systematically into lower-income areas). However, a review of statistics on loan recipients' income levels in lower-income areas suggests that merging banks have higher proportions of lower-income loan recipients in

(text continued on p. 223)

Figure 9.24 **Denial Rates by Lender Type in Selected Northeastern Cities, Home-Purchase Loans, 1996**

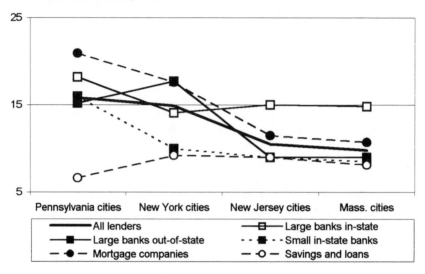

Note: Figures depict denial rates as percentage of approved and denied loans only.

Figure 9.25 **Market Share in Lower-Income Areas of Selected Northeastern Cities, Home-Purchase Loans, 1996**

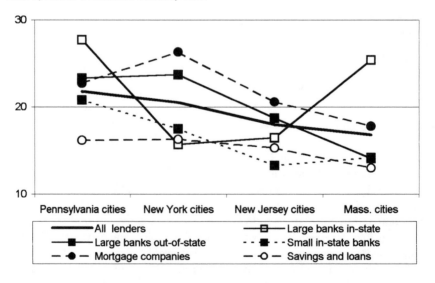

Note: Lower-income areas here are the third of every city's census tracts with the lowest 1990 median incomes. Figures denote percentage of all applications.

Figure 9.26 **Minorities in the Applicant Pool of Selected Northeastern Cities, Home-Purchase Loans, 1996**

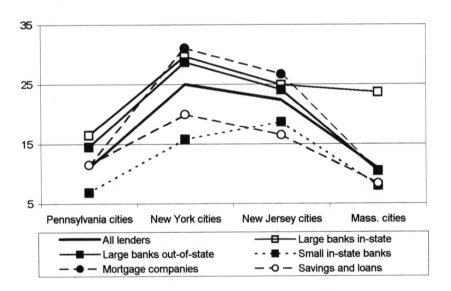

Note: Figures denote percentage of all race-identified applicants.

Table 9.12 **Fair-Share Scores by Lender Type for Loans Made, Purchase Loans in Eastern Cities, 1996**

	All lenders	Non-bank lenders	All commer-cial bks	Small in-state banks	Large in-state banks	Large out-of-state banks with branches	without branches
Ratio of minority-area to other-area loans among purchase loans							
Northeastern cities							
Pennsylvania cities	33.6	30.6	36.0	33.7	49.6	48.3	28.7
New York cities	28.5	30.0	26.9	17.6	26.4	63.8	23.0
New Jersey cities	67.1	87.4	38.9	48.1	NA	29.3	30.6
Massachusetts cities	42.4	42.5	42.4	31.2	80.2	NA	44.7
NE cities median	**38.0**	**36.6**	**37.5**	**32.4**	**49.6**	**48.3**	**29.6**
Southeastern cities							
North Carolina cities	28.0	30.8	25.3	20.9	22.9	NA	41.4
Georgia cities	16.1	21.0	10.9	9.5	NA	9.3	18.6
Mississippi cities	9.2	11.0	7.7	7.9	NA	NA	6.2
SE cities median	**16.1**	**21.0**	**10.9**	**9.5**	**22.9**	**9.3**	**18.6**
Ratio of lower-income area to other-area loans among purchase loans							
Northeastern cities							
Pennsylvania cities	43.8	37.2	49.4	45.3	80.8	71.3	38.8
New York cities	42.2	43.8	40.5	26.8	39.4	100.1	39.5
New Jersey cities	30.3	25.1	41.3	56.5	NA	35.0	37.7
Massachusetts cities	61.2	68.1	56.8	43.4	92.5	NA	55.2
NE cities median	**43.0**	**40.5**	**45.4**	**44.4**	**80.8**	**71.3**	**39.1**
Southeastern cities							
North Carolina cities	52.6	66.9	40.3	34.8	38.2	NA	63.5
Georgia cities	44.5	47.0	41.7	21.9	NA	22.0	31.2
Mississippi cities	21.0	26.1	16.9	15.1	NA	NA	20.3
SE cities median	**44.5**	**47.0**	**40.3**	**21.9**	**38.2**	**22.0**	**31.2**

Note: All ratios are adjusted for available owner-occupied units in every census tract. Italicized ratios fall below the fair-share benchmarks of 33 for minority areas and 50 for lower-income areas. The methodology used here is introduced in chapter 7.

lower-income areas than do other lenders. This implies that merging banks' good fair-share performance is not due to their financing of gentrification.

Probit Analysis

Tables 9.13 to 9.15 present selected results from probit analyses of these four states. Minority applicant coefficients are depicted in Table 9.13. In the all-lender estimations, Native American and African-Americans have extremely similar, statistically significant coefficients in all four city clusters. Hispanic applicants are at a disadvantage in three states and at an advantage in the other, Pennsylvania. The Asian-American coefficient is insignificant in three states, and positive and significant in the fourth (Pennsylvania). No clear pattern of significance for minority applicants is apparent for lender types.

Table 9.14 sets out coefficients for loan applications on homes in minority neighborhoods. In Pennsylvania, minority neighborhoods are at a slight statistical advantage in four of the six equations reported, including that for all lenders. Probits for the other three states come to precisely the opposite conclusion—several estimations for each state, including those for all lenders, find that minority neighborhoods are at a statistical disadvantage in loan applications. Table 9.15 shows that lower-income neighborhoods are at a statistical disadvantage for all lenders in three states—Pennsylvania is again the exception. Lower-income applicants are consistently at a disadvantage relative to other applicants.

Disadvantage calculations for the Northeastern states are presented in Table 9.16 and shown graphically in Figures 9.27 to 9.30. Overall disadvantage performance is very similar in every state except Pennsylvania, which has a net advantage when race and lower-income scores are summed. Correspondingly, every lender type registers a significant disadvantage level in every state but Pennsylvania. There are two common threads for all four city clusters. First, merging banks without in-state branches have large disadvantage scores—in three city clusters, their disadvantage scores are worse than any other lender type's. Second, merging banks with in-state branches generally have low disadvantage scores—in Pennsylvania they register a net advantage.

Southeastern Cities

The Southeastern home-purchase loan market is dominated by commercial banks, as are the Midwestern and Northeastern markets examined here. Figure 9.21 shows that Southeastern savings and loan associations have been losing market share rapidly, especially to mortgage companies. Mortgage companies' market share almost doubled between 1992 and 1996, and their market volume more than tripled. Southeastern home-loan markets grew tremendously between 1992 and 1995, as Figure 9.22 illustrates—this region's 102 percent growth rate is just behind that of the Southwest.

(text continued on p. 230)

Table 9.13 **Coefficients for Applicant Race, Probit Equations for Home-Purchase Loans in Northeastern Cities, 1996**

	All lenders	Small in-state banks	Large banks w/in-state branches	Large banks w/no in-st. branches	Savings and loans	Mortgage com-panies
Pennsylvania Cities						
Native American	-0.232	-0.25	-0.263	-0.459	0.766	-0.265
	(0.085)***	(0.195)	(0.203)	(0.164)***	(0.446)*	(0.172)
African-American	-0.090	-0.221	0.022	-0.240	-0.267	-0.060
	(0.021)***	(0.051)***	(0.057)	(0.045)***	(0.047)***	(0.042)
Asian-American	0.260	0.045	0.313	0.135	0.080	0.315
	(0.046)***	(0.097)	(0.138)**	(0.085)	(0.082)	(0.116)***
Hispanic	0.109	0.087	0.223	0.051	-0.211	0.067
	(0.032)***	(0.073)	(0.076)***	(0.069)	(0.071)***	(0.069)
New York cities						
Native American	-0.258	-0.486	-0.054	-0.194	-0.176	-0.379
	(0.063)***	(0.182)***	(0.145)	(0.165)	(0.163)	(0.012)***
African-American	-0.213	-0.234	-0.313	-0.331	-0.374	0.0004
	(0.015)***	(0.053)***	(0.030)***	(0.046)***	(0.046)***	(0.024)
Asian-American	0.143	0.055	0.216	0.088	0.147	0.088
	(0.022)***	(0.080)	(0.042)***	(0.060)	(0.049)***	(0.050)*
Hispanic	-0.094	-0.048	-0.205	-0.046	-0.124	-0.023
	(0.019)***	(0.070)	(0.040)***	(0.056)	(0.050)**	(0.031)
New Jersey cities						
Native American	-0.259	-0.127	-0.188	-0.437	-0.339	-0.216
	(0.105)**	(0.226)	(0.285)	(0.216)**	(0.775)	(0.014)
African-American	-0.276	-0.191	-0.240	-0.165	-0.410	-0.253
	(0.022)***	(0.054)***	(0.060)***	(0.050)***	(0.174)**	(0.028)***
Asian-American	-0.030	0.112	0.145	-0.001	-0.120	-0.041
	(0.031)	(0.054)**	(0.072)**	(0.064)	(0.207)	(0.048)
Hispanic	-0.089	-0.041	-0.073	-0.079	-0.231	0.006
	(0.025)***	(0.053)	(0.065)	(0.050)	(0.200)	(0.034)
Massachusetts Cities						
Native American	-0.447	-0.209	-0.267	-0.438	-0.390	-0.404
	(0.044)***	(0.364)	(0.173)	(0.163)***	(0.117)***	(0.054)***
African-American	-0.251	-0.357	-0.254	-0.485	-0.482	-0.171
	(0.045)***	(0.183)*	(0.193)	(0.132)***	(0.098)***	(0.063)***
Asian-American	0.064	-0.089	0.165	0.068	0.200	0.058
	(0.052)	(0.241)	(0.202)	(0.157)	(0.126)	(0.071)
Hispanic	-0.161	-0.069	-0.14	-0.085	-0.181	-0.162
	(0.017)***	(0.097)	(0.064)**	(0.059)	(0.040)***	(0.022)***

***Denotes significance at a 1% confidence level, ** significance at 5%, * at 10%.
Note: Standard errors are shown in parentheses below each coefficient.

Table 9.14 **Coefficients for Minority Neighborhoods, Probit Equations for Home-Purchase Loans in Eastern Cities, 1996**

	All lenders	Small in-state banks	Large banks w/in-state branches	Large banks w/no in-st. branches	Savings and loans	Mortgage com- panies
Pennsylvania cities	0.056	-0.038	0.043	0.086	0.101	0.106
	(0.016)***	(0.033)	(0.045)	(0.036)**	(0.041)**	(.034)***
New York cities	-0.039	0.075	-0.145	-0.161	-0.044	0.028
	(0.014)***	(0.045)	(0.034)***	(0.044)***	(0.042)	(0.023)
New Jersey cities	-0.149	-0.137	-0.141	-0.101	-0.15	-0.129
	(0.020)***	(0.043)***	(0.054)***	(0.043)**	(0.152)	(0.055)**
Mass. cities	-0.059	-0.028	-0.134	-0.182	-0.117	-0.018
	(0.020)***	(0.099)	(0.076)*	(0.072)**	(0.047)**	(0.028)
North Carolina cities	-0.067	-0.05	-0.041	-0.067	-0.052	-0.06
	(0.01)NR***	(0.050)	(0.057)	(0.040)*	(0.048)	(0.02)NR***
Georgia	-0.018	0.064	0.013	-0.223	0.02	0.068
	(0.020)	(0.076)	(0.074)	(0.049)***	(0.057)	(0.038)**
Mississippi	-0.038	-0.155	NA	0.048	0.189	-0.002
	(0.030)	(0.059)***		NR	(0.087)**	(0.049)NR

*** denotes significance at the 1% level, ** at the 5% level, * at the 10% level.

Note: NR means an equation is statistically unreliable. Minority neighborhoods consist of the one quarter of census tracts in every metropolitan area with the highest proportion of minority residents.

Table 9.15 **Coefficients for Lower-Income Applicants and Neighborhoods, Probit Equations for Home-Purchase Loans in Eastern Cities, 1996**

	All lenders	Small in-state banks	Large banks w/in-state branches	Large banks w/no in-st. branches	Savings and loans	Mortgage com- panies
Pennsylvania cities						
Lower-income applicants	-0.022	-0.009	-0.012	-0.020	-0.022	-0.023
	(0.004)***	(0.009)	(0.013)	(0.010)**	(0.011)**	(0.009)**
Lower-income areas	-0.014	-0.028	0.04	-0.031	-0.076	-0.054
	(0.015)	(0.030)	(0.043)	(0.034)	(0.037)**	(0.030)*
New York cities						
Lower-income applicants	-0.021	-0.043	-0.019	-0.01	-0.022	-0.014
	(.004)***	(0.01)***	(0.008)**	(0.011)	(0.010)**	(0.0062)**
Lower-income areas	-0.130	-0.055	-0.063	-0.025	-0.122	-0.141
	(0.012)***	(0.040)	(0.03)**	(0.039)	(0.036)***	(0.020)***
New Jersey cities						
Lower-income applicants	-0.021	0.003	0.009	-0.04	-0.016	-0.023
	(0.005)***	(0.011)	(0.014)	(0.011)***	(0.039)	(0.0074)***
Lower-income areas	-0.091	-0.078	-0.076	-0.091	-0.091	-0.101
	(0.020)***	(0.042)*	(0.055)	(0.042)**	(0.146)	(0.028)***
Massachusetts cities						
Lower-income applicants	-0.027	0.028	-0.043	-0.039	-0.023	-0.024
	(0.0059)***	(0.03)	(0.022)**	(0.019)**	(0.014)*	(0.0081)***
Lower-income areas	-0.078	-0.264	-0.023	-0.130	-0.130	-0.058
	(0.021)***	(0.10)***	(0.078)	(0.070)*	(0.048)***	(0.029)**
North Carolina cities						
Lower-income applicants	0.001	0.008	0.011	-0.016	-0.005	0.009
	(0.004)NR	(0.015)	(0.016)	(0.012)	(0.014)	(0.006)NR*
Lower-income areas	-0.101	-0.078	-0.113	-0.042	-0.090	-0.083
	(0.01)NR***	(0.048)	(0.059)*	(0.039)	(0.046)*	(0.02)NR***
Georgia cities						
Lower-income applicants	-0.024	-0.012	-0.012	-0.024	-0.031	-0.014
	(0.005)***	(0.017)	(0.018)	(0.011)**	(0.012)***	(0.007)*
Lower-income areas	-0.051	0.033	-0.038	-0.114	-0.187	-0.015
	(0.021)**	(0.071)	(0.075)	(0.049)**	(0.053)***	(0.030)
Mississippi cities						
Lower-income applicants	-0.015	-0.034	NA	0.030	-0.041	-0.005
	(0.008)NR**	(0.016)**		(0.030)	(0.022)*	(0.01)NR
Lower-income areas	-0.133	0.046	NA	-0.221	-0.274	-0.171
	(0.03)NR***	(0.060)		(0.114)*	(0.080)***	(0.05)NR***

*** denotes significance at a 1% confidence level, ** significance at 5%, * at 10%.
Note: Standard errors are shown in parentheses below each coefficient.

Table 9.16 **Net Borrower Race/Lower-Income Disadvantage in Northeastern Cities, 1996**

	All lenders	Small in-state banks	Large banks w/in-state branches	Large banks w/no in-st. branches	Savings and loans	Mortgage com-panies
Equiproportional borrower characteristics						
Pennsylvania cities						
Lower-income disadv.	-19.4	0.0	0.0	-6.3	-19.0	-15.4
Minority disadv.	14.1	-22.1	52.0	-56.3	37.2	49.2
Total disadvantage	-5.3	-22.1	52.0	-62.6	18.1	33.8
New York cities						
Lower-income disadv.	-28.7	-14.3	-16.0	0.0	-27.3	-28.0
Minority disadv.	-48.7	-60.7	-54.4	-60.0	-34.5	-30.0
Total disadvantage	-77.4	-75.0	-70.4	-60.0	-61.8	-58.0
New Jersey cities						
Lower-income disadv.	-22.2	-11.7	0.0	-54.6	0.0	-24.5
Minority disadv.	-86.0	-31.3	-33.8	-74.0	-39.0	-46.8
Total disadvantage	-108.2	-43.1	-33.8	-128.7	-39.0	-71.3
Massachusetts cities						
Lower-income disadv.	-22.0	-44.1	-14.3	-34.0	-29.4	-17.3
Minority disadv.	-95.3	-35.7	-36.4	-122.7	-123.9	-70.9
Total disadvantage	-117.3	-79.8	-50.7	-156.7	-153.3	-88.2
States' own borrower characteristics						
Pennsylvania cities						
Lower-income disadv.	-6.8	0.0	0.0	-5.9	-22.4	-17.5
Minority disadv.	8.0	-16.0	10.6	-6.6	-8.7	20.5
Total disadvantage	1.2	-16.0	10.6	-12.5	-31.1	3.0
New York cities						
Lower-income disadv.	-33.5	-13.2	-18.0	0.0	-31.8	-33.4
Minority disadv.	-33.1	-23.5	-63.1	-68.2	-48.8	-16.9
Total disadvantage	-66.6	-36.7	-81.1	-68.2	-80.6	-50.3
New Jersey cities						
Lower-income disadv.	-23.5	-11.3	0.0	-53.5	0.0	-23.8
Minority disadv.	-55.3	-32.9	-36.7	-30.3	-39.0	-2.7
Total disadvantage	-78.8	-44.3	-36.7	-83.7	-39.0	-26.5
Massachusetts cities						
Lower-income disadv.	-22.6	-44.6	-15.1	-34.9	-30.0	-17.8
Minority disadv.	-25.8	-15.3	-23.3	-46.8	-43.7	-15.3
Total disadvantage	-48.4	-59.9	-38.4	-81.7	-73.7	-33.1

Source: Author's probit equations using 1996 HMDA home-purchase loans.
Note: Methodology is explained in the text.

Figure 9.27 **Residential Lending Disadvantage in Pennsylvania Cities, Home-Purchase Loans, 1996**

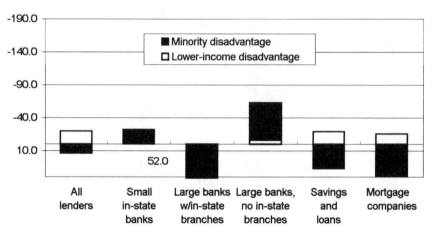

Note: Disadvantage is shown per 1,000 hypothetical borrowers.

Figure 9.28 **Residential Lending Disadvantage in New York Cities, Home-Purchase Loans, 1996**

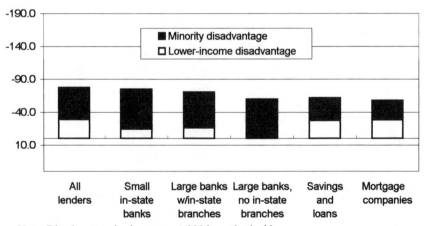

Note: Disadvantage is shown per 1,000 hypothetical borrowers.

Figure 9.29 **Residential Lending Disadvantage in Massachusetts Cities, Home-Purchase Loans, 1996**

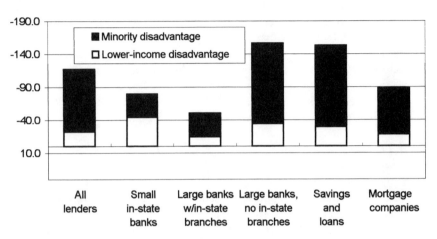

Note: Disadvantage is shown per 1,000 hypothetical borrowers.

Figure 9.30 **Residential Lending Disadvantage in New Jersey Cities, Home-Purchase Loans, 1996**

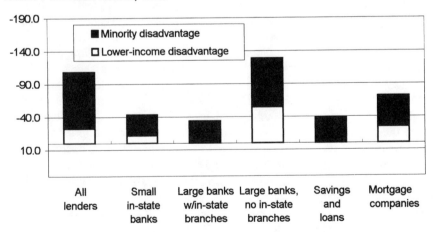

Note: Disadvantage is shown per 1,000 hypothetical borrowers.

The financial infrastructures of eight Southeastern cities are shown in Figure 9.31. These population-weighted figures are remarkably similar, since the cities depicted range from large to small. Further, the pattern in these cities is unique. The credit union counts are low—equivalent to Southwestern cities and below the northern regions. Investment offices appear with about the same frequency as in the Southwestern and Northeastern regions. The other financial office types—bank and thrift branches, loan brokerages, pawnbrokers, and check-cashers—appear in population-adjusted levels well above those anywhere else. The Southwestern region has similar numbers of loan brokers, but many fewer bank branches. Some cities in the two northern regions have similar numbers of bank branches, but many fewer informal financial offices. Most Southeastern cities shown here have double the number of per-capita financial offices found in the Northeast and Southwest.

Acquiring Banks and Merger Activity

While its plentiful financial offices might belie the fact, the Southeastern region is home to some of the most aggressive acquiring banks. Heading the list are NationsBank and First Union. As discussed above, NationsBank has used mergers as an expansion strategy. Most recently, it merged with Boatmen's Bancshares of Missouri in September 1997; prior to that, its major acquisitions included Bank South of Atlanta, Georgia, in January 1996 and C&S/Sovran Corporation of Atlanta in December 1993.[12] In May 1998, its proposed merger with BankAmerica shocked the business world. In addition to the markets already discussed here, NationsBank has branch networks in Tennessee, Kentucky, and Delaware.

First Union has been moving aggressively to overtake NationsBank. In November 1997 it took over Signet Banking Corporation of Virginia; and a month later, as noted above, it agreed to merge with CoreStates of Philadelphia. It operates branch operations in South Carolina, Tennessee, Washington, D.C., Georgia, and Florida. First Union entered the New Jersey market through its January 1996 takeover of First Fidelity Corporation of Newark.

While these two North Carolina banks dominate acquisition activity in this region, the other two large Southeastern banks included here have expanded beyond their home-state markets. Suntrust Bank, headquartered in Atlanta, has bought up community banks elsewhere in Georgia since 1969; it operates commercial banks in Tennessee, in Florida, and in Alabama. SouthTrust, headquartered in Alabama, has a branch network encompassing Alabama, Florida, Georgia, Mississippi, North Carolina, South Carolina, and Tennessee.

The three Southeastern states encompassed here fall into three different categories of bank acquisition patterns. North Carolina is home to acquiring banks, with minimal presence of out-of-state banks; in this respect it resembles Minnesota and Pennsylvania. Georgia is both a target state and an acquiring state—in this respect, it resembles California, though its in-state institutions are less well ensconced. Mississippi is a target state.

Figure 9.31 **Financial Offices per 100,000 Population in Selected Southeastern Banking Markets, 1996**

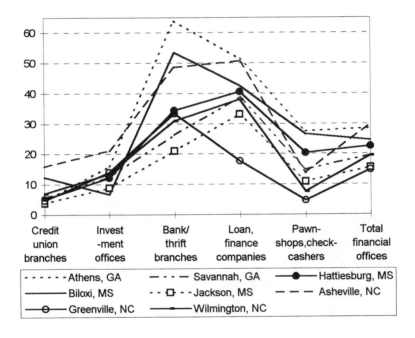

Denial Rates, Market Share, and Fair Share

Residential loan denial rates are as high in the Southeastern city clusters examined here as in the Southwestern states. Further, as Figure 9.32 demonstrates, denial rates vary widely by lender type. Small in-state banks, large banks in-state, and savings and loans have low denial rates; but those for mortgage companies and merging banks without in-state branches are substantially higher. Mortgage companies also have large relative proportions of minority applicants, as Figure 9.33 shows; and small in-state banks and large banks in-state have relatively few minority applicants.

The fair-share scores for these Southeastern city clusters (Table 9.12) reveal a bifurcated pattern. North Carolina's fair-share scores are generally above both the minority and lower-income benchmarks; the exceptions are its small and large in-state banks, which fail the minority benchmark of 25 percent for loans made. Georgia's lenders overall pass the lower-income hurdle, but universally fall short in their minority fair-share scores. Mississippi's lenders universally fail to meet either race or income benchmarks.

Probit Analysis

Coefficients from the probit equations for Southeastern cities appear in Tables 9.14, 9.15, and 9.17. Surprisingly, given the fair-share performance, this region's probits seldom found minority neighborhood to be statistically significant (Table 9.14); however, lower-income neighborhoods are consistently negative and significant, with sometimes sizable coefficients (Table 9.15). Table 9.17 contains coefficients for applicant race. Throughout these Southern markets, African-Americans are invariably at a disadvantage in residential loan markets. In North Carolina and Georgia, Hispanic applicants are also chronically at a disadvantage, as are Native Americans in North Carolina.

As before, overall and lender-by-lender results are conveniently summarized in the disadvantage calculations displayed in Table 9.18 and illustrated in Figures 9.34 to 9.36. North Carolina has the highest disadvantage levels, due almost entirely to racial difference. The other states' also have substantial, but more variable, levels of disadvantage, due to a combination of minority and lower-income factors. Note that in all these city clusters, the disadvantage levels calculated with the equiproportional method are well below those calculated with actual own-state proportions of loan applicants. Small in-state banks perform worst among lender types in two states, North Carolina and Mississippi; in Georgia, that distinction goes to merging banks with in-state branches. Mortgage companies post the lowest disadvantage scores in every state, except for merging banks without in-state branches in North Carolina.

(text continued on p. 238)

Figure 9.32 **Denial Rates by Lender Type in Selected Southeastern Cities, Home-Purchase Loans, 1996**

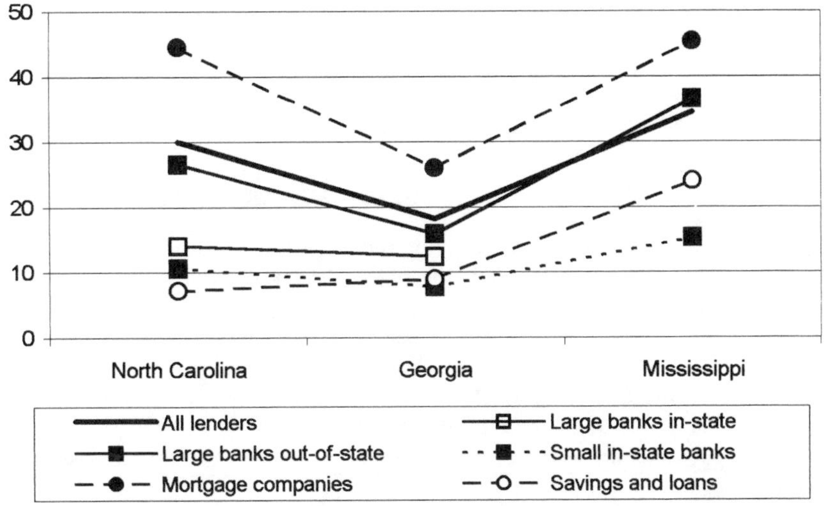

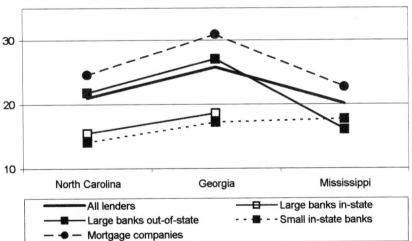

Note: Figures depict denial rates as percentage of approved and denied loans only.

Figure 9.33 **Minorities in the Applicant Pool of Selected Southeastern Cities, Home-Purchase Loans, 1996**

Note: Figures denote percentage of all race-identified applicants.

Table 9.17 Coefficients for Applicant Race, Probit Equations for Home-Purchase Loans in Southeastern Cities, 1996

	All lenders	Small in-state banks	Large banks w/in-state branches	Large banks w/no in-st. branches	Savings and loans	Mortgage com-panies
North Carolina Cities						
Native American	-0.234	-0.495	-0.116	-0.367	-0.363	-0.175
	(0.05)NR***	(0.203)**	(0.256)	(0.146)**	(0.178)**	(0.07)NR***
African-American	-0.456	-0.661	-0.470	-0.382	-0.468	-0.414
	(0.01)NR***	(0.042)***	(0.049)***	(0.031)***	(0.039)***	(0.01)NR***
Asian-American	0.099	-0.214	-0.288	0.317	0.230	0.128
	(0.05)NR**	(0.121)*	(0.105)***	(0.135)**	(0.159)	(0.071)NR*
Hispanic	-0.139	-0.312	-0.341	-0.043	-0.363	-0.051
	(0.03)NR***	(0.109)***	(0.133)***	(0.079)	(0.103)***	(0.034)NR
Georgia Cities						
Native American	-0.145	-0.385	-0.028	-0.074	-0.348	-0.030
	(0.085)*	(0.358)	(0.452)	(0.198)	(0.219)	(0.122)
African-American	-0.225	-0.496	-0.454	-0.337	-0.354	-0.101
	(0.014)***	(0.049)***	(0.052)***	(0.034)***	(0.035)***	(0.019)***
Asian-American	0.085	0.181	-0.111	0.294	-0.117	0.097
	(0.040)**	(0.172)	(0.127)	(0.076)***	(0.096)	(0.068)
Hispanic	-0.072	-0.204	-0.543	-0.027	-0.019	-0.086
	(0.034)**	(0.134)	(0.133)***	(0.072)	(0.079)	(0.052)*
Mississippi Cities						
Native American	0.052	-0.592	NA	-0.067	-0.099	0.342
	(0.12)NR	(0.341)*		(0.44)NR	(0.302)	(0.18)NR*
African-American	-0.210	-0.560	NA	-0.343	-0.188	-0.043
	(0.02)NR***	(0.042)***		(0.09)NR***	(0.060)***	(0.033)NR
Asian-American	0.283	-0.203	NA	-0.058	0.165	0.305
	(0.09)NR***	(0.147)		(0.38)NR	(0.166)	(0.22)NR
Hispanic	0.031	-0.356	NA	NA	0.168	0.225
	(0.113)	(0.247)			(0.317)	(0.018)NR

*** denotes significance at a 1% confidence level, ** significance at 5%, * at 10%.
Note: Standard errors are shown in parentheses below each coefficient.

Table 9.18 **Net Borrower Race/Lower-Income Disadvantage in Southeastern Cities, 1996**

	All lenders	Small in-state banks	Large banks w/in-state branches	Large banks w/no in-st. branches	Savings and loans	Mortgage companies
Equiproportional borrower characteristics						
North Carolina cities						
Lower-income disadv.	-16.9	0.0	-17.0	0.0	-13.5	-13.9
Minority disadv.	-84.7	-163.6	-109.9	-53.0	-117.6	-57.4
Total disadvantage	-101.6	-163.6	-126.9	-53.0	-131.1	-71.3
Georgia cities						
Lower-income disadv.	-16.1	0.0	0.0	-26.1	-41.6	-4.7
Minority disadv.	-34.3	-49.6	-99.7	-41.5	-35.4	-7.6
Total disadvantage	-50.4	-49.6	-99.7	-67.6	-77.0	-12.3
Mississippi cities						
Lower-income disadv.	-27.7	-10.8	NA	-33.2	-58.0	-28.6
Minority disadv.	7.3	-135.2	NA	-34.3	11.2	30.8
Total disadvantage	-20.4	-146.0	NA	-67.5	-46.8	2.2
States' own borrower characteristics						
North Carolina cities						
Lower-income disadv.	-19.8	0.0	-19.9	0.0	-15.9	-16.3
Minority disadv.	-92.3	-124.0	-90.2	-74.2	-12.8	4.0
Total disadvantage	-112.1	-124.0	-110.1	-74.2	-28.7	-12.2
Georgia cities						
Lower-income disadv.	-12.8	0.0	0.0	-18.9	-29.1	-4.6
Minority disadv.	-47.8	-105.2	-107.6	-83.3	-75.0	-18.0
Total disadvantage	-60.6	-105.2	-107.6	-102.2	-104.2	-22.6
Mississippi cities						
Lower-income disadv.	-23.4	0.0	NA	-19.0	-39.3	-29.5
Minority disadv.	-35.7	-97.5	NA	-53.5	-59.3	0.0
Total disadvantage	-59.1	-97.5	NA	-72.5	-98.7	-29.5

Source: Author's probit equations using 1996 HMDA home-purchase loans.
Note: Methodology is explained in the text.

Figure 9.34 **Residential Lending Disadvantage in North Carolina Cities, Home-Purchase Loans, 1996**

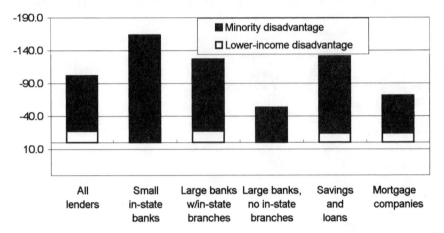

Note: Disadvantage is shown per 1,000 hypothetical borrowers.

Figure 9.35 **Residential Lending Disadvantage in Georgia Cities, Home-Purchase Loans, 1996**

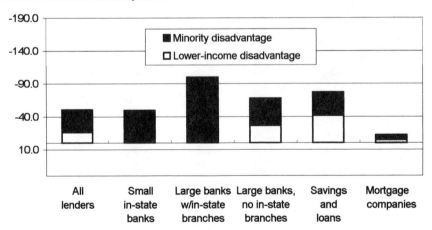

Note: Disadvantage is shown per 1,000 hypothetical borrowers.

Figure 9.36. **Residential Lending Disadvantage in Mississippi Cities,
Home-Purchase Loans, 1996**

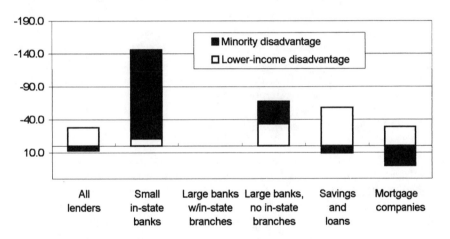

Note: Disadvantage is shown per 1,000 hypothetical borrowers.

Banking Infrastructure, Credit Flows, Discrimination, and Bank Consolidation

The aim of this chapter was to encompass numerous cities from every U.S. region in a representative study of credit-market access. The many statistical relationships and econometric results obtained here invite further empirical experimentation. It is hoped that the results presented here will open up an extended discussion about the methodology and implementation of multiregional, multidimensional studies of credit-market outcomes, particularly studies using publicly available data. The relentless advance of desktop computing power, together with the growth of affordable economic databases, is opening the door to the wide dissemination of advanced methods for assessing bank performance—methods that only a decade ago required a mainframe computer and tens of thousands of dollars on data acquisition and conversion.

This concluding section focuses narrowly on two questions at the heart of our study. What are the likely effects of bank mergers and consolidation on the social efficiency of the banking system—that is, on access to credit? And are these effects more pronounced in some geographic areas than in others? We first discuss the relationship of financial infrastructure and consolidation, and then probe our econometric results in more depth.

Financial Infrastructure and Consolidation

Differences in financial infrastructure from region to region are striking. The formal and informal financial infrastructures are slim in the Southwest, on a population-adjusted basis. Both are robust in the Mountain/Great Plains states and the Southeast; and formal financial infrastructure is strong but informal infrastructure slim in the Midwest and Northeast. We speculated above that some differences, such as the greater frequency of credit-union offices in the Midwest and Northeast, can be traced to differences in migration and industrial development patterns. Further research on this historical background is crucial, especially as this will enrich contemporary understanding of the links between financial institutions and populations.

Apart from the role of history, some portion of the differences in financial infrastructure undoubtedly arise because of the differential pace of bank consolidation in different states and regions. Recall that the Southeastern cities examined here had the most bank branches per capita, while the Southwest had the fewest. And indeed, between 1981 and 1996 our three Southeastern states lost 15 percent of operating banks, whereas the Southwestern states in our study lost 32 percent.

Table 9.19 provides more suggestive evidence on this point. Its first two columns show that the Southeast has had the lowest annual rate of loss of operating banks since 1990, while the Northeast and Southwest have experienced the most rapid loss rate. However, this fragmentary evidence is far from convincing—the Northeastern states, with a healthy number of 1996 bank branches, lost the largest percentage of banks in the 1980–96 period, 36 percent (the Mountain/Plains and Midwestern states lost 29 percent). Further, the premise that the Southeast is overbanked and hence ripe for substantial consolidation *because* it has a high per-capita number of bank branches may not be correct. The last two columns of Table 9.19 set out 1991 and 1996 statistics on the number of operating banks per person in this study's five regions. These statistics show that the Southeast has the third lowest regional banks-per-person total. The lowest banks-per-person level is found in the Northeast; next comes the Southwest—though California, considered alone, has statistics approximately equal to this region's. But these statistics would suggest that the regions most ripe for further consolidation and mergers are the Mountain/Great Plains states and the Midwest.

Bank consolidation patterns may help to explain patterns in bank outcomes that otherwise appear simply anomalous. Consider Figures 9.37 and 9.38, which present estimates of regional checking account costs (Figure 9.37) and bank service charges (Figure 9.38) from the Federal Reserve bank cost survey discussed in chapter 6. Note that the Northeastern and Southern regions in this Federal Reserve survey consistently have the highest costs and service charges. If the number of bank offices and operating banks alone determined costs, then the Northeastern and Western regions should have the lowest costs recorded here. But instead the Midwest is consistently the most economical region in terms of banking costs.

However, Table 9.19 sheds different light on the results in these two figures: two of the three regions with the lowest number of banks operating per person, the Northeast and Southeast, are precisely those with the highest banking costs. The third region is the Southwest, in which banking costs have risen rapidly since 1995. Could the paradox of higher banking costs even with many banking offices be explained by the presence of fewer banking firms—that is, could old-fashioned monopoly power still be a factor in the futuristic financial-services market of the present? Chapter 10 explores this question at length.

Probing Our Probit Results

The multidimensional character of our investigation together with our multiple-market approach generates an inherent complexity that even the "disadvantage method" presented here does not tame. In this final subsection we present some further probit and "disadvantage" results that highlight this chapter's key results.

One striking conclusion from this chapter's probit equations is the widespread significance of the coefficients for all minority applicants. Another is the persistent disadvantage of African-American loan applicants in market after market and equation after equation. Figure 9.39a displays average coefficients for African-American

(text continued on p. 245)

Table 9.19 **Bank Density and Changes in Bank Populations**

	Change in banks operating, 1980-90 (average annual %)	Change in banks operating, 1990-96 (average annual %)	Banks per 100,000 persons, 1991	Banks per 100,000 persons, 1996
Southwestern	-0.44	-4.29	3.49	2.48
Mtn/G. Plains	-1.52	-3.67	13.91	10.42
Midwestern	-1.80	-3.35	11.38	8.93
Northeastern	-1.91	-5.09	1.53	1.11
Southeastern	-1.17	-2.44	3.88	3.00
U.S.	-1.45	-3.81	4.79	3.59

Note: Bank population figures are drawn from the FDIC web site, and human population estimates for 1991 and 1996 are drawn from the U.S. Census Bureau web site.

Figure 9.37 **Bank Transaction Account Charges by Region, 1995**

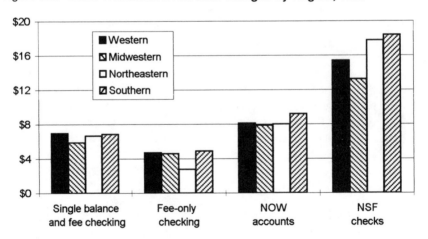

Source: Board of Governors (1996b).
Note: NSF means "not sufficient funds." Figures measure cost per occurrence.

Figure 9.38 **Bank Service Charges by Region, 1995**

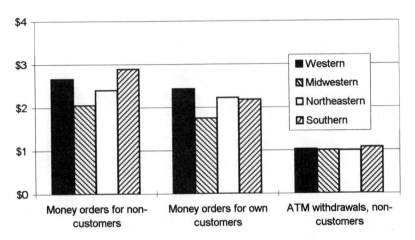

Source: Board of Governors (1996b).
Note: Figures measure cost per occurrence.

Figure 9.39a **Average African-American and Hispanic Coefficients, All-Lender Probit Equations by Region, 1996**

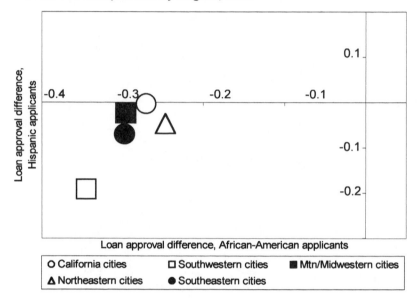

Loan approval difference, African-American applicants

O California cities   □ Southwestern cities   ■ Mtn/Midwestern cities
△ Northeastern cities   ● Southeastern cities

Note: Insignificant coefficients are counted as zero.

Figure 9.39b **Average Native and Asian-American Coefficients, All-Lender Probit Equations, by Region 1966**

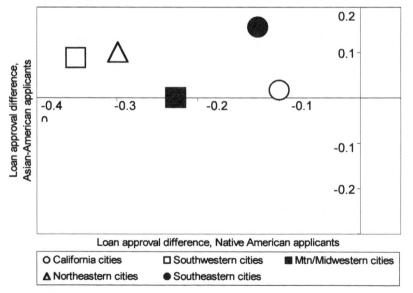

Loan approval difference, Native American applicants

O California cities   □ Southwestern cities   ■ Mtn/Midwestern cities
△ Northeastern cities   ● Southeastern cities

Note: Insignificant coefficients are counted as zero.

Figure 9.40 **Average Regional Disadvantage Scores by Lender Type, Home-Purchase Probit Equations, 1996**

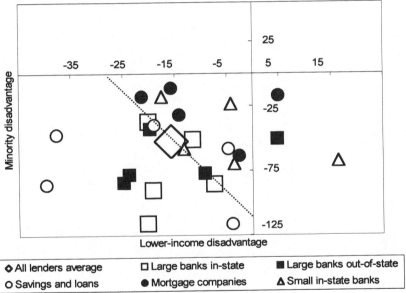

Figure 9.41a **Average Native American and African-American Coefficients, Probit Equations by Lender Type, 1966**

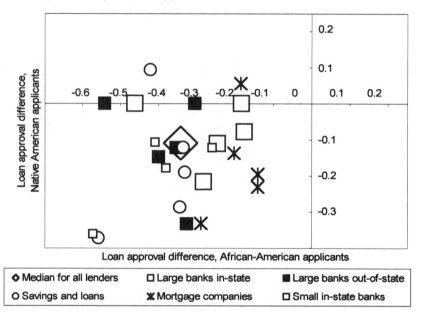

Figure 9.41b **Average Hispanic and Asian-American Coefficients, Probit Equations by Lender Type, 1966**

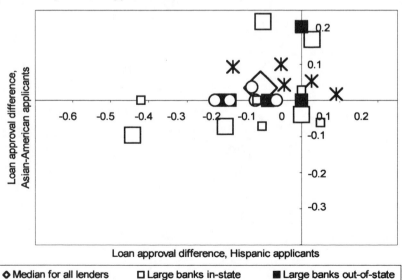

and Hispanic borrowers in each region. The average African-American coefficient is no more than –0.25 in any region, indicating a disadvantage of 25 percent. The Hispanic coefficient takes on a small negative average value in four regions, but a larger one of almost –0.20 in the New Mexico–Texas average. The average coefficients shown for Native American applicants in Figure 9.39b are all negative, with a wide range extending from just over –0.10 in California cities to just over –0.35 in the New Mexico–Texas cities. Note that Asian-American applicants' average coefficient is zero in the Mountain/Midwestern region, and positive in the other four regions. In evaluating these averages, keep in mind that the coefficients for Asian-American and Hispanic applicants, in particular, frequently take on both negative and positive signs in our detailed results.

Beyond these results for all lenders, we have emphasized here a credit-market "horse race" among different lender types. As we have seen, no one horse wins or loses the racial/lower-income disadvantage race in most markets. Nonetheless, certain patterns emerge. These broad patterns were summarized in Table 2.2 in chapter 2; here we go into more depth.

Figures 9.40 and 9.41 summarize the outcomes of these horse races diagrammatically. In Figure 9.40, low-income and minority disadvantage are measured along the X and Y axes, respectively. The average 1996 regional disadvantage scores for each lender type are mapped into this X-Y space. Each lender type is assigned a different symbol. This facilitates visual inspection of patterns for each lender cluster—for example, the large white boxes that symbolize acquiring banks.

All but three data points in Figure 9.40 fall into the Southwestern quadrant, indicating both net lower-income and net minority disadvantage. But how then to evaluate these patterns? As a point of reference, the all-lenders average across all regions is depicted as an oversized black diamond. A dashed line is drawn diagonally through this diamond; this line can be considered to represent tradeoffs of lower-income against minority disadvantage that leave applicants in these markets at a constant level of disadvantage. Lines with other slopes or curves could be drawn; the point of such a line is to separate behavior that is better than average from behavior that is worse than average. With this reference point in hand, we can consider the various sectors. All but one of the savings and loan points fall outside the average–disadvantage line. And all but one of the large banks' points fall along or outside of the average–disadvantage line. At the same time, mortgage companies fall entirely inside the average–disadvantage line, as do most small in-state banks.

Figures 9.41a and 9.41b provide additional visual evidence for minority-applicant coefficients in Model 1 probit equations. Again black diamonds for all-lenders' averages provide points of reference. Figure 9.41a shows regional averages by lender type for the two minority categories most likely to be negative and significant—Native and African American. Here, mortgage companies' averages are consistently low; with one exception, savings and loan averages indicate consistently large negative coefficients for both applicant groups.

Table 9.20 **Average Regional Disadvantage Scores by Lender Type, Probit Equations for Home-Purchase Loans, 1995 and 1996**

	All lenders	Small in-state banks	Large banks w/in-state branches	Large banks w/no in-state branches	Savings and loans	Mortgage com-panies
California cities						
Income disadvantage	-15.9	-4.7	-2.6	1.3	-2.3	-16.8
Race disadvantage	-48.3	-54.8	-43.6	-45.1	-46.1	-29.1
Total disadvantage	-64.2	-59.4	-46.2	-43.8	-48.4	-45.9
Other Southwestern cities						
Income disadvantage	-26.4	8.2	-22.5	-12.4	-32.7	-6.8
Race disadvantage	-65.0	-52.7	-66.0	-54.8	-70.1	-52.6
Total disadvantage	-91.4	-44.5	-88.5	-67.2	-102.8	-59.5
Mountain/Midwestern cities						
Income disadvantage	-13.7	-7.8	-3.0	0.8	0.2	-6.3
Race disadvantage	-65.4	-69.4	-35.6	-62.6	-95.7	-43.7
Total disadvantage	-79.1	-77.2	-38.7	-61.8	-95.5	-50.0
Northeastern cities						
Income disadvantage	-32.9	-16.1	-7.6	-20.1	-34.2	-32.9
Race disadvantage	-50.2	-46.3	-25.4	-67.6	-45.6	-18.4
Total disadvantage	-83.1	-62.4	-33.0	-87.7	-79.8	-51.3
Southeastern cities						
Income disadvantage	-23.0	-0.9	-2.1	-4.9	-15.6	-15.3
Race disadvantage	-35.9	-110.7	-117.4	-90.9	-51.5	-0.6
Total disadvantage	-59.0	-111.6	-119.5	-95.8	-67.1	-15.9

Note: The figures shown here represent average disadvantage scores for Model 1 probit equations for 1995 and 1996 home-purchase loans, estimated separately. The lower (more negative) the score, the worse the disdvantage.

Table 9.21 **Relative Lender Performance Against Market Average, Home-Purchase Loans in Seventeen Markets, 1995 and 1996**

	1996 Loans			1995 Loans		
	Lower-income disadvantage	Minority disadvantage	Total disadvantage	Lower-income disadvantage	Minority disadvantage	Total disadvantage
All lenders average	-8.1	-45.2	-53.3	-28.4	-54.5	-82.9
(calculated with merging banks divided into two groups in probit equations)						
Difference between all-lenders avg and:						
Small in-state banks	1.9	-6.5	-4.7	5.4	-9.5	-4.1
Large banks with in-state branches	1.9	13.6	15.5	5.3	-2.9	2.4
Large banks without in-state branches	-1.4	-13.3	-14.7	8.7	-5.1	3.7
Savings and loans	-3.0	-15.5	-18.5	-4.5	2.7	-1.8
Mortgage companies	0.7	21.8	22.4	-12.6	19.3	6.7
All lenders average	-15.0	-48.2	-63.2			
(calculated with merging banks treated as one group in probit equations)						
Difference between all-lenders avg and:						
Small in-state banks	9.5	-12.0	-2.5			
All merging banks	1.0	-5.0	-4.0			
Savings and loans	-0.9	0.2	-0.7			
Mortgage companies	-9.6	16.8	7.2			

Source: Coefficients from probit equations for loan approval, chapter 9.

Note: An average disadvantage is computed for each market and then subtracted from every lender group's score. The resulting difference is then summed across all market areas and divided to get an average for every lender type. A positive average means that the lender group did better than the average market performance; a negative average, worse.

Among commercial banks, small banks' average coefficients are (again with one exception) further to the southwest than the overall (indicating more disadvantage for African-American and Hispanic borrowers) than the all-lenders' average. Merging banks in-state have a pattern of relatively small coefficients, while merging banks out-of-state have generally high negative coefficients.

Figure 9.41b uses the same scale as Figure 9.41a to depict regional/lender-type coefficient averages for Hispanic and Asian-American applicants. Again mortgage companies perform best—all but one of their gray dots are clustered together northeast of the all-lenders' diamond. Savings and loan associations and small in-state banks also have tight clusters of regional averages, generally close to the origin. The regional averages for the two large bank groups are more dispersed; those for merging banks in-state, in particular, are widely spread out.

We now turn back to disadvantage analysis. Table 9.20 presents disadvantage scores by region and lender type explicitly; unlike Figures 9.40 and 9.41, which contain 1996 data, Table 9.20 shows averages for 1995 and 1996 regressions (run separately). The all-lenders averages show that income disadvantage is most significant in the Northeastern and Southwestern city clusters analyzed here, and lowest in the Mountain/Midwestern and California market areas. Racial disadvantage is most significant in the Southwestern and Mountain/Midwestern states, on average. So overall, disadvantage scores are highest in the Southwestern (New Mexico and Texas) cities, followed closely by the Northeastern and Mountain/Midwestern markets included here. The disadvantage averages for each lender type are widely variable. Merging banks with in-state branches, for example, perform worst in the Southeast and best in the Northeastern and Mountain/Midwestern areas.

The data shown in Table 9.20 suggest that a comparison of different lender types may be biased if it ignores the relatively large differences in disadvantage levels among regions. Table 9.21 calculates disadvantage scores for different lender types relative to regional averages for all lenders. So a positive score indicates less disadvantage than is found on average in each region; a negative score indicates more disadvantage. Results drawn from 1995 and 1996 Model 1 probits are shown separately. In both years, the best relative disadvantage performance is turned in by mortgage companies; large banks with in-state branches also have good relative performances in both years. In 1996, savings and loans and large banks without in-state branches had poor relative performance. In 1995, savings and loans also performed poorly, but small in-state banks did somewhat worse. This table also shows the analytical conclusions that follow when all large merging banks are combined into one category. When this is done, large merging banks are actually the worst-performing sector, on average, followed by small in-state banks and savings and loans.

We might close this section by mentioning one empirical experiment that failed, but with results of interest in evaluating the social-efficiency aspects of merging banks' and other banks' credit-market performance. This experiment focused on small in-state banks that were making HMDA-reported loans in 1992 but ceased reporting under HMDA by 1996 (in most cases because they had closed). Figure 9.42 depicts the 1992 disadvantage scores for these lenders. A comparison of these scores with those for other lender groups in 1992 does not find that these closed banks were uniformly better or worse than other lender groups in social-efficiency terms. For example, closed banks outperform merging banks in-state in eight city clusters in 1992—especially in California, New Mexico, and the Southeast—but perform less well in seven cases.

Conclusion

This chapter has uncovered substantial evidence that minority applicants and areas, as well as lower-income applicants and areas, are at a considerable disadvantage in obtaining loan approval throughout every region of the United States. African-Americans' chances of loan approval are worse than those of other applicants in virtually every Model 1 probit equation run here. The almost certain feature of any American credit market is that African-American applicants will be at a statistically significant disadvantage. Native American applicants are also chronically disadvantaged, and Hispanic applicants are frequently disadvantaged. Redlining (area) effects, while smaller in magnitude than person-specific effects, are regularly significant in lending markets.

The disadvantage technique developed here, using race and lower-income coefficients for 1995 and 1996, leads to the conclusion that savings and loan associations performed worst on average in the many equations run here. Mortgage companies, on balance, scored best in the disadvantage index. This result for mortgage companies must be treated with care. There is reason to suspect that mortgage companies are more likely than other lenders to have onerous terms and conditions, about which HMDA data provides no information. The high fair-share scores reported for these lenders in this chapter suggest that in some cases they may be working in lower-income and minority neighborhoods to provide credit at higher terms than other lenders who will not lend there. At the same time, while some mortgage companies may impose exploitative terms on their borrowers, most compete head-to-head in the mainstream mortgage market. Only the presence of extensive data on key terms and conditions of HMDA-reported loans can resolve this problem.

The assessment of small in-state banks' performance depends on how they are compared. When they are compared with *all* large merging banks, their performance is the same as or slightly better than their large-bank competitors. When they are compared with the two subgroups of large merging banks, small in-state banks do less well. Large merging banks with in-state banks generally perform well relative to other lenders, while merging banks without local branches perform badly in disadvantage terms. This result in itself constitutes

Figure 9.42 **Disadvantage Scores for Commercial Banks Closed After 1992, All City Clusters, 1992**

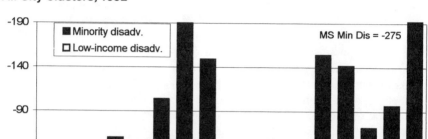

Note: City clusters are distributed left to right in their order of introduction in this chapter. Figures show net disadvantage per 1,000 hypothetical borrowers.

yet more evidence that local market structure—the presence of bank branches in localities where lenders lend—matters.

In broad terms, this chapter has added to the large body of empirical literature that suggests that loan applicants who are minorities, who have relatively low incomes, and who seek loans on homes in minority or lower-income neighborhoods are at a systematic disadvantage in every region of the United States. Model 1 cannot identify whether the minority disadvantage registered here is due to personal discrimination, to structural differences between white and minority applicants, or to other factors. But whether this difference arises because some groups are treated unfairly or have fewer economic resources, the outcome is the same—credit-market outcomes will at best reproduce, and at worst amplify, structural inequality that divides the United States along income and racial lines ever more deeply. This chapter also makes the contrasting point that these structural differences in credit-market outcomes are not fatally necessary. In many markets, our econometric results suggest that one or more lender groups have initiated practices that reverse minority and lower-income disadvantage. That different lenders might "read" a situation differently, or act differently, follows naturally from our twin core assumptions that economic outcomes are uncertain and that financial structures matter. Efforts to identify and understand reversals of this sort are crucial.

10

Bank Concentration, Strategic Interaction, and Access to Credit

Introduction: Why Should Concentration in Banking Markets Matter?

The econometric investigation in chapter 9 has focused on whether different types of lender behave differently in credit markets, with special attention to merging banks. We found that merging banks with in-state branches generally perform well, as measured by our racial and lower-income disadvantage index; but merging banks offshore—without in-state branches—perform badly. The focus was on the behavior of large merging banks versus other lenders in residential credit-markets modeled the same from one place to another. In reality, of course, markets differ in numerous characteristics. Among these, one is of special importance for our investigation of the impact of bank mergers—the degree of monopoly power that exists in local banking markets. Model 1 per se pays no attention to monopoly power. This chapter modifies Model 1 to allow us to consider the link between the degree of bank concentration and credit-market outcomes. Here we address the specific question: What is the effect of market concentration per se on outcomes in urban credit markets?

We first develop some insights into the possible importance of market concentration among banks. We then report on probit results incorporating banking-market concentration factors for ten California cities; probits are run for 1995 and 1996 separately. The 1990 census data and 1995 and 1996 HMDA data used in the probit analysis of ciapter 9 are supplemented here by some measures of banking market concentration published by Laderman (1995). This empirical experiment suggests that increasing concentration in banking markets reduces the probability of loan approval, all else being equal. This evidence is of special interest because the influence of increasing market concentration on access to credit has not previously been explored. The results shown here illustrate the broad point made throughout this work—the ongoing bank merger wave has social consequences and costs that have been all but ignored to date, but which deserve close attention from citizens, banks, and regulators.

Economic Aspects of Banking-Market Concentration
and Market Power

How could a changing degree of concentration affect outcomes in credit markets? A market's degree of concentration refers to whether a small number of firms account for a large share of total activity therein. Concentrated markets may feature one monopoly supplier, a few suppliers (oligopoly), or many suppliers with several firms that have dominant market shares. The coexistence of very large and very small firms within a given industry poses a puzzle for economic theory—in standard models, it is assumed that all firms will adopt best-practice technology, and this will lead to all firms' reaching approximately the same (efficient) size. So when one firm or several firms are large relative to their competitors, they must have privileged access to technology, information, capital, or all three. The coexistence of large and small firms can also be explained by theorizing that the large and small firms actually occupy different market niches because their products differ in significant ways. In banking, large and small banks do use different information and production technologies; and large and small banks often sell significantly different products, some of which go under the same name.

Historically, economists have criticized concentrated markets because the firm or firms that dominate these markets are able to charge higher prices and provide lower volumes than under conditions of perfect competition. As discussed in chapter 5, some economists do not regard concentration as a problem because they disagree that concentration will lead to persistent exploitative outcomes. In their view, monopolists who charge exploitative prices will soon be exposed to market entry; and agreements to collude among oligopolists are unstable because every cartel member has an incentive to undercut the agreed collusive price. So whether concentration in any specific markets leads to the exercise of market power depends on the constraints under which participants in those markets operate. Here we elaborate further on why market concentration might matter for credit-market outcomes.

It is useful to start with the cases of pure monopoly—one seller in one market—and pure competition. When a firm's goal is to maximize profit and when it has no competitors to worry about, it will sell fewer goods, and charge its customers more for each good, than if it had competitors. It will thus earn monopoly profits and restrict supply. When a profit-maximizing firm faces a large number of competitors, on the other hand, it must charge a price sufficiently low that its customers will not shift their business to its competitors; and when the price pressure exerted by competitors is maximized, this firm will earn zero profits (above whatever normal rate of return is obtained on invested capital).

Market concentration has an effect when a small number of large firms achieve excessive profits in a given market. The very presence of large firms is not enough to generate excess profits and restricted supply. Two structural elements in these markets are crucial. First, do those who buy from the large suppliers in this market have other alternatives? Second, are the monopoly profits earned in this market available to new entrants?

Monopoly profits in a given market may arise in part because the suppliers are providing something buyers need and can get nowhere else. In this case, monopolists and oligopolists have power over buyers. How much power depends on whether any close substitutes exist for what the monopolist sells, and on whether the monopoly's customers will face significant barriers or costs in switching markets. These barriers could arise because of discrimination, but they might also be due to transaction costs or informational barriers. In sum, the more nearly unique the product and the fewer options the monopoly's customers have, the higher monopoly profits can be in a given market.

So in the markets for loans and banking services, do those served by banks have other options? The answer is different for different types of customers. Chapter 4 has described the strategic shift in banking, which has been triggered by—and has contributed to—a redefinition of market boundaries and instruments. As noted, banks' deposit customer base is being segmented into several relatively distinct components, each with a different financial capacity (and hence revenue potential, from the intermediaries' perspective). Different levels of financial capacity translate into different cost and return possibilities for bank customers. Those with money market and 401(k) funds and credit cards have more leverage—more market power—than those struggling to meet minimum deposit balances. And the alternatives to bank-provided deposits, checks, and loans that are available to those with fewer resources will invariably cost more, impose more risk, or be less secure. Financial wealth, income, and race are all highly correlated, so minority and lower-income households have fewer cost-competitive financial-services alternatives to what banks offer than do white and upper-income households. In sum, a portion of banks' customer base in both the deposit and loan markets are relatively captive customers; another portion are highly mobile.

What about the second question: Are monopoly profits available to new banking-market entrants? Suppose monopoly profits exist because firms can indeed charge higher-than-competitive prices and earn excessive profits. Whether new firms will enter this market depends on several factors. For one thing, entering a market involves fixed costs; if these are substantial relative to the monopoly profits that any entrant could hope to share, entry will not occur. Second, entry may not occur if the large firms earning excess profits in a given market can threaten any new entrants with retaliation. Even if monopoly profits exist and do not require excessive fixed costs, the reaction of this market's existing monopoly supplier (or oligopolistic suppliers) to new entrants is crucial. Is this firm willing to share its monopoly profits more broadly—or will the monopolist cut prices to punish entrants and drive them out? Third, new entrants might not enter a monopolized market they regard as excessively unstable; in this case, the customer base being exploited by dominant firms may disappear due to structural change.

These factors all clearly apply to the case of banking. Fixed costs are high in banking. Retaliation by established large banks is likely. And customer bases are being continually redefined and redivided these days.

The upshot is that there is good reason to believe that the market power that potentially accrues to large firms in concentrated markets may be important in banking. Large banks with market power can exercise it in the case of customers who offer them only low revenue potential, and who lack low-cost or secure alternatives to banking services.

Strategic Interaction and Market Concentration in Banking

Thus far we have emphasized how market power can lead to certain classes of *individual customers'* facing higher costs, being less secure, and so on. However, the existence of market concentration may also have consequences for different *market areas.*

Any scenario of competition among price-setting oligopolists (large firms) involves strategic coordination. Strategic coordination refers to the interactions among the various competitors' pricing and selling approaches. It is certainly true that whether oligopolistic banks enjoy monopolistic profits depends on whether they can successfully collude by holding prices above competitive levels. Collusion presents difficulties because firms in the market may be tempted to defect and take short-term gains; and these firms may also need to deter new entrants, as noted above. This well-known game-theoretic scenario can give rise to many different outcomes over time, which we do not explore further here. Instead we focus on another set of strategic considerations that has been largely overlooked in the credit market literature.

Strategic interaction also comes into play in lenders' decisions on where to lend. Whether banks will lend in a given area depends, in effect, on where other banks are lending. This matters because arguably the returns on these institutions' loans in a given market area depend on the pattern of loan flows there. The building blocks for these arguments have already been put in place; see the discussion surrounding Figure 7.1. To review, agents with informational advantages often have reasons to hide information they possess; and time-using economic processes have uncertain, and not merely risky, outcomes—a fact causing distress to the agents who must have invested capital in hopes of achieving positive outcomes. Financial intermediaries have the recurring problem of being uninformed about their applicants' true capacities and intentions; but their very *raison d'être* as lenders forces them to commit loans over time in the face of uncertainty and of possibly flawed or misleading information. Further, banks must make a lot of decisions of this sort, and quickly. Consequently, banks may use all sorts of information as signals about whether loans to particular kinds of borrower in particular geographic areas are likely to work out or to go bad.

As Figure 7.1 points out, many different kinds of information are used as proxies about which loan applicants and which geographic areas should be bet on. This figure differentiates between presumptive and behavioral signals, which can be obtained via either public or private channels. Public information is cheaper than private information; and since behavioral signals are superior to presumptive signals, the best sort of information is public behavioral information. One source of information of this sort is the geographic distribution of the loans made by other (competing) lenders. Knowing where the other firms have put their money may be useful and lead to an "imitation effect" in local lending patterns. Note that for any given lender, if other lenders have done costly (private) research, then those other firms' loan patterns presumably reflect the conclusions of that research; so lending where other lenders lend is a way of capturing some of the value of information someone else has paid for. This imitation effect could be at work even if lenders are pursuing fee-based income by making loans they can sell off. If some lenders are making lots of loans (and hence generating fee-based income) in a given area, other lenders may want a piece of the action. One can imagine scenarios in which knowing where other lenders are active might generate a negative imitation effect within a given landscape—in some cases, information on where other lenders are operating may lead lenders to focus on somewhat different areas.[1]

If lenders are dealing with areas about which there is substantial uncertainty, lending where other lenders lend may also be sensible due to spillover effects. Section 3 of chapter 1 argued that spillover effects are important in bank/community dynamics. Spillovers arise whenever the returns or costs of an economic transaction are not exhausted by the parties to that transaction. The more important spillovers are in molding those outcomes, uncertainty about outcomes is certainly greater. In an urban credit market, a bank's decision to make a loan in a community generates a clear benefit to the borrower—but it may also have either of two spillover effects in the surrounding community (Dymski 1995). For one thing, there may be a refurbishment effect from home turnovers—that is, incoming owners have a tendency to "spruce up" their new homes. This refurbishment enhances the value of new owners' assets, but also the value of nearby homes and businesses. Second, there is a liquidity effect—the turnover of houses put on the market in a given community increases the "liquidity value" of housing assets there. A prospective homeowner seeking housing within a given metropolis will, all things being equal, buy a home in a community where housing assets are readily bought and sold; for in a mobile nation, this ensures that one can "get one's money out" when it is time to move on.

The sale of any one home will generate a small spillover; whether this spillover is captured by other homeowners or lenders depends on the overall geographic pattern of loans in a metropolis. Note that imitation-effect competition and spillovers can be mutually reinforcing. Loans by any lender in a given community may lead other lenders competing for metropolitan market share to seek out a piece of that community's loan market; and these net loan flows may, in turn, enhance the value of that community's assets (and reduce default probability), validating the original decision to follow the leader.

Summary

In sum, strategic cooperation can play out many different ways in urban loan markets. As we have seen several times, the economic theory relevant to urban credit markets does not lead to firm predictions, but instead suggests the range of possible outcomes in the real world. These ideas support the coevolutionary view of the bank/community relationship, introduced in chapter 1 and contrasted with the passive view of this relationship. There is clearly an implicit connection between strategic interaction and market concentration. The character of strategic interaction depends on the characteristics and strategies of active lenders at a given place and time. When a small number of firms dominate market share, their choices and strategies dominate the path-dependent dynamics associated with spillover-ridden markets. A small number of large lenders can make a market bloom or leave it fallow.

Market Concentration and Access to Credit in Ten California Cities

In chapters 7 to 9 we explored the relationship between banking-market concentration and financial outcomes indirectly, using our "horse race" approach and a variety of descriptive statistics. A 1995 study by Elizabeth Laderman of the Federal Reserve Bank of San Francisco offers an opportunity to confront directly the question of whether market concentration per se affects access to credit. Laderman calculated a variety of market-structure variables for a variety of Western urban markets for 1982 and 1992; among these variables are number of operating banks, deposit volumes, and HHI scores.[2] Of the markets examined by Laderman, many fall outside of the states examined here, and some are small markets. However, many of the mid-size and large markets she incorporates are in California. Since California cities are incorporated into our study already, the effects of market concentration on credit-market outcomes can be evaluated using a subset of Laderman's California banking markets.

Model 2: Design

Laderman's HHI data can be used to assess whether the probability of loan approval varies with the structural factors she identifies, especially the degree of banking-market concentration as measured by the HHI. The ten California cities selected here are Bakersfield, Fresno, Modesto, Riverside–San Bernardino, Sacramento, San Diego, Santa Barbara, Santa Cruz, Santa Rosa, and Stockton. Los

Angeles was avoided because of its size, and San Francisco because of its possibly unique circumstances. Using only California cities holds constant many factors that vary between metropolitan areas in different states—for example, states' bank charter and branching regulations, their merger-entry rules, the composition of in-state and out-of-state lenders, and local economic conditions. With these factors held constant, the importance of HHI per se comes to the fore.

The point of departure for our estimation here is Model 1. We construct Model 2 by adding four structural variables, differing from city to city, which are based on Laderman's reported data. These are

- The logarithm of the 1982 HHI index,
- The percentage change in the HHI index between 1982 and 1992,
- The percentage change in operating banks, 1982–1992,
- The logarithm of 1992 bank deposits.

Using the logarithm of the 1982 HHI index and of 1992 bank deposits scales these figures appropriately for our probit equation. The two percentage-change variables are multiplied by 0.01; but they are *not* logged, because they sometimes take on negative values.[3] The first two variables in this list describe market concentration per se, as it evolved in the period 1982–1992. The third variable controls for changes in the number of bank competitors per se. Since the number of banks and the degree of concentration are independent, adding this variable ensures that the coefficients for the HHI variables do not include effects attributable to changes in the number of banks. The fourth variable is a scale variable, whose inclusion controls for differences in the size of the ten cities included in this estimation.

Table 10.1 presents the values of the first three of these variables for the ten California cities included here. The last two columns of Table 10.1 contain city-by-city data on loan approval rates, to permit comparisons of approval rates with HHI levels. A perusal of these data suggests no obvious relationship between banking-market concentration and access to credit (as measured by the approval rate for loan applications). However, a simple comparison of this sort can be misleading, because these cities differ in many ways apart from banking-market HHI. For example, these cities have widely different proportions of minority applicants (the 1995 home-purchase applicant pool varies from 42 percent minority in Riverside–San Bernardino to 86 percent in Santa Rosa); they also differ in income, age of housing stock, density, and so on.

Of course, probit analysis, like regression, is designed precisely to untangle the effects of multiple factors on a single determined variable. The idea of the Model 2 probit is to determine whether increases in market concentration and in market size (as measured by deposit volume), and the sheer number of bank lenders, affect access to capital as measured by the probability of loan approval. By adding these variables to our baseline model, these effects are captured net of

Table 10.1   **Recent Changes in Banking-Market Structure, Ten California Cities**

	Banking mkt HHI level:		% Ch., 1982-92, in:		1995 home-purchase loans (%):	
	in 1982	in 1992	HHI level	No. of banks	Approved and made	Withdrawn, incomplete, other
Fresno	1489	1796	20.6	-24.1	61.0	19.9
Riv./S.Bernard	1339	1698	26.8	15.4	70.4	17.5
Bakersfield	1280	1567	22.4	-27.3	75.3	14.3
Santa Barbara	808	1544	91.1	-28.0	65.8	20.5
Santa Cruz	1951	1288	-34.0	-28.6	69.8	18.0
Sacramento	1347	1241	-7.9	-13.5	74.9	15.0
Stockton	3385	1217	-64.0	-12.0	72.5	15.9
Modesto	971	1178	21.3	-32.1	59.5	20.0
San Diego	828	1084	30.9	-5.6	68.8	19.0
Santa Rosa	1091	878	-19.5	7.4	70.1	17.8

Source: Laderman (1995); 1995 HMDA data.

Note: In column 4, a positive sign for percent changes in HHI levels means more concentration; in column 5, a negative sign means fewer commercial banks operating. One hundred minus columns 6 and 7 equals the percentage of 1995 applications denied.

all the other factors incorporated into Model 1. Since the four variables added here are all the same for each of the ten cities, our procedure replaces the intercept terms of the previous models with several variables specific to each city. The probit estimation then determines, in effect, whether each of these individual factors contributes independently to the location of every city's intercept term.

In addition to the HHI-related variables added in Model 2, we should point out the presence of two variables already present in Model 1, which test for strategic interaction among banks in their credit-market behavior. One variable, identified as V15 in Appendix 8A, tests whether home-purchase loan applications in that 50 percent of census tracts with the highest loan volume are more or less likely to be approved than loans in lower-volume census tracts; the other, (V16 in Appendix 8A), tests whether home-purchase loan applications in that 50 percent of census tracts with the highest average loan amounts are more or less likely to be approved than loans in lower-loan-value census tracts.

The discussion in the previous section pointed out that strategic interactions among banks could work out many different ways. Banks might seek out loan opportunities in underserved niches in a metropolis; or they might seek out loan opportunities in areas where many other lenders are active. These two variables admittedly offer only crude first approximations to the question of whether lender strategic interaction matters; but they are a first approximation, nonetheless. In the estimated equations summarized in chapter 9, at least one of these variables is typically significant. Because of the special connection suggested in the previous section between market concentration and strategic interaction, the coefficients for these variables will be discussed explicitly here.

Model 2: Results

Model 2 was estimated separately for 1995 and 1996 data. Several versions of Model 2 were run; and Model 1 was also run on the same data. These experiments all suggest that variables included in both Model 1 and Model 2 take on very similar coefficient values in both models; and that the variables included in Model 2 enhance the explanatory power of Model 1. The results for all lenders are presented in Table 10.2. This table presents the results of four separate probits—1995 and 1996 probits for all home-purchase loans, including those with conventional and FHA/VA financing, and 1995 and 1996 probits for conventional loans only.

Note first in Table 10.2 that most Model 1 variables are statistically significant and have the expected coefficients in these probits. Interestingly, the Asian-American coefficient is invariably negative and significant here. Also of special interest are the two bank strategic-interaction variables. The loan-volume term, which tests for whether lenders make loans in tracts where other lenders are making loans (holding several of these tracts' other characteristics constant), is invariably positive and significant; its value ranges from 3.8 percent to 10.8 percent. The loan-value term is negative in one of two all-loans equations, but positive and significant in both conventional-loans equations.

All four market-structure variables are significant in each of the four equations shown, with one exception. The expected signs for these variables are: log of 1982 HHI index, −; change in HHI, 1982–1992, −; 1992 deposits, +; change in banks, 1982–1992, +. A review of these results shows that the 1982 HHI variable takes on the anticipated positive sign in the conventional-loans equation, but a negative sign in the all-loans equation. The 1982–1992 HHI change variable is negative and significant in three of four cases; 1992 deposits are positive and significant only once, and negative and significant twice; and the change in banks variable is negative in 1995 but positive in 1996.

Table 10.2 thus presents solid evidence that banking concentration, as measured by two HHI variables, significantly affects the probability of home-purchase loan approvals; and so does the size of any city's deposit base and changes in its bank population. Similar results were derived for equations run with sub-sets of the data used here—for minority and white applicants separately, for commercial banks only, for large merging banks only, and so on. The differences in signs of the market-structure variables among these equations are somewhat surprising. However, it should be kept in mind that the 1992 deposits variable is a proxy for the size of the market; the shift from positive to negative of this variable's coefficient between 1995 and 1996 represents factors unmeasured here that increased relative lending in bigger markets in 1995, but decreased it in

Table 10.2 **Probit Results for Model 2 in Ten California Cities, for All Lenders, Home-Purchase Loans, 1995 and 1996**

Variables:	All Loans, Conventional and FHA/VA				Conventional Loans only			
	1995 Data		1996 Data		1995 Data		1996 Data	
	Estim.	Std. Err.	Estim.	Std. Err.	Estim.	Std. Err.	Estim.	Std. Err.
Intercept	0.034	(0.254)	-1.043	(0.225) ***	1.621	(0.278) ***	1.055	(0.387) ***
Applicant characteristics								
Native American	-0.256	(0.050) ***	-0.256	(0.046) ***	-0.280	(0.059) ***	-0.310	(0.086) ***
African American	-0.284	(0.020) ***	-0.053	(0.018) ***	-0.398	(0.028) ***	-0.024	(0.031)
Asian American	-0.039	(0.020) **	-0.263	(0.018) ***	-0.014	(0.022)	-0.399	(0.040) ***
Hispanic American	-0.015	(0.012)	0.023	(0.011) **	-0.175	(0.015) ***	-0.196	(0.022) ***
Female	0.015	(0.012)	0.002	(0.010)	0.039	(0.014) ***	0.027	(0.019)
Loan/Income ratio	-0.018	(0.002) ***	-0.002	(0.000) ***	-0.015	(0.002) ***	-0.048	(0.006) ***
Log(Applic. Income)	0.048	(0.013) ***	0.105	(0.011) ***	0.114	(0.015) ***	0.075	(0.019) ***
Loan rank (4 levels)	0.048	(0.008) ***	-0.040	(0.006) ***	0.023	(0.010) **	-0.006	(0.010)
Loan/Inc rank (4 lev)	0.052	(0.007) ***	0.069	(0.005) ***	0.014	(0.008) *	0.037	(0.010) ***
Low-income applicants	-0.003	(0.014) **	-0.137	(0.013) ***	-0.020	(0.017) ***	-0.173	(0.024) ***
Census tract characteristics								
Residential density	0.137	(0.001) ***	0.000	(0.001)	0.133	(0.004) ***	-0.002	(0.002)
Pct of owner occup's	-0.031	(0.027) **	0.121	(0.022) ***	-0.057	(0.027) ***	0.097	(0.036) ***
High-minority areas	-0.081	(0.013) ***	-0.030	(0.012) ***	-0.067	(0.017) ***	-0.064	(0.024) ***
Low-income areas	-0.101	(0.015) ***	-0.090	(0.013) ***	-0.129	(0.018) ***	-0.090	(0.025) ***
High-loan activity areas	0.108	(0.015) ***	0.038	(0.010) ***	0.099	(0.017) ***	0.047	(0.019) **
Areas w/high loan amts	-0.056	(0.011) ***	0.002	(0.010)	0.033	(0.014) **	0.091	(0.019) ***
Market concentration factors								
Log of 1982 HHI index	0.071	(0.027) ***	0.470	(0.055) ***	-0.177	(0.029) ***	-0.184	(0.094) *
Change in HHI, '82-92	-0.073	(0.026) ***	0.086	(0.023) ***	-0.312	(0.028) ***	-0.197	(0.039) ***
Deposits, 1992	0.017	(0.031) **	-0.224	(0.027) ***	0.008	(0.036)	-0.314	(0.050) ***
Change in banks, '82-92	-0.170	(0.008) ***	0.039	(0.016) **	-0.326	(0.008) ***	0.044	(0.027) *
No of observations	130,467		159,004		85,759		97,669	
Proportion of approvals	0.859		0.853		0.826		0.825	
Log likelihd for normal	-52338		-64521		-38432		-44099	
Pearsn Chi-Sq: Pr>Chi-Sq	0.000		0.001		0.000		0.000	
L.R. Chi-Sq: Pr >Chi-Sq.	1.000		1.000		1.000		1.000	

*** denotes significance at the 1% level, ** at the 5% level, * at the 10% level.

1996. The change-in-banks variable also appears to be responding to different forces in the two different years.

Most surprising are the positive coefficients for HHI variables in the two all-purchase-loans equations—especially because these HHI variables take on anticipated signs in the conventional-loans-only equations. However, on further reflection this apparent anomaly can be understood. The conventional-loans equations produce the expected signs—access to capital declines as market concentration increases. This is the classic pattern anticipated in the long structure-conduct-performance tradition in industrial organization, wherein firms operating in markets with higher degrees of monopoly are more discriminating about the quantity and terms of contracts they will strike with their customer base. The basic insight is that since the customer has few other places to turn, the customer has little—or at least restricted—choice. Conventional loans are booked to be sold off, in the main, using standard creditworthiness criteria. When VA/FHA loans are added to conventional loans, the relationships set out in Table 10.2 sometimes reverse signs. This may be due to two reasons: First, VA/FHA loans may be easier to place and process in more concentrated banking markets; second, VA/FHA loan applications behave very differently from conventional loans, and hence are effectively white noise muddying relationships more clearly observed for conventional-loan applications only. Further study of these market-structure variables and effects is warranted. The key point established in the probits shown in Table 10.2 is that local market-structure effects are consistently significant in residential-credit markets. Market concentration very much matters even in the era of particle finance.

How quantitatively important are these market-concentration effects? A benchmark here is provided by the coefficients for minority applicants' race: These are as large as –40 percent in Table 10.2. Are market-concentration factors this important? Answering this question requires some manipulation of the raw results in Table 10.2; Table 10.3 contains the results of these adjustments.[4]

Table 10.3 shows how three market-structure variables affect the probability of loan approval in the two all-lenders equations for conventional loans that were shown in Table 10.2. Note that differences in 1982 HHI have an impact on loan approval that ranges from –7 percent in Stockton in both years, due to its high 1982 concentration level, to a 4 percent higher probability of approval in Santa Barbara due to its low 1982 concentration level. The 1982–1992 change in HHI has an even larger impact on the probability of loan approval; this effect ranges from an estimated 20 percent boost to loan approval rates for Stockton (due to this city's huge 1982–1992 reduction in HHI levels) in 1995, to an estimated –15 percent effect (also in 1995) on Santa Barbara approval rates as that market became more concentrated. The 1982–1992 change in banks has slightly smaller effects, ranging from +5.0 percent to –10.5 percent in 1995, and from +1.4 percent to –0.7 percent in 1996. The net effect of these market-structure effects is recorded in the far right column in Table 10.3. The highest positive net effect estimated is a 10.2 percent boost to the probability of loan approval in Santa Rosa in 1995, and a 5.8 percent boost in Stockton in 1996. The largest negative net effect of these market-structure variables on loan approval is –33.6 percent in 1995 and –12.6 percent in 1996; both scores are registered for Santa Barbara, due to its increasing concentration and its loss of banks operating locally.

For conventional loans, the net effect of these market-structure variables on the probability of loan approval, in sum, is negative in eight of ten cities in 1995, and in six of ten cities in 1996. A calculation of the effect of these same variables on loan approval for all loans, not shown here, comes to similar conclusions: The net probability of loan approval is less in five cities in 1995, and in

Table 10.3a **Estimated Effect of Banking-Market Structure Variables on Home-Purchase Approval Rates in Ten California Cities, 1995 and 1996**

| (in percent) | Effect on probability of loan approval of: | | | Net estimated |
	1982 HHI	Change in HHI, 1982-1992	Ch. in no. of banks, '82-'92	effect of mar- ket structure
Estimates for all lenders, conventional loans only, 1995				
Fresno	-0.76	-6.43	-7.89	-15.08
Riv./S.Bernard.	0.06	-8.37	5.03	-3.28
Bakersfield	0.40	-7.00	-8.92	-15.51
Santa Barbara	3.94	-28.42	-9.16	-33.64
Santa Cruz	-2.84	10.60	-9.34	-1.58
Sacramento	0.01	2.46	-4.40	-1.93
Stockton	-7.07	19.98	-3.92	8.99
Modesto	2.53	-6.65	-10.51	-14.63
San Diego	3.75	-9.65	-1.84	-7.74
Santa Rosa	1.63	6.09	2.42	10.15
Estimates for all lenders, conventional loans only, 1996				
Fresno	-0.79	-4.06	1.06	-3.79
Riv./S.Bernard.	0.06	-5.28	-0.68	-5.90
Bakersfield	0.42	-4.42	1.20	-2.80
Santa Barbara	4.10	-17.94	1.23	-12.62
Santa Cruz	-2.95	6.69	1.26	5.00
Sacramento	0.01	1.55	0.59	2.16
Stockton	-7.35	12.62	0.53	5.79
Modesto	2.63	-4.20	1.41	-0.16
San Diego	3.90	-6.09	0.25	-1.94
Santa Rosa	1.70	3.85	-0.33	5.22

seven cities in 1996. A simple calculation allows us to measure how these market-structure shifts affected these ten California cities as a whole. For each city, the number of 1995 home-purchase loan applicants is multiplied by the net effect of market-structure variables on loan-approval probability. The product that results indicates the number of applicants who can be considered either approved or not approved for home-purchase loans due solely to these market-structure effects (holding constant the other variables included in Model 2). Summing across all ten cities suggests that the three market-structure variables shown in Table 10.3 led to 2.3 percent (3,760) of all home-purchase loan applicants' being set aside in 1995; and 5.8 percent (9,630) of all home-purchase loan applicants were set aside in 1996.[5]

In sum, Tables 10.2 and 10.3 provide strong evidence that market structure in general, and the degree of banking concentration in particular, is an important determinant of access to credit. Table 10.3 shows that the relative effects of banking-market concentration on the probability of loan approval, in some cities,

Table 10.3b **Estimated Effect of Banking-Market Structure Variables on Home-Purchase Approval Rates in Ten California Cities, 1995 and 1996 (in percent)**

(in percent)	Effect on probability of loan approval of:			Net estimated effect of market structure
	1982 HHI	Change in HHI, 1982-1992	Ch. in no. of banks, '82-'92	
Estimates for all lenders, all home-purchase loans, 1995				
Fresno	0.30	-1.51	-4.10	-5.30
Riv./S.Bernard.	-0.02	-1.96	2.62	0.64
Bakersfield	-0.16	-1.64	-4.64	-6.44
Santa Barbara	-1.58	-6.65	-4.76	-12.99
Santa Cruz	1.14	2.48	-4.86	-1.24
Sacramento	0.00	0.57	-2.29	-1.72
Stockton	2.84	4.68	-2.04	5.47
Modesto	-1.01	-1.56	-5.46	-8.03
San Diego	-1.51	-2.26	-0.96	-4.72
Santa Rosa	-0.65	1.43	1.26	2.03
Estimates for all lenders, all home-purchase loans, 1996				
Fresno	2.01	1.77	0.94	4.73
Riv./S.Bernard.	-0.15	2.31	-0.60	1.55
Bakersfield	-1.07	1.93	1.06	1.92
Santa Barbara	-10.46	7.83	1.09	-1.54
Santa Cruz	7.53	-2.92	1.11	5.72
Sacramento	-0.03	-0.68	0.53	-0.18
Stockton	18.78	-5.51	0.47	13.74
Modesto	-6.71	1.83	1.25	-3.63
San Diego	-9.96	2.66	0.22	-7.09
Santa Rosa	-4.33	-1.68	-0.29	-6.30

are comparable to some applicant race effects. So banking-market structure generally, and bank concentration specifically, clearly deserves much closer attention in studies of access to credit. These probit results suggest that market concentration reduces access to credit systematically, just as applicant minority status does. More thorough study is warranted, as is regulatory concern about the continuing impact of market concentration on local market outcomes.

These striking results are paradoxical in light of recent trends—for how can it be that *banks'* market concentration so consistently affects lending outcomes, when the markets for residential credit have apparently become so much more open in recent years? Several responses to this question can be proposed. First, while many more nondepository firms now operate in local residential credit markets than before, it is by no means the case that commercial banks have at the same time become less important in these markets. Instead, banks have been gaining market share in mortgage markets at the expense of the collapsing thrift industry. So commercial banks are not universally losing their grip on residential credit markets to nonbank competitors; the opposite appears to be true in many locales.

A second response is that the diversity of mortgage companies in any given credit market may be more apparent than real. Many mortgage companies' reported loans are derived from their participation as financiers in specific new-homes projects; so mortgage companies' credit is not as widely available as it would appear from the sheer number of these nonbank lenders' loans in any given year. Third, many lenders now make loans by recourse to relatively standardized terms; so the presence of ever more lenders in residential credit markets may not enhance opportunities for credit-market access. Finally, the market structures of the nonbank sectors that compete with banks are often moderately or even highly concentrated. In many locales, the consumer seeking credit may have to choose which monopolistic market she will contend with.

Table 10.4 provides some explicit data on different lenders' market concentration for the California cities used in the HHI probit equations in this chapter. The data are unconventional. The HMDA data for 1995 themselves are used to generate quasi-HHI estimates by lender group. Turn first to the HMDA-based HHI estimates for commercial banks only. These quasi-HHI figures are derived by calculating the market share of each bank in the 1995 home-purchase loan pool, squaring each market share, and adding the resulting figures together. Note that the quasi-HHI figures are surprisingly close to those provided by Laderman for 1992—the Laderman 1992 and quasi-1995 estimates of HHI are highly correlated (0.875). This gives a degree of confidence in the quasi-HHI estimates for mortgage companies and savings institutions. The quasi-HHI estimates for savings institutions are remarkably high—several exceed the 1,000–HHI benchmark suggested by the Federal Reserve for moderately concentrated banking markets. The mortgage companies' quasi-HHI figures indicate less concentration—but as argued above, this may not mean a significant improvement in choices and market access for consumers seeking residential credit.

Discussion: Concentration and Access to Credit

This chapter first discussed the possible influence of market concentration and bank strategic interaction on access to credit, and then reported on an empirical test of these factors in ten California credit markets. Probit equations using several measures of market structure, including two variables specifically measuring market concentration (HHI), were run. These probits indicate clearly that access to capital, as measured by the probability of loan approval, becomes less as banks' market concentration becomes more. Market concentration per se, changes in the degree of concentration, and changes in the number of banks operating locally are all significant determinants of the probability of loan approval; and the coefficients attached to these variables are, in some cases, nearly as large as those associated with individual race.

Table 10.4 **Market Characteristics by Lender Type, 1992 Federal Reserve Data and 1995 Home-Purchase Loans in Ten California Cities**

	Federal Reserve Data			Commercial Banks		
	1992 banking market characteristics:			5 largest lenders:		No. of
		% Ch in HHI,	% Ch in No.	HHI for 1995	% of all banks'	1995 comm.
MSA	HHI, 1992	1982-1992	of Com.Bks.	HMDA Loans	1995 loans	bank lenders:
Fresno	1796	20.6	-24.1	2212	76.3	52
Riv./S Bernard.	1698	26.8	15.4	1818	69.6	97
Bakersfield	1567	22.4	-27.3	2058	73.4	40
Santa Barbara	1544	91.1	-28.0	1516	76.8	42
Santa Cruz	1288	-34.0	-28.6	1288	65.3	41
Sacramento	1241	-7.9	-13.5	1199	62	70
Stockton	1217	-64.0	-12.0	924	56.1	48
Modesto	1178	21.3	-32.1	1153	67	39
San Diego	1084	30.9	-5.6	1078	68.5	83
Santa Rosa	878	-19.5	7.4	1120	67.2	46

	Mortgage Companies			Savings Institutions		
	5 largest lenders:		No. of active	5 largest lenders:		No. of active
	HHI for 1995	% of mort. co's'	1995 mortg.	HHI for 1995	% of all thrifts'	1995 thrift
MSA	HMDA Loans	1995 loans	co. lenders:	HMDA Loans	1995 loans	lenders:
Fresno	821	54.1	81	1121	70.8	33
Riv./S Bernard.	322	36.6	135	593	53.4	97
Bakersfield	514	49.8	76	1329	36.7	32
Santa Barbara	1869	71.3	49	1882	84.4	25
Santa Cruz	1321	66.7	39	1378	72	30
Sacramento	452	45.6	99	925	64.8	53
Stockton	590	51.0	72	1103	67.1	39
Modesto	531	50.1	59	1054	70.1	28
San Diego	492	44.3	108	1162	70.9	68
Santa Rosa	855	56.4	53	986	64.2	33

Source: Upper left quadrant, Laderman (1995); other data, 1995 HMDA data.

Note: The HHI for 1955 HMDA loans is derived by summing the square of the market-share percentages of the top five lenders in each lender category. Figures for active lenders reflect institutions reporting home-purchase loans under HMDA in 1995.

Further investigation of market-structure effects should be pursued before firm conclusions are drawn; these probit results clearly suggest that investigation into these effects is warranted. And since race coefficients comparable to those observed here have generated a continuing firestorm of controversy over the possibility of racial discrimination in credit markets, perhaps a controversy over the implications of market concentration in banking is not out of the question, before the banking industry's transformation is a *fait accompli.*

11
Conclusions

Introduction: Don't Worry, Be Happy?

Fueled by 1.7 mergers per business day since 1981, the scope and scale of the consolidation trend among commercial banks is remarkable. Not only has the numerical pace of bank mergers quickened since 1981, this pace has remained high to the present day. Further, these mergers increasingly involve megabanks both as acquirers and as targets.

For many industry analysts and much of the press, this trend in banking is as unstoppable as the weather. Distinguished financial economists such as Franklin Edwards and Frederic Mishkin have consistently developed several arguments that, taken together, not only justify bank mergers and megamergers, but interpret them as a key to rescuing the banking industry from obsolescence. First, both scholars have suggested that small banks as currently configured are not economically efficient institutions. In a coauthored 1995 article, they observed that when noninterest revenues are eliminated from bank profit flows, banks' return on assets has been negative since 1980. Since large banks are most efficient at fee-based activity, implicitly these authors are suggesting that only a drastic reduction in the number of small banks can rescue the industry from profitless stagnation. Mishkin made this point more strongly in a 1998 essay: "The restrictions on competition in the past which helped many small banks stay in business may have produced more small business lending than is socially optimal. The implicit subsidy to small banks from the restrictions on competition might have been passed onto some small businesses who would not have obtained loans otherwise" (16).

Second, changing the financial structure (by allowing mergers) will improve, not worsen, the allocation of credit. This point is implicit in the passage by Mishkin. Edwards wrote in 1988:

> the entire argument that we should be concerned about the effects of a revised financial structure on credit allocation is spurious. . . . Institutions will have offices in many locations and will quite naturally shift credit to areas and borrowers with the greatest need. Borrowers (of a given credit standing) who

are willing to pay more for credit will receive the credit. Since borrowers who are willing and able to pay more presumably have more productive (or higher-yielding) uses for the credit, the result is a more efficient allocation of credit. Credit will flow to its most productive uses. (133)

It has also been argued that one large bank with a portfolio of loans made in different geographic areas will be less risky than a set of smaller banks, each of which has made loans in just one of these areas. A regional downturn that would sink one or more of these small banks will only dent the earnings of the large one.

Third, mergers constitute no threat to the achievement of efficient banking market outcomes; to the contrary. Edwards writes, "The concentration occurring in banking is accompanied by a broadening of the relevant range of competition to include nonbanks in most product markets served by banks" (1988, 113). Indeed, "If anything, the acceptable concentration-ratio (or HHI) levels specified in the current Antitrust Guidelines are unnecessarily restrictive for the maintenance of competitive markets, and the importance attached to potential entry is too little" (140).

These arguments have some holes. It is true that small banks are risky because they are less capable of diversifying their loan portfolios. But large banks' potential for loan losses from participating in lending manias is at least as great as small banks'. While smaller institutions have been implicated in lending problems in the past two decades, large banks have been burned more severely by a string of loan crises: the LDC debt crisis, the commercial real-estate bubble, bridge loans for mergers and acquisitions, to name three.[1] Just over a decade ago, all three of the largest U.S. banks today, Chase, Citi, and BankAmerica, survived near-death experiences.

Large banks' lending problems have been especially severe precisely because large banks have been able to lend such large amounts, especially when competing for market share in fashionable "emerging" markets. This happened again in the East Asian crisis of 1997–1998. This crisis caught Citicorp with 20 percent of its overseas assets in East Asia; BankAmerica, 9 percent; and Chase, 8 percent. BankAmerica was placed on credit review by Moody's Investors Service in January 1998 because of concerns about its Asian subsidiary, especially after its stock price lost almost 24 percent of its value in December 1997. Other aspects of the vulnerability of large integrated banks to the global financial instability in 1997 and 1998 were discussed at the end of chapter 5.

And even though small banks are more risky because they are tied to local economic conditions, they remain viable as profit-earning firms. Katherine Samolyk at the Cleveland Fed disaggregated 1982–1994 bank call-report data by state and bank size to determine which types of banks are performing best. She found that local economic conditions do contribute to disparities in banks' profitability, asset quality, capitalization, and lending; but controlling for local economic health, small banks (those with assets of $100 million to $1 billion in

1987 dollars) had the best performance over the 1983–1994 decade, whereas the largest institutions were less profitable. Large banks had many more nonperforming loans than did small banks operating in the same markets. Small banks affiliated with multibank holding companies performed better than unaffiliated small banks. In sum, concludes Samolyk, "the experience of the 1980s [suggests that] banks *can* be too large" (1994, 3). Other micro-level studies also suggest that small banks have been consistently more profitable than large banks (see Berger, Hanweck, and Humphrey 1987 and Goudreau and King 1991).

What of the allocation of credit? It is comforting to assume that markets work well all the time in a disembodied, disinterested way. But many markets periodically malfunction. Factor markets, especially credit and capital markets which require long-term commitments, are replete with the problems of uncertainty and asymmetric information and with principal-agent tensions. The idea that markets can solve problems where social policy should fear to tread, in short, is naive. As we have argued here, credit flows where it does for many complicated reasons, which are historically informed and path dependent; participants in U.S. credit markets cannot reasonably be viewed as unaffected by the peculiarly American history of social segregation and difference; and credit markets reflect structures of regulation and oversight as much as pure opportunities for sound credit. In this world in which we live, to borrow Minsky's phrase, every premise must be subject to full and rigorous investigation. Concentrating more and more resources in the hands of a smaller and smaller number of decision makers will not solve the problem of fundamental uncertainty, nor will it guarantee the obsolescence of discrimination, nor will it preclude bad judgment or poorly considered efforts to seize market share. Human beings will be no less fallible than they've proven to be in the past.

This volume has also presented evidence, in chapters 6 and 10, that mergers and banking concentration are not neutral and may have some deleterious effects in banking markets. This evidence also suggests that rumors of the death of banking generally, and small banks specifically, have been greatly exaggerated. While Edwards and Mishkin suggest that only fee-based income has kept banks from collective insolvency, the fact remains that during the last seven years of record profits for the commercial banking industry, lending-based income has exceeded fee-based income every year. Really what these and other analysts are urging is not the elimination of an inherently nonviable intermediation structure, but a new structure which they judge more suited to the economic circumstances of the new millennium. For despite all the evidence reviewed here that banking remains primarily local, the media and many experts have in mind a disembodied world of aspatial financial relationships cut off from all geographic reference points. Here today, gone tomorrow. This is the sort of world that mobile global capital is creating, a world in which industrial production is shifted rapidly from site to site on the basis of cost, in which large multinational firms coordinate the activities of sub-contractors in flexible accumulation processes, in which yesterday's industrial giant is today's cash cow and tomorrow's factory-building-turned-condominium. The banking firms best suited for this flexible, space-shifting world, it is argued, are banks whose geographic and market reach allows them to move resources around this world, in the amounts and contractual forms needed, like chess pieces on a chess board.

Meanwhile, the business press writes about mergers as if reporting on baseball games: that is, the rules of the game are well understood, so it's only necessary to report the scores as the long season continues. The arguments of experts such as Edwards and Mishkin are accepted as gospel truths. Consider these excerpts from a *Wall Street Journal* article of April 13, 1998, written by Steven Lipin and Anita Raghavan, on the NationsBank/BankAmerica and Banc One/First Chicago NBD mergers:

> More than one factor drives the merger frenzy, but the backdrop is simply that the U.S. has a capacity glut in financial services. Some buyers are slashing overhead and laying off employees. . . . [M]oreover, providers of financial services face heavy spending because of the cost of staying technologically abreast and dealing with the year-2000 computer-conversion problem. . . . Merging can ease such spending burdens. While the prices being paid for acquisitions have soared, buyers' share prices have also risen, giving buyers the currency with which to find partners.

The "currency with which to find partners" is now devalued, as discussed in chapter 5, due to the downturn in bank stock prices after June 1998. While this has led to a pause in the action, it is important to remember that the entire bank merger game has gone forward with minimal attention to its effects on the welfare of consumers and communities. Bank equity owners and managers appear as the protagonists in merger dramas; those actually engaged in banking practices are only good as framing shots for six o'clock news stories on how the markets reacted. Yet despite this failure to engage with the substance of the issue, three core questions about the bank merger movement deserve an answer—the three questions at the core of this book:

- What are the causes of the bank merger wave, and why is it proceeding with such vigor?
- How well are U.S. banking markets performing today in "social efficiency" terms?
- What are the likely consequences of the merger wave in banking?

The remainder of this chapter recapitulates *this* study's answers to these questions. Chapter 12 suggests some appropriate policy responses.

The Causes of the Bank Merger Wave

The beginnings of the current merger wave are found in the juncture of three events in the 1980s: the election of President Ronald Reagan and his market-oriented administration, the deregulation of the banking industry, and the savings and loan debacle. These events provided, respectively, a market-friendly regulatory environment, the removal of constraints on aggressive behavior, and a set of distressed insured institutions requiring suitors.

The bank merger wave is typically defended as allowing acquiring banks to be safer and sounder by attaining operating efficiencies that derive from economies of scale and scope. However, economies of scope have remained elusive; their existence has not been definitively established in any study. Further, industrial-organization studies of banking find that economies of scale are exhausted at small asset sizes; so while a $250-million-asset bank can function more efficiently than a $25-million-asset bank, a $40-billion-asset bank is not inherently more efficient in per-unit cost terms than a $250-million-asset bank.

An analysis of the components of bank return on assets illustrates that operational efficiency and profitability are only loosely related. In particular, an increase in firm scale can yield a higher return on assets even with no improvement in operational efficiency. The access of larger banking firms to centralized capital markets provides the means needed to pursue returns of this sort. Wall Street has both mounted an attack on bank balance sheets—through its mutual funds, commercial-paper markets, bond markets, and so on—and at the same time come to the support of banks its analysts deem the fittest in the brave new financial world.

Regulatory attitudes toward bank mergers have shifted due to the influence of the "new learning" approach, according to which prices may be competitive even in monopolistic markets. In this view, more market concentration is not problematic as long as entry by outside competitors is possible. In the "structure-conduct-performance" view previously used, market concentration leads to consumers' exploitation. Further, the view of many economists that equity markets are efficient makes it acceptable to substitute equity-market event studies for operating studies in determining the efficiency and desirability of alternative banking developments.

Paired with the interest in bank mergers by Wall Street is a more lenient stance toward mergers on the part of bank regulators. Fed economists have authored numerous studies raising serious questions about the advisability of larger and fewer banking firms. While these questions have gone begging answers, Federal Reserve Board members and policy-makers have put more permissive merger rules in place.

The opening provided by changing regulatory philosophy and stance has been seized by banks' redefining their strategies and the markets they serve. The New Deal system, in which banks operating under price ceilings maximized their customer bases by cross-subsidies between larger (wealthier) and smaller (poorer) units, has given way to a brave new financial world in which these cross-subsidies have been eliminated. The new dominant strategies in banking are fee-based banking and upscale retail banking, both of which seek to sell multiple products to captured customers. Banks committed to upscale retail banking must, once they have saturated their given deposit customer base with financial products, expand geographically to increase their profit flows systematically. Acquiring banks pursuing upscale retail banking have been the driving force behind the merger wave. Large acquiring banks' way has been smoothed by the watered-down criteria that federal regulators now use to measure market monopoly in banking, and also by their advantage over small banks in *capital-market access*. Wall Street, which believes in whatever generates fees, has eagerly supported megabanks' equity issues and share swaps; these banks' ability to manipulate and expand their equity bases has been the key component in their market extension and acquisition strategies.

The State of Play in Banking and Bank Consolidation

The banks' merger wave has been transforming the face of American banking so rapidly that any accounting will be out-of-date before the ink dries on this page. Considering all approved mergers and using the June 30, 1998, balance sheets shown in Table 9.1, the ten largest U.S. bank holding companies as of October 1998 are: Citigroup, $739 billion in assets (Table 9.1 does not incorporate an estimate of the assets of Travelers Group); BankAmerica, $572 billion; Chase Manhattan, $367 billion; J.P. Morgan, $281 billion; Banc One, $246 billion; First Union, $229 billion; Wells Fargo, $186 billion; Bankers Trust $173 billion; Fleet Financial, $101 billion; and National City, $81 billion. What is next? The current equity-market swoon may have slowed the merger wave; but some idle speculation suggests the many possibilities, based on diverse rationales: First Union with Fleet, to create a depositor base along most of the Eastern seaboard? Fleet with Chase, to create a Northeastern giant? First Union with Fleet and Chase? Banc One with U.S. Bancorp to create a Midwestern-Northwestern conglomerate that can go head-to-head with Wells/Norwest? Why not Chase with Wells Fargo/Norwest, and BankAmerica/NationsBank with Banc One, so two conglomerates can compete coast to coast?

The Strategic Fragmentation of Banking?

Knowing which way the merger ball will bounce next requires knowing the strategic plans banks are mapping out. This has become difficult for two reasons. First, with dependence on Wall Street for rapid growth, as pointed out in chapter 4, comes a built-in instability in the pace and character of the bank merger wave. These mergers combine a flavor-of-the-week aspect with Wall Street's "can you top this?" chutzpah. For example, despite its notable record of growth by merger, the price of NationsBank stock languished relative to other leading banks' in 1997. Similarly, Wells Fargo's stock price sank in 1997 due to its difficulties in absorbing First Interstate. But not soon enough, all was forgiven for NationsBank, as it merged with Barnett Banks and ultimately BankAmerica; and Wells's stock price spurted on takeover rumors (possible suitors included U.S. Bancorp), culminating in a deal with Norwest, as described in chapter 4. And while bank stocks dived in mid-1998, they will rise again, permitting the game to continue.

Second, these megamergers are pushing holding companies into different directions, and forcing strategic fits that seem increasingly more and more questionable. The Citibank/Travelers Insurance Group merger, for example, creates an integrated financial services company with a commercial bank component. The BankAmerica/NationsBank merger, on the other hand, creates a retail banking giant with global presence and extensive corporate capabilities. The Banc One/First Chicago NBD combination sets up a regional banking powerhouse. Which of these directions is definitive? How do these combinations relate to the merged Morgan Stanley/Dean Witter, Discover? In which markets will Citigroup and Banc One compete in the year 2000? These questions have no clear answers yet; all these players are banking on the future.

More troubling is that the push to get big is getting in the way of strategic focus. The best example of a possible mismatch is the Wells Fargo/Norwest merger. Wells has been among the most aggressive banks in reducing full-service branch offices, replacing them with supermarket branches, and attracting customers to on-line banking. Norwest, on the other hand, has bucked this trend, maintaining a strong network of bank branches and using them to draw customers. This has been a notably successful strategy, too: Norwest averages 3.8 products per customers; traditional banking accounts for less than 40 percent of its earnings stream, as it sells everything from mortgages to insurance and brokerage products (*Wall Street Journal,* June 8, 1998). How are these two incompatible approaches to upscale consumer banking to mesh?[2]

Fragmentation in the Provision of Access for Banking Customers?

While large banks are moving in different directions organizationally, they have united in their search for high-value-added customers. Every week seems to bring a new initiative aimed at strengthening ties with revenue-generating customers while ensuring that other customers pay higher marginal costs for the banking services they receive. At the same time, these large banks are under intense scrutiny, especially in the preapproval phases of their megamerger proposals; so they are simultaneously taking steps to reassure customers about their reinvestment efforts.

These divergent pulls and pushes sometimes give the impression that large banks are moving in different directions at once. Consider some of Wells Fargo's initiatives in the past year. In September 1997, Wells opened twenty business centers throughout California, each staffed by several small-business specialists (*San Diego Union-Tribune,* September 26, 1997). This real initiative was followed in June 1998 by Wells' announcement of a small-business lending program for African-American entrepreneurs (*San Diego Union-Tribune,* June 18, 1998). Investigation by reporters and community activists revealed, however, that Wells had no new program; it was instead making an effort to identify more African-American borrowers with its current rules and procedures. Days earlier, Wells Fargo announced that it would tighten its rules for free checking (*San Diego Union-Tribune,* June 4, 1998). According to reporter Penni Crabtree, "WF is cleaning house of some of its less profitable consumer checking accounts. . . . Beginning July 1, WF customers who maintained free checking accounts at low levels will pay a monthly fee of $9 unless they maintain a daily minimum balance of $1,000 or sign up for direct deposit of Social Security checks." This move was expected to affect some 150,000 checking account customers, or about 3 percent of the bank's 5.5 million checking accounts. It is "aimed at clients who have free checking accounts—gained through waivers, promotions or agreements through Wells or other banks that have since merged with Wells." Similarly, in late May 1998, the preapproval period of the BankAmerica/NationsBank merger, these two banks announced that they would set aside $350 billion over ten years for reinvestment. This effort too was greeted with skepticism by activists because of the lack of specific details about how this money would find its way into low-income communities; California activists were especially worried about the fate of the BankAmerica Community Development Bank, a subsidiary that BankAmerica has used as the focal point of its community-reinvestment lending in the 1990s.

Meanwhile, in June 1998 both Wells Fargo and NationsBank introduced hybrid asset-management accounts designed to meet banking and investment needs for the upscale customers for whom they are preparing to do renewed battle in what analysts like to call the "lucrative California market." Actually, this search for upscale retail customers is now a global one. For example, two days before the "big bang" in Japanese financial markets on April 1, 1998, Citibank ran multipage ads in leading Japanese newspapers offering a new multiproduct, reduced-fee account for customers who could open accounts with deposits of at least 1 million yen (about $7,800).

The Social Efficiency of the Banking System

How socially efficient is the banking system? And how will mergers affect this social efficiency level? The question of how well the banking system facilitates access to transaction services, credit, and capital for those who have faced barriers to opportunity cannot be answered comprehensively. Consequently, we have focused on how different types of banks and nonbanks react to racial and income differences in the communities they serve.

This study has first used fair-share measures to examine the performance of banks and other lenders in lower-income and minority neighborhoods. Overall, most lender groups failed to meet fair-share benchmarks. Large merging banks, especially those without in-state branches, perform poorly in fair-share tests. This study then develops a probit model which tests for the determinants of the probability of loan approval using HMDA data for home-purchase loans. This model is set up to evaluate two propositions. First, does access to credit vary significantly by lender type and by region; second, do large merging banks perform differently than in-state banks and nonbank lenders in providing this access? The focus of interest in this multi-variable probit model are four race- and income-related variables: applicant race, applicants with low relative incomes, location of a home in a minority census tract, and location of a home in a lower-income census tract.

Results for our probit equations suggest that access to credit varies considerably among regions; and this access is generally less in larger cities with higher proportions of minority applicants. The estimated equations for in-state banks, large merging banks, and nonbank lenders alike chronically have significant negative coefficients for minority applicants, for high-minority areas, and for lower-income areas; that is, our probit results suggest that all lenders are less likely to lend to minorities, all else being equal, and less likely to lend in high-minority and lower-income areas.

Given that many lenders are sensitive to race and income variables in probit equations, how do different lender groups in different financial markets compare? A disadvantage method is developed here to allow such probit-based comparisons. This method makes use only of statistically significant coefficients generated by probit equations, and controls for differences in applicant-pool demographics. This method suggests that large merging banks' disadvantage, overall, is at average levels. Mortgage companies generate the least disadvantage for minority and lower-income applicants and areas, while thrifts generate the most.[3] When merging banks are split into those with and without in-state branches, out-of-state large banks' average performance in disadvantage terms is poor. While the performance of different lender types varies widely from place to place, on average there is certainly no reason to think that the replacement of small in-state banks by large merging banks will improve access to credit for minority and lower-income applicants and areas.

Our review of many cities' experience shows that racial differences matter literally everywhere, as do income differences, in access to credit. Racial and income denial gaps have fallen slightly, but remain sizable in virtually all of the diverse markets we study here. Regional differences in credit availability are significant. The differential approval and denial rates among the city clusters examined here demonstrate that banking remains local—where you are matters for what you can do—and in turn that various other characteristics of local banking markets, especially differences in financial infrastructure, matter. The problem of intermarket differences in financial structures and outcomes deserves much more study.

The Likely Effects of Bank Consolidation on Consumers and Communities

Evidence generated in other studies and pulled together here suggests that bank mergers and consolidation may have effects contrary to consumer and small non-financial firms' interests. To a large extent, banking markets remain local; but consolidation increases the opportunities for monopolistic pricing. Consumers earn lower rates of interest on deposits in more concentrated banking markets; and evidence collected by the Federal Reserve shows that consumers pay higher fees at large banks and at banking institutions owned out-of-state. Banks' fees for consumer financial services have not fallen in the past few years despite apparent gains in computer technology during this period. Large acquisition-oriented banks in particular have aggressively increased bank fees; so the increasing dominance of these banks suggests banking consumers will pay higher average fees.

The bank merger wave is accompanied by the growth of standardized financial services and contracts, on the one hand, and by the growth of the informal financial sector, on the other. Banks are actively courting higher-income, higher-balance customers capable of generating fees from multiple products, while charging higher fees to lower-balance (and hence lower-income) customers for basic products. The informal sector—check-cashing stores, pawnbrokers, and loan brokers—has grown in the wake of banks' market shift. Studies of this sector indicate that it often charges exploitative prices.

A second probit model is developed here to consider whether banking-market concentration affects access to credit. This proposition is tested by incorporating four measures of banking-market structure into our basic probit model for a sample of ten California metropolitan areas. These measures include the level of banking-market concentration in 1982, the so-called Herfindahl-Hirschman Index (HHI), and also the change in the HHI between 1982 and 1992, for each of these ten market areas.

Results of this probit with 1995 and 1996 data suggest strongly that access to credit varies inversely with market concentration in these ten market areas. The more concentrated are these markets, the lower the probability of loan approval, all else held equal. This result obtains for the credit market as a whole, for white and minority borrowers separately, for all banks, and for large acquiring banks. The estimated magnitude of these market-structure effects is large, with the probability of loan approval being positively or negatively affected by 15 percent or even more by the degree of concentration in local banking markets. These results show that banking-market concentration, and especially increasing concentration, can have effects on access to credit nearly as large as those for applicant race. The large disadvantage found here and in many other studies for minority applicants has, of course, generated a national policy debate over the sources of these race effects, their significance, and possible remedies. The large and statistically robust effects found here for banking-market concentration suggest the need for a similar national consideration of what might cause this sensitivity of credit-marketoutcomes to market concentration, how large these market-concentration effects are, and what to do about them.

The consequence of larger banks' shift to standardized information will be to increase the disadvantage of smaller businesses, relative to larger ones, in gaining access to credit. At the same time, smaller banks are much more likely to use localized knowledge in their small-business lending, and are more hospitable lenders for smaller businesses. But insofar as large banks are buying up small banks in every market in the country, smaller businesses will be, at the least, inconvenienced by the ripple effects of the bank merger wave, if not displaced from their prior relationships with banks as credit and transactions-services suppliers.

Some analysts and bank supervisors have argued that the replacement of smaller banks by larger ones, even if accompanied by branch closures, will not adversely affect small business or customers in inner-city areas. This argument rests on two points: that large banks will be able to meet small-business needs well using credit-scoring methods that are analytically neutral; and that if some portions of the banking market are not being served, new banks will emerge de novo to fill these holes. Both points are speculative at best. For one thing, new entrants into the banking field may have difficulty succeeding. Kimball (1997) finds, for example, that small-niche banks are much riskier than larger banks; and a study by Whalen (1994; reported in the same volume as Peek and Rosengren 1996) suggests that a high proportion of de novo banks in New England have either failed or failed to thrive. For another, credit scoring may not be a panacea that somehow will eliminate discrimination and redlining effects from lending outcomes. Indeed, the poor performance of out-of-state merging banks in this study suggests the opposite. It is perhaps wisest to be guided by Helen Ladd's observation that "the different credit scoring models deserve research scrutiny as well, to be sure that they are not simply substituting discrimination in the form of adverse impact for discrimination in the form of disparate treatment" (1998, 59–60).

Bank Concentration and the Social Efficiency of the Banking System

Even if the bank merger wave was stopped in its tracks today, it has already changed U.S. banking irrevocably. Even while banking markets remain local, as demonstrated here and in studies reviewed here, consolidation is changing the character of banking itself. The dynamic of acquisition, market consolidation, downsizing, and share buy-back has proceeded at a remarkable pace. As we have seen, the list of the largest banking firms in the United States shifts quarterly. Under the new Regulation Y, the pace of consolidation has quickened.

It is no use to mourn the death of the heroic local bank, as depicted so poignantly in Jimmy Stewart's holiday movie classic. In some markets, small banks evidently are stalwarts in maintaining fair and equitable access to credit; and credit unions and other niche institutions provide important alternatives to the megabank even today. But our study has found that small in-state banks often perform poorly relative to other lender types in the disadvantage indices calculated here. This suggests an answer to the puzzle of why there has been no sustained public outcry in response to the bank merger wave. More specifically, while community advocates have often used megamergers as opportunities to negotiate reinvestment packages for affected markets, advocates have seldom cried out in protest at the death of small commercial banks. The answer is perhaps that small banks have too infrequently performed well in providing access to minority applicants, minority communities, and lower-income applicants—that is, to the sort of bank customers most likely to energetically protect their rights.

In his in-depth study of three bank mergers in St. Joseph County, Indiana, Nesiba (1995, chapter 5) argues that bank mergers per se do not pose a threat to reinvestment; however, he notes that this conclusion depends on acquiring banks' need to adhere to the Community Reinvestment Act. In his view, acquiring banks have a strong incentive to perform well under the CRA, largely because their future acquisition plans depend on maintaining good CRA performance. Nesiba notes that large acquiring institutions have typically been the targets of reinvestment protests in the past, and thus seek to avoid more protests in the future; and they bring with them a wealth of experience in providing loans for low-to-moderate-income areas.

Our analysis agrees with Nesiba's emphasis on the importance of the CRA, but must be more sanguine about the relationship between reinvestment and bank consolidation. The evidence reviewed here does not support a conclusion that more consolidated banking markets pose no threat to reinvestment and to access to credit for minorities and lower-income households. Evidence reviewed in this volume suggests that merging banks often perform relatively well in credit-market disadvantage terms; but they sometimes do not. And our evidence also suggests that access to credit is less in more concentrated banking markets, all else being equal. Further, large merging banks often perform poorly in our fair-share tests compared to other lenders.

Nesiba's conclusion that acquiring banks will perform well to avoid CRA protests and to facilitate future expansion is also too strong. For one thing, once consolidation nears its logical resting place, acquiring banks' primary motivation for CRA compliance—maintaining the ability to merge further in the future—will be eliminated. Beyond this, regulatory signals may be changing, as Chairman Greenspan's recent comments (and those of other Federal Reserve officers such as Thomas Hoenig) make clear. The revisions to Regulation Y go some distance toward uncoupling reinvestment behavior and the right to acquire or branch across state lines. The Federal Reserve's willingness to use CRA "satisfactory" ratings in lieu of extended comment periods is troublesome, given bank regulators' chronic pattern of finding most banks should be rated "Satisfactory" or better. Here we should keep in mind Nesiba's observation, based on interviews with bank managers, that much loan activity in lower-income neighborhoods is done specifically to comply with the CRA.[4]

This heightens the importance of the "social efficiency" approach suggested in this study. Since banks' institutional structure is in rapid flux, and no one sector can be counted on to deliver credit and capital in the requisite volumes to underserved communities, the performance of the banking system—or any of its component parts—should be evaluated in part based on whether it facilitates access to credit and capital for those with inherited disadvantages of income and wealth.

Some will greet this suggestion with skepticism and annoyance; after all, why should banks alone be held accountable for enhancing social mobility in a country whose politicians have been busily reducing the amount of redistribution through the tax and transfer system, cutting lifeline welfare programs, and providing ever more public services only on a "fee for use" basis? This complaint is valid, as far as it goes, but perhaps irrelevant. The premise of American society as a "classless democracy" where "anyone has a chance to make it" depends on the existence of ladders of opportunity available to all—not just to those with family wealth, those with privileged access to informal sources of credit and capital, or those with the right connections or last names. Ladders of opportunity must be jealously guarded; and opportunity comes through the factor markets, the labor and credit/capital markets, which control income flows for every economic unit.

The institutions controlling access to credit and capital thus have a social responsibility to make a portion of their awards of credit and capital on a redistributive basis. The banks may consider these loans "community reinvestment" or "social lending," as they will; but within the architecture of the economy as a whole, it is crucial that these and other mechanisms for economic mobility not be closed off. And as Alan Greenspan pointed out in mid-1998, U.S. commercial banks and bank holding companies are the recipients of some unique public support. Community reinvestment is part of a de facto quid pro quo for deposit insurance and the banking safety umbrella. To see this, consider why the Community Reinvestment Act succeeded where legislation on plant closing has failed.

12
Ten Recommendations for Public Policy

Introduction

In framing recommendations, it is useful to put the current trajectory of the banking industry into perspective. This industry for years was completely sheltered from market forces by a scheme of market segmentation and specialization. As Alan Greenspan has reminded Congress recently (see chapter 5), commercial banks have always enjoyed certain privileges under law. Among these are deposit insurance and the banking safety umbrella. Protection was traded for stability. In the mid-1970s Congress added to this balance the obligation to engage in community reinvestment. This historic compromise was sorely tested in the 1980s. When the U.S. macroeconomic environment deteriorated sufficiently, the industry was marketized only to be thrown into a broad-based crisis. The locally based institutions specializing in housing finance—the savings and loan associations—went into systemic default. The money-center banks at the heart of the commercial-banking system fell into a double lending trap, the LDC debt crisis on the one hand and the Texas/Oklahoma oil-patch collapse on the other. The banking "franchise" was worth very little, in effect, for a large share of the population of banking firms.

Housing finance was then resuscitated by government-sponsored securitization—a strategy that cut Wall Street into the (fee-based) action. The money-center banks that barely survived the twin debt crises were, in turn, brought back to life as of 1987 through a Wall Street–sponsored sale of their nonperforming loans, and a Wall Street sale of new equity. These banks would not have survived if not for the long reach of the banking safety umbrella. In effect, government has always stood firmly behind one half of the compromise; and somewhat reluctantly, it has not forsaken the other half.[1] Umbrella protection remains in place, and so does an altered competitive terrain in which competitive protections have been partially set aside.

The competitive environment is being transformed in particular by aggressive large banks who are vigorously pursuing merger targets under the tutelage of Wall Street acquisition specialists. Technological change and market centralization has given an edge to intermediaries who make decisions on the basis of standardized information and who work with standardized instruments. Those flourishing in this environment tend to see their ascendancy as a historical inevitability. The old ways surely must simply be set aside. Wall Street has in any case always been uniformly cynical about community reinvestment, which is at best irritating and at worst a social misallocation of capital. There is evidence that Federal Reserve policies buy into this view: that restoring the value of the banking franchise means freeing the fit—the large and acquisition-oriented—to ensure their own survival through merger and market expansion.[2]

But as Emmons and Greenbaum (1998) point out, the competitive advantage of broker-oriented firms in the current environment does not mean that intermediaries that specialize in working with small firms and less wealthy households are obsolete. A need for them remains. The historic compromise remains in place, at least in principle: to eliminate community reinvestment concerns on the grounds that they are competitively inconvenient logically implies that deposit insurance and the safety umbrella should be eliminated because they confer unfair competitive advantage. If the large banks leading the merger wave do not want this, then they must redouble their efforts to make credit accessible where it has not been, to lower barriers based on race and geography. This study shows that these barriers are high literally everywhere in the United States. More than vague promises and the prospect of socially neutral computer-driven assessment technologies are needed to provide assurance that these barriers are being taken seriously. If this end of the historical quid pro quo is discarded, then the United States is one step closer to resembling those nations in which government policies do not expand opportunity but protect privilege.

So what recommendations are appropriate? Here we might ask, what is the consumer's interest? The answer is simple: The consumer's interest is in equitable credit patterns; equitable and adequate branch patterns; and nondiscriminatory availability of affordable services. Many policy steps are needed to achieve these goals, beyond those that pertain directly to the topic of this report.[3] The ten policy recommendations made here fall into four clusters: those pertaining to merger policy per se; those pertaining to the Community Reinvestment Act (CRA) in light of the transformation of U.S. banking; those that link the CRA and merger policy; and those pertaining to the banking safety umbrella.

Merger Policy

1. Use traditional structural criteria, applied market by market, to judge merger applications.

A reduced set of criteria, such as the fast-track provision of the revised Regulation Y, should rarely, if ever, be used. Each market is different, and circumstances vary considerably from one locale to another; so the effect of a merger in any given market must be evaluated separately. A presumption in favor of the right to merge does consumer interests no good, since it flies in the face of research by Federal Reserve economists to the effect that banking markets remain local, and the effects of market power significant, even in the late 1990s.

2. Consider additional grounds for evaluating mergers—specifically, the net projected cost to consumers.

This net projected cost would equal changes in financial services, plus or minus changes in service availability, plus or minus changes in service costs. Sufficient actual institutional experience that the figures needed for making these calculations are in hand. At the very least, this net projected cost could be set against the net projected gain in cash flow for the acquiring bank, to derive a true net social benefit or cost from any proposed merger.

3. Approve mergers on a conditional basis, using the criterion that approval depends on consumers in specific classes—those who are lower-income and minority, and who reside or own businesses in lower-income and minority neighborhoods—being kept at least as well off after as before the merger in question.

Since the organizational changes associated with mergers are effectively irreversible, the "conditionality" will have to take the special form of a set of contingent commitments for performance on the part of acquiring banks. These commitments might include funds to be invested in low-rent housing projects, or funds to build community infrastructure in lower-income neighborhoods. These commitments might also involve promises to maintain or open branches in underserved neighborhoods. The number of contingent commitments implemented would then be tied to the acquiring banks' postmerger performance—the number of offices closed, the roster of services and fees to be provided to customers, and so on.

Community Reinvestment Act Policy

4. The Community Reinvestment Act (CRA) should be extended to nonbank firms providing home mortgage credit.

We have shown that entities not regulated under the CRA play a large part in the home mortgage market. This study has found that mortgage companies' disadvantage performance is generally better than that of other lender types; but we have also found that mortgage companies in several regions focus on minority and lower-income customers—primary constituents of the CRA itself. Extending CRA's mandate to nonbank lenders is thus an appropriate safeguard.

5. *Special regulatory vigilance should be given to small, isolated banking markets whose residents have lower incomes—especially cities and towns in rural areas, on the one hand, and inner-city market areas, on the other.*

This vigilance should be given both in connection with merger approval and in ongoing evaluation under the Community Reinvestment Act. These markets are especially vulnerable to isolation and to being cut off from access to capital.

6. *Reporting under HMDA should be broadened to include small business loans for all banks above some cutoff asset size, such as $1 billion. CRA performance criteria should then be broadened as well to include quantitative targets for delivering credit to small businesses, especially those operating in lower-income neighborhoods and areas.*

The relationship between small business lending and bank mergers is controversial. Regulators should take seriously the empirical evidence that small businesses may be negatively affected by banking mergers and consolidation. The time-honored principle that the best defense is a good offense suggests that regulators would be prudent to set up special criteria for large merging banks vis-à-vis small-business lending and relationships. Large banks with solid programs in place would be able to document their success; others would be given an incentive to become more responsive to small-business customers.

The Community Reinvestment Act and Bank Merger Policy

7. *Establish a mechanism wherein consumer and community advocates can participate directly in merger approval processes, rather than only being able to comment on already formulated plans that have been made privately.*

Local groups have a good idea of which types of institutions and programs are best serving diverse local needs. Given the United States's growing income and ethnic diversity, a well-functioning, accessible, and fair credit market is a public good in any community; and as such, it deserves protection.

8. *When prospective mergers encompass underserved markets or underserved consumer groups within markets, approval should be linked to definite plans by acquirers to reduce disparities such as racial denial gaps or below-par credit flows.*

These plans should involve specific targets and timelines in specific market areas within the broad and often multistate scope of the merging firms.

The blanket commitments often made now often involve huge but nonspecific dollar commitments. Neighborhood redevelopment and commercial revitalization must, however, take root market by market. Reinvestment planning should be similarly detailed—indeed, it should be undertaken with as much seriousness of purpose as goes into the acquiring bank's postmerger marketing strategy.

9. *As large banks control more of the total U.S. banking market, they should take more responsibility for ensuring that the markets they work in are accessible to the full spectrum of American society.*

Require that acquisition-oriented banks whose size and rate of asset growth exceeds some level—say, $25 billion in assets and a 100 percent gain in asset size over the past five years—take responsibility for putting in place a secondary market mechanism that would buy, package, and sell off loans made by banks that operate in underserved market areas such as inner cities and lower-income rural areas. A mechanism of this sort is proposed in Dymski and Veitch (1996c). Investment bankers and brokerages that have underwritten at least some minimum dollar-volume of banking equity issues for acquiring banks could perhaps also be obliged to participate in this institution-building process.

Banking Safety Umbrella Policy

If the special role of large banks in reinvestment activity suggested above—that is, if large banks do not serve broad-based customer markets with instruments that increase access to credit and provide low-cost transaction accounts—then more profound changes in banking law should be considered. If present trends continue, institutions committed to working with lower-balance, smaller economic units will only be able to provide instruments that will make most people dependent on them with costlier transactions and more expensive credit and capital. As Emmons and Greenbaum suggest, banking law should be changed to make those financial firms that work with smaller economic units, and that are at a disadvantage in a world of standardized information and arm's-length credit assessment, more competitive.

10. *Banks' special protections, deposit insurance and the safety net, should be limited to banks providing broad-based customer markets with instruments that increase access to credit and provide low-cost transaction accounts.*

There are several ways to achieve this. Large banks have the capacity, and this study has found that large merging banks sometimes perform

very well in minority and lower-income disadvantage terms. Local commitment matters; this study has also found that large merging banks with
in-state branches perform better in disadvantage terms than do offshore
merging banks and, in some cases, small in-state banks. But large banks
often do poorly in fair-share terms.

So large merging banks are squarely on a cusp, caught between market forces
driving them up-market and a social reinvestment movement pressuring them to
remain committed down-market. The question is, can merging banks remain
committed to social efficiency goals while imposing participation requirements
that are increasingly exclusive? The fork in these institutions' road draws ever
nearer. The suggestion made here about this moment of decision is simple: If
large banks want to compete head-to-head with investment banks and mutual
funds for well-to-do clients and well-established firms, and if they no longer
have a corporate commitment to meeting the social responsibilities implicit in
the deposit insurance and lender-of-last-resort protections they have accepted,
they should shed these protections.

Contemporary economists have already broached the possibility of reserv-
ing federal subsidies and guarantees for socially responsible financial firms.
It is implicit in the recently revived Depression-era notion of "narrow banking"; see Phillips (1994). The narrow banking idea suggests limiting deposit
insurance to banks that provide transaction accounts and invest only in short-
term Treasury (or investment-grade) securities. This idea is a good starting
point, but does not go far enough. For as this study has documented, barriers
to equal access to credit also remain a systematic problem across the United
States. And these barriers, whether due to personal discrimination or structural inequality, demand action if the gap between those with wealth and
financial resources and those without them is not to deepen even more. In
effect, this discussion suggests that leveling the playing field requires more in
any reconfigured banking license than the transaction services featured in the
narrow-banking scheme. Credit-market inequalities should not be forgotten.
Asking the reconfigured, socially efficient bank to do more than the narrow
bank might require stronger advantages than just exclusive claim to deposit
insurance; hence the notion of restricting the banking safety umbrella to
banks committed to providing credit to economic units that lack ready access
to centralized credit and equity markets.

If a withdrawal of the safety-umbrella protection from large merging banks is
not advisable, there are other ways of expanding the role of smaller banking
institutions in the brave new financial world. Some have already been suggested,
while others come readily to mind: small banks operating in lower-income areas
could be allowed to engage in equity participation in local projects; banks making significant, continuing commitments to reinvestment could be given special
treatment vis-à-vis reserve requirements; and so on. In any event, banking regu-

lators and Congress should put approvals of large bank mergers on hold until they resolve how the banking system will meet its social efficiency responsibilities.

If the current merger movement is too far gone to permit a regulatory pause at this point, those interested in socially efficient banks need not despair. Banking history dictates that credit-market fiascoes requiring substantial federal intervention have occurred in cycles far shorter than a decade since the end of the Bretton Woods system in 1971. It is reasonable to presume that new fiascoes will call forth substantial governmental support before the new millennium has faded into memory. Perhaps then policy-makers and regulators will reconsider the merits of letting the large get larger simply because centralized equity markets desire it. Perhaps then social-efficiency criteria will become more than an asterisk on the page of financial progress. It is never too late, just as it is never too early, to discover a calculus that weighs economic causes and social consequences more evenly than the U.S. bank merger wave of the 1990s has done.

Notes

Chapter 1

1. The term "bank" has several different meanings for economists. Any institution that issues deposits and creates credit is a bank; so mutual savings banks and savings and loan associations qualify as banks in this sense. The term "depository institution" is a synonym for the term "bank." The term "commercial bank" is reserved for institutions chartered specifically as such by federal or state authorities. The term "thrifts" refers to mutual savings banks and savings and loan associations. When used as an adjective, the term "bank" should be interpreted as "commercial bank"—for example, the term "bank assets" refers to commercial bank assets.

2. Rist (1940) and Kregel (1998) offer two insightful discussions of the Banking and Currency Schools in monetary theory.

3. Fundamental uncertainty, a concept introduced into economics by John Maynard Keynes (1936, chapter 12), refers to a situation in which agents must make decisions spanning the present and future without reliable information about the future.

4. If the Banking School view is so obviously a sensible way of understanding credit markets and banking firms, why has the Currency School view remained the dominant view among banking analysts? We might offer a conjecture. The language of financial market efficiency is a heady brew; once one imbibes a little, it is hard to stop. Some of efficient-market theorists' key definitions are also self-referential. For example, the test of whether financial markets are efficient is whether financial prices reflect all useful information; but the test of whether information is useful is whether it is reflected in prices. So once financial markets are understood as efficient, it is hard to think differently. The analytical task shifts from determining whether outcomes in a given case are or are not efficient, to determining how to explain these outcomes as efficient. It becomes hard to imagine how anything could happen other than what has happened.

5. Spillovers exist when the return to a given activity by any economic unit depends on the level of economic activity conducted by other economic units. Paul Krugman (1995) has written most compellingly recently of the importance of spillovers in urban outcomes.

Chapter 2

1. Figures released by Federal Governor Laurence Meyer on April 29, 1998, suggest that the top twenty-five banks controlled 51 percent of domestic commercial-banking assets in 1996 and 52.7 percent in 1997. Meyer's figures also showed the top twenty-five banks' asset share growing steadily; it stood at 33.1 percent in 1980.

2. Smith and Walter (1998) estimate that more than $4.5 trillion in mergers and acquisitions were completed worldwide in 58,000 transactions. Just under half occurred in the United States. Financial services firms accounted for 42 percent of merger activity inside the United States, 50 percent outside it.

3. *American Banker,* November 14, 1996. This article quotes James McLaughlin of the American Bankers Association: "If we continue to see protests against institutions that have sterling records, there may well be a backlash."

4. Large banks' figures for earnings and revenue indicate double-digit growth, year over year; but these figures are difficult to evaluate because these institutions' asset bases are also growing rapidly due to mergers.

5. Single "balance and fee" checking accounts are accounts where holding a certain balance can result in a fee waiver. NOW accounts are interest-bearing checking accounts.

6. In the figures reported here, results for large merging banks with and without in-state branches are reported, but not the composite large merging banks category. There are 101 results, not 102, because Mississippi had in-state large merging banks (as defined here) in 1996.

7. These 1995 results are drawn from probit analyses done independently with 1995 data. Other 1995 results are not reported in this summary; and they are reported only selectively in other chapters. Similarly, probits were done independently using 1992 data. The results for 1995 and 1996 are, in general, very similar; this provides a way of checking on the reliability of the results reported here.

Chapter 3

1. This decision has had an ironic side effect on bank competition. The two-sided definition of "banking" has insulated institutions conducting partial bank-like activities from banking supervision. The mutual funds and nonbank lenders that made serious inroads on banks' savings and credit markets in the 1970s and 1980s, described below, operated outside the umbrella of banking regulation.

2. The HHI for any given market is derived by taking the market share of every banking firm therein, squaring it, and summing over all banks. Holder (1993a) provides a useful introduction to bank antitrust law and to the HHI. Laderman (1995) demonstrates that the HHI can be reexpressed as $HHI = NV + 10,000/N$, where N is the number of banks in the market and V is the variance of these firms' market share. The HHI will rise unambiguously as V rises, and it will fall as N rises if N is less than 100 divided by the square root of V.

3. This segmentation also included the provision of housing finance, which was left to specially charted intermediaries (savings and loan associations and mutual savings banks) whose asset purchases were restricted almost entirely to locally generated mortgages on owner-occupied residential real estate. The historical perspective discussed here is developed at length in Dymski, Epstein, and Pollin (1993) and in Dymski and Veitch (1996a).

4. This "prudent person" principle was the root of many jokes about banks—"bankers only lend money to those who don't need it," the "3–6–3" rule of bank management, and so on.

5. These Fed policy shifts also coincided with the onset of the free-market-oriented Reagan administration. The influence of President Reagan was immediately felt despite his not appointing any Federal Reserve governors until 1982 and not controlling a majority of board appointees until 1986. Of course, President Reagan *did* control Department of Justice executive appointees, and hence policy; and his Justice Department was singularly lenient in antitrust enforcement.

6. By no means did these changes signal the Fed's advocacy of a widespread merger wave. Savage (1984) argued that, based on available evidence about bank size and efficiency, "a major merger movement cannot be justified as necessary to avert widespread bank failures" (1).

7. The Department of Justice took account of thrifts only at a 20 percent level; so in principle, its merger guidelines should have been stricter than those of the Federal Reserve.

8. This view originated with Harold Demsetz (1974), who asserted that a monopolistic market structure can be explained by greater efficiency, not the exercise of market power. Later this argument was completed by the contestable markets hypothesis, which points out that Demsetz's interpretation holds as long as the presence of potential competitors forces monopolist firms to charge competitive (or entry-deterring) prices. The contestable-markets view was treated definitively in Baumol, Panzar, and Willig (1982). Its implications for antitrust law were explored in Landes and Posner (1981).

9. Berger, Kashyap, and Scalise (1995) argue that the banking industry will stabilize at about 4,000 organizations in the near future.

10. The Douglas amendment to the 1956 Bank Holding Company Act (Savage 1993, 1079) requires home state approval before an in-state bank can be acquired by a bank headquartered in another state.

11. See Serwer (1995) and Grant and Barlyn (1995). Throughout this book, mergers are dated based on when they have been announced, and hence when they are covered most vigorously by the business press.

12. In June 1995, First Union paid $5.4 billion for First Fidelity of New Jersey, in the largest bank merger in U.S. history until then. This merger brought First Union's asset total to $124 billion.

13. The figures cited define size in terms of total deposits held, as reported in the *American Banker* of April 28, 1997.

14. The *American Banker* article lists NationsBank separately from NationsBank South; the two institutions' year-end 1996 deposit totals were $80.8 billion and $46.8 billion, respectively. The latter bank, based in Atlanta, is the new manifestation of Bank South.

Chapter 4

1. Rhoades (1996, Table 5) provides a list of major bank acquisitions.

2. In market-extension mergers the merging bank is to operate in new geographic market areas; in horizontal mergers the merging bank takes over assets previously operated by target banks in markets where it already operates.

3. Many studies of economies of scale in banking have also tested for the presence or absence of economies of scope. Most such inquiries have found that operating economies of scope are either nonexistent or very small in scale. See, for example, Rezvanian et al. (1996).

4. Under the Bank Holding Company Act, a bank holding company may retain any investment held by a company it buys for a period of two years, renewable for up to three more years (Meyer 1998). One might speculate that some of the aggressive acquisitions now taking place that nominally contradict the Glass–Steagall Act, like those mentioned in this paragraph, are being undertaken on the assumption that Congress will eliminate Glass–Steagall within this five-year period. If it does not, Citigroup, for example, would have to sell off Traveler's insurance underwriting business. Note that throughout this volume, mergers are often dated on the basis of their announcements, as reported in the business press. Technically, many of these mergers are not finalized until months later.

Using announcement dates provides a consistent way of discussing mergers that have been approved and mergers that have been proposed but not yet approved.

5. The Cobb–Douglas functional form assumes that output varies smoothly and in the same direction when inputs are increased or decreased. The translog functional form allows output reversals. In effect, the first form can generate only "L-shaped" cost functions, whereas the second can accommodate "U-shaped" functions.

6. Specifically, these studies found weak evidence of positive cost complementarities between total deposits and total loans for larger banks and of negative cost complementarities between these same variables for banks with less than $100 million in total deposits. Complementarities are measures of whether a given proportional increase in one item (total loans) leads to a higher or lower proportional increase in costs for another item (total deposits). Positive complementarities mean higher-than-proportional increases, and negative ones mean lower-than-proportional increases.

7. Srinivisan (1991) points out that FCA data do not extend to the $1 billion-and-up large banks that have accounted for most interstate acquisitions.

8. Kaparakis et al. (1994) tested for inefficiency in a 1986 sample of all banks with $50 million or more in assets, and concluded that bank inefficiency increases with bank size. Hunter and Timme (1995) conducted a study of the 317 commercial banks with $1 billion or more in assets (in non-unit-banking states) for the period 1983–1990, and found both that economies of scale are unimportant for these large banks and that this result holds even after allowing for fixed inputs. Rezvanian et al. (1996) studied cooperative banks in the period 1989–1991 and found significant economies of scale for this contingent of small, real-estate-based depositories, especially up to the level of $100 million in total assets. So economies of scale are captured at relatively small institutions. Positive but statistically insignificant economies of scope were also found.

9. These statements, of course, involve judgments by the author of acquirers' relative success, not their intentions; and even if the subjective impression captured in Table 4.2 is right, changing competitive conditions could bring changes quite rapidly.

10. Berger and Mester (1997), in their comprehensive empirical assessment of bank efficiency, also point out the ambiguity of the concept of banking efficiency. They adopt different measures of efficiency based on a cost approach and a profit approach, and obtain different results in their effort to measure the degree of bank efficiency.

11. Efficiency is no less ambiguous in the case of bank mergers per se. Savage (1993) argues that two merging banks are unlikely to provide lower-cost services even when they share a common market area. For one thing, the direct costs of servicing customers are substantial, independent of branch office costs. For another, banks may not pass along post-merger economies to their customers.

12. One obvious source of reduced profits is inefficiency in operations. Losses of this sort are termed "X-inefficiency." While X-inefficiency cannot be precisely measured, DeYoung (1994c) has found that X-inefficiency is substantially greater at large banks (those with over $1 billion in assets) than at small banks, when all else is equal.

13. The too-big-to-fail doctrine holds that large banks will not be allowed to fail because their demise would destabilize the financial system. The elaborate efforts made by the Federal Reserve in the wake of the Franklin National Bank failure in 1974 and of the Continental Illinois failure in 1985 suggested the plausibility of this doctrine. See Hetzel (1991).

14. While the evidence they assembled for the 1981–1986 period provides no support for the authors' deposit-insurance too-big-to-fail thesis, they suggest that this thesis may have been operative during the early 1990s megamergers.

15. Indeed, Hawawini and Swary (1990) argue that bank managers have an incentive to pursue mergers that do not enhance bank profitability (on average), because they are rewarded on the basis of sales volume rather than on the basis of profitability.

16. This fear arises because the market value of bank takeover–target stocks has climbed well above book value. Hence these shares can only be bought at a premium. So acquirers cannot swap shares on a one-for-one basis with the owners of the takeover-target stock; instead acquirers must "sweeten" the deal by either paying out cash, and taking on new debt, or by offering a one-for-some-stock swap that works to their own shareholders' disadvantage.

17. *Business Week*'s article on the merger between banking giants NCNB and C&S/Sovran (itself the product of several prior mergers) was entitled "Hugh McColl's masterwork: So far, NationsBank is a model merger" (April 27, 1992: 94). Since studies of banking performance show that a merger of this type is unlikely to yield real economies of scale or scope, for whom is it an ideal model? The answer does not appear to be consumers.

18. Gorton and Rosen (1991), however, make the opposite argument: They assert that bank failures in the 1980s were a means of reducing banking-system capacity, but mergers were not, because of the defensive strategies of entrenched bank managers.

19. Cornett and Tehranian (1992) find systematic empirical evidence that both interstate and intrastate bank mergers produce significant increases in the cash-flow returns to stockholders.

20. *American Banker,* April 16, 1997.

21. *American Banker,* November 26, 1996. The *American Banker* of November 25, 1996, discussed the share-buyback programs initiated by First Bank Systems in February 1996, by PNC on August 15, and by Chase Manhattan in October 1996—and went on to note that each of these programs had subsequently raised concerns about insider trading.

Chapter 5

1. Consider the statement made before Congress in 1993 by John LaWare, a member of the Federal Reserve Board, in support of federal interstate banking legislation: "Interstate banking is now a reality and has been for some time. For years, both domestic and foreign banks have maintained loan production offices outside their home states, have issued credit cards nationally, have made loans from their head offices to borrowers around the nation and the world. . . . [D]ifferences among the states impeded the interstate delivery of services to the public and reduced the efficiency of the banking business."

2. A 1994 study by Beshouri and Nigro (1994) provides indirect evidence for the local character of banking markets. These authors find that securitization for small-business loans has proceeded slowly, and is unlikely to grow in the future because of the idiosyncratic and localized character of information about these loans' risk and return.

3. Simons and Stavins (1998) come to the same conclusion in an article summarized in chapter 6.

4. At least some Federal Reserve researchers have produced studies skeptical of equity markets' capacity to efficiently evaluate risk. For example, Randall (1989) reviewed the stock prices of forty bank holding companies reporting large losses in the 1980s. He found that these companies' stock prices did not fall while they were accumulating extremely risky assets—in particular, "oil patch" loans which came under pressure when oil prices collapsed in the early 1980s. Gilbert (1990) points out some methodological limitations in Randall's study, but Randall's basic point stands: Stock-market prices can only properly adjust for risks that can be anticipated; therefore, stock markets can only imperfectly compensate for risk-taking.

5. There is little doubt that the savings-and-loan crisis was worsened by unscrupulous executives manipulating the deposit-insurance system to their advantage (Mayer 1990). Whether deposit insurance itself was the root problem is another matter, not addressed here.

6. Alton Gilbert (1990) reviews a number of proposals for increasing the effectiveness of market discipline of bank risk. Among these are ideas for using market evaluations of financial instruments such as equities and subordinated debt to provide feedback for bank managers. Gilbert notes that all but one study of bank equity markets have shown that bank stock prices respond negatively to increasing bank risk. The one study that challenges the view that markets can evaluate risk is of some interest—it is discussed below. Further, evidence from other studies has been more mixed, as the studies reviewed in this section demonstrate.

7. The authors themselves conclude: "Our focus on stock market returns, rather than the actual accounting experience of individual banks, leaves open the possibility that we have captured the market's expectations, but not the reality, about the long-run effects of interstate banking" (245).

8. In a related analysis, these same authors (Demsetz, Saidenberg, and Strahan, 1996) argue that stock-market price shifts can discipline bank behavior and prevent excessive bank risk-taking.

9. The Southern Finance Project (1991) analyzed the Bank of America/Security Pacific merger and found that concentration ratios were above the Justice Department's "highly concentrated" rating level in seventy-five of ninety-nine counties in the states in which these banks operated. Nonetheless, the merger was approved.

10. In these 205 cases, mitigating factors were cited that offset the HHI score itself. These mitigating factors were strong remaining competition; misleading HHI; potential competition; convenience and needs considerations; and procompetitive effects on the market. In the first category, competition from thrifts was cited most often, followed by numerous remaining commercial-bank competitors.

11. Thomson (1990) sets out the conceptual rationale for this approach.

12. Some provisions are also made in the revised Regulation Y to enhance public access to information about merger proposals, in particular through the Internet.

Chapter 6

1. Interestingly, this concern has been voiced not just by community activists, but by the business press; for example, "Small business loans to shrink with industry," *American Banker,* March 14, 1996, and "Bank Mergers Reduce Loans to Small Firms," *Wall Street Journal,* March 10, 1997. This literature is reviewed in Board of Governors (1996a).

2. Journalistic studies of the informal financial sector, such as Green and Nostivitz (1992) and Hudson (1996a, 1996b), argue that this sector is exploitative of its low-income customers.

3. As of March 1996, the average income of households in Los Angeles County public and assisted housing was $10,229.

4. *American Banker,* November 14, 1996.

5. Findings for this survey are reported in Hannan (1994) and Board of Governors (1996a and b, 1997).

6. Consumer groups, however, have long noted that the Federal Reserve cost survey may understate consumer price increases by understating the importance of large banks.

7. Elizabeth Laderman of the Federal Reserve Bank of San Francisco concluded (Laderman 1996) that the merger of BankAmerica with Security Pacific in 1992 was relatively benign in its effects on California consumers in that the deposit-rate "gap" in California—the lower deposit rates paid on California small-denomination deposits than on deposits elsewhere in the United States—did not worsen afterward. This is an optimistic interpretation; one might instead ask why this rate gap did not shrink further in light of increased interstate competition among banks and increased competition for higher-balance deposit customers (especially customers able to purchase certificates of deposit).

Chapter 7

1. This discussion draws on Dymski and Veitch (1992, 1996a, 1996b).

2. Grant writes of Texas' loss of in-state–owned banking capacity: "The engine that drove the commercialization and industrialization of the state, and provided the early entrepreneurs with the seed money to build some of today's leading businesses, is gone" (1996, 251).

3. The contemporary theory of asymmetric information makes much of this. See, for example, Stiglitz and Weiss (1991).

4. All lenders other than large banks are categorized as commercial banks, savings and loans, or mortgage companies based on the regulatory agency they identify in their disclosure of data under HMDA.

5. The ProCD phonebook program, sold commercially, was selected for use because it contains a comprehensive listing of businesses by address and SIC code. Other programs would yield slightly different patterns. Data drawn from this phonebook program required considerable preparation prior to use, because firms in the same line of business are classified differently in different geographic areas. The SIC codes used here were as follows: 5932G for pawnbrokers; 6099D, 6099F, and some instances of 7389 for check-cashers; 6062 and 6063 for credit unions; 6035 for thrifts; 6029 for commercial banks; 6162 and 6163 for mortgage and loan brokers; and 6211A, 6211B, and 6211C for investment and mutual fund offices.

6. The statistics shown in the first two columns of Table 7.1 are drawn from U.S. Census data; those shown in the last column are taken from Nolle (1995). Population totals are for metropolitan statistical areas (MSAs), with the exception of Los Angeles data, which include the city of Los Angeles only. The information on state interstate-banking policies is taken from various Federal Reserve publications; it reflects policies in force as of 1993. This year represents a midpoint for the lending data analyzed here.

7. Dymski and Veitch (1996a, 1996b) find a close correlation between the racial and income character of neighborhoods and the character of local financial infrastructure. Bank branches are located disproportionately in upper-income and low-minority areas. Informal financial offices are, by contrast, located more heavily in lower-income and high-minority areas. Further, there is some evidence of a geographic separation in Los Angeles's financial infrastructure: Bank branches tend to be located in close proximity to one another, but are seldom found near check-cashing stores or pawnbrokers. New bank branches are opened in areas that already have large numbers of bank branches; closed bank branches are typically located in places with low numbers of branches.

8. All HMDA loans reported here have been subjected to several screening tests. Applications are excluded if they were withdrawn or incomplete; if applicants did not report incomes, or reported zero incomes; and so on. Screening of this sort, done routinely, makes raw figures invariably higher than figures reported here. Due to the large number of results, this volume does not include tables of summary statistics. The SAS programs used to generate results shown here are available on request from the author.

9. This total includes five branches of Texas Commerce Bank, which was purchased in 1986 by Chemical Bank of New York.

10. This adjustment is made in the following way: Obtain a figure that expresses the number of applications per owner-occupied home. Next, compute the same figure for this city's nonminority area. Then divide the former figure by the latter figure and express as a percentage.

11. While the lender will not suffer in the event of borrower default, the widespread incidence of FHA defaults in the lender's market area could have adverse spillovers for the default rate on the lender's conventional loans in that market area.

12. The "nonconventional" loan category encompasses FHA loans and two other categories: Veterans Administration (VA) guaranteed loans, which are available for some veterans; and Farmers Home Administration (FmHA) insured loans, which are sometimes used for home acquisition in metropolitan areas. VA and FmHA loans constitute a minute share of the market for home-purchase loans. They are included here in analyses of "all purchase loans."

Chapter 8

1. Technically, probit analysis is not a regression technique. The dependent variable in probit models is not continuously distributed, and, in consequence, probit error terms are not distributed as per the classical statistical model. Probit models are also inherently nonlinear, whereas regression models are typically linear. Whereas estimated coefficients derived from regression equations with continuously distributed dependent variables are considered to have statistical properties, the coefficients derived from probit equations have, at best, asymptotic properties. Asymptotic properties become meaningful as the amount of data investigated increases; that is, probit analysis requires a large volume of data to generate meaningful results. Long (1997) presents an up-to-date and thorough discussion of probit models.

2. The problem of leaving out independent variables that might matter is termed "omitted variable bias" in econometrics. This bias may arise because the effects of variables *included* in the analysis can be over- or underestimated when these *included* variables partly capture the influence of *excluded* variables.

3. The latter method is preferred here because it avoids preselection bias, which arises when one assumes a distinction is empirically important in a test of whether it is.

4. Galster (1992) provides a comprehensive survey of studies that criticize the redlining model. Clark (1993), Cloud and Galster (1993), and Dymski (1996) provide reviews of literature on housing and credit market discrimination and redlining.

5. For example, Ladd (1998) writes in her review of this literature, "Based on that [Boston] study, it is clear that mortgage lenders discriminate against minorities. The fact that minorities may have higher default rates on average than whites is irrelevant to the interpretation of the race coefficient in such models."

6. See Rachlis and Yezer (1993).

7. See Berkovec et al. (1994) and Brimelow and Spenser (1993). Quercia and Stegman 1992 review this literature.

8. Carr and Megolugbe (1993) and Browne and Tootell (1995) defend the conclusions of the Boston study. Galster (1993) and Ferguson and Peters (1995) counter the default-rate critique.

9. Glennon and Stengel (1994) argue that since the controversial Boston study "represents only one study, in one city, at one point in time," it should be replicated elsewhere. But they go on to observe that "the intense publicity and controversy generated by the release of the Boston Fed study" make it "virtually certain that such a follow-up effort will never take place" (36).

10. Some economists who have become skeptical of HMDA studies have suggested that "audit" studies, in which white and minority subjects pose as housing or credit applicants in real-world experiments, are better suited for tests of personal discrimination. However, audit studies have their own limits. They are suitable only for capturing relatively egregious bias, not more subtle bias; and they ignore structural elements of discrimination altogether.

11. The author has designed Model 1 using only the variables that are available on the HMDA CD-ROMs available through the Federal Reserve. Thus the specification used

here could be copied by any researcher with access to the HMDA CD-ROMs and appropriate software.

12. Ladd (1998) uses the term "statistical discrimination" and provides references.

13. See the model developed in Dymski (1995).

14. Perle, Lynch, and Horner (1993) use 1982 Detroit data to show that while lending flows appear sensitive to area racial composition in an equation-8.1 model with four variables, they no longer are in an 11–variable model. Schill and Wachter (1993) take this approach one step further; they use an equation-8.2 model with 1990 (application-level) HMDA data to study race effects in Philadelphia and Boston. They find that individual race is a consistently significant determinant of loan denial. But while neighborhood racial composition significantly determines loan denial rates in the absence of neighborhood "quality" variables, it becomes insignificant when seven neighborhood "quality" variables (including the proportion of residents on welfare) are added.

15. Greene (1990) discusses the statistical difficulties associated with limited dependent variables.

16. See Greene (1990, 682–83). Greene warns that goodness-of-fit tests based on the F-distribution, especially the "R-squared" measure commonly used for classical regression analysis, is inappropriate in the case of the probit model. The likelihood-ratio test for the probit model is analogous to the "R-squared" measure.

17. Here we rely on two results from probability theory. First, $P(A + B) = P(A) + P(B)-P(AB)$, where $P(A)$ means the probability of event A and $P(AB)$ means the probability that both events A and B will occur. Second, $P(AB) = P(A \mid B)P(B)$, where $P(A \mid B)$ means the probability that event A will occur given ($\mid$) that event B has occurred. A special case of this last result is the case of $P(ABCD)$; Lindgren (1976, 43) shows that $P(ABCD) = P(A \mid BCD) P(B \mid CD) P(C \mid D) P(D)$. This is the algorithm used here, with appropriate substitutions for A, B, C, and D.

18. This follows from the fact that $P(A \mid B) = P(AB)/P(B)$.

19. Note that in here and elsewhere in this study, the Y-axes in closely related figures are set to the same scale to permit "eyeball" test comparisons of results.

20. Further evidence supporting the significance of regional variations in financial structures is provided by the Federal Reserve's survey of 1995 banking costs (Board of Governors 1996b).

21. The technique used to identify financial-infrastructure "type" is as follows: First, the unweighted average number of financial offices of every type was computed for each region. This resulted in five infrastructure profiles, each consisting of one "average" for each category of financial office, shown in Tables 7.2 and 7.7. Next, the difference between the actual population-weighted number of offices in any given city and the "average" for each of the five regions was computed for each category of financial office. These differences were squared and then summed for each city/region combination. So, for example, the difference between the financial infrastructure of, say Greenville, NC, and the Northeast regional average was computed, as was the difference between this city and the Southeast regional average. It was then determined which regional average each city was closest to; and the resulting pattern of city/region matches was evaluated. Only in the Southwest, Southeast, and Mountain/Great Plains areas did most metropolitan areas have financial infrastructures that resembled the average for their own region more than the average for another region. The majority of Northeastern and Midwestern cities' infrastructures were closest to other regions' averages.

22. Indeed, there may be an interesting parallel between the informal financial sector in the South, oriented toward an excluded working poor that was historically largely African-American and Appalachian, and the rise today of an informal financial sector in the Southwest, oriented toward servicing an excluded working poor that includes Hispanic, African-American, and some Asian-American households.

23. In practice, it is difficult to cleanly separate economic and social factors; see Dymski (1995 and 1997). The central problem is that some variables used by lenders—for example, income stability and credit history—are both potentially correlated with borrower social characteristics and, at the same time, unavailable to the researcher.

24. This method of choosing among methods of grouping financial infrastructures mimics information-theoretic techniques in statistics.

Chapter 9

1. Spiegel, Gart, and Gart (1996) provide a detailed history of the history and recent acquisitions of seventeen of the banks classified as large merging banks in this study.

2. This technique completely disregards coefficients whose degree of significance falls short of 10 percent. While such coefficients may contain meaningful information, no simple method exists for determining whether this near-significance is due to true statistical insignificance or to small sample size; hence, they are not incorporated here.

3. The lower-income applicant total can deviate from 333 because the delineation of lower- and upper-income is done before applications are submitted to all missing-values screens.

4. The information set out here for bank acquisition activity is drawn largely from the Federal Reserve System's National Information Center of Banking Information. This center records Federal Financial Institutions Examination Council (FFIEC) data (http://www.ffiec.gov/nic).

5. Boatmen's also entered Oklahoma via acquisition in 1982, Tennessee in 1984, Arkansas in 1993, and Illinois in 1995.

6. The figures illustrating denial rates and market share in this chapter include only lenders for whom patterns exist.

7. Model 1 is fully described in chapter 8 and its appendices.

8. The probit coefficients discussed in the text are for statistically significant variables, unless otherwise indicated.

9. For example, a lender that made strong affirmative efforts to identify African-American applicants might have a large negative African-American coefficient if these applicants differed from other applicants in ways important for creditworthiness but independent of the economic variables incorporated in Model 1. We might note that the variation found here for race and low-income variables is greater than for virtually every other variable in Model 1; indeed, most other variables have stable coefficients from one equation to the next within any market area.

10. U.S. Bancorp purchased West One Bancorp of Boise in December 1995.

11. There are some exceptions to this assertion, as there are in California: Keycorp of Cleveland has a market presence in upstate New York, and Comerica of Detroit purchased Empire Federal Savings of New York in 1990. Fleet also has some holdings in upstate New York due to its 1988 purchase of Norstar Bancorp of Albany.

12. C&S/Sovran itself resulted from the 1991 merger of Citizens and Southern Corporation of Atlanta (with branches in Florida) and Sovran Financial Corporation of Norfolk (with branches in Maryland and Washington, D.C.).

Chapter 10

1. Two examples come to mind. One is the case of new exurban communities (such as Temecula or Lancaster in California) in which numerous developers are simultaneously building subdivisions. Developers and lenders often have tied-in relationships: Potential

buyers at a given development may be channeled to one or more lenders (or in some cases, such as Kaufman Broad of California, the developer and the mortgage company may be the same). A lender attempting to enter these exurban home-loan markets might be advised to find its own subdivisions rather than muscling in on other lenders' turf. A second example is the case of niche lending in established urban markets. A new niche lender may be better advised to expand the geographic (or customer-type) range of markets handled by current lenders rather than engaging in head-to-head competition for a fixed number of asset sales within already established niches.

2. These calculations cannot be taken directly from published figures for deposits because of formula adjustments used by the Federal Reserve (see pages 41–42 and notes 6 and 7 to chapter 3).

3. Both sets of adjustments generate independent variable values close to one, allowing a more efficient estimation of the equation's parameters.

4. Specifically, the coefficients on 1982 HHI must be adjusted because logged, not raw, HHI values are used in the probit equation. The adjustment for this variable was done as follows: The average 1982 HHI for all ten cities was computed and calculated as a logarithm; then the difference between this logged average and the logarithm of each city's HHI score was calculated; then this difference was multiplied by the 1982 HHI coefficient generated in the probit regression. A much simpler adjustment was required for the HHI-change and bank-change variables: The coefficients had to be multiplied by 100 to be compatible with a percentage-change format.

5. When this calculation is done for probits using all home-purchase loans, not just conventional loans, the results remain negative, but are smaller: –0.5 percent overall in 1995 and –2.2 percent in 1996.

Chapter 11

1. One recent article (Zimmerman 1996) points up the vulnerability of regionally undiversified banks by showing that California community banks' earnings slumped in the wake of the state's severe early-1990s recession. These banks had problems because they shifted into real-estate lending, filling the vacuum left by the crippled thrift industry, just before California's real-estate market went into a deep tailspin. This point is well taken; but it leaves open the question of how much bank earnings would have been affected if most of these community banks had been replaced by a few large bank lenders.

2. Another potential source of incoherence arises from the anything-goes attitude of the Federal Reserve described in chapter 5. For example, Zions Bank of Utah recently entered the California market via merger; it purchased Grossmont Bank of San Diego, First Pacific National Bank of Escondido, and Sumitomo Bank of San Francisco. The logic of this move is not transparent. Zions' management may see a ripe opportunity to buy into the California market, but why do so when equity prices are so high?

3. We repeat once more that the evaluation of relative performance conducted here does not include information about the terms and conditions of loans. Such information might lead us to reconsider this conclusion about mortgage companies' generally superior performance in minority and lower-income access to credit.

4. It has been shown that loans in low-income communities do not necessarily carry higher default risk—that is, they are hardly outside the pale of normal business practice. Mills and Lubele (1993) reviewed 2,231 loans by seven lenders in large MSAs and found that single-family community development loans generally performed better than did these lenders' overall single-family loan portfolios.

Chapter 12

1. This support was in evidence most recently when Community Reinvestment Act regulations were toughened to include quantitative performance criteria as of January 1996 (60 FR 22156, May 4, 1995).

2. Edwards and Mishkin (1995) argue that banks can maintain adequate profit levels either by expanding into new and riskier areas of lending or by pursuing new off-balance-sheet activities. While either course of action involves considerable risk, these authors are not unduly concerned about systemic or even individual banking risks. In their view, regulatory monitoring, structured capital requirements, and activity diversification will suffice to prevent the recurrence of 1980s-style crises. This approach to regulation is precisely that adopted in the 1991 Depository Institution Deregulation and Monetary Control Act, which followed the blueprint set out in Kaufman (1990).

3. A comprehensive set of recommendations for proconsumer, procommunity financial reform is set out in Dymski, Epstein, and Pollin (1993).

Bibliography

Akhavein, J.D., Allen N. Berger, and David Humphrey. "The Effects of Megamergers on Efficiency and Prices: Evidence from a Bank Profit Function." *Review of Industrial Organization* 12, no. 1 (February 1997): 95–139.

Amihud, Yakov, and Geoffrey Miller. *Bank Mergers and Acquisitions.* Boston: Kluwer Academic, 1998.

Baumol, William J., John C. Panzar, and Robert D. Willig. *Contestable Markets and the Theory of Industrial Structure.* New York: Harcourt Brace Jovanovich, 1982.

Benston, George. "Mortgage Redlining Research: A Review and Critical Analysis." *Journal of Bank Research* 12 (1981): 8–23.

Benston, George J., Gerald Hanweck, and David Humphrey. "Scale Economies in Banking." *Journal of Money, Credit and Banking* 14, no. 1 (1982): 435-456.

Benston, George J., William C. Hunter, and Larry D. Wall. "Motivations for Bank Mergers and Acquisitions: Enhancing the Deposit Insurance Put Option versus Earnings Diversification." *Journal of Money, Credit and Banking* 27, no. 3 (August 1995): 777–789.

Berger, Allen N. "The Profit-Structure Relationship in Banking: Tests of Market-Power and Efficient-Structure Hypotheses." *Journal of Money, Credit and Banking* 27, no. 2 (May 1995): 404–432.

———. "The Efficiency Effects of Bank Mergers and Acquisitions: A Preliminary Look at the 1990s Data." In *Bank Mergers and Acquisitions,* ed. Yakov Amihud and Geoffrey Miller. Boston: Kluwer Academic, 1998.

Berger, Allen N., and Timothy Hannan. "The Price-Concentration Relationship in Banking." *Review of Economics and Statistics* 71, no. 2 (May 1989): 291–299.

Berger, Allen N., Gerald A. Hanweck, and David B. Humphrey. "Competitive Viability in Banking: Scale, Scope, and Product Mix Economies." *Journal of Monetary Economics* 20, no. 3 (December 1987): 501–520.

Berger, Allen N., and David Humphrey. "The Dominance of Inefficiencies over Scale and Product Mix Economics in Banking." *Finance and Economics Discussion Series No. 107.* Washington, DC: Board of Governors of the Federal Reserve System, January 1990.

Berger, Allen N., William C. Hunter, and Stephen G. Timme. "The Efficiency of Financial Institutions: A Review and Preview of Research Past, Present, and Future." *Journal of Banking and Finance* 17, nos. 2–3 (April 1993): 221–249.

Berger, Allen N., Anil K. Kashyap, and Joseph M. Scalise. "The Transformation of the U.S. Banking Industry: What a Long, Strange Trip It's Been." *Brookings Papers on Economic Activity,* no. 2 (1995): 55–218.

Berger, Allen N., and Loretta Mester. "Inside the Black Box: What Explains Differences in the Efficiencies of Financial Institutions?" *Journal of Banking and Finance* 21, no. 7 (1997): 895–947.

Berger, Allen N., Anthony Saunders, Joseph M. Scalise, and Gregory F. Udell. "The Effects of Bank Mergers and Acquisitions on Small Business Lending." *Finance and Economics Discussion Series,* 1997–28. Washington, DC: Board of Governors of the Federal Reserve System, 1997.

Berkovec, James, Glenn Canner, Stuart Gabriel, and Timothy Hannan. "Race, Redlining, and Residential Mortgage Loan Performance." Working Paper 94–1, Department of Finance and Business Economics, School of Business Administration, University of Southern California, January 1994.

Beshouri, Christopher, and Peter Nigro. "Securitization of Small Business Loans." Working Paper 94–8, Economic and Policy Analysis. Washinton, DC: Comptroller of the Currency, December 1994.

Board of Governors of the Federal Reserve System. *Report to the Congress on the Availability of Credit to Small Business.* Washington, DC, 1996a.

———. *Annual Report to the Congress on Retail Fees and Services of Depository Institutions.* Washington, DC, June 1996b.

———. *Annual Report to the Congress on Retail Fees and Services of Depository Institutions.* Washington, DC, June 1997.

Born, Jeffrey A., Robert Eisenbeis, and Robert S. Harris. "The Benefits of Geographical and Product Expansion in the Financial Services Industry." *Journal of Financial Services Research* 1 (1988): 161–182.

Boyd, John H., and Stanley L. Graham. "Investigating the Banking Consolidation Trend." Federal Reserve Bank of Minnesota, *Quarterly Review* (spring 1991): 3-15.

Bradbury, Katherine L., Karl E. Case, and Constance R. Dunham. "Geographic Patterns of Mortgage Lending in Boston, 1982–87." Federal Reserve Bank of Boston, *New England Economic Review* (September/October 1989): 3–30.

Bradford, Calvin. "Financing Home Ownership—The Federal Role in Neighborhood Decline." *Urban Affairs Quarterly* 14, no. 3 (1979): 313–335.

Brimelow, Peter, and Leslie Spenser. "The Hidden Clue." *Forbes,* January 4, 1993.

Browne, Lynn E., and Geoffrey M.B. Tootell. "Mortgage Lending in Boston—A Response to the Critics." Federal Reserve Bank of Boston, *New England Economic Review* (September/October 1995): 53–78.

Brunner, Allan D., and William B. English. "Profits and Balance Sheet Developments at U.S. Commercial Banks in 1992." *Federal Reserve Bulletin* 79, no. 7 (July 1993): 650–673.

Calomiris, Charles W. "Is Deposit Insurance Necessary? An Historical Perspective." *Journal of Economic History* 50, no. 2 (June 1990): 283-295.

Canner, Glenn. "Redlining and Mortgage Lending Patterns." *Research in Urban Economics* 1 (1981): 67–101.

Canner, Glenn, and D. Smith. "Home Mortgage Disclosure Act: Expanded Data on Residential Lending." *Federal Reserve Bulletin* 77 (November 1991): 863–864.

Carr, James H., and Isaac F. Megolugbe. "The Federal Reserve Bank of Boston Study on Mortgage Lending Revisited." *Journal of Housing Research* 4, no. 2 (1993): 277–314.

Caskey, John P. *Fringe Banking: Check-Cashing Outlets, Pawnshops, and the Poor.* New York: Russell Sage Foundation, 1994.

———. *Lower Income Americans, Higher Cost Financial Services.* Madison, WI: Filene Research Institute, Center for Credit Union Research, 1997.

Cebenoyan, A. "Multiproduct Cost Function and Scale Economies in Banking." *Financial Review* 23 (1988): 499–512.

Chamberlain, Sandra L. "The Effects of Bank Ownership Changes on Subsidiary-Level Earnings." In *Bank Mergers and Acquisitions,* ed. Yakov Amihud and Geoffrey Miller, 137–172. Boston: Kluwer Academic, 1998.

Chang, Angela, Shubham Chaudhuri, and Jith Jayaratne. "Rational Herding and the Spatial Clustering of Bank Branches: An Empirical Analysis." Federal Reserve Bank of New York, Research Paper no. 9724 (August 1997).

Clark, Jeffrey A. "Economies of Scale and Scope at Depository Financial Institutions: A Review of the Literature." Federal Reserve Bank of Kansas City, *Economic Review* (September/October 1988): 16-33.

———. "Economic Cost, Scale Efficiency, and Competitive Viability in Banking. *Journal of Money, Credit and Banking* (August 1996): 342–364.

Clark, William A.V. "Measuring Racial Discrimination in the Housing Market: Direct and Indirect Evidence." *Urban Affairs Quarterly* 28, no. 4 (June 1993).

Cloud, Cathy, and George Galster. "What Do We Know About Racial Discrimination in Mortgage Markets?" *Review of Black Political Economy* 22, no. 1 (summer 1993): 101–120.

Consumer Federation of America. "Bank Fees on Consumer Accounts: The Fifth Annual National Survey." (June 1988). Mimeo.

———. "Check Cashing Outlet Fees: Still High and Climbing." (December 1989). Mimeo.

Cornett, Marsha M., and Hassan Tehranian. "Changes in Corporate Performance Associated with Bank Acquisitions." *Journal of Financial Economics* 31, no. 2 (April 1992): 211–234.

De Cossio, Francisco, Jack W. Trifts, and Kevin P. Scanlon. "Bank Equity Returns: The Difference Between Intrastate and Interstate Bank Mergers." In *Proceedings of a Conference on Bank Structure and Competition.* Chicago: Federal Reserve Bank of Chicago, 1987.

Dedman, B. "The Color of Money." *Atlanta Constitution,* May 1–4, 1988.

Demsetz, Harold. "Two Systems of Belief About Monopoly." In *Industrial Concentration: The New Learning,* ed. Harvey J. Goldschmid, H. Michael Mann, and J. Fred Weston, 164–84. Boston: Little, Brown, 1974.

Demsetz, Rebecca S., Marc R. Saidenberg, and Philip E. Strahan. "Banks with Something to Lose: The Disciplinary Role of Franchise Value." Federal Reserve Bank of New York, *Economic Policy Review* 2, no. 2 (October 1996): 1–14.

Demsetz, Rebecca S., and Philip E. Strahan. "Historical Patterns and Recent Changes in the Relationship Between Bank Holding Company Size and Risk." Federal Reserve Bank of New York, *Economic Policy Review* 1, no. 2 (July 1995): 13–26.

DeYoung, Robert. "Determinants of Cost Efficiencies in Bank Mergers." Working Paper 93–01, Economic and Policy Analysis. Washington, DC: Office of the Comptroller of the Currency, August 1993.

———. "Do Regulators Read the Literature? Bank Merger Regulation, 1963–1990." *Southern Economic Journal* 61, no. 1 (July 1994a): 69–85.

———. "Fee-Based Services and Cost Efficiency in Commercial Banks." Working Paper 94–3, Economic and Policy Analysis. Washington, DC: Office of the Comptroller of the Currency, April 1994b.

———. "X-Efficiency and Management Quality in Commercial Banks." Working Paper 94–1, Economic and Policy Analysis. Washington, DC: Office of the Comptroller of the Currency, January 1994c.

Dunham, Constance. "Interstate Banking and the Outflow of Local Funds." Federal Reserve Bank of Boston, *New England Economic Review* (March/April 1986): 7–19.

Dymski, Gary A. "The Theory of Credit-Market Redlining and Discrimination: An Exploration." *Review of Black Political Economy* 23, no. 3 (winter 1995): 37–74.

———. "Why Does Race Matter in Housing and Credit Markets?" In *Frontiers of Re-*

search on Discrimination, edited by Patrick L. Mason and Rhonda Williams. Boston: Kluwer Academic, 1997.

Dymski, Gary A., and John M. Veitch. "Race and the Financial Dynamics of Urban Growth: L.A. as Fay Wray." In *City of Angels,* ed. Gerry Riposa and Caroline Dersch, 131–58. Los Angeles: Kendall/Hunt Press, 1992.

———. "Taking it to the Bank: Credit, Race, and Income in Los Angeles." In *Residential Segregation: The American Legacy,* ed. Robert D. Bullard, Charles Lee, and J. Eugene Grigsby III, 150–179. Los Angeles: Center for Afro-American Studies, UCLA, 1994.

———. "Financial Transformation and the Metropolis: Booms, Busts, and Banking in Los Angeles." *Environment and Planning A* 28, no. 7 (July 1996a): 1233–1260.

———. "Financing the Future in Los Angeles: Great Depression to 21st Century." In *Rethinking Los Angeles,* ed. Michael Dear, Eric Hise, and Eric Schockman. Beverly Hills: Sage, 1996b.

———. "Credit Flows to Cities." In *Reclaiming Prosperity: A Blueprint for Progressive Economic Reform,* ed. Jeff Faux and Todd Schafer, 227–235. Armonk, NY: M.E. Sharpe, 1996c.

Dymski, Gary A., Gerald Epstein, and Robert Pollin. *Transforming the U.S. Financial System: An Equitable and Efficient Structure for the 21st Century.* Armonk, NY: M.E. Sharpe, 1993.

Dymski, Gary A., John M. Veitch, and Michelle White. *Taking It to the Bank: Race, Poverty, and Credit in Los Angeles.* Los Angeles: Western Center on Law and Poverty, 1991. Reprinted in United States Senate, Committee on Banking, Housing, and Urban Affairs. *Report on the Status of the Community Reinvestment Act: Views and Recommendations,* vol. 2 of 2, November 1992. Washington, DC: USGPO.

Edwards, Franklin R. "The Future Financial Structure: Fears and Policies." In *Restructuring Banking and Financial Services in America,* ed. William S. Haraf and Rose Marie Kushmeider, 113–155. Washington, DC: American Enterprise Institute, 1988.

Edwards, Franklin R., and Frederic S. Mishkin. "The Decline of Traditional Banking: Implications for Financial Stability and Regulatory Policy." Federal Reserve Bank of New York, *Economic Policy Review* 1, no. 2 (July 1995): 27–45.

Egan, Jack. "Chasing After Bank Stocks." *U.S. News and World Report,* September 11, 1995.

Elliehausen, Gregory E., and John D. Wolken. "Banking Markets and the Use of Financial Services by Small and Medium-Sized Businesses." Staff Study 160. Board of Governors of the Federal Reserve System. Washington, DC, 1990.

———. "Banking Markets and the Use of Financial Services by Households." *Federal Reserve Bulletin* 7 (March 1992).

Emmons, William R., and Stuart I. Greenbaum. "Twin Information Revolutions and the Future of Financial Intermediation." In *Bank Mergers and Acquisitions,* ed. Yakov Amihud and Geoffrey Miller, 37–56. Boston: Kluwer Academic, 1998.

Evanoff, Douglas, and Philip Israilevich. "Productive Efficiency in Banking." Federal Reserve Bank of Chicago, *Economic Perspectives* (July/August 1991): 11-32.

Fama, Eugene. "Banking in the Theory of Finance." *Journal of Financial Economics* 6, no. 1 (1980): 39–57.

Ferguson, Michael F., and Stephen R. Peters. "What Constitutes Evidence of Discrimination in Lending?" *Journal of Finance* 50, no. 2 (June 1995): 739–748.

Furlong, Fred. "Interstate Banking in the West." *FRB San Francisco Weekly Letter* 94–15, April 15, 1994.

Galster, George C. "Research on Discrimination in Housing and Mortgage Markets: Assessment and Future Directions." *Housing Policy Debate* 3, no. 2 (1992): 637–683.

———. "The Facts of Lending Discrimination Cannot Be Argued Away by Examining Default Rates." *Housing Policy Debate* 4, no. 1 (1993): 141–146.

Galster, George C., and W. Mark Keeney. "Race, Residence, Discrimination, and Economic Opportunity: Modeling the Nexus of Urban Racial Phenomena." *Urban Affairs Quarterly* 24, no. 1 (1988): 87–117.

Gates, William. "Baked Beans and Bacon from a Hole in the Wall." *The Independent,* November 10, 1996.

Gilbert, R. Alton. "Market Discipline of Bank Risk: Theory and Evidence." Federal Reserve Bank of St. Louis, *Review* 72, no. 1 (January/February 1990): 3–18.

Gilligan, Petty. "Small Business Lending." Federal Reserve Bank of Boston, *New England Banking Trends* 5, no. 1 (winter 1997).

Glennon, Dennis, and Mitchell Stengel. "An Evaluation of the Federal Reserve Bank of Boston's Study of Racial Discrimination in Mortgage Lending." Working Paper 94–2, Economic and Policy Analysis. Washington, DC: Comptroller of the Currency, April 1994.

Gorton, Gary, and Richard Rosen. "Overcapacity and Exit from Banking." Wharton School Working Paper, University of Pennsylvania, November 1991.

Goudreau, Robert E., and B. Frank King. "Commercial Bank Profitability: Hampered Again by Large Banks' Loan Problems." Federal Reserve Bank of Atlanta, *Economic Review* (July/August 1991): 39–54.

Grant, Joseph M. *The Great Texas Banking Crash: An Insider's Account.* Austin: University of Texas Press, 1996.

Grant, Linda, and Suzanne Barlyn. "Here Comes Hugh." *Fortune,* August 21, 1995.

Green, Mark, and Glenn Von Nostivitz. "Survival of the Fattest: Bank Mergers Are Taxing Consumers." *The Nation* 254, no. 3 (January 27, 1992): 81–84.

Greene, William H. *Econometric Analysis.* New York: Macmillan, 1990.

Greenspan, Alan. Remarks at the Annual Convention of the American Bankers Association. Honolulu, Hawaii, October 5, 1996.

Greenspan, Alan. Testimony Before the Senate Committee on Banking, Housing, and Urban Affairs, June 17, 1998.

Gropper, David. "Empirical Investigation of Changes in Scale Economies for the Banking Firm, 1979–86." *Journal of Money, Credit and Banking* 23, no. 4 (November 1991): 718–727.

Guttentag, Jack M., and Susan L. Wachter, "Redlining and Public Policy," *Monograph Series on Finance and Economics,* no. 1. New York: Solomon Brothers Center for the Study of Financial Institutions, 1980.

Hannan, Timothy H. "Bank Commercial Loan Rates and the Market for Commercial Loans." Working Paper. Washington, DC: Board of Governors of the Federal Reserve System, 1989.

———. "Bank Commercial Loan Markets and the Role of Market Structure: Evidence from Surveys of Commercial Lending." *Journal of Banking and Finance* 15, no. 1 (February 1991): 133–149.

———. "Recent Trends in Retail Fees and Services of Depository Institutions." *Federal Reserve Bulletin* 80 (September 1994): 771–781.

Hannan, Timothy, and Robin Prager. "Do Substantial Horizontal Mergers Generate Significant Price Effects? Evidence from the Banking Industry." Washington, DC: Board of Governors of the Federal Reserve System, 1996.

Hawawini, Gabriel A., and Itzhak Swary. *Mergers and Acquisitions in the U.S. Banking Industry: Evidence from the Capital Markets.* New York: North Holland Elsevier Science, 1990.

Hetzel, Robert L. "Too Big to Fail: Origins, Consequences, and Outlook." Federal Reserve Bank of Richmond, *Economic Review* 77, no. 6 (November/December 1991): 3–15.

Hoenig, Thomas M. "Rethinking Financial Regulation." Federal Reserve Bank of Kansas City, *Economic Review* 81, no. 2 (second quarter 1996): 5–14.

Holder, Christopher L. "Competitive Considerations in Bank Mergers and Acquisitions: Economic Theory, Legal Foundations, and the Fed." Federal Reserve Bank of Atlanta, *Economic Review* (January/February 1993a): 23–36.

———. "The Use of Mitigating Factors in Bank Mergers and Acquisitions: A Decade of Antitrust at the Fed." Federal Reserve Bank of Atlanta, *Economic Review* (March/April 1993b): 32–44.

Huck, Paul, and Lewis Segal. "New Data on Mortgage Lending." Federal Reserve Bank of Chicago, *Chicago Fed Letter,* no. 119 (July 1997): 1, 4.

Hudson, Michael. "Cashing In on Poverty: How Big Business Wins Every Time." *The Nation,* May 20, 1996a.

Hudson, Michael, ed. *Merchants of Misery.* Monroe, ME: Common Courage Press, 1996b.

Humphrey, David B. "Why Do Estimates of Bank Scale Economies Differ?" Federal Reserve Bank of Richmond, *Economic Review* (September/October 1990): 38–50.

———. "Delivering Deposit Services: ATMs Versus Branches." Federal Reserve Bank of Richmond, *Economic Quarterly* 80, no. 2 (spring 1994): 59–77.

Hunter, William C., and Stephen G. Timme. "Core Deposits and Physical Capital: A Reexamination of Bank Scale Economies and Efficiency with Quasi-Fixed Inputs." *Journal of Money, Credit and Banking* 27, no. 1 (February 1995): 165–186.

Hunter, William C., and Larry Wall. "Bank Merger Motivations: A Review of the Evidence and an Examination of Key Target Bank Characteristics." Federal Reserve of Atlanta, *Economic Review* (September/October 1989): 2-19.

Jayaratne, Jith, and Christine Hall. "Consolidation and Competition in Second District Banking Markets." Federal Reserve Bank of New York, *Current Issues in Economics and Finance* 2, no. 8 (July 1996): 1–6.

Kaparakis, Emmanuel I., Stephan M. Miller, and Athanasios G. Noulas. "Short-Run Cost Inefficiency of Commercial Banks: A Flexible Stochastic Frontier Approach." *Journal of Money, Credit and Banking* 26, no. 4 (November 1994): 875–894.

Kaufman, George G., ed. *Restructuring the American Financial System.* Boston: Kluwer Academic, 1990.

Keeton, William R. "Do Bank Mergers Reduce Lending to Businesses and Farmers? New Evidence from Tenth District States." Federal Reserve Bank of Kansas City, *Economic Review* 81, no. 3 (third quarter 1996): 63–76.

Kennickell, Arthur B., and Myron L. Kwast. "Who Uses Electronic Banking? Results from the 1995 Survey of Consumer Finances." *Finance and Economics Discussion Series,* 1997–35. Washington, DC: Board of Governors of the Federal Reserve System, 1997.

Keynes, John Maynard. *The General Theory of Employment, Interest, and Prices.* London: Macmillan, 1936.

Kim, H. "Economies of Scale and Economies of Scope in Multiproduct Financial Institutions: Further Evidence From Credit Unions." *Journal of Money, Credit and Banking* 22 (1986): 504–525.

Kim, Sunwoong, and Gregory D. Squires. "Does Anybody Who Works Here Look Like Me—Mortgage Lending, Race, and Lender Employment." *Social Science Quarterly* 76, no. 4 (December 1995): 823–838.

Kimball, Ralph C. "Specialization, Risk, and Capital in Banking." Federal Reserve Bank of Boston, *New England Economic Review* (November/December 1997): 51–73.

Kregel, Jan. *The Past and Future of Banking.* Rome: Bancaria Editrice Spa, March 1998.

Krozner, Randall S., and Philip E. Strahan. "The Political Economy of Deregulation:

Evidence from the Relaxation of Bank Branching Restrictions in the United States." Federal Reserve Bank of New York, Research Paper no. 9720, June 1997.

Krugman, Paul. *Development, Geography, and Economic Theory*. Cambridge: MIT Press, 1995.

Kwast, Myron L., Martha Starr-McCluer, and John D. Wolken. "Market Definition and the Analysis of Antitrust in Banking." *Finance and Economics Discussion Series* 1997–52. Washington, DC: Board of Governors of the Federal Reserve System, October 1997.

Ladd, Helen F. "Evidence on Discrimination in Mortgage Lending." *Journal of Economic Perspectives* 12, no. 2 (spring 1998): 41–62.

Laderman, Elizabeth. "Changes in the Structure of Urban Banking Markets in the West." Federal Reserve Bank of San Francisco, *Economic Review* 1 (1995): 21–37.

———. "The California 'Rate Gap' Since the BankAmerica-Security Pacific Merger." Federal Reserve Bank of San Francisco, *FRBSF Economic Letter*, no. 96–31 (October 25, 1996).

Laderman, Elizabeth, and Randall Pozdena. "Interstate Banking and Competition: Evidence from the Behavior of Stock Returns." Federal Reserve Bank of San Francisco, *Economic Review*, (spring 1991): 32-47.

Landes,W.M., and Richard A. Posner. "Market Power in Antitrust Cases." *Harvard Law Review* 94 (1981): 937–996.

LeCompte, R., and S. Smith. "Changes in the Cost of Intermediation: The Case of Savings and Loans." *Journal of Finance* 45 (1990): 1337–1346.

Liang, Nellie, and Donald Savage. "New Data on the Performance of Nonbank Subsidiaries of Bank Holding Companies." Staff Study 159. Washington, DC: Board of Governors of the Federal Reserve System, February 1990.

Lindgren, Bernard W. *Statistical Theory*. 3d edition. New York: Macmillan, 1976.

Litan, Robert E. *What Should Banks Do?* Washington, DC: The Brookings Institution, 1986.

Long, J. Scott. *Regression Models for Categorical and Limited Dependent Variables*. Advanced Quantitative Techniques in the Social Sciences Series, no. 7. Thousand Oaks, CA: Sage, 1997.

Mayer, Martin. *The Greatest-Ever Bank Robbery: The Collapse of the Savings and Loan Industry*. New York: Charles Scribner's Sons, 1990.

Mester, Loretta. "Efficient Production of Financial Services: Scale and Scope Economies." Federal Reserve Bank of Philadelphia, *Business Review* (1987): 15–25.

Meyer, Laurence. Testimony Before the Committee on Banking and Financial Services, U.S. House of Representatives. Washington, DC: Board of Governors of the Federal Reserve System, April 29, 1998.

Mills, Edwin, and Luan Lubele. *Sound Loans for Communities: An Analysis of the Performance of Community Reinvestment Loans*. Chicago: Woodstock Institute, October 1993.

Mishkin, Frederic. "Bank Consolidation: A Central Banker's Perspective." In *Bank Mergers and Acquisitions*, ed. Yakov Amihud and Geoffrey Miller, 3–20. Boston: Kluwer Academic, 1998.

Moore, Robert R. "Has Consumer Credit Growth Jeopardized Bank Profits?" Federal Reserve Bank of Dallas, *Financial Industry Issues* (first quarter 1996): 1–6.

Munnell, Alicia H., Lynn E. Browne, James McEneaney, and Geoffrey Tootell. "Mortgage Lending in Boston: Interpreting HMDA Data." Working Paper no. 92–7. Boston: Federal Reserve Bank of Boston, 1992.

Nakamura, Leonard I. "Information Externalities: Why Lending May Sometimes Need a Jump Start." Federal Reserve Bank of Philadelphia, *Business Review* (1992/1993): 11–20.

Nesiba, Reynolds F. "Interstate Banking and Community Reinvestment: An Evaluation of How Bank Mergers and Acquisitions Influenced Residential Lending Patterns in St. Joseph County, Indiana, 1985–1993." Unpublished Ph.D. dissertation, Department of Economics, University of Notre Dame, 1995.

Nolle, Daniel E. "Banking Industry Consolidation: Past Changes and Implications for the Future." Working Paper 95–1, Economic and Policy Analysis. Washington, DC: Comptroller of the Currency, April 1995.

Noulas, Athanasios G., Subhash C. Ray, and Stephen M. Miller. "Returns to Scale and Input Substitution for Large U.S. Banks." *Journal of Money, Credit and Banking* 22, no. 1 (February 1990): 94–108.

Oliver, Melvin L., and Thomas M. Shapiro. *Black Wealth/White Wealth: A New Perspective on Racial Inequality.* New York: Routledge, 1995.

Orlow, Daniel K., Lawrence J. Radecki, and John Wenninger. "Ongoing Restructuring of Retail Banking." Federal Reserve Bank of New York, Research Paper no. 9634, November 1996.

Peek, Joe, and Eric Rosengren. "Small Business Credit Availability: How Important Is Size in Lender?" April 1995, in the *Effects of Bank Consolidation On Small Business Lending.* Joint Hearing before the Committee on Small Business, House of Representatives, 104th Cong., 2nd Sess. Boston, March 4, 1996, pp. 115–154. Washington, DC: USGPO, 1996.

Peristiani, Stavros. "Do Mergers Improve the X-Efficiency and Scale Efficiency of U.S. Banks? Evidence From the 1980s." Federal Reserve Bank of New York, Research Paper no. 9623, June 1996.

Perle, Eugene D., Kathryn Lynch, and Jeffrey Horner. "Model Specification and Local Mortgage Market Behavior." *Journal of Housing Research* 4, no. 2 (1993): 225–244.

Phillips, Ronnie J. *The Chicago Plan and New Deal Banking Reform.* Armonk, NY: M.E. Sharpe, 1994.

Phillips, Susan. "Supervisory and Regulatory Responses to Financial Innovation and Industry Dynamics." Remarks at the BAI Seminar on Regulatory Changes. Washington, DC, November 25, 1996.

Piloff, Steven J., and Anthony M. Santomero. "The Value Effects of Bank Mergers and Acquisitions." In *Bank Mergers and Acquisitions,* ed. Yakov Amihud and Geoffrey Miller, 59–78. Boston: Kluwer Academic, 1998.

Pouschine, Tatiana. "Dangerous Medicine." *Forbes,* August 5, 1991.

Quercia, Roberto G., and Michael A. Stegman. "Residential Mortgage Default: A Review of the Literature." *Journal of Housing Research* 32, no. 2 (1992).

Rachlis, Mitchell B., and Anthony M.J. Yezer. "Serious Flaws in Statistical Tests for Discrimination in Mortgage Markets." *Journal of Housing Research* 4, no. 2 (1993): 315–36.

Radecki, Lawrence. "Potential Employment Effects of the Restructuring of Retail Banking." Federal Reserve Bank of New York, *Economic Policy Review* 3 (February 1997): 75–78.

Randall, Richard. "Can the Market Evaluate Asset Quality Exposure in Banks?" Federal Reserve Bank of Boston, *New England Economic Review* (July/August 1989): 3–24.

Rawls, John. *A Theory of Justice.* Cambridge: Harvard University Press, 1974.

Rezvanian, Rasoul, Seyed Mehdian, and Elyas Elyasiani. "Economies of Scale and Scope in Small Depository Institutions: Evidence from U.S. Cooperative Banks." *Quarterly Review of Economics and Finance* 35 (spring 1996): 39–55.

Rhoades, Stephen A. "Mergers and Acquisitions by Commercial Banks, 1960–83." Staff Study 142. Washington, DC: Board of Governors of the Federal Reserve System, January 1985.

————. "Evidence on the Size of Banking Markets from Mortgage Loan Rates in Twenty Cities." Staff Study 162. Washington, DC: Board of Governors of the Federal Reserve System, February 1992.

————. "A Summary of Merger Performance Studies in Banking, 1980–93, and an Assessment of the 'Operating Performance' and 'Event Study' Methodologies." Staff Study 167. Washington, DC: Board of Governors of the Federal Reserve System, July 1994.

————. "Market Share Inequality, the HHI, and Other Measures of the Firm-Composition of a Market." *Review of Industrial Organization* 10, no. 6 (December 1995): 657–674.

————. "Bank Mergers and Industrywide Structure, 1980–94." Staff Study 169. Washington, DC: Board of Governors of the Federal Reserve System, January 1996.

Rist, Charles. *History of Monetary Theory from John Law to the Present Day.* Trans. Jane Degras. New York: Macmillan, 1940.

Rose, Peter S. "The Impact of Mergers in Banking: Evidence from a Sample of Federally Chartered Banks." *Journal of Economics and Business* 39 (1987): 289–312.

————. *The Interstate Banking Revolution: Benefits, Risks, and Tradeoffs for Bankers and Customers.* Westport, CT: Greenwood Press, 1989.

————. "The Diversification Effects of Bank Mergers." Mimeo, 1994.

Samolyk, Katherine. "Bank Performance and Regional Economic Growth: Evidence of a Regional Credit Channel." Federal Reserve Bank of Cleveland, Working Paper 9204, February 1992.

————. "U.S. Banking Sector Trends: Assessing Disparities in Industry Performance." Federal Reserve Bank of Cleveland, *Economic Review* 30, no. 2 (second quarter, 1994): 2–17.

Savage, Donald T. "The Implications for Bank Merger Policy of Financial Deregulation, Interstate Banking, and Financial Supermarkets." Staff Study 137. Washington, DC: Board of Governors of the Federal Reserve System, February 1984.

————. "Interstate Banking: A Status Report." *Federal Reserve Bulletin* 79 (December 1993): 1075–1089.

Schill, Michael H., and Susan M. Wachter. "A Tale of Two Cities: Racial and Ethnic Geographic Disparities in Home Mortgage Lending in Boston and Philadelphia." *Journal of Housing Research* 4, no. 2 (1993): 245–276.

Serwer, Andrew E. "Why Bank Mergers Are Good for Your Savings Account." *Fortune,* October 2, 1995.

Shaffer, Sherill. "Bank Competition in Concentrated Markets." Federal Reserve Bank of Philadelphia, *Business Review* (March/April 1994): 3–16.

Shlay, Anne. "Financing Community: Methods for Assessing Residential Credit Disparities, Market Barriers, and Institutional Reinvestment Performance in the Metropolis." *Journal of Urban Affairs* 11, no. 3 (1989): 201–223.

Simons, Katerina, and Joanna Stavins. "Has Antitrust Policy in Banking Become Obsolete?" Federal Reserve Bank of Boston, *New England Economic Review* (March/April 1998): 13–26.

Sloan, Allen. "Big Boys with Their Bigger Toys." *Newsweek,* September 11, 1995.

Smith, Roy C., and Ingo Walter. "Global Patterns of Mergers and Acquisition Activity in the Financial Services Industry." In *Bank Mergers and Acquisitions,* ed. Yakov Amihud and Geoffrey Miller, 21–36. Boston: Kluwer Academic, 1998.

Southern Finance Project. "The Bigger they Come: Megamergers and Their Impact on Banking Markets." Mimeo. Charlotte, NC, September 1991.

Spiegel, John, Alan Gart, and Steven Gart. *Banking Redefined: How Superregional Powerhouses Are Reshaping Financial Services.* Chicago: Irwin Professional, 1996.

Srinivasan, Aruna. "Review of *The Interstate Banking Revolution,* by Peter Rose." Federal Reserve of Atlanta, *Economic Review* (March/April 1991): 42-46.

———. "Are There Cost Savings from Bank Mergers?" Federal Reserve Bank of Atlanta, *Economic Review* (March/April 1992): 17–28.

Srinivasan, Aruna, and Larry Wall. "Cost Savings Associated with Bank Mergers." Working Paper 92–2, Federal Reserve Bank of Atlanta, February 1992.

Stengel, Mitchell, and Dennis Glennon. "Evaluating Statistical Models of Mortgage-Lending Discrimination: A Bank-Specific Analysis." Working Paper 95–3, Economic and Policy Analysis. Washington, DC: Comptroller of the Currency, May 1995.

Stiglitz, Joseph E., and Andrew Weiss. "Credit Rationing in Markets with Imperfect Information." In *New Keynesian Economics,* vol. 2, ed. Gregory Mankiw and David Romer, 247–276. Cambridge: MIT Press, 1991.

Strahan, Philip E., and James Weston. "Small Business Lending and Bank Consolidation: Is There Cause for Concern?" Federal Reserve Bank of New York, *Current Issues in Economics and Finance* 2, no. 3 (March 1996): 1–16.

Tannenwald, Robert. "Cyclical Swing or Secular Slide? Why Have New England's Banks Been Losing Money?" Federal Reserve Bank of Boston, *New England Economic Review* (November/December 1991): 29–46.

Thomson, James B. "Using Market Incentives to Reform Bank Regulation and Federal Deposit Insurance." Federal Reserve Bank of Cleveland, *Economic Review* (1990), 1–18.

United States Department of the Treasury. *Modernizing the Financial System: Recommendations for Safer, More Competitive Banks.* Washington, DC: USGPO, February 1991.

United States v. Philadelphia National Bank, 374 U.S. 321 (1963).

Wall, Larry D., Alan K. Reichert, and Sunil Mohanty. "Deregulation and the Opportunities for Commercial Bank Diversification." Federal Reserve Bank of Atlanta, *Economic Review* (September/October 1993): 1–25.

Whalen, Gary. "Wealth Effects of Intraholding Company Bank Mergers: Evidence from Shareholder Returns." Economic and Policy Analysis Working Paper 94–4. Washington, DC: Comptroller of the Currency, May 1994.

Wheelock, David C., and Paul W. Wilson. "Evaluating the Efficiency of Commercial Banks: Does Our View of What Banks Do Matter?" Federal Reserve Bank of St. Louis, *Review* 77, no. 4 (July/August 1995): 39–52.

Williams, Richard A., and Reynolds F. Nesiba. "Racial, Economic, and Institutional Differences in Home Mortgage Loans: A Case Study Analysis of St. Joseph County, Indiana." Mimeo. University of Notre Dame, 1994.

Zimmerman, Gary C. "Factors Influencing Community Bank Performance in California." Federal Reserve Bank of San Francisco, *Economic Review,* no. 1 (1996): 26–42.

Index

About the Author

Gary Dymski is associate professor of economics at the University of California, Riverside, and a research associate of the Economic Policy Institute. He is on the editorial boards of the *International Review of Applied Economics* and *Geoforum* and is coeditor of *Transforming the U.S. Financial System* (M.E. Sharpe, 1993) with Gerald Epstein and Robert Pollin, and *New Directions in Monetary Macroeconomics* (University of Michigan Press, 1994) with Robert Pollin.